Self and Society
in the Films of
Robert Wise

ALSO BY JUSTIN E.A. BUSCH

The Utopian Vision of H.G. Wells
(McFarland, 2009)

Self and Society
in the Films of
Robert Wise

Justin E.A. Busch

McFarland & Company, Inc., Publishers
Jefferson, North Carolina, and London

LIBRARY OF CONGRESS CATALOGUING-IN-PUBLICATION DATA

Busch, Justin E. A.
    Self and society in the films of Robert Wise / Justin E. A. Busch.
        p.   cm.
    Includes bibliographical references and index.

    ISBN 978-0-7864-5915-5
    softcover : 50# alkaline paper ∞

    1. Wise, Robert, 1914–2005 — Criticism and interpretation.
I. Title.
PN1998.3.W569B78   2010
791.4302'33092 — dc22   2010023050

British Library cataloguing data are available

Front cover: Natalie Wood as Maria in *West Side Story,* 1961
(United Artists/Photofest)

Manufactured in the United States of America

McFarland & Company, Inc., Publishers
  Box 611, Jefferson, North Carolina 28640
    www.mcfarlandpub.com

Table of Contents

Acknowledgment

The Margaret Herrick Library of the Academy of Motion Picture Arts and Sciences is indeed, as its publicity materials claim, "a cinephile's wish come true." The friendly, knowledgeable, and helpful staff is equally an author's wish come true. I could have spent a month there, but had only a day, during which I was able to examine in detail Jerry Goldsmith's manuscript scores for the music to *Star Trek: The Motion Picture*, making possible a much fuller understanding of the musical structure which plays such a significant role in my analysis of that film. I had intended to provide specific examples drawn from my research, but while the cooperation provided by the library staff was exemplary the corporate copyright holder of the music was, shall we say, less supportive, and I have perforce foregone the examples. I hope to visit the Library again some day; in the interim, I extend my heartfelt gratitude for the assistance I received.

Introduction:
Style and Substance

I don't look for stories in any particular area. I want a good spanking yarn that I think I can make into a damned good movie. (Robert Wise)[1]

Measured by popular acclaim, Robert Wise is among the most successful of directors. *The Set-Up* took the Jury Award at the Cannes Festival. *West Side Story* and *The Sound of Music* both received Best Direction awards from the Director's Guild of America, acknowledgments echoed by Golden Globe Awards for Best Film and capped with double Academy Awards (Best Direction and Best Picture, which latter award also went to Wise as producer of each). Further Academy Award nominations went to *I Want to Live!* (Best Direction) and *The Sand Pebbles* (Best Film); from 1951 to 1979, Wise's films garnered over 60 Academy Award nominations. Wise's box office record is similarly impressive. *West Side Story* made a sizeable profit, *The Sound of Music* retains its place among the highest grossing films of all time,[2] and *Star Trek: The Motion Picture* remains the top ticket seller (and, adjusted for inflation and less stringent accounting methods, probably the greatest moneyspinner) of the many films in that highly successful franchise. Although Wise directed a few fiscal flops (*Star!* being the most obvious example), by far the majority of his films have been well-received at the box office. Nor did these successes lead to an outsized ego and petulant outbursts, either on or off the set. By all accounts Wise was one of the truly humane people in the Hollywood film industry. No scandal attached to his name; nor did disgruntled performers from his films hasten to bewail his harsh treatment of their foibles. Quite the contrary; many are Wise's collaborators, before and behind the camera, who have testified to his patience and kindness. One such may stand for the others.

1

John Houseman, producer of *Executive Suite*, personally selected Wise, whose work he had known for some years, over many better known directors, precisely because of Wise's geniality. "Among Robert Wise's particular virtues," Houseman said, "were those of coolness and modesty. No director with a visible ego could have handled a cast made up of what might well have been the largest collection of stars ever assembled for a dramatic picture — except possibly *Grand Hotel*."[3] Wise worked with, not against, his collaborators, and the result shows in the serene balance of his films, minor and major alike, a balance visible across Wise's entire spectrum of works, a spectrum including films on a wide range of topics covering most of the major genres. Both at the box office and within the industry, both among audiences and his fellow film makers, Robert Wise commanded wide respect.

Rather the reverse is true when one considers Wise's reception among serious critics. Academic writers on film have very largely ignored his work, and neither he nor any among his films has been the subject of such monographs as pullulate around the films of, say, Bergman, Kurosawa, or Hitchcock, or even more recent, and far less versatile, directors such as Quentin Tarantino.[4] Nor does it appear that many critics or theorists regard Wise as deserving of their attention, save perhaps negatively. Andrew Sarris altogether denied Wise the presumably precious appellation of "auteur," and David Thomson dismissed Wise as a "mediocrity or worse," asserting that "his better credits are only the haphazard products of artistic aimlessness given rare guidance." Thomson condemns what he sees as "a restless, dispiriting search among subject areas— war, epic, musical, science fiction, horror, crime, Western — that has never caught up with interest."[5]

Thomson's comments suggest an important reason for the lack of attention given to Wise by film commentators. Wise is seen not as an auteur, but as a journeyman, or even a studio hack, grinding out conventional pictures on demand. Wise himself has recognized the charge, and offered his own response:

> I've been taken apart sometimes for not having a really consistent style, [...], but that's exactly what I wanted. I try to address each script in the cinematic fashion I think is right for that given script, and since I've done such different kinds of stories, there's no straight stylistic line in my work.[6]

Clearly Wise is, at least in his own eyes, akin to what Raymond Durgnat called the "anti-auteur — the man who delights in adopting different themes and styles for each of his films."[7] Even if true, though, this will not quiet critics such as Thomson, or indeed most auteurists, since the objection will immediately follow that the problem lies in the very fact that Wise has chosen such diverse subjects, rather than finding his particular subject (or style) and concentrating on developing it.

I argue a position contrary to that of most of Wise's academic or theory-driven critics. Wise may be no auteur as the term is normally understood, but there is indeed a method to his subjective eclecticism, one which does not simply encourage what has been perceived as a lack of stylistic consistency, but even requires it. Many of Wise's films, especially the early studio assignments, are generic and conventional, save in their presentation; it is primarily through Wise's directorial choices that the well-worn stories derive their effectiveness. Thus, for example, the grainy look of *The Desert Rats*, which is by no means entirely due to the use of stock footage; Wise put a great deal of consideration into its appearance. Careful choice and use of specialized lenses likewise added surprising depth and verisimilitude to *The Captive City*. The use of mirrors and panes of glass as subtle reminders of the two levels of personality embedded in one child adds much to *Audrey Rose*, and the use of infrared film stock and unusual lenses in *The Haunting* helps make this among the most visually entrancing of black and white horror films. Examples could be multiplied, but the point would be the same; as Sidney Lumet, another director who has been accused of lacking stylistic consistency, commented, "That's what style is: the way you tell a particular story." What matters is the manner in which the presentation is grounded in the events being presented, "its organic connection to the material."[8]

This stylistic eclecticism is not accidental. The heart of Wise's work lies not in a particular set of visual mannerisms, but in a concern for a type of experience and a particular approach to presenting those experiences. Wise's films often have neither hero nor villain in the larger-than-life sense; rather, virtually all of them are about the confrontation of an ordinary, professionally trained person, or a small group of such people, with circumstances which run directly counter to their understanding of their professional role(s). That is, Wise takes a person who has a job to do, and who is fully competent, perhaps even excellent, at meeting the normal requirements of that job, and confronts them with a situation in which competence, excellence, and heroism are not merely inadequate but irrelevant, or even destructive. Nor is this all. Underlying this approach is a strong suspicion that the social structure undergirding the professionalism in question may itself be not merely inadequate to the demands placed upon it, either by the individual or by the forces which have created the dilemma faced by that person, but a directly contributory factor in the crisis which underlies the particular film. These two elements, singly or in combination, dominate many of Wise's films, and all of the important ones. As my discussion will demonstrate, Wise's development of these two elements allows us to understand why he is not, and could not have been, an auteur in the full-blown stylistic sense of a Hitchcock or a Bergman. Nonetheless, these films collectively form an important body of work, unjustly neglected, which offers a profound reflection on the nature of humanity under modern Western capitalism and its concomitant social and political relations.

Considering the different films, the basic reasoning behind Wise's stylistic eclecticism should already be clear, although I will be developing it at much greater length as the book unfolds: different professions have different approaches, and the surroundings of a person engaged in each will likewise differ. Stylistically, it would be difficult to determine the directorial link among many of Wise's films, yet in many cases the appearance of the film is a major part of its appeal, and the appearance is driven by Wise's response to the circumstances of the story. The seedy arena and locker room frequented by a small-time professional boxer (*The Set-Up*) will share little with that of a top-secret state-of-the-art biological research facility (*The Andromeda Strain*), for example, and the attitudes, expressions, and behaviors of the denizens of those worlds will likewise differ. To present the settings identically would be to deny those differences, to eradicate the emotional distinctions which the characters themselves would feel. If the feelings of those portrayed differ, so should the cinematic examination thereof. There is thus a method here which it would be unfair to ignore. Wise's choices are just that: decisions designed to enhance the impact of a particular story and approach thereto. This, too, must be accounted a kind of auteurism, even if not in the conventional theoretical sense, for it clearly represents a specific outlook realized in particular ways.

There is a second aspect of Wise's cinema more closely attuned to conventional auteurist expectations, something which is indeed true of each and every one of his films: the pace and rhythm with which they unfold. Wise's films do not move quickly, ever; even Wise's camera, however mobile overall, rarely moves rapidly, either physically or through zooms (two quite striking ones in *The Haunting* are among the chief exceptions, and are themselves driven by the surrounding circumstances). Wise's underlying approach has been described as documentarian, but this is more than a simple matter of visual style. Many of his films, whether the manner of the visuals is naturalistic, atmospheric, or even expressionistic, refrain from insisting upon a particular emotional or moral response through their overt cinematic presence. Wise's subjects are often melodramatic, perhaps even operatically intense, at heart, but the manner of presentation is rarely so; his films draw their strength from a calm, even at times subdued, combination of visual, textual, and histrionic elements, one which offsets, and thereby highlights, the specific factors in the story which intensify the drama. His films suggest; they do not insist. The moral or political conclusions of Wise's motion pictures are quietly reinforced, not punctuated, by their pacing, which allows, even encourages, the viewer to work through the problems on their own. As an illustration, take *The Day the Earth Stood Still*, a film with an avowed message. Apart from Klaatu's spaceship (about which we are told, but which we in fact never see moving at hypersonic speeds), the only machines we see moving rapidly in the entire film are the police and military units preparing to surround Klaatu's ship and, later, hunting him through the streets of Washington. The camera observes, sometimes very carefully indeed, yet it does not participate in the excitement generated by the on-screen movements; there are no rapid cuts ratcheting up the tension, no zooms or swish pans or urgent dollies to and fro. Thus implicit in both the title and the sequence which provides the title — the half hour during which virtually everything mechanical on Earth loses power — is the idea that those most affected will be the military profession-als, whose chief requirement is power, power to move and power to strike. The pacing tells the story as much as anything else, yet no attention is ever called to the fact.

This aspect of Wise's approach was noticed quite early on. François Truf-faut, in a 1954 review of Wise's 1953 film *So Big*, singled out this very ele-ment as an indication of Wise's status — as an auteur, no less. Describing the film as "a kind of masterpiece," Truffaut went on to applaud its detachment: "The emotion is contained throughout, but this very reserve is an added clev-erness of the *auteur* calculated to encourage the tears the women in the audi-ence apparently cannot restrain."[9] In most of his films, and in all of the best ones, Wise leaves room in the presentation for the viewer to become involved, to help create the moral and emotional space within which the action will reverberate. In short, Wise does not, as Hitchcock would prescribe, play the audience like an organ, but rather invites them to exercise their own imagi-nations in exploring the subject at hand: film as chamber music, even when the subject is huge and the scope is vast.

It will at once be seen how this approach reflects Wise's approach to those with whom he worked. Collaboration does not always entail respect, but the evidence says strongly that Wise indeed treated his casts and crews with respect, quietly encouraging their best work but never resorting to tan-trums or insults to obtain it.[10] Wise's films, then, do stem from his person-ality, but his personality was not such as to insist upon predominance, either individually or professionally.

Is this enough to make Wise into an auteur? I do not know; nor does the question strike me as especially important. What matters are the works themselves, not the reputation of the creator(s) thereof. Auteurist theory is often used as a kind of shorthand, such that all films, however minor, by a director awarded the accolade are scrutinized desperately for clues support-ing that director's assigned status; instead of considering the films as films, the auteurist considers them as products of someone whose eminence as a director is already recognized. The flaws in this approach are amply evident and widely admitted, yet somehow the prestige accorded to recognized auteurs remains a determining factor in much critical assessment. But such a theory, like any other theory, is merely a tool, and if it gets in the way of recognizing major achievements by even comparatively minor figures it is not fulfilling its function properly. It is my contention that many of Wise's films are worth examining on their own terms, terms which do indeed fit within a larger vision, whether or not that vision is consistent enough in style and substance to warrant being considered as an example of auteurism.

This book, then, is not a survey of Wise's entire cinematic output, but rather of those films which best embody a particular aspect of that output, and of certain among those films in detail. Wise worked within the studio system, and at times, especially early in his career, took assignments simply because that was his job. Thus, for example, in between such major works as *The Body Snatcher* (1945) and *The Set-Up* (1949), Wise also honed his craft through *A Game of Death* (1945), *Criminal Court* (1946), and *Mystery in Mexico* (1948), minor efforts by any standards. Others among his films, though often quite entertaining, appear to me to stand outside his central concerns. In both cases, the films require little or no commentary (or such commentary as I might offer would be redundant, merely echoing the same point, made in the same way, regarding another film).[11] Above these films are yet others, which, though perhaps significantly flawed, remain intriguing in unexpected ways, and deserve at least a degree of acknowledgment. And some are important films, operating on multiple levels, which demand, and amply reward, close consideration.

Accordingly, I shall begin with a mosaic of somewhat more than a dozen samples drawn from throughout Wise's career. After a preliminary consideration of the central elements which shape and guide Wise's overall approach, I will offer overviews of the relevant elements in each film, indicate the thematic threads connecting the various films, explore the questions of professionalism and its problems as developed therein, and suggest at least some of the social critiques underpinning the film. These discussions will be shorter or longer as the film in question demands; not every film is as complex as the best, and not every film requires extensive analysis in support of my points. Nor will I repeat myself unduly; if the discussion of one film has covered in detail a specific point I am making about Wise's work I shall merely indicate, rather than again discuss, the presence of that element in subsequent sections, trusting the reader to make additional connections for her or himself. The stage having thus been set, I shall, in the second chapter, revisit the central social components of Wise's work in greater detail, using a comparison with the great Swedish director Ingmar Bergman to indicate the breadth and limitations of Wise's overall achievement. With that in mind, I will then explore four further films in greater depth (*The Body Snatcher, The Day the Earth Stood Still, Odds Against Tomorrow,* and *The Andromeda Strain*); these films demonstrate, in various ways, Wise's view of the essential isolation of the individual within the hierarchical system of professionalism, the social structures which shape that hierarchy as currently constituted, and the contradictions within the system itself. These discussions will be followed by separate chapters offering detailed, at times almost shot-by-shot, readings of four of Wise's greatest films, one from each of his most productive decades: *Born to Kill, Executive Suite, The Sand Pebbles,* and *Star Trek: The Motion Picture.* These four films offer, respectively, his most powerful depiction of the shattering consequences of untrammeled individualism, his most complex dissection of hierarchies of power, his clearest and most extensive examination of the fatal consequences of political and military adventurism, and his most optimistic vision of the possibilities, and processes, of overcoming the kinds of problems pointed up in the earlier films. In each of these films Wise masterfully employs an extraordinarily cohesive and complex palette of cinematic elements to great result, and my examinations will be correspondingly and increasingly wide-ranging and expansive.

Although this is a book about a single director, it is not an analysis of that director's psyche through his films. I shall not, therefore, strain to discover hitherto unnoticed stylistic links among the films, though some do exist. The bulk of the book will instead be committed to exploring the types of situations and characters which propel Wise's films and which precluded him from an overriding concern with developing a particular style. Thus I do not discuss the production history of the films, as opposed to their historical context, which may indeed be quite important. I do not compare any of the films to its original source, be it a stage play, a poem, or a novel; each of these originals is a work in its own medium, and I treat the films simply as films. Nor shall I use the films as an illustration of any pet theories, although I shall use elements of such theories freely to the degree that they illuminate the films. In encountering academic cinematic analysis, one frequently gets the impression that the film is being used to demonstrate *that* the theory works rather than the theory being used to show *how* the film works; too often the reading of a given film is twisted to make the film fit the theory, a process which I find unhelpful at best, rather than allowing the film to shape the theoretical boundaries. No theory can cover all aspects of even a single art, let alone of all the arts, and thus no theory is likely to account for every aspect of film, itself a commingling of several arts. The best aesthetic discussions are those which open new or deeper ways of experiencing the works at hand, so where I find a theory, or some component thereof, useful in opening up fresh understandings of the film under consideration I shall happily apply and acknowledge it in the hopes of assisting the viewer to see the film more completely. To the degree that I succeed in this, I will have attained my own modest theoretical goals.

There may be doubts about some of my comparisons or contextual links; it is unlikely, it will be said, that Wise or any of his collaborators had this or that idea or writer or film in mind when creating their own work. On one level — the purely factual — I tend to agree with the concerns this objection reflects; exact and specific *influences* are rare, and difficult to ascertain with certitude. On another, more important, level — of, if you will, cultural *confluences*— I disagree profoundly; there are great patterns of human thought and practice, whether conscious, unconscious, or coincidental, and elements of widely disparate human creations can often be used to illuminate (but not simply to explain away!) elements of others. What matters are the conversations thoughtful viewers coming from different backgrounds can have regarding the work at hand, and any relevant manner of encouraging those conversations strikes me as worth applying. One of the marks of good, and especially great, works of art is their ability to sustain quite distinct, yet extensive, interpretations, to share different kinds of meaning with different kinds of explorers, to answer different questions at different times, or sometimes even simultaneously. Obviously these interpretations, to be relevant, need to be grounded in the work at hand (hence my often detailed descriptive passages); almost as obviously they need to be internally coherent (to claim that an object stands for one thing in the opening scene and something quite opposed in the closing scene needs very great justification indeed, for example). But coherence is found in many ways, not all of them purely factual.

Robert Wise has to a degree been a victim of his own success; had he never made *The Sound of Music*, or had that film been less successful at the box office, he might well be regarded more seriously by academic writers and critics. As with Steven Spielberg in our own time, his popular successes have overshadowed his weightier films, and his work has been treated as all of a piece, none of it worthy of sustained thought (ironically enough, this dismissal itself entails a sort of reverse auteurist approach). It will be clear that I disagree with this assessment; if this book succeeds even partially, it will encourage others to look at the films again with an eye toward appreciating, rather than simply dismissing, their many excellent qualities. I can add nothing to Robert Wise's popular renown, nor do I need to do so; I hope, though, to add something to his posthumous critical reception in return for the complex range of pleasures the best of his films have given me and so many others.

Chapter One

Competence and Crisis

Art cannot change the world, but it can contribute to changing the consciousness and drives of the men and women who could change the world.
(Herbert Marcuse)[1]

Preface

What follows is a brief thematic survey of the various aspects of the clash between internal competence and external challenges in several of Wise's films, greater and lesser alike. These short essays do not pretend to offer either a complete traversal of Wise's output or a comprehensive examination of every element in every one of the films selected as examples. Nor should their respective lengths be taken as necessarily reflecting any corresponding assessment of the relative importance or aesthetic quality of the films under discussion — though I do at times suggest such assessments. Rather, the following 15 essays should be thought of as collectively forming something of an extended prelude to the more detailed discussions which follow, with each essay serving as a window onto some particular aspect of Wise's achievement. Any film could be discussed at greater length; the best films could each generate a book in themselves. This is simply a beginning.

Some preliminary remarks on Wise's work as a whole may be helpful in orienting the reader. Three central ideas wind their way through Wise's output, expressed either thematically (that is, as a substantial element in the action itself) or implicitly (that is, as a reasonable extrapolation from the setting or the action). The first and most important, which I laid out in the Introduction, has to do with the role of, and the limits on, professionalism. The second, also already mentioned in the Introduction, is broader than the first, and involves the relationship between individuals and the settings within which they carry out their actions. This provides the basis for much of Wise's social criticism, for a setting which warps professionalism and cripples imagination is a setting which harms, or even destroys, individuals, and Wise is deeply concerned with individual freedom and self-expression. The third, perhaps less frequently found, and certainly less extensively developed, though not therefore less important than the first two, has to do with the vital role in overcoming those limits played by and through active imagination, especially moral imagination. I shall have considerably more to say about this element as my discussion unfolds; for now it should suffice to indicate that Wise offers not only criticism but, at times, both implicit and more or less explicit visions of a means of transcending the situation being criticized, visions embedded within the action itself.

These three ideas are developed alongside, and occasionally within, a surprisingly harsh worldview, which may, for the sake of convenience, be described as Hobbesian, paralleling as it does the philosophical outlook of the English philosopher Thomas Hobbes (1588–1679). Wise did not make philosophical films as such, and he avowed no link to Hobbes, yet Hobbesian views, among the most influential in modern thought, foreshadow much that is found in his films. Hobbes is the philosopher of authority *par excellence*; having lived through the turmoil leading to, and climaxing in, the English Civil War, he was especially aware of, and worried by, the causes and consequences of social and political chaos. There is in Hobbes a grave distrust of the uncontrolled individual, a distrust grounded in an awareness of the appetites—for money, sex, power — which can drive even an otherwise civilized person to commit quite heinous deeds and to treat other persons as means to the desired ends without any concern for the consequences for those others. Hobbes sees all too clearly the social chaos which must result if such an attitude becomes universal, and he demands strong political controls to prevent such a catastrophe. We see Hobbesian fear particularly in Wise's crime films and Westerns (as in those of many other directors; Hobbesian fears drive more than one director or screenwriter), where individuals acting upon their desires and lusts with little or no regard for others sow widespread havoc, destruction, and death. This fear drives Hobbes's insistence upon the need for strict, powerful, and if necessary violent external controls. "Of all Passions," he wrote, "that which enclineth men least to break the Lawes, is Fear."[2] Or, as Jeremy Rodock, in Wise's 1956 Western *Tribute to a Bad Man*, put it, explaining the need to hang horse thieves, "It's fear that keeps men honest." We see a similar concern for control, this time writ large, in *The Day the Earth Stood Still*, with its demand for supranational dominion over weapons of mass destruction, particularly atomic weapons. There is truth in Hobbes's fears, and Wise confronts that truth directly; much of Wise's work, upon consideration, turns out to be unexpectedly dark in outlook and tone.

Yet it would be wrong to see Wise purely as a Hobbesian filmmaker, or as advocating stringent political authority in a Hobbesian vein. Countering Hobbesian fears about untrammeled individualism is a belief in the possibility of individual and social progress, progress rooted deeply within what is best about human beings as individuals. From the middle 1950s on, Wise's films give ever greater heed to comprehending the social background of human motivations, and with expanding the sense of justice and mercy such an understanding can generate (*Tribute to a Bad Man* is pivotal here, as part of Rodock's trajectory as a character is the softening of his reliance on overly harsh methods of punishment). In fact, this growing emphasis on compassion is not merely a complement to Wise's awareness of the dangers of human moral and emotional atomism and isolation, but a direct consequence of that awareness; the way forward cannot be taken alone but requires that individuals come together in their comprehension of their own damaged condition and the reasons therefore. As Eric Hoffer wrote, human beings "draw together when we are aware that night must close in on all living things; that we are condemned to death at birth, and that life is a bus ride to the place of execution. All our squabbling and vying are about seats in the bus, and the ride is over before we know it."[3] Wise's films starkly delineate the squabbling and vying, but seldom lose sight of the social forces shaping those fights. As seen from this perspective, fundamental human sympathy is warped by power-based human institutions; what is needed to correct the problems depicted is therefore not rigid control but the creation of fresh institutions, ones which reflect, encourage, and channel that natural possibility — possibility, but never certainty — of goodness. The paramount need is community: community of knowledge, of understanding, and of actions based upon these. There is an optimism here which also holds its place in Wise's outlook, albeit an optimism tempered by an awareness that one cannot simply remove social constraints and expect freedom to flower. This side of Wise's perspective is most directly expressed through the role of children in his films, who are almost invariably signifiers of moral stability and the possibility of positive social change (the central exhibit, of course, being *The Sound of Music*). Optimism is less commonly found than its darker counterpart, but it remains present as a possibility in all but the grimmest of Wise's films.

This is not a book on philosophy, and I shall not greatly expand upon these points, yet the presence of such ideas, or descendants thereof, will from time to time be noted, either by me or by the thoughtful reader. The tension between the wish for total freedom and the need for some social controls upon those who would act as if they had such freedom is a long-standing one in American (and world) politics. Wise often depicts that tension, and the varying questions and answers it generates, in his films. Thus the third of the three thematic elements I noted above — professionalism, the relationship between individual and society, and the importance of imagination — links directly with the struggle between freedom and social control, and allows us to see how professionalism tends to support the latter and imagination to press for the former, and sets the stage for following Wise's examinations of these conflicts, personal and political alike.

All of the foregoing is set within a yet larger context, a steadfast secular humanism. Nowhere does Wise call the viewer's attention to this fact, yet acquaintance with a significant number of his films makes it clear. While individuals in Wise's films may hold religious beliefs of one sort or another, almost nowhere is this more than a character trait. Religion is at most simply another profession. Nothing flows from it; the events of the films occur without being influenced in any way by divine forces. Even the ghost stories are made largely without reference to divinity; the supernatural powers are simply forces we do not comprehend, pointing to nothing beyond themselves (a partial exception to this is found in *Audrey Rose*, which exception I will discuss when attending to that film). Wise's films, unlike those, say, of his close contemporary Ingmar Bergman, to whom I will recur in Chapter Two, find no anguish in the silence, or absence, of a deity; the action takes place entirely on the level of human thought and emotion, in a world in which deity is simply irrelevant — unheard, unseen, and unmissed. As I say, Wise does not call anyone's attention to this secularism, but it has important consequences, to which I shall return later.

With these broad guidelines in place, we may now turn to the films themselves.

The Curse of the Cat People (1944)

Gunther von Fritsch fell behind schedule on this Val Lewton sequel and was replaced by Wise, who was already serving as the film's editor. Despite the accidental nature of Wise's first assignment as director, the film fits the profile of many of his later works. Amy Reed (Ann Carter), child of Oliver and Alice (Kent Smith and Jane Randolph), survivors of *The Cat People*, develops a friendship with Irena, the deceased cat woman (and Oliver's first wife) from the earlier film. Amy's parents and teacher respond to her stories with cool rationality, refusing to credit them as anything more than the fantasies of a lonely girl. Frustrated, Amy runs away from home and seeks refuge with an elderly actress who has also befriended her, only to face death at the hands of the actress's estranged daughter. Irena saves her, and in the process Amy's father comes to realize that there is more to the story than fantasy, at which point Irena can at last rest in peace.

The clash between imagination and practicality is limned quite soon; Amy, on a kindergarten field trip to Sleepy Hollow, is following a butterfly, the beauty and freedom of which has entranced her. One of her classmates, a well-meaning but obtuse boy, cries out that he will "get it" for her, which he promptly does; he swoops it up in his cap, and presents the crushed remains to Amy, for which effort he is rewarded with a slap, the reason for which he of course has no idea. His action is in fact the negation of the very thing which appealed to Amy; in possessing the physical object he has eliminated the freedom which it symbolized. In response to Amy's action, her parents meet with the teacher, who is inclined to take the matter less seriously than Mr. Reed. The latter, though, is not concerned about the incident but about what he thinks it portends; "It may seem stupid of me," he tells Miss Callahan, Amy's teacher (Eve March), "but it's not the slap I'm worried about, it's the reason[....] Amy slapped Arnold because he hurt the butterfly, and — it was her friend." Miss Callahan thinks this "a harmless fancy," but Mr. Reed disagrees; "Amy has too many fancies and too few friends, and it worries me. It doesn't seem normal." Shortly afterward he expands on the point to his wife: "I know what can happen when people begin to lie to themselves, imagine things. I love Amy too much to let her lose herself in a dream world where butterflies become pals. I saw what happened to Irena with her cat people." Here he is referring to Irena (Simone Simon), his wife in the first film, who thought herself doomed by a curse to turn into a sort of were-cat; he didn't believe in the curse in the first film, and he doesn't believe it here, despite all sorts of suggestive evidence to the contrary. Such things aren't normal, and therefore don't happen.

But even Miss Callahan's understanding is limited by normality. After Amy has revealed knowledge of Irena to Mr. Reed, he takes her outside and asks her if Irena is in the yard; despite the threat of punishment if she persists in her story, Amy affirms her friend's presence. Mr. Reed punishes his daughter, and afterward talks with Miss Callahan, who is conveniently visiting the Reed home. Miss Callahan quotes from Robert Louis Stevenson's "Unseen Playmate," and suggests that having an imaginary friend is a normal aspect of childhood. "No," Mr. Reed insists, "this is different. This is worse. It isn't just a childish fantasy." Miss Callahan's reply is efficient and pragmatic; "It couldn't be anything else," she assures him, proceeding to provide a quick lecture on child psychology in support of her position. Amy, meanwhile, runs away from home, necessitating a search; with her life in danger, she is saved by Irena's apparition, and is reunited with her parents. Mr. Reed vows to be more understanding, and the film closes with his asking Amy if Irena is in the garden again. As he asks, his eyes shift toward the garden, but he does not turn his head; the viewer is left to determine whether he is refusing to look because he is afraid of what he might see, or of what he might not see. Amy avers Irena's presence, and her father, still without looking, admits, or claims, "I see her too, darling." Amy's face lights up, and her father carries her inside as Irena fades away and the film ends.

The action and imagery are beautifully balanced between normality and fantasy; although the fact of the film's being a sequel to one with more overt supernatural elements does imply that Irena may indeed be a genuine spirit of some sort, at no time is the viewer forced to any conclusion regarding Irena's reality. Yet there is a fascinating and subtle complication which extends beyond the screen images, one grounded in the very nature of film: whenever Amy sees Irena, so do we; if Amy's experiences are hallucinations, so too are ours. It may, and quite sensibly would, be objected that what Amy sees must be shown if we are to understand the plot. But we are implicated even as we object, for the mere fact of having chosen to watch the film at all means that, at least for the time spent watching, we have chosen fantasy over reality. Amy's visions do not exist, because they are cinematic inventions, but in being moved by them (and the film is very successful on an emotional level) we perforce give credence to the dissatisfaction with quotidian reality which would give rise to such visions (we could not have been touched emotionally without seeing the film; we would not see the film if we were completely satisfied with our surrounding reality). This tension is key; at no time are we allowed to dismiss Irena as simply a child's fantasy, and every denial of the imaginative is answered by its affirmation. Thus, for example, Amy's birthday party is virtually spoiled because she has placed the invitations in the bole of an old tree in the backyard rather than mailing them — but we learn that she did so because her father had, some years before, told her it was a magic mailbox. At the party, now limited to the family, Amy is given more coaching in magic by her father, a contradiction she is quick to recognize.

> *Mr. Reed:* Amy, make a wish. Wish real hard, and blow out the candles, and your wish will come true.
> *Amy:* But wishes don't come true.
> *Mr. Reed:* Certain wishes do.
> *Amy:* But you told me in the garden that the wish about the tree couldn't come true.
> *Mr. Reed:* Well, this is different.

His lame response indicates that he, rather than Amy, has not yet learned the most vital lesson: that without an imaginative counterpart, normality is all but unbearable. It is the fantastic element which supports Amy, and which, in the end, will save her life. Whether or not it is objectively real is irrelevant, but those who fail to recognize its importance will risk losing far more than they gain. Those in whose lives there is no art — no fantasy — are impoverished beyond measure, but recognizing this requires also that we transcend our own normality in the interests of invention. In one form or another, it is this idea which lies at the heart of many of Robert Wise's films.

Mademoiselle Fifi (1944)

Wise's first solo directing effort was a studio assignment, but again questions of professionalism play a major role, this time attached to class distinctions. The central character, Elizabeth Rousset (Simone Simon) is a laundress (her profession changed, for obvious reasons, from prostitution in each of the original Guy de Maupassant stories which were combined to form the screenplay). Boarding a coach traveling through occupied France during the aftermath of the Franco-Prussian War, Elizabeth finds herself in the company of a revolutionary, a priest, and several respectable bourgeois couples. While the coach is stopped at an inn, Elizabeth draws the unwelcome attentions of the Prussian officer whose nickname provides the film's title. She refuses his advances, and he refuses to allow the coach to proceed. After some time, the others prevail upon her to sacrifice her honor to their convenience; after she has done so, and the coach is allowed to proceed, they treat her with contempt. At a second encounter with the Prussian officer where he attempts to exert further control over her, Elizabeth kills him.

The film's propagandistic elements are evident; almost as clear is the structure of commercial relations which drive its plot. Elizabeth Rousset already fulfills one function which her social "betters" choose not to fulfill themselves, that of keeping their clothes clean. By implication she is already engaging with bodily wastes of various sorts. Those who are served almost inevitably come to regard it as the duty of those serving to obey them in matters outside of the purview of the initial contractual relations, and thus it is no surprise that the wealthier couples soon abandon any consideration for Elizabeth's situation and see her purely instrumentally. It is thus only a short leap of classification to presume that she can fulfill another function: serving the bodily lusts and, again by implication, bodily discharges of the Prussian officer. Those who serve exist to be used; Elizabeth Rousset serves, and therefore she exists to be used.

Class and political attitudes now converge. Having served her purpose, Elizabeth, like any other object, must now be put back in her place. Having fulfilled the desires of the hated occupiers, Elizabeth, like any collaborator, must now be reviled. Each attitude justifies the other, and each allows the one holding it to avoid considering their own role in creating the foundational situation. Elizabeth is, in essence, discarded, her own humanity dismissed; after all, the reasoning runs, were she fully human she would neither serve nor surrender. That she has been coerced into both conditions (service through economic pressure, and sexual submission through direct personal pressure which she is ill-equipped to resist) is not so much dismissed as irrelevant as not seen at all. Her own behavior is structurally determined; she has been conditioned to serve, and carries out her conditioning all too well. Thus Elizabeth is complicit in her own servitude. She has been defined socially, and come to define herself professionally, as one who serves. Her body operates to carry out tasks which others wish to avoid, and when thrown into a situation where such service includes surrendering itself sexually, it, and she, can offer, initially, only limited resources of resistance. Her own professionalism has foundered on the contradictions of servitude, a fact of which she becomes increasingly aware after her first encounter with the Prussian.

Extreme circumstances breed extreme reactions, and thus it is no surprise that, when the Prussian takes a further opportunity to avail himself of Elizabeth's body, she kills him. In essence she has simply carried her professional duties to their limit; confronted with personal dirty laundry (the man who, with society's encouragement, raped her), she cleans it in the most effective way possible (she removes not merely the dirt but the agent responsible therefore). She then flees to a church whose bells are being kept silent until freedom once more becomes possible; her action being taken as a blow for freedom, the bells ring even as she is given refuge. Contemporary audiences would simply have noted that a German had been killed for France, but far more interesting is the fact that what is being celebrated is in fact a blow by and for an individual against her own servitude. It is a point Wise would develop, in greater detail and at greater length, in subsequent films.

The Set-Up (1949)

Stoker Thompson (Robert Ryan) is an over-the-hill boxer still struggling to make his living in the ring, even though his best days, never very good to begin with, are well behind him. He goes on because he continues to dream of achieving the success which has thus far eluded him. Having been boxing for 20 years, since he was 15, he literally cannot imagine doing anything else: "If you're a fighter, you gotta fight," he tells his increasingly unhappy wife Julie (Audrey Totter). His manager arranges with a local gangster for Stoker to throw a fight to the gangster's favored boxer, but doesn't even bother to tell Stoker, so certain is he that Stoker will lose (the titular set-up). Stoker instead wins, and has his right hand broken by the gangster for having welshed on the arrangement.

Despite the setting and much of the on-screen action, including the stunningly filmed and edited final bout, *The Set-Up* is only tangentially about boxing *per se*. Rather, it is about power, or, more often, the lack of it, and what it does to individual dreams and desires. Practically any one-on-one sport would have sufficed, though the violence inherent in boxing serves well as a central metaphor, as does the limited space available in a boxing ring. Wise makes especially good visual use of this toward the film's climax, as Stoker realizes he is trapped, both literally and figuratively, by his situation; as he scuttles through the empty arena, the shadows cast by the ropes around the ring form a rigid grid, silently reminding the viewer that Stoker was always enframed, even when he thought he was most free.

Stoker is trapped by more than gangsters and ominous shadows. He is trapped by his own limitations, both of ability and of self-knowledge; he is what he does, and he is not very good at what he does, but he cannot admit this even, or perhaps especially, to himself or his wife. "Two hours after the fight," Julie reminds him regarding his last defeat, "you still didn't know who I was." Stoker's response is to dismiss the last fight and extol his chances in the next one. He outlines a well-worn scenario; if he can land just one real punch on his much-younger opponent tonight, he'll knock him out, which will mean a rematch (a hundred and fifty dollars), maybe even a "top spot" (five hundred dollars, maybe even six hundred). That's real money, he tells Julie, money enough to let him invest in a younger boxer and train him, or to open a bar or a cigar store. Julie tries to make him see her real fears, which have nothing to do with money: "It makes no difference to me if you go back to the docks or drive a garbage truck or — or go on relief even[....] [I]t's better than havin' you with your brains knocked out, Bill. It's better than havin' you dead."[4] Stoker, who endures the physical violence, fails completely to understand its emotional impact on Julie; "Maybe you can go on taking the beatings," she tells him; "I can't." He leaves for the fight.

In a certain sense, this is what Stoker *must* do, for the alternative is to admit that he has failed at the only thing he has ever done, failed at the profession by which he is defined, both by himself and by others. Even in speculating about possible future options, Stoker's list is sparse, not only limited but unrealistic; there is no reason whatsoever to believe that he would be any more successful as a small shopkeeper than as a boxer. Stoker may not be much as a boxer but he would probably be less as anything else, for he lacks training, education, and imagination. In a society in which making money is paramount, Stoker has turned to the only resource he has available: his own body. He has converted himself into an object to be marketed and used like any other. Like any such object, he has a limited shelf life, and he is reaching that limit now.

Here the main theme of *The Set-Up* intersects with a secondary, but still significant, motif. The film is also about time, about confronting the ineluctable manner in which individuals face the decay and loss of hopes and possibilities. Wise anchors this theme in the simplest manner possible; the action of the film takes place in exactly the film's running length, a fact signaled by numerous shots of, or containing, clocks of one sort or another (or, sometimes, just the ticking of a clock). This is not simply a gimmick, but a fundamental aspect of Stoker's situation. His time as a boxer is running out, and with it his time to find a new path, a new sense of self. It is this pressure which he at last begins to feel and, more importantly, to acknowledge, as the film proceeds.

Stoker lives in a world of exaggerations and illusions covering up a harsh reality. He and Julie are staying in Paradise City, which is anything but paradisiacal. The dance hall between the hotel and the arena is named Dreamland. When Julie walks about the city streets instead of attending Stoker's fight, she passes under neon signs advertising "Dancing" and "Prescription Drugs"; although belonging to two separate establishments the signs are juxtaposed, the former above the latter, in such a way as to equate the two products, each a means of overcoming pain. She passes the dance hall, the dancers seen as gyrating shadows on an opaque window next to a sign proclaiming the presence of "Sammy Combs and his World-Famous Orchestra," an accolade whose truth may be doubted, as may the hall's claim to providing a "refined atmosphere." As Stoker prepares, he listens to Gunboat Johnson (David Clarke), one of his fellow fighters, warm up for his own fight by obsessively repeating, as he evidently has done many times before, a story of a man who began with a long string of defeats but rose to become a champion (Gunboat will be knocked out less than two minutes into his second round, quite probably suffering brain damage in the process). Stoker's trainer, Gus (Wallace Ford), relaxes after prepping the fighters by reading a pulp magazine entitled *Thrilling Love*, the contents of which, one suspects, do not reflect the reality of his life.

Illusions are the dark side of imagination, for they require it even as they warp it. Pure imagination is a transformative engagement with reality, whereas illusions subvert reality, or deny it. Illusions thus require ever-stronger supports to maintain themselves or they eventually crack, crumble, and give way to reality. Unfortunately, illusions, feeding upon imagination, often find just enough hope to keep going, to overwhelm far stronger evidence which contradicts them. Illusions are internal, deriving much of their strength from the person's need to believe in them; the less satisfactory a person's inner life is, the more likely he or she will be to succumb to illusions of one sort or another, each addressing some experienced deficit in reality. Hence Gunboat's concentration on history, which reveals that one man did overcome a string of defeats to become a champion, rather than on his own deficiencies as a fighter. Hence the insistence of Tony (Phillip Pine) on using the Bible as a guide to the afterlife, despite what he admits as the million-to-one odds of it being accurate; as Stoker notes in vague approval, "Everybody makes book on something." Imagination builds upon as many facts as it can obtain; illusion ignores as many as it must. Imagination energizes; illusion enervates.

Stoker's illusions are under great pressure from reality. Julie's increasing distaste for his profession, growing from her love for him, is one warning. Another comes in the form of the inert bodies carted from the ring, or the battered faces weary with defeat (though here there are still those who win, since somebody must, wins taken as carrying greater evidentiary weight than do the losses). A third is visible in the faces of those sitting around the ring, people for whom Stoker, Gunboat, and the other fighters are indeed simply objects for their amusement. Stoker sees the first of these as he enters the arena and steps up to watch a moment of the current bout; a close-up focuses on Stoker but is dominated by a man's head screaming, "kill 'im, kill 'im."

Stoker is a commodity. It may be argued that he has freely chosen this role (though this would lead into deep debates about the nature both of freedom and of choice), but the consequences are the same however he has arrived at this position: he exists, to those who plunk down their money and purchase a ticket, not as a person but as a thing. The same, of course, is true of his opponent, Tiger Nelson (Hal Fieberling), who represents an investment on the part of a local gangster. The interchangeability of the two men, of any two fighters, is indicated by the crowd, which begins by rooting largely for Nelson, the expected winner, but shifts toward rooting for Stoker as his victory looks more likely; toward the end, one respectably dressed woman is seen, close-up, screaming, "Stoker, Stoker, kill him, kill him," an obscene smile stretching across her face, and then later, in an extreme close-up, the tightest in the film, as just a mouth urging the same action.[5]

These people see Stoker and Nelson as providing a return on their investment (the price of a ticket), good or bad in proportion to the violence offered. His humanity is of no account, his evident pain and exhaustion merely part of the thrilling show for which good money has been paid. Stoker's own manager likewise sees him through purely monetary lenses, and thus has no compunction about selling him out on the expectation that he will perform (poorly) as he has done before. A thing is presumed to have no motivations, and its character is of interest only inasmuch as it can be expected to perform in accordance therewith: "There's no percentage in smartening up a chump," he declares as the reason for not telling Stoker about the arrangement (when he tells him later, it is only because he is becoming afraid that Stoker might win and is trying to get Stoker to take the fall by offering him an extra 30 dollars). To enter into such a system is to become subject to its internal processes, to lose one's freedom (things are not free); near the end of the fight Stoker and Nelson are battering each other so furiously that they are unaware of the bell and must be torn apart by the referees and handlers. To speak of freedom here is not merely a misnomer, it is a brutal joke; these men have been reduced to machines carrying out functions determined by others. Stoker's life, like that of most people, is shaped and largely controlled by money — by his need for it (he must earn to eat, if nothing else), by his dreams about it (his aforementioned hopes of investing in another boxer), and by his place in relation to the fiscal desires of others (he asks why his fight has been scheduled after the main event and is told bluntly, "The radio. Gotta go with the main early."). And then, of course, there is the fact that considerable sums have been wagered on his presumably pre-arranged defeat by his opponent that night, sums which will be lost through his unexpected victory ("I paid for something tonight. And I didn't get it," the gangster Little Boy [Alan Baxter] murmurs). The lost investments will require recompense, in the form of a violent beating and the destruction of Stoker's ability to fight and thus his ability to earn money.

Practically everyone sees Stoker as a means to an end, be it profit or entertainment. The one who does not is Julie, who in place of illusion has imagination, and who thus provides what hope the film has for the future. She understands, because she can envision, the consequences should Stoker continue being battered, whether he wins or loses (early in her walk about the city, she overhears a boxing match on the radio, and shudders in horror as she imagines it to be Stoker's bout; upon discovering that it is Gunboat's defeat being reported, she sags in Pyrrhic relief). While Stoker is fighting she is strolling the city, perhaps contemplating leaving him, or even suicide (she spends much time standing on a bridge staring down at the trains and buses passing below), but as the night lengthens she returns to the commercial strip and purchases some food to have waiting for him when he returns. She sees Stoker stagger from the alley where he has been crippled by the thugs and runs to him, and it is with their rejoining that the film reaches its ambiguous ending. Stoker rasps out his realization that he can no longer fight, and his expression contains a mix of sadness and relief. "I won tonight," he tells her, still proud of his last victory, though we realize that he is as much proud of having refused to take a fall as of actually defeating Tiger Nelson. "We both won tonight," she replies, her tear-streaked face radiant; "we both won tonight."

If they did, it is hardly an unmixed victory. *The Set-Up* refuses to take the easy way out, and there is at the end no certainty whatsoever of a happy continuation (an ambulance is on its way, and Julie and Stoker, neither of them employed, will soon have to pay the medical bills, for example).[6] Within the confines of a brief film in a limited setting, Wise has explored a wide range of social and emotional implications, gaining insights which would be developed at even greater length elsewhere, especially in *Odds Against Tomorrow* and *The Sand Pebbles*.

The House on Telegraph Hill (1951)

A studio assignment Wise originally demurred at taking, this is something of a rehash of elements from Alfred Hitchcock's *Suspicion* and *Rebecca*, the principal difference being that the husband is, in fact, a murderer. Victoria Kowelska (Valentina Cortesa), while in a concentration camp, befriends Karin Dinackowa; when the latter dies, Victoria decides to assume her identity to get to the United States, where Karin has relatives. There she meets Alan Spender (Richard Basehart), a friend of the family who woos and wins her, but who proves to have ulterior motives. Several attempts to kill her misfire, the last fatally for Spender himself, who accidentally drinks the poisoned orange juice he has prepared for Victoria.

What is of interest here is not the suspense plot, but the fact that the central characters represent, with one partial exception, inversions of Wise's usual concern. As with the more complex central figures in *Born to Kill*, whose harsh detachment from normal social interactions I will examine in Chapter Three, these are all people without external professions, at least of readily discernible nature, though this film goes even further than the earlier one in detaching its principals from ordinary job-related connections. Indeed, Cortesa's character doesn't even have her own identity for a substantial portion of the film. Nor does she do anything even remotely joblike, either explicitly or implicitly. Likewise her new husband; although he refers to having work to do, the nature of this work is never specified. Major Marc Anders (William Lundigan), who succors Victoria and to whom she eventually confesses her secret, does have a job (his military rank and status are relevant only as a means of connecting his character with Cortesa's), but it is, apart from one minor aspect, driven entirely by the needs of the plot, of singular unimportance; he himself notes that, although he is nominally the senior partner in his firm, customers prefer to deal with the older junior partners.

Only the nursemaid (Fay Baker) to Cortesa's inherited son can be said to have a profession, although the reason for her devotion to the boy is left unclear.[7]

Once these differences between this film and others in Wise's career have been noted, though, it remains clear that the basic structure remains typical, albeit on a purely personal level: the problems of each of the central characters stem in large part from the self-presentational choices they have made, from what they profess to be. Victoria poses as a mother to a boy she has never met (he was sent away from Europe while still extremely young, and thus does not remember his actual mother), and is unaware that he is the heir to a large sum. Spender has posed as a caring but distant relative to the boy, which in turn ensures that when an actual close relative (the putative mother) appears he will have to take drastic measures to handle the threat she presents. The professional problems are therefore in each case quite literally problems based on a profession; each character is confronted with difficulties stemming from the foundational falsehood on which the rest of their actions rest. The difference between this film and most of Wise's others is one of emphasis rather than subject. In the other films the professionals are, on the whole, what they claim to be, and the question is whether the training which allows the claim to be made at all is adequate to the circumstances; here the absence of training creates the increasing desperation underlying actions subsequent to the initial falsehood.[8] Only when the falsehoods are admitted can the desperation be ameliorated, the circumstances be overcome, and the characters restored, or admitted, to their proper professions. Each of the characters has committed the error of mistaking their situation (or job) for their vocation, and until this error is rectified they will remain detached from, and uncomfortable with, the world in which they carry out the actions associated with their position. Wise will revisit this sort of problem, in greater detail and with greater success, in later films.

The Captive City (1952)

As Wise moved into the 1950s, his films began, like those of many other directors, to take on what has been described as a documentary appearance, eschewing stylization in favor of a grittier naturalism (a stripped-down approach which serves to make the occasional movements away from it all the more striking and effective). Typical of these films is *The Captive City*, made for Wise's own production company on a tight budget (250,000 dollars), and filmed entirely on location. It follows the story of Jim Austin (John Forsythe), co-owner and editor of a small circulation newspaper who has uncovered, confronted, and is now escaping from, an organized criminal gambling ring. As befits the subject, there is no true resolution; rather, Austin simply tells his story, concluding with a plea to the audience to do their part in fighting organized crime. An epilogue features Senator Estes Kefauver making the same point. Kefauver had been head of the Senate Committee to Investigate Organized Crime in Interstate Commerce from 1950 to 1951; the hearings he chaired, some of which were televised, had captured widespread interest and made him a far more recognizable figure than any of the performers in the film, adding to its documentary appeal.

Yet there is more here than immediately meets the eye. The corruption already seen in *The Set-Up* was limited, local, and personal. Here it has metastasized across an entire city, with the willing, if often unwitting, participation, of many of the citizens. Wise and screenwriters Karl Kamb and Alvin Josephy, Jr. have themselves uncovered a serious social problem, though perhaps not the one against which Kefauver warns at the end. Crime takes two forms here: physical (a photographer who takes the wrong sort of photograph is beaten up; a private investigator who learns too much is murdered), which is socially unacceptable and universally condemned, and economic (various people are seen abetting the criminal organization because doing so is profitable). This latter practice is not only widely accepted, it is even to a degree necessary, or at least seen as such; ordinary people have a hard enough time making ends meet, and must seize any reasonable opportunity to make more money. Gambling itself takes advantage of this fact; by far the majority of gamblers, legal or otherwise, are in fact harming themselves by spending too much of what little they have in a vain attempt to acquire more, either because they genuinely need it or because they have become convinced they do (the creation of this conviction being simply an echo of the methods of modern advertising's relationship with the drive to acquire ever more commodities). Hence the blind eye turned by many citizens to illegal economic activities on the part of others; all recognize that such illegal activities are often merely shadow forms of much larger and more successful activities on the part of those who control society. In a society in which money is essential to survival, everything else takes second place. When the centrality of money is partially obscured, as it is in the United States, there is still room for outrage when the activities involved go beyond the merely fiscal to include violence. Hence the odd nature of many such warning films as this: the ostensibly evil nature of the minor activity (here, gambling) is in fact developed, and can be developed only through an emphasis on another activity altogether (here, murder), because the first activity is too closely linked to the economic character of society to be condemned outright.

That this is so, and that the film recognizes the fact, is made clear as Austin's campaign begins to be noticed. The citizens are not behind Austin, and the town's business leaders are least supportive; the first thing they do is start pulling their advertising from the newspaper in an attempt to pressure Austin to call off his crusade (thus pointing up another rarely noted oddity: what we descriptively label as a "newspaper" is in fact an advertising circular which also provides news; the ratio is invariably weighted in favor of the advertisements, as without the income derived therefrom no newspaper could exist in the first place). In other words, both the average citizen and the business leaders know and welcome what Austin never acknowledges: that business benefits directly from the flow of extra money, however that money is obtained. Ordinary citizens acquire more goods, and the business community acquires more profits; there is little reason seen by members of either to change the system or their behavior within it, whatever the consequences. Corruption is therefore inherent in the system even as it attacks corruption most strongly; or, rather, the system itself requires a degree of complicity from those who participate in it, such that to participate is to be corrupted, and even, to a degree, to will that corruption upon oneself. Here we see the reason for the enormous emphasis on self-interest in modern capitalism, an emphasis given voice by several characters in the film. Any fundamental change toward equality in the present structure of human relations would require a repudiation of what we have been trained to regard as being in our self-interest. It rarely being rational to act against our own self-interest, we assume that actions to change the present structure of human relations would be irrational. It is only when we more closely examine what we have been trained to take as our self-interest and recognize that in many cases it is in fact quite the opposite that we can shift our perspective on the rationality of the actions we have previously chosen to take in the service of that imposed concept of self-interest.

There is a link here with Wise's interest in the role of imagination, in this case moral imagination; so long as we remain trapped within our own narrow circle of egoism, unable to develop within ourselves an empathetic understanding of the situation and needs of others, so long as we will be unable to comprehend the need for change, whether on our part or that of the society within which we live. Only if we can step outside of ourselves as it is presently constituted can we hope to see ourselves, and our surroundings, clearly enough to make the appropriate decisions. One of the results of shared public experiences, whether artistic (e.g., a film) or political (e.g., a Senate Committee hearing) can be to aid in this recreation of our inner selves, this expansion of our moral horizons.

But such changes are neither instantaneous nor guaranteed; attaining them requires considerable effort, and makes for discomfort. The ordinary person is not a crusader, and tends to feel awkward in the presence of one, especially if they know both that the crusader's claims are plausible and that accepting and acting upon those claims would entail a change in their own behavior. Austin encounters this, and learns that all one can do is strive without certainty of success. In this regard, *The Captive City* parallels but exceeds Frank Capra's *Mr. Smith Goes to Washington*, in which the eponymous protagonist stands up for what is right only to learn that "the people" to whom he is appealing not only don't care, they downright disapprove. Capra, desperate to believe in the redemptive power of democracy, resorts (as in others among his films) to an implausible *deus ex machina*, here the breakdown of Senator Paine. Wise admits instead that, without a genuine change in the conditions in which political and economic decisions are made and actions are taken, no such resolution is possible, save rarely and in isolation; his hero is in fact fleeing for his life (the main action of the film is told in flashback). Capra's film is far better (John Forsythe, though crisp and competent, is no James Stewart, and Wise has no Claude Rains at all, among other obvious comparisons), but Wise's is more honest in its conclusions.

The Desert Rats (1953)

It is in the nature of war films to confront their characters with extreme situations. *The Desert Rats* is in many ways typical: the raw recruits must learn to be professional soldiers under the tutelage of a harsh but ultimately admirable career officer, Captain (later breveted Major and then Lieutenant Colonel) MacRoberts (Richard Burton). The complications here are, first, that one of those raw recruits is the alcoholic former tutor of MacRoberts, Bartlett (Robert Newton), a self-admitted coward who signed up while drunk, and, second, that MacRoberts is an Englishman commanding Australian troops. Aided by excellent performances, Wise develops Richard Murphy's somewhat episodic (though Oscar-nominated) screenplay through pinpoint editing, careful composition, and the gritty cinematography of Lucien Ballard in such a manner that an otherwise fairly routine war picture looks and feels much more complex and effective than a bare description would indicate.

As in many of Wise's films, the pseudo-documentary feel is key. The film begins with dramatic music over the Twentieth Century–Fox logo.[9] Newsreel-style lettering gives the date and place of the film: 1941— Libyan Desert, North Africa. We see the commander of the Afrika Corps, Erwin Rommel (James Mason, reprising his role from *The Desert Fox*, a film deemed by many to be rather too sympathetic to the Nazi officer), making plans to take the Suez Canal. Rommel and his officers speak in German, without subtitles, adding to the documentary effect. A narrator (an uncredited Michael Rennie) intrudes, setting the scene and explaining that the only thing standing in Rommel's way is an Australian garrison besieged at Tobruk. A massive assault is shown under the credits, and we know the men involved, the titular desert rats, will face worse before the film is over.

The pseudo-documentary approach works here, as in many others among Wise's films, by allowing the film to slide into far less traditionally realistic elements almost unnoticeably. The process is visible quite early on; Bartlett, having been too drunk to march from the dock to the camp, receives a ride from his old pupil MacRoberts. Having been dropped off, he turns and sees the other men straggling toward their barracks. Naturalistically speaking, the scene makes little sense, as Bartlett has been dropped off in the middle of the desert (something that might be the barracks area is barely visible in the far background). Emotionally, though, the setting is entirely appropriate, and thus realistic on a deeper level than mere fact. Bartlett's isolation and fear are powerfully suggested by the dimly lit, wide-open space around him, accented by the constant lightning-flicker of German artillery on the far horizon; simultaneously, the lack of discipline and hope among the green troops is encapsulated by their slow trudging in no order at all toward no visible destination. The filming here takes on a noirish cast which is no longer documentary in nature, but which we accept because we've already been eased into taking the film's overall approach as being true to the "facts." This alternation between naturalistic imagery (including stock footage) and segments filmed with much richer highlights, taking on at times an almost dream-like sheen, will continue throughout the film.

MacRoberts's credo begins as that of military professionals everywhere: "Only a line officer knows that *any* decision he makes in battle may involve somebody being killed or wounded. His job is to follow orders and make decisions, without letting sentiment, loyalty, friendship or anything else interfere." He sees himself as simply an agent of a larger tactical purpose. He expects his men to accept his approach, and for a time he is, despite occasional grumblings from those under his command, successful in leading the men to ever more daring and dramatic feats of combat. The facts on the ground, so to speak, support his presuppositions concerning the relative places of a trained commander and his men.

But MacRoberts's approach to his task is flawed by his own self-reliance; he takes personal responsibility for every detail, and inevitably discovers that he cannot live up to his expectations regarding himself. Hints that he is covering up his own uncertainties appear occasionally, but the crisis comes at the film's evident climax. He has been tasked with leading the defense of a strategically important hill, where his troops are suffering extensive casualties as the three days originally envisioned extends to eight. At last he snaps. Learning of the parlous state of the troops under his command as regards ammunition and casualties, he lashes out, "I don't give the orders, I just obey them." But this is no longer enough, as he admits: "Headquarters told me to hold; I can't!" Exhausted, he decides to order a retreat. Having a keen grasp of the facts of the situation, MacRoberts is incapable of imagining any response to those facts other than the one he has ordered. Despite his expertise, both presumed and repeatedly proven, his decision is wrong.

The two elements of MacRoberts's situation and character provide the base on which the film rests, and it proves to be an unexpected one. Almost lost amidst the alternating scenes of tactical exposition and the ensuing battles is an intriguing fact: that MacRoberts, the central professional soldier, fails in the end, saved from his own act of despair only by the collective action of his men and the convenient arrival of the relieving force. Once again, Wise manages to suggest that individual professionalism, no matter how dressed up in powerful speeches and courageous acts, is in the end not enough; the individual must be transcended to achieve the results most desired by that individual. It is a lesson one would think obvious in wartime, yet a point often ignored by the more hero-centered sort of war films.

The lesson is pointed up through a powerful yet subtle detail of staging. MacRoberts's chief statement of his outlook comes at the beginning of an extended scene with Bartlett, who is pleading for mercy on behalf of an officer MacRoberts has ordered court-martialed for abandoning his post in battle, even though the ostensible abandonment was the result of an effort to rescue his commanding officer. Bartlett is standing in a dugout, MacRoberts striding the ground above him; MacRoberts is clearly in control, every bit the hard-nosed commander. Yet Bartlett, knowing his own weaknesses, holds a kind of moral equality with MacRoberts, an equality suggested by subsequent events. A German air attack frightens Bartlett, a fact noticed by MacRoberts, who joins him in the dugout, where Bartlett expresses his fear and his own sense of failure of nerve. The ensuing dialogue is filmed is a series of alternating two-shots, allowing neither to dominate until MacRoberts brusquely rejects Bartlett's plea and leaves the dugout, resuming his dominant position.

This visual balance is reversed during MacRoberts's crisis. Having learned that the Germans are again on the move, he begins the process of ordering a pull-out. Bartlett, by now serving as something of an orderly to MacRoberts, questions him, and we see that MacRoberts has reversed his opposition to allowing considerations external to the tactical situation to play a role in command decisions. Angry at Bartlett's suggestions that his decision to retreat is not the one he really wants to make, especially given the tactical realities, MacRoberts explodes angrily: "You drunken old fool! There're over a hundred men out there and I'm responsible for them. If I order them to stay they'll all be killed. It's senseless to ask 'em for what they haven't got. I can't do it and I won't do it!" Bartlett's response is somber but to the point; "I'm old, I'm a drunk, and maybe I'm a fool," he says. "But I do know what I'm talking about. Don't take all this on yourself, Tammy. Everybody needs help sometimes. Let *them* help you. Ask them." MacRoberts, imprisoned by his putative knowledge and his assumption of a particular professional role, cannot; "No," he responds. "I've had it. I can't." Violently, he orders Bartlett to carry out his orders to call for a withdrawal. The entire scene is filmed as an inversion of the earlier one; even as MacRoberts condemns Bartlett the latter is seen, for the only time in the film, standing above MacRoberts, taking the superior position. The two-shots emphasize Bartlett's moral authority, derived from self-knowledge rather than adherence to external rules; those from Bartlett's position angle downward toward MacRoberts; those from MacRoberts's side are slightly below his eye level.

The order is given, but MacRoberts finds that the men have refused to obey it. They are armed and awaiting the German advance, with Bartlett having taken the forward warning post by himself. Inspired by these actions, MacRoberts rallies the men, following a German artillery barrage, to "Fix bayonets," the sign of impending close combat. His heroic stance turns out to be unnecessary; the German barrage has ceased because the Germans have been forced to retreat by the advance of an Allied relief force from the east. The film ends in a blaze of major-key martial music as the men celebrate their salvation.

It is possible to come away from *The Desert Rats* with the intended sense of military heroism duly honored. This impression is not entirely mistaken; the soldiers do perform their tasks above and beyond the call of duty while remaining ordinary men with all their foibles and weaknesses. Yet at the same time, there is a strong sense here of the role that luck, rather than will, plays in such matters; had the relief forces been delayed by even an hour, the defending troops would have been annihilated.[10] Nor is MacRoberts's future assured; he knows, and we know, that he *did* place the call to headquarters announcing the pullback, and that this could well be taken by higher officers behind the lines as a sign that he has lost his fighting edge.[11] This is not, though, the focal point of the action. What matters at the film's climax is not MacRoberts's fate *per se*, but that MacRoberts's men, acting collectively, have decided to disobey his orders in the service of the greater cause. The amateurs have superseded the professional, for they have arrived independently at the conclusion from which he started (the necessity of subordinating individual loyalties to military exigency), and have done so in the only manner that sustains moral weight: through free choices shared with others. No person acts in a vacuum, and choices taken without consideration of the needs and situations of others are morally vicious. MacRoberts had failed to understand that such actions as those taken by his men, while they can be commanded, are most meaningful, and most powerful, when freely chosen, and this can come about only through a collective understanding and choice shared among genuine individuals. Hence the centrality of Bartlett's cowardice and drunkenness; these attributes render him an outsider to the traditional military virtues, making his eventual decision to fully participate in the combat MacRoberts sought to avoid all the more potent. It is no accident that it is Bartlett, not the sergeant who usually conveys MacRoberts's orders, who informs the men of the true situation; their collective decision to act upon his words signifies the shared humanity, rather than obedience, of the soldiers. *The Desert Rats*, then, while a comparatively minor war film, is profoundly humanistic in a way that many others are not. Rather than relying on overheated portrayals of amatory passion fueled by impending combat, or depicting excessively heroic individual actions more suited to legend than history, it grounds itself on the shared experience of combat and the tensions it creates within ordinary men. As such, it remains considerably more relevant and watchable than many of its contemporaries.

Run Silent, Run Deep (1958)[12]

Surging forward on a broodingly dramatic score by Franz Waxman, Wise's last war film of the 1950s, although in many ways fairly conventional in plot and character motivation, is an excellent example of his ability to increase the emotional intensity of a film with small but telling details. The story is not complex. Having commanded one submarine lost to enemy action, Commander P.J. Richardson (Clark Gable) convinces the navy to give him command of the *Nerka*, whose Executive Officer, Lieutenant Bledsoe (Burt Lancaster), had expected the position. Tensions and conflicts ensue, with various among the crew taking the side of one or the other of the officers. Richardson achieves his vengeance against the Japanese destroyer which he believes to have sunk his submarine, but at the cost of mortal injuries; Bledsoe demonstrates his command capability by following through on Richardson's plans, after which he and the crew commit Richardson's body to the sea, implicitly burying the internal conflicts with it.

As with *The Desert Rats*, the power of the film comes not from the story, effective though it is, but from the way Wise uses the intense realism of the setting. Wise sailed aboard an actual submarine while preparing the film, and had the set constructed to scale, using as much navy surplus equipment as possible. The restrictions this placed on blocking and camera movement work to good advantage, emphasizing the various characters not merely as war movie stereotypes (which most certainly are) but as individuals, each of whom is constantly grating on the nerves of everyone else. Assisting this tension are the many close-ups, which, especially on the big screen, gradually create and maintain the claustrophobic nature of the surroundings even within a large movie house. Filming in black and white added a further dimension of emotional realism; even muted color would have been too lush for such a stark plot. Yet for all of the film's documentary aspects, its core is limned through quite other means, and it is here that Wise's directorial approach and touch manifest themselves most effectively.

The key here is imagination, though our first glimpse of its working is presented misleadingly. An intertitle informs us that a year has passed since the opening events. We see Richardson brooding, presumably over the loss of his command, in an office at Pearl Harbor. His adjutant Mueller (Jack Warden) arrives and sets up some toy ships on the desktop. The two play through an attack on a destroyer of the *Akikaze* class, the type of ship which sank Richardson's previous command, Richardson evidently growing more intensely involved as the game unfolds. Within seconds the destroyer has been "sunk," making, as Mueller tells Richardson, "two hundred times you sunk Bungo Pete in two hundred days. He only sunk you once." Richardson, though, admits the important distinction: "Just once. But that wasn't on a desk." Moments later, on learning that yet another submarine has been lost in the same area as his was, his frustration boils over, and he flings the toys to the floor. The action is symbolically significant; Richardson is renouncing fantasy and ready again to challenge reality — yet the challenge will succeed only because of the fantasy, the imaginative game, in the first place.

Richardson obtains command of the *Nerka*, and the desktop game gives way to larger and more serious ones as he takes the crew through a series of drills, their purpose adumbrated by the earlier game but still unknown to either crew or the first-time viewer. In fact, the purpose is simple: to allow the *Nerka* to sink a Japanese destroyer with a head-on torpedo shot (a "bow-shot") even as the destroyer attacks the submarine. The technique is, to say the least, unorthodox, and has evolved in Richardson's mind over, and by means of, those months of play; the imaginary act will make possible the real triumph. Applying his technique, though, will require another, more serious act contravening reality, this time Richardson's own professional duties. His orders are explicit; he is to avoid the territory in which four submarines have been lost. He will disobey.

The process is approached obliquely, in a manner foreshadowing the eventual climax of the film. The *Nerka* encounters a Japanese submarine, but Richardson, to the disgruntlement and anger of the crew, orders that no action be taken. In fact, his decision makes sense; taking on such a target would be difficult at best, possibly requiring considerable expenditure of the limited supply of torpedoes, and should the submarine escape it would report the encounter, leading to heightened surveillance and a riskier mission later on. But Richardson, like MacRoberts in *The Desert Rats*, is too confident of his own tactical rectitude to bother informing the crew (one third of them are "new men"). Thus it is that the next encounter, with a tanker escorted by a *Momo* type destroyer, is initially greeted with little enthusiasm or excitement among the crew. Even when Richardson orders an approach, it is at first dismissed by one crew member as "just sightseeing." His approach is serious; it is, in fact, the final component of the series of drills. The tanker is torpedoed and the *Nerka*, remaining on the surface, is sighted by the escort, which turns to attack. All works as planned by Richardson; the *Nerka* dives and fires as the Japanese ship approaches, and the latter is indeed sunk. The crew celebrates; their commanding officer is indeed a cool-headed man and they no longer need fear being led by a coward.

Not all of them are so sanguine, though. Kohler (Joe Moross), the crew member standing in relation to Bledsoe where Mueller stands in relation to Richardson, comes to Bledsoe to express his anxieties.

> *Kohler:* I've seen all kinds of captains[....] But I never saw one run away from a Jap sub before, then take on a destroyer with a shot I didn't even know was in the book. There has to be a reason. That bow shot didn't just happen. The drills were planned for it[....] I never heard of a bow shot being set up where it wasn't used in desperation. It's all like some experiment.
> *Bledsoe:* Suppose a bow shot was the only way he thought he could get an *Akikaze*. [This is clearly a speculative statement, not a question.]
> *Kohler:* An *Akikaze* isn't a *Momo*, there's a hell of a difference.[13]
> *Bledsoe:* This *Akikaze*'s in the Bungo Straits.
> *Kohler:* But that's impossible, the orders say to avoid it.
> *Bledsoe:* I know.

The tension underlying the film has moved to a new level, and the relations between Bledsoe and Richardson are now less stable than before (a fact signaled by the rising and falling camera movements, ostensibly motivated by the motion of the submarine yet rarely seen elsewhere).

Bledsoe occupies the pivot point between the two elements driving the film. On the one hand, he is the man responsible for seeing that rules and regulations are followed to the letter, which duty he accepts and acknowledges; here he is a man of fact and explicit knowledge. On the other, he is facing a captain who, albeit within the bounds of military protocol, which necessarily leaves much leeway to commanders on the field of battle, has decided to disobey direct orders based on what may be an entirely illusory tactical advantage; here he must decide his own attitude toward imagination, which by definition operates within boundaries which are vague and quite possibly unknowable, at least directly — only someone who has crossed a boundary can be certain of its parameters, and by then the decision to cross may be irrevocable.

Bledsoe's dilemma is pointed up in two related scenes. In the first, prompted by Richardson's decision not to attack a convoy, which would give away his position, he confronts the commander with his realization that the ship is being taken into the Bungo Straits. The relative positions of the two men assure us that Bledsoe has the upper hand morally, if not factually; until the climactic moment he remains standing, towering over Richardson. Bledsoe admits Richardson's command prerogative, but denies validity to the assumptions on which the decision is based. He warns Richardson of the personal consequences should the decision be wrong; "If you should fail, and somehow come out of this alive," he says, "there won't be a desk small enough for you this time." Richardson's response, delivered softly and with more than a hint of weariness, highlights the difference between the two officers; "That's strange, Jim," he says, "I never even thought of failing." For the moment imagination, which is all that we have to go on when contemplating future outcomes of present actions, is overriding fact, in this case the destruction of four previous submarines. Bledsoe presses his attack; "You've got a lot of guts, sir," he says, "with other peoples' lives." Richardson at last grows angry; "That's my decision, and my responsibility." "To whom, sir," Bledsoe inquires sarcastically, "to a crew that died a year ago?" Richardson leaps up furiously; "Yes!" he shouts, "To a dead crew, a dead sub!" Here Richardson's moral imagination is operating at its broadest; he is making decisions about the future, an unknowable realm which exists, and necessarily can exist, only in speculation, on behalf of persons who no longer exist, who are literally part of the dead past, but to whom he feels indebted. The staging, bringing him at last to a level equal with Bledsoe's, reveals Wise's sympathy with his decision and his reasons.

Bledsoe is dissatisfied, but shortly afterward is forced to declare his true allegiances. A group of petty officers asks him to take over command based on Richardson's decision to disobey orders. Bledsoe is coldly furious, and will have none of it. "We might as well make up our minds right now," he tells them, "we're going to follow his orders." Cartwright, an officious junior officer (Brad Dexter) is bitter about the situation; "Where? To the bottom?" Bledsoe's answer is uncompromising: "If that's what he's got in mind, that's where we'll go. This boat, any boat, has *one* captain." He orders the group to break up. The rules are clear, and however much he dislikes them, Bledsoe knows, at least for the moment, where his professional responsibility lies.

Imagination, moral or tactical, has a vital role to play, but it cannot be the sole focus of action. Richardson has neglected, in his obsession with past and future, to consider properly the claims of the present — that is, of reality. For this he and the *Nerka* pay a high price. Another convoy is sighted, accompanied by an *Akikaze*, and this time the order to attack is given. Although a supply ship is sunk, the assault on the destroyer is foiled by aircraft and what appears to be one of the *Nerka*'s own torpedoes gone rogue. Diving, the *Nerka* is battered by depth charges; Richardson is injured and three crew members killed, and Richardson is forced to order the bodies, along with miscellaneous rubbish, to be ejected from the torpedo tubes. Again imagination defeats superficial realism, for the Japanese destroyer commander, taking the jetsam and corpses as indicative of fact, calls off his attack. As the destroyer departs, an unusual sound is heard by the sonar operator. "What is it, sir?" he asks Richardson; "I can't make that out." Richardson has no immediate answer.

The pendulum, having swung Richardson's way, now swings back. Soon after the attack, while inspecting damaged equipment, Richardson passes out. His recovery, while prompt, is only partial, but its nature provides yet another visual clue to the balance between fact and imagination required here. His awakening is not at all realistic, at least in the manner of the rest of the film. The unusual sound is heard once more, with the sound man's voice repeating the question, "What is it, sir, I can't make that out," again and again. The screen echoes the words; the image is so blurry no detail can be discerned.

What is uncertain now is the direction the ship will take. Richardson's imagination-driven attempt having apparently failed, it is now Bledsoe's regulation-driven turn. The putative failure gives him the opening. It is clear that the tactical advantage identified by Richardson which allowed his decision to override orders no longer exists, if it ever did; any further action along those lines would be dereliction of duty. "We're through playing with lives, Captain," Bledsoe announces, his words delivered far more calmly than MacRoberts's at the similar crisis in *The Desert Rats* but otherwise bearing the same message of imaginative failure and exhaustion: "This boat's had it, it's the end of the line." As Richardson responds with disbelief, he is shown in an unusual two-shot dominated by Bledsoe's back, a veritable blank wall of resistance. Bledsoe calls in Cartwright, waiting just outside the compartment for this very eventuality, and declares that he will be in command for the voyage home. As Cartwright leaves, Richardson chastises Bledsoe, the accompanying two-shot again signaling the situation; both are seen from behind, but Richardson's back is pressed against hanging ropes on the far left of the screen, while Bledsoe's back occupies the central portion of the image. Wordless opposing close-ups emphasize the tension, but as Bledsoe leaves, Richardson sags in physical and mental defeat.

Fortunately for Bledsoe he will be offered a chance to reconsider his position. As for MacRoberts earlier, and as will be the case again for Captain Collins in *The Sand Pebbles*, lucky timing plays a role. As the crew is repairing the *Nerka* preparatory to returning home (a prospect viewed with mixed feelings among them), it so happens that a radio in the officers' mess is tuned to Tokyo Rose, who announces the sinking of the *Nerka*, mentioning several crew members by name. Bledsoe realizes that the Nerka's trash, dumped overboard without proper weighting by the none-too-bright cook, has been picked up by coastal fishermen, and that information, correlated with the detritus left over from the faked sinking, has given the Japanese the illusion that the submarine is indeed gone. Bledsoe reverses course and resumes the attack.

Thematically, what remains is the reconciliation of imagination and fact. Bledsoe leads the attack, but it is Richardson who at last recognizes the odd sounds heard earlier as the sign of a hidden Japanese submarine, the actual force which sank the earlier American submarines. He staggers back to the bridge and warns Bledsoe, and the two of them devise a plan of attack which, needless to say, succeeds. Bledsoe explicitly hands command back to Richardson for the actual attack, and Richardson manages to issue the last two orders before collapsing as the Japanese submarine explodes and bombers arrive to avenge it.

The coda to the film is Richardson's burial at sea. Strictly speaking, it is unnecessary, the main action having concluded; a simple shot of the submarine returning to Pearl Harbor would have done. Emotionally, though, this short scene is vital, lest we take away the impression that fact has truly triumphed over imagination. Rather, Bledsoe offers a few words in memory of Richardson, then concludes with a suitably non-denominational religious formulation: "Unto Almighty God we commend the soul of our shipmate departed, and we commit his body to the deep in the sure and certain hope of the resurrection unto eternal life, when the sea shall give up her dead in the life of the world to come." The last words of the film, then, are explicitly grounded in imagination (hope is not, and indeed can never be, the same as knowledge), reminding the viewer that very little of any significance in life is grounded solely in matters of fact; our deepest commitments, our greatest fears and highest hopes, require a leap into the unknown, a leap which carries with it always the possibility of failure. *Run Silent, Run Deep* is in many ways an extremely realistic film, but its realism operates at a deeper level than on mere matters of fact. This point will recur, still more powerfully, at the conclusion of Wise's last meditation on the scope and nature of imagination, *Star Trek: The Motion Picture*.

I Want to Live! (1958)

Barbara Graham (Susan Hayward), a hard-living woman with a criminal record, is accused of murder; although insisting on her innocence throughout the process, she is tried, convicted, and executed. That, in a nutshell, is the plot of the film, based on a series of newspaper articles regarding the real Barbara Graham, which won Wise his first Academy Award nomination as Best Director (although Wise lost, Susan Hayward won for Best Actress). Wise takes no stands on Graham's guilt or innocence; years later he admitted to being uncertain regarding his own feelings about her. But he, like many of those who had witnessed the process of her execution, found the manner in which it was carried out cruel and degrading, and it is this which informs the film's overall feel and approach. While much of the film has dated more noticeably than many of Wise's other films of the 1950s, the final act, the preparation for and carrying out of the execution, remains appallingly powerful, aptly described by Richard Keenan as "still among the most harrowing scenes dealing with the depiction of capital punishment ever filmed."[14]

From the very first moments of the film we know, even without any historical knowledge, that Barbara Graham is doomed. Deep shadows, unstable camera angles, and pounding jazz capture the frenetic disorder in which she lives. As Theodor Adorno observed, "Jazz, like everything else in the culture industry, gratifies desires only to frustrate them at the same time." Barbara's life is an entire sequence of frustrated desires which seem to be on the verge of being granted — love, money, marriage, and, eventually, a commutation or a pardon; the jazz score (among the earliest in a Hollywood film) conveys the emptiness at the heart of her life quite effectively. She is trapped both by the expectations of others and her desperate attempts to live up to her own artificially stimulated desires; her actions, though intended as expressions of freedom, merely replicate the destiny of a multitude of similar women (and, for that matter, men). "However much jazz subjects ... may play the non-conformist, in truth they are less and less themselves. Individual features which do not conform to the norm are nevertheless shaped by it, and become marks of mutilation. Terrified, jazz fans identify with the society they dread for having made them what they are."[15] Barbara's attempts at living what she takes to be a normal life, like her desperate search for happiness, cannot escape the vortex of external expectation and condemnation into which she has both fallen and leapt.

As Barbara's scheduled execution grows closer, the music gradually dwindles in importance, eventually disappearing almost entirely.[16] What had previously moved quickly now slows to a crawl, and Wise increasingly turns to his documentary style as the professionals, those whose job it is to supervise and carry out the court's decision, take over. The last long segment of the film is taken up almost entirely with the preparations for an execution and the series of brief reprieves which strip Barbara of her thus far carefully sustained composure. Wise, who witnessed an execution himself prior to filming the sequences, concentrates on the minutiae of the process, the turning of levers and filling of containers and testing of window blinds, all of it with the sound magnified unnaturally, literally echoing the intense emotions with which a person condemned to death approaches their final day. The men arranging a death are not themselves inhuman; if anything, they show a certain detached sympathy for the woman they will soon kill, and perhaps a kind of regret at their own subsumption into the machinery of death. But their job requires that they repress whatever feelings they may have. Barbara becomes an object, in their eyes and hers, however much they may express their sympathy for her situation, for they must, as professionals, detach themselves from the consequences of their tasks and concentrate solely on carrying those tasks out most efficiently, and she must concentrate on retaining such dignity as she can. It is this which lies at the heart of much opposition to the death penalty: the way the process strips away the humanity not merely of those to be killed but also of those who must carry out the state's order of execution.

The final moments of the process are filmed in extreme detail, with increasingly precise close-ups of the objects and mechanisms associated with an execution. The executioners grow colder in their expressions; the press representatives and official witnesses, by contrast, who bear no responsibility for the death they are about to see, take their places around the gas chamber with unseemly haste. Several times the telephone rings, first with this momentary delay and then with another order to go ahead, stretching out the action almost intolerably; it is a tribute to Wise's sense of pacing (and the overall sound design, also nominated for an Academy Award) that these delays are invariably jarring, yet never seem gratuitous. Step by step, close-up by close-up, almost invariably without any camera movement at all, Wise unfolds the execution through to the final death spasms.

I Want to Live! is a double-edged title, applying first to Barbara's mistaken identification of sheer activity with living, her misguided attempt to replace a life which is meaningful with a series of ostensibly fun or stimulating behaviors (that is, actions molded not by free choice but by insensate responses to dehumanizing social structures), and then to Barbara's hopes for a reprieve. The film itself, though uneven, is among Wise's most somber, holding out little hope for the characters or the system in which they are embedded. That Barbara believes, evidently quite strongly, in both god and religion (she is a Roman Catholic, and shows no religious doubts whatsoever), may offer some comfort to her, but has no impact otherwise. That Ed Montgomery (Simon Oakland), the reporter who first convinced the public to despise her and who then grew convinced of her innocence, has made every effort to save her, likewise has no impact, even though she sends him a note, which he reads after her execution, thanking him for his work on her behalf. That the professionals, from the warden through to the technicians of death, regret what they must do is similarly of no avail, for they carry out their duties nonetheless, and will presumably continue to do so in the future. Action is either devoid of emotion or futile, ending either in dehumanization or death. It is no surprise that *I Want to Live!* was followed by *Odds Against Tomorrow*, Wise's bleakest and harshest film; together, the two offer a grim assessment of the possibilities for finding personal redemption in an atomistic society in which isolation from other human beings is mistaken for individualism.

West Side Story (1961)

West Side Story, designed by Wise's regular collaborator Boris Leven, is often visually striking, using color particularly well, and the performances are powerful, especially that of Natalie Wood as Maria. It was a well-deserved success, making colossal sums for its investors and winning ten Academy Awards. Nor, despite being officially co-directed by Jerome Robbins, is it entirely atypical of Wise's overall interests; as a call "for reconsideration of the social conditions in our society that promote racial hostility and violence,"[17] it echoes the harsher depiction of such conditions in Wise's immediately preceding film, *Odds Against Tomorrow* (which I examine in greater detail in the next chapter), and it allowed him considerable scope to depict the devastation which commonly accompanies group hatred.

Following a brief overture, *West Side Story* begins strikingly; vertiginous helicopter shots of New York City emphasize the massive scale of the surroundings and the comparatively trivial presence of the individuals living, or perhaps simply trapped, therein. Images of captivity abound: the shots through the chain link fence surrounding the tennis court where the action begins, for example, or the isolated little girl sitting within a self-created oculus of thickly drawn chalk lines.[18] The theme is carried over verbally after an incipient fight between the two gangs, the Jets and the Sharks, is broken up by the police. Lieutenant Schrank (Simon Oakland) refers to the neighborhood as "my territory," Jets member Action (Tony Mordente) insists that "A gang dat don' own a street is nothin',"[19] and Jets leader Riff (Russ Tamblyn) declares, "We fought hard for this turf and we ain't gonna give it up!," adding that "this turf is small, *but it's all we got!*" The theme is familiar from other Wise films; the less one has the more fiercely one will defend it, even to the point of irrationality. Thus, confronted by the influx of Puerto Rican immigrants into "his" territory, Riff advocates direct measures: "We're gonna clean them Sharks up once'n for all so they ain't *never* gonna set foot on our turf again, an' we're gonna do it in one all-out fight!" Once territory becomes more important than lives, everything else follows; the turf wars of Jets and Sharks are, and were, intended to be seen as small scale versions of contemporary tribal, religious, and national conflicts (patriotism, as George Jean Nathan remarked, "is often an arbitrary veneration of real estate above principles").[20]

What is perhaps most notable here is the absolute impotence of the authority figures. The police, presumably charged with maintaining order and promoting social cohesion, are shown as thugs spewing racist epithets and abusing their limited power; as Schrank says to Shark leader Bernardo (George Chakiris) after insulting him degradingly, "When I got a badge, whatta you got?" The other adults are no better, if less offensive, appearing mainly as trivialized weaklings (the goofy dance hall host Glad Hand [John Astin] and the sensible but ineffective shopkeeper Doc [Ned Glass]). It is not that the adults are overwhelmed by the problems they face, but rather that they form a significant component of those problems, whether through corrupt action or irrelevant inaction. The point is made explicit in the "Officer Krupke" musical number, in which the Jets act out a series of encounters between Riff and various representatives of authority (Krupke, a judge, a psychiatrist, and a social worker), each ending in a different conclusion, all of them contradictory and none of them useful.

It is this absence of trustworthy authority which creates the central structural tension of the film. The adults have evidently abdicated responsibility almost altogether. The New York City we see is all but devoid of living beings other than the film's characters; apart from Schrank and Krupke, civic authority is represented solely by posters, looking like something from *1984*, advertising a mayoral candidate. The bleak imagery intensifies the sense of desolation and hopelessness driving the emotional action. On a more personal level, we hear about parents, but none plays any constructive role in the lives of their children; this is a world of teenagers and (very) young adults lacking guidance, save from their respective gangs. Absent this guidance, the gang members lack also the impetus toward moral, political, and social involvement with others beyond their tiny strips of territory; instead they repeat, on a small scale, the behaviors of the worst side of the adult world, that of racism, sexism, greed, and violence. As Maria says of the forces which are leading inexorably to disaster, "It is not us. It is everything around us." The New York City seen here, strewn with detritus and ruled by violence, is every bit as post-apocalyptic as that of later science fiction films.

So the kids, and we, perforce turn to the gangs for structure and focus, an effort doomed to failure. Gangs are inherently anti-individualistic; bigotry of any sort vitiates consideration of persons as individuals. The Jets in particular are poorly off in this regard, scarcely a one of them having more than a descriptive moniker in place of a name; Riff, Ice, Action, Mouthpiece, Gee-tar, and so on. Only Tony, no longer a member, is identified by name rather than nickname, and even he has no significant family links. Members of the Sharks do, mostly, have names, but this is only a slight improvement, as both the Jets and the Sharks are grounded in territorial racism (the members of each gang variously describe their opposites as "spics," "micks," "polacks," and so on). Identity derives from membership; as the song lyrics (not directly quotable here for reasons of copyright) indicate, the gang functionally replaces the family, serving in fact even more effectively as a means of personal and social control. Riff quickly emphasizes the strength of this control, convincing Tony (Richard Beymer), a former Jets member now holding a job, to serve as his second in challenging the Sharks to the showdown; "without a gang," he says, "you're an orphan." Tony reluctantly acquiesces, and the two engage in a lighthearted but ominous exchange. "Womb ta tomb," says Riff; "Birth ta earth," replies Tony. In other words, the gangs not only provide structure, they require specific behaviors every bit as much as would the outer authorities, and in just as violent a manner. The gangs contradict the very reason they have come into being; a person trapped in a violent and indifferent society does not become free by entering a different trap.

It takes some time for this problem to become clear; at first, Leonard Bernstein's eclectically enthusiastic orchestral score and the exuberant choreography of Jerome Robbins combine with Wise's sharp-edged cuts on motion to create a sense of play, as if we're watching some sort of stylized dance competition (Wise would attempt to realize a similar vision nearly thirty years later in *Rooftops*, with far worse music and much less success). Gradually the contradiction is brought out, first at the dance attended by members, or affiliates, of both gangs. Wise limns this through a startling use of the Panavision aspect ratio. As Tony, who has arrived to join Riff in issuing the aforementioned challenge, meets Maria, sister of Shark leader Bernardo, Wise blurs the central two-thirds of the screen, leaving only Tony and Maria in focus at the opposing edges of the picture; the frenetic energy of the dancers, expressing their gang loyalties through choice of partners, remains present but secondary to the connection between two individuals who, as yet, have only their sense of attraction on which to base their actions. A series of alternating shots show the two approaching each other, the dancers still out of focus save when they impinge directly on the space occupied by the two central characters. The music then becomes less edgy and the scene darkens as the two dance; presently the remaining dancers drift into slow motion as Maria and Tony speak to each other, discovering their shared humanity and nascent love. Here and elsewhere when considering Maria and Tony, Wise abandons the visual realism of much of the rest of the film, obtaining thereby a heightened emotional realism in a manner we have seen before. The truth here is not one of location but of deep human interaction, interaction framed by and oppugnant to the setting in which it will attempt to thrive.

That the success of newfound love is doubtful becomes quickly evident; as Tony and Maria start to kiss the lights flash back on, the dancers resume normal motion, and Maria's brother Bernardo violently shoves Tony away from her. "Couldn't you see he's one of them?" he asks. "No; I saw only him," Maria replies. Bernardo orders Maria to be taken away; Maria is startled and begs to stay, but Bernardo's argument, unconsciously echoing that of Riff to Tony earlier, is conclusive: "Please, we are family. Now go." She goes. Tony, though, is entranced, and, hearing a first mention of Maria's name, murmurs it softly; as he does so we see, behind him, only the shadows of dancers, again indicating the relative unreality of gang concerns.

The foregoing descriptions should serve also to indicate the manner in which the film has dated most noticeably. Vital to its success is the audience's acceptance of the gang members as not essentially vicious, as perhaps even, in some manner, sympathetic. This sympathy was easier to obtain in 1961 than today, for drugs and gunplay were neither so common nor so widely reported as they have since become (apart from a brief reference to marijuana in the "Officer Krupke" number, drugs make no appearance at all). Thus the conclusion of the film, with members of each gang joining forces to carry Tony's body away and the belligerent Schrank and Krupke watching silently, seems now increasingly forced, an implausibly optimistic ending grafted on to a tragedy grounded in deep-set animosities.[21] We have not seen any real sign of the moral imagination which must accompany such a transformation; rather, most of the surviving characters, apart from Maria, have been seen as intransigent in their detestation of their opposites. In this respect, the obliteration of the central figures at the end of *Odds Against Tomorrow* rings truer, and seems more likely to evoke a sense of ongoing revulsion at bigotry, than does the finale of *West Side Story*. If a few deaths were all it took to awaken a sense of shared humanity, we would live in a pacifist paradise by now. What is needed will be an ongoing and expanding series of individual rejections of prejudice coupled with similarly significant changes in the social structure within which those choices are made; without both components the possibility of progress remains bleak. The social criticism of *West Side Story* is largely offered in glib generalities, however trenchant the specific events may be. Wise had examined the social character of violence before, and would return to it again; despite the tunes, *West Side Story* is related more to *Born to Kill* and *The Sand Pebbles* than to either of its later musical theater companions, but those films are less compromised in their portrayals.

The Haunting (1963)

Were there any doubts about Wise's ability to adjust his cinematic approach to the circumstances of the story, *The Haunting* should lay them to rest; his final black-and-white film is as visually striking as *Odds Against Tomorrow*, yet in a very different manner. Here Wise uses one of the most mobile cameras of his career, a camera which, assisted by infrared film and experimental lenses, drifts and cranes and peers through the bric-a-brac and sumptuous set design of Hill House in a decidedly unstable manner, one utterly appropriate to Nelson Giddings's open-ended and often deliberately ambiguous screenplay — "Add up all these — these wrong angles," one of the putative researchers, says, "and you get one big distortion in the house as a whole." The filming more than amply reflects that distortion.

The Haunting begins with an ominous narration accompanied by even more ominous images of a gloomy old house. The narration continues after the credits, gradually infused with a more personal tone, eventually giving way to a face-to-face encounter between the elderly owner of Hill House and an enthusiastic academic. Thus it is that we meet the professional investigator of psychic phenomena, the garrulous, urbane, and slightly pompous Dr. John Markway (Richard Johnson), "a trained anthropologist, a respected member of the University faculty." It is he who will engineer the confrontation with the supernatural that forms the core of the film, but it is others who will most directly experience the consequences of that confrontation. Experts and investigators often forget the genuine human beings who form the subjects of their researches; Markway's quest for knowledge is perhaps more benign than that of Dr. MacFarlane in *The Body Snatcher*, but the results are only slightly less deadly.

Despite his role in the lengthy initial build-up, and perhaps contrary to his own expectations, Dr. Markway is not entirely the center of attention. Indeed, he turns out to be largely irrelevant, not only in his professional academic capacity but even in his presumptive status as leader of the group of ghost hunters he attempts to assemble to investigate Hill House; only two of the six assistants who had originally agreed to work with him remained committed. We get a sense of his limitations very early on, when he offers a demonstration of the peculiar construction of the house, which is, or so he assures his listeners, such that doors always close of their own accord. He opens one and prompts the others to watch, only to be confounded by the door's staying open. A few moments later, ostensibly guiding the others to the dining room, he stumbles into a broom closet. Although he laughs these fumbles off, the point is being made: his knowledge and control of the situation are much less than he takes them to be. Markway is the most prominent of Wise's overwhelmed professionals.

The true center of the film is occupied by Eleanor Lance (Julie Harris), a downtrodden, naïve, and timid woman ridden with guilt about her dead mother, who has had scarcely any life, inner or outer, of her own. She is the opposite of Markway; where he is overconfident she is uncertain, where he is enthusiastic she is hesitant, where he is forceful she is withdrawn. Her exact character is a matter of some debate, for she is in essence a person with no qualities, being defined by what she is not rather than by what she is (her character is thus related to that of Victoria Kowelska in *House on Telegraph Hill*, save that her lack of self-assertion is imposed rather than chosen). At Hill House she meets Theodora (Claire Bloom), a confident, attractive, and seductive lesbian, to whose overtures she reacts ambivalently.

Patricia White has offered a strong argument that Eleanor's suppressed lesbianism motivates much of what happens at Hill House.[22] While this sexual tension is surely part of the overall situation, there is more to the film. As Markway's opening narration points out, "Hill House was born bad," and in fact the first death, the manner of which will recur in the last, takes place even before the woman (the wife of Hugh Crain, the original builder) sets foot in, or even sees, the house. An equally strong case could be made, I think, for the idea that Hill House represents the literalization of the idea of possession(s). Hugh Crain deliberately located it in the most remote part of New England he could find, sequestering his wife from sex and society, only to lose her (in the 1860s, the presumptive era when the house was constructed, most married women were indeed little more than the property of their husbands, both legally and socially). Keeping the house, Crain remarries with predictable results: the second wife also dies, hurtling down the stairs under highly irregular circumstances. Crain moves to England, leaving his daughter in the care of a nurse. Significantly, the daughter lives out her life in the house for decades, scarcely ever leaving it[23]; she possesses the house, it is true, but it possesses her as well, in that she is as much a part of it as any of the heavy Victorian furniture and massive amount of bric-a-brac scattered throughout it. She dies of natural causes (or so it would appear), beating on the wall of her bedroom as her nurse-companion dallies with a (male) farmhand somewhere below. The companion inherits the house, but is driven to hang herself in the library. She leaves the house to yet another woman, who lives elsewhere, and it is that woman who is approached by Dr. Markway with his investigative scheme.

Eleanor Lance's situation is complex, but it is noteworthy that she has no home of her own and is dominated by her sister, whose living room doubles as Eleanor's bedroom. When we first see her she is embroiled in a dispute with her sister over whether or not she, Eleanor, will be permitted to use a car (which is half hers anyway) to travel to meet with Dr. Markway. Eleanor takes the car surreptitiously, and drives out to Hill House, fantasizing about having her own apartment and speculating on the nature of what lies ahead. There is an absence of self-identity evident in her thoughts, which, given in a voice-over (a technique restricted to Eleanor's on-screen appearances) are constantly driven by her lack of certainty about any aspect of her future life.

At Hill House (photographed on infrared film so as to have an especially uncanny appearance) Eleanor feels an immediate connection ("It's staring at me"), stressed by an intense close-up of her blinking eyes, after which comes an equally strong revulsion: "Get away from here," she thinks, "get away at once. It's my chance. I'm being given a last chance[....] Anyone has a right to run away." Her personal situation then reasserts itself: "But you are running away, Eleanor," she realizes, the third person revealing that she thinks of herself less as a person than as an object. "And there's nowhere else to go." Nowhere but forward; she drives to the front of the house and enters, pushing aside brooding fears: "It's waiting for me. Evil. Patient."

I have considered Eleanor's introduction to Hill House at some length because it suggests that what will happen is already in some measure determined by her life beforehand, not merely the emotions she will feel upon meeting and interacting with Theodora. It is not merely what Eleanor may eventually repress that matters, but the emptiness inside her, an emptiness prone to panic and fear and desire she cannot yet fully comprehend. Eleanor is the human equivalent of Hill House itself, empty and lonely; Hill House, then, will take possession of her, even if it must scare away those who would be her friends. Patricia White sees this similarly, but with a different emphasis; "The film, resisting the visualization of desire between women, displaces that desire onto the level of the supernatural, Theo's seduction of Eleanor onto the 'haunting.'"[24] But the desire of the house for Eleanor, and her ambivalence regarding it, exists well before she, or we, meet Theodora.[25] Theodora herself will acknowledge the point; "It wants you, Nell," she comments after the two women have their first shared encounter with the force of the house; "the house is calling you." One might see here a classic love triangle in which one angle happens to be occupied by a supernatural force, yet one which is just as obsessive in its attachment as a person might be. Hence the equivocation I noted above between two senses of possession, the natural and the supernatural. To possess in either sense is to control, and where possession is of fundamental importance any attempt to counter it will be resisted with all possible strength.

That night Eleanor and Theodora are tormented by a variety of peculiar sounds, especially tremendous booming knocks, sounds unheard by either Dr. Markway or the fourth member of the party, Luke (Russ Tamblyn), the ne'er-do-well relative of the house's owner, there to keep an eye on the property he expects to inherit and profitably exploit someday. The next morning a message scrawled in chalk on a wall is found: "Help Eleanor Come Home." As Eleanor has just been telling Dr. Markway, who has been flirting with her and to whom she obviously feels some attraction, that she is excited by the prospect of finding something extraordinary at Hill House and scared he will send her away, the message is especially disturbing, and Eleanor's response is especially revealing. "It's my name, it belongs to me, and something is using it," she wails to Dr. Markway. Eleanor is deeply uncertain of her identity, but at least she knows her name, one of the few things in her life she can truly call her own.

Eleanor knows more than she realizes, though, more even than Dr. Markway realizes there is to be known. Later that day, Eleanor is staring up at the house's main tower, imagining a death about which we have not otherwise heard. "That's where she did it," Eleanor thinks, "from that window. Climbing out through the bars, hanging on for an instant. Hanging on." A moment later a rapid vertical zoom from the tower's perspective, one of the fastest camera movements in the entirety of Wise's work, nearly hurls Eleanor over the balcony. She is saved by Dr. Markway, who grasps her in something of a parody of a romantic clinch. His suggestion that perhaps she should leave is met with a strong demurral, even after she realizes that his concerns are for the experiment rather than for her. Theodora and Luke arrive, with Luke commenting on the tableau, and Dr. Markway, perhaps to assuage his own conscience, prompts Theodora to move in with Eleanor. Again the latter's reaction is revealing; "Oh, but that's my room, my very own room." Dr. Markway, oblivious to the emotional undercurrents, insists, and Theodora is only too happy to oblige.

The next scene is key, both for the lesbian energy reading of *The Haunting* and my own (the two are not so much incompatible as angled differently). Theodora has convinced Eleanor to take a drink (or several), and Eleanor is tipsy enough to let out some of her own dreams, albeit in the form of lies. Asked by Theodora where she lives, she describes a dream rather than reality. "I haven't had it long enough to believe it's my own," she says. "It's a little apartment[....] I live alone. I'm still furnishing it. Buying one thing at a time to make sure I get everything absolutely right. Took me two weeks to find the little stone lions I keep on the mantle." The description could fit her mental space as well as the imaginary apartment (the stone lions come from a pair, much larger, she saw while driving up to Hill House); Eleanor is discovering and creating herself one thing, one thought, at a time. Her rapid changes of mood are evidence of this; she has no secure base from which to choose one action, or even one state of mind, over another. Theodora's comment that she needs to get Eleanor back to her apartment as soon as possible provokes an angry outburst about the others picking on Eleanor. She throws herself back against the pillow and declares, "I don't want to leave Hill House. Ever, ever, ever."

That night she hears voices, murmuring just below the level of intelligibility. Clutching Theodora's hand for comfort, she stares in fear at a pattern in the plaster which takes on an increasing resemblance to a face. Hearing a child whimper, she grows angry: "I will take a lot from this filthy house for his sake, but I will not go along with hurting a child, no I will not."[26] She verbalizes her resolve, convincing herself at last to scream as she switches on a light. It is then that she discovers that she has moved in the night to a fainting couch across the room from the two beds, in the furthest of which Theodora is just waking up. "Whose hand was I holding?" Eleanor asks, holding her hand out in terror. The scene is filmed very carefully, such that we scarcely see Eleanor's hand connected to her body, either because it is all we see (the first shots are startling cuts from hand to face and back again) or because the angle is such as to exclude Eleanor's elbow; the hand becomes an alien object which does not belong to her.

Markway's reaction the next morning is in essence a pep talk combined with a lecture on not fearing the unknown. His professional enthusiasm aroused, he is determined to keep Eleanor there for the sake of his experiment.[27] He needs her, and is not above making an implicit personal appeal; "There's certainly something going on in Hill House. We're getting close, Eleanor, very close to finding out what it is." He is closer to one aspect of the mystery than it occurs to him to see. Eleanor at last reveals the nature of her guilt about her mother; the old woman, an invalid for over a decade, had pounded on the wall to command Eleanor's attention the night she died, but Eleanor had been too exhausted to respond. In Eleanor's eyes, all her years of submission, servitude, and care had come to naught in that moment. In the eyes of the house, it is precisely this fact, so similar to one of the deaths which had already occurred, which makes Eleanor family, if you will. Markway succors her verbally while leading her on emotionally. "Goosebumps," she says as she shivers. "There isn't by any chance a cold spot [a supernatural manifestation of which we have already seen an example] in this room, is there?" Markway denies the presence of one, but the viewer by now sees it in Markway's heart, which is open more to the supernatural than the natural (he has not bothered to tell Eleanor that he is married, even as he toys with her).

Additional tensions spill over into a spat between Theodora and Eleanor, climaxing in harsh words from the latter, who derides Theodora as unnatural, one of "Nature's mistakes." Theodora, who has discerned Markway's flirtation with Eleanor and wants to warn her that he is married, never gets to do so, for the argument is interrupted by the arrival of Grace Markway (Lois Maxwell), who has come to warn her husband that a reporter has learned of his project and that his reputation as a serious academic is threatened. Markway is unwilling to stop his work, and encourages her to leave, but she, having expected this, announces that she is joining the ghost hunters and will be disappointed if she does not see a ghost. Markway assures her that there is nothing "romantic" at Hill House (she clearly suspects otherwise), but Eleanor, prompted by jealousy, interjects that "There's the nursery," the room where Abigail Crain died, the one room in the house which has remained locked throughout the investigation. Grace, who is even more of a skeptic than Luke, is thrilled, and announces her intention to stay there; Dr. Markway attempts to dissuade her by assuring her he has no key, but the door, of course, is now wide open (its menace jabbed home with a horizontal zoom shot into the darkness).

Catastrophe soon follows. Huddled in the parlor the four ghost hunters are trapped by a force pressing at the door, which bulges as if about to give way. Grace Markway disappears from the nursery, and Eleanor at last surrenders to the house's desire, running through the darkened hallways until she reaches the library where Abigail Crain's assistant had hung herself. She climbs a tottering spiral staircase toward the balcony whence the woman had leapt, Markway slowly following, the fragmented and unbalanced shots of her hand on the railing and her bare feet on the steps attesting to her unsettled mind. As Eleanor is coaxed away from the top, Grace Markway, spooked and confused by the atmosphere of the house and looking quite disheveled and distraught, opens a trap door, startling Eleanor into fainting.

As Eleanor recovers downstairs, Dr. Markway is determined that she must leave; at last, but too late, he has recognized the consequences for her should she stay, though he still sees them principally in relation to himself. "I can't take any more chances," he assures her; "I realize now what a terrible thing I was asking of you all." Eleanor is anguished and pleads with him to reconsider; "It isn't fair," she says. "I'm the one who's supposed to stay here, she's taken my place." Playing her last card, she admits to having lied about her apartment. There isn't one; everything she owns is in her car. "So you see, there's no place you can send me. I have to stay here." Markway and the others will have none of it, and hustle her down the stairs and out the front door. Sadly, she says to Markway, "It's the only time anything's ever happened to me." Getting in the driver's seat, she brushes off Luke's attempt to take over; "I'll drive, it's my car. At least half mine." At the last minute she calls out to Theodora, who is clearly touched; the last encounter between the two is poignant. "I thought you weren't going to say good-bye," Theodora says breathlessly; "Oh, Nellie my Nell, please be happy. Everything's going to be all right." Markway brusquely bids Eleanor farewell yet again.

Luke, though, has forgotten the key to the outer gate, which he steps out to get from Markway. Eleanor smiles secretly. "What fools they are," she thinks. "The house tricks them so easily." She puts the car into motion, easily outrunning the others, desperate to stop her. "So now I'm going. But I won't go. Hill House belongs to me." At precisely that moment the steering wheel jerks in her hand, suddenly making her aware of the price she must pay to fulfill her desires. For a moments she fights it, only to relax suddenly as she thinks, "It's happening to you, Eleanor. Something at last is really, really, really happening to me." Moments later, startled by Mrs. Markway, who runs in panic across the road, she smashes the car head-on into a tree, the same tree, as Dr. Markway portentously reveals a few moments later "where the first Mrs. Crain was killed in an 'accident.'" Markway cannot resist the opportunity to pontificate further, and he makes what amounts to a graveside speech, ending with a reference to "Poor Eleanor." Theodora is less certain, for it is she who has seen most deeply into Eleanor's heart. "Maybe not, 'poor Eleanor.' It was what she wanted, to stay here. She had no place else to go. The house belongs to her now, too. Maybe she's happier." As the film ends Eleanor's last voice-over is heard describing the solidity of the house and the fact that "We who walk here walk alone." It is impossible to tell her emotional state from either her words or her tone.

Is Eleanor simply a repressed lesbian, and can the events of the film be so easily explained? I have indicated reasons for seeing much more here. Eleanor's relation with Theodora is indeed uneven, and there is no doubt that part of the reason is Eleanor's ambiguity about, and fear of, any kind of physical relation with another woman (especially since she has her heart set on, and has been falsely encouraged by, Dr. Markway). Repression does play a role, to be sure, but it is not conclusive. The last words between the two women suggest neither anger nor revulsion on Eleanor's part, and only concern and friendship, if not love, on Theodora's part. Eleanor's name-calling during the earlier clash between the two was triggered at least as much by what she saw as Theodora's interference as by Theodora's advances, and her words were meant to wound, in the manner of angry words from a child denied a treat, rather than to express her deepest convictions regarding sexuality; they are the stereotypical responses of an ignorant person with a limited expressive range. They voice confusion, not hatred.

The real key here, I think, is found in Eleanor's emotional isolation and confusion; remember, she has spent the last eleven years, her entire adult life, taking care of her ailing mother, and thus has no friends, no love, no job, and no room of her own. She is not just lonely; she is profoundly ill-equipped to engage with the world. *The Haunting* is not only frightening but also, perhaps even especially, a very melancholy film, as much about the pain of a life empty of meaning and an imagination starved of viable material upon which to work as the search for the supernatural. Eleanor's relation with Hill House is remarkably similar to that of many an abused woman with her abuser; the latter provides at least a sense that the woman being abused is truly desired ("He wouldn't be so jealous if he didn't love me," and similar sad fallacies), and the abuser often acts so as to isolate her, to control her, to possess her. Had Eleanor been able to respond positively to Theodora she might have been able to save herself, but her negative response is rooted not so much in repression as in a lack of self-knowledge, a lack of imagination about the possibilities of human love. Eleanor's life is so devoid of positive stimuli that the only way for her to feel alive is to die. Hill House, unlike Theodora or Dr. Markway, told Eleanor who she really was; unfortunately, Eleanor listened.

The Sound of Music (1965)

Having been so successful with his first adaptation of a stage musical, Wise was soon asked to direct another. That fact, the opening helicopter shots, and the participation of screenwriter Ernest Lehman are virtually the only similarities between the two. Nonetheless, Wise's typical approaches to problems involving authority and individualism do appear also in his second musical, albeit in muted form. In fact, *The Sound of Music* begins, lightheartedly, with a professional problem: the clear absence of a true vocation to the convent on the part of Maria (Julie Andrews). The film's first question, sung by the chorus of nuns, therefore concerns her true character and what to do with and about it. This is balanced by a similar problem regarding the Baron Von Trapp (Christopher Plummer). The Baron's ostensible professional role as a former captain in the Imperial Austro-Hungarian navy is purely a plot element (it sets up the conflict with the Nazis which will motivate the family's flight from Austria); the real question is how he will come to learn his true profession as a loving father (in fact, his behavior during his first meeting with Maria suggests that his approach to discipline is not all that different from that of the fascists). The answer, of course, is through falling in love with Maria, a circumstance for which he is unprepared either by class or experience. In the course of his sentimental education, he must learn also that allowing his children to become public performers is not merely an expedient but a valuable goal in itself, for musical performance can be as much an expression of individuality as it is a money-making venture. He must move, a few generations behind the rest of the industrialized world, from the feudal to the capitalist era, metaphorically speaking. The answers to the questions involving the Baron and Maria all turn out, conveniently, to be the same; each must escape a professional structure which denies individuality in order to discover, and then become, who they truly want to be.

Wise and screenwriter Ernest Lehman made a particular, though only partly successful, effort to remove the more saccharine elements from the original stage version. "We made every effort to find ways of not getting too cute," Wise later said. "We felt they overdid the folksy stuff in the play, so we toned that way down."[28] Along with the folksy stuff they also reduced the presence of the Baron's friend Max Detweiler (Richard Haydn), self-described as "a very charming sponge." In some ways this is regrettable, as the glimpses of amoral self-centeredness his character does provide suggest the more turbulent currents running beneath, but ignored by, the film's general development.

Max is something of a professional manager, although apparently not one of the more successful ones. He has attached himself to Baron Von Trapp and Elsa, a baroness presumed to be Von Trapp's eventual second wife (Eleanor Parker, very good in another underutilized part), and makes full, knowing, and slightly cynical use of the connection. "I like rich people," Max declares; "I like the way they live. I like the way *I* live when I'm with them." He is the epitome of a conventional conservative, a person for whom the present system is working, who takes no interest in whether it works for anyone else, and who therefore sees no reason for change. For such people, it really doesn't matter what system they exist under, so long as they see no diminution in their own pleasure within it. "What's going to happen's going to happen," he advises Von Trapp apropos the Nazi elements in Austria and the looming *Anschluss*; "Just make sure it doesn't happen to you." This provokes an angry outburst from the Baron; Max, startled, defends himself by denying any personal involvement. "You know I have no political convictions," he reminds Von Trapp. "Can I help it if other people do?" The Baron's answer is unequivocal. "Oh, yes, you can help it," he insists quietly but firmly. "You must." A short while later the Baron acknowledges his awareness that the world in which he grew up, and to which he avows allegiance, is ending.

The film makes little more of this tension; the Nazis are villains, yes, but with minimal presence or moral weight beyond swastika flags and the officious Herr Zeller (Ben Wright). Even the defection of Liesl's boyfriend from young love to Nazi Party loyalty is almost offhand, and certainly does not have any great emotional impact on either her or the audience (the real confrontation stemming from his change of heart comes not with Liesl but with the Captain). The Nazis are obstacles to be overcome rather than aspects of foundational political problems. Max Detweiler's comment to the children after the *Anschluss*, that "The thing to do these days is to get along with everybody," seems excusable in its context only because we haven't seen any of the actual destruction attendant upon the takeover (there are, so far as one can tell, no Jews at all among the film's characters, major or minor — though it is also unlikely that a Catholic former Austro-Hungarian Imperial naval officer such as Captain Von Trapp would in fact have numbered many Jews among his personal associates and friends). Nor do we see any hint of Austrian complicity in the *Anschluss*; the eager throngs who greeted Hitler's entrance are invisible here.

Critics have generally decried the unwillingness of *The Sound of Music* to delve into the tensions underlying its situation.[29] This is not entirely fair; few musicals demonstrate an interest in the political or economic conditions of the world in which they are set or in which they are made, and most, having made less money than this one, are let off lightly for their detachment (Mark Sandrich's highly regarded *Top Hat* certainly exhibits no interest in, or even awareness of, the Depression, for example). Nor indeed is it easy for a form which relies on the audience's willing suspension of disbelief in its basic approach to then draw them back into a serious consideration of fundamental realities, especially given the triviality of most of the music involved. This fact would become clearer with Wise's third musical.

Star! (1968)

Despite reprising the director, associate producer, and leading performer from *The Sound of Music*, and despite a promising opening weekend, *Star!* tanked at the box office, and it has remained little seen since then.[30] In retrospect it holds up about as well as either of Wise's previous musicals, and it appears to be finding a respectful audience on DVD, but its comparative failure is not entirely a mystery; *The Sound of Music* positively reeks of sincerity; *Star!*, on the other hand, is predicated on the importance of insincerity. Professionalism plays an important role here, but in an unexpected and atypical manner.

Star! opens with an overture. The musicians enter a pit beneath a large stage with a closed curtain. Stereotypical sounds of warming up are heard, and the tuning A is sounded, whereupon we see the conductor enter and begin the music. The curtain opens upon a scrim printed with the names of many of Gertrude Lawrence's shows. Following the overture, the 20th Century–Fox logo and fanfare appear, attached to what appears to be a featurette from 1940 about Gertrude Lawrence. Yet despite the sepia-tinting and small Academy-ratio screen image, it is, or should be, immediately clear that this is no period piece. Nor is it especially accurate, as Gertrude Lawrence herself (Julie Andrews) makes clear when she suddenly bobs up (now in color) in front of the image and laughs at the absurdity of the commentary.

The point has been made, and the rest of the film will develop it: *Star!* is about artificiality, the triumph of image over reality. The newsreel is a fake — but is a fake we already know to be a fake, because the staged overture has already signaled that the entire film is itself a play — that is, a game, serious perhaps but not real. This artificiality is endemic to the musical, but here it is embedded in the very foundations of the narrative. Nor is this all; the small-screen/large-screen dichotomy serves also to suggest that what we create is in some manner larger than life, more important than reality. This, though, is precisely the problem.

It is a problem misunderstood by many among *Star!*'s first viewers. Pauline Kael complained that "there's no difference in point of view between the gray, grainy, small screen fake documentary, with its mixture of actual and simulated newsreels, and the wide-screen, 70-mm, color movie."[31] She's right descriptively, but has missed the point analytically. The similarity is fundamental here; the reality is in the performances, not in what they purport to portray. Hence, again, she is right to note that "although the documentary is supposed to be in production in 1940, it's not in any recognizable style of that date," but she's wrong to use this as a criticism. The entire film, "fake" and "real" parts alike, is grounded in the idea that what matters is what one creates, not its relation to fact. The putative documentary contains many shots which assume the presence of a camera in places it would, to say the least, have been unlikely to be, and many of its sequences are lit and shot far more expressively than would have been many studio films of its supposed era. The documentary is a fake, but so is its subject; the "Gertrude Lawrence" shown therein — and in *Star!* itself — is herself largely a creation compiled from her performances. *Star!* is an atypical musical, in that *all* of its numbers are stage productions. The real-life sequences, shorter and fewer than the stage extravaganzas, thus come to be seen as scarcely relevant connectors; Gertrude Lawrence exists principally to perform, and everything else is subordinate to that. In the end, we believe in the stage productions more than in the dramatic situations surrounding them.

This interplay between image and reality is directly evident in another way; there are several scenes in which there is a momentary but undeniable ambiguity as to whether what we are seeing is a stage backdrop or an actual location.[32] Likewise the shift between documentary and reality in the "Jenny" number; the documentary narrator expresses doubts about the staging, doubts apparently echoed in Julie Andrews's (or Gertrude Lawrence's) own mind when she slides down a rope in black and white, rips through a barrier, and finds herself in color. The doubts are then laid to rest (save, perhaps, unexpressed doubts about aesthetic taste) by the "actual" production — which is then given a standing ovation by the documentary crowd.

What we have in *Star!*, then, is professionalism run amok. Gertrude Lawrence, the character, exists to perform; it is her vocation, and her curse.[33] By the end of the film, it is entirely unclear whether the shows she has been in coincidentally reflect her life or whether her life has taken its cue from the shows she's been in. After all, most of the scenes we see are indeed from shows in which the historical Gertrude Lawrence did appear — but the scenes taken therefrom have been carefully selected for a dramatic purpose. The climax of this interrelation comes in the aforementioned Jenny number, with its insistence on the dangers of being too certain about what one wants in life (a theme echoed throughout the film).

So *Star!* is faced with an intriguing problem, one it does not overcome with complete success. There is an emptiness at its heart, an emptiness which is nevertheless a vital aspect of its dramatic structure. This is surely a part of the reason for the film's failure at the box office; audiences found no obvious point of sympathy. In this regard, *Star!* was simply ahead of its time; several decades of films with unsympathetic protagonists have made audiences more receptive to such a portrayal.[34]

Star! faces a peculiar paradox, one rooted deeply in its central character's profession: the more it succeeds on its own grounds, the more it will fail on conventional grounds. That is, the more it manages to create the sense of its main character as being largely an assemblage of performances the less likely it will be that the audience will make the identification, positive or negative, which usually attends narrative success. The key to this is found only at the end of the film. Having married producer Richard Aldrich, Lawrence expresses doubts (as she had done, and in the same words, immediately after her first marriage). Aldrich comments that divorce is easy in the United States, and Lawrence reacts: did he really mean that? "I mean everything I say," he replies. "Well I don't," she continues; "I just think I do at the time." In essence, this is the mantra of the successful performer; one believes entirely in the role one is playing and the manner in which one is playing it, or at least creates the illusion that one so believes, even though one is at the same time aware that the exigencies of performance will change from night to night (dropped lines, missing props, varied audience reactions, and so on), and that the roles (who one "is") will change from play to play. Thus Lawrence's summation in the film's last lines is both accurate and symptomatic: "I know the only things that matter are understanding, and happiness, and being absolutely genuine all the bloody time." Understanding, for a professional performer, is a matter of the moment. Happiness is the sense of achieving identity with the role at which one is aiming. Being genuine is being persuasive to an audience; the more genuine one is as an actor, the less of oneself as an individual separate from one's part will shine through. Lawrence is all of these things performatively, which means that she is none of them really. *Star!* is in effect a film about not the triumph of style over substance but the identity of style and substance. One is one's performance.

This provides a final clue as to why *Star!* is not, and *could not have been*, entirely successful on anything like traditional terms. Gertrude Lawrence (the character, it should go without saying) acts as she has learned to act in order to succeed; she follows her profession wherever it leads, only to discover, along with the audience, that it leads to self-contradiction. *Star!* is thus neither a cinematic *Bildungsroman*, with Gertrude Lawrence coming to discover and refine her personality, nor an anti-*Bildungsroman*, with Lawrence arriving at some sort of secure self-deception, a self-deception seen as such by the audience. Rather, it is a series of set-pieces linked, almost accidentally, by the presence of the (more-or-less) same person. To the extent that Gertrude the performer succeeds in being what the role requires, she is not developing as a person — yet the more successful she is in each role the more she as a person becomes defined by that role (hence the links between her "real" life and the events in her shows). *Star!* is, necessarily, unable to develop its central character save pointillistically, almost kaleidoscopically, with the elements being disconnected, or only loosely linked. To have done otherwise would have required a very different movie, one much less honest about the chaos at the heart of the professional performer's life, where professionalism ensures a kind of success which is also failure; it undercuts itself even as it elevates itself (the veracity of the portrayal is confirmed daily by the struggles of movie stars and other celebrities to balance their professional lives with their private ones, struggles which often end in retirement, addiction, or failure). *Star!* limns the dangers of allowing professionalism to override basic human needs. For all the glamour of its stagings, it presents a contrapuntally bleak view of the possibilities of balancing one's public and personal lives.

The Hindenburg (1975)

To describe this minor but generally enjoyable film as a tragedy would be to inflate its claims considerably, yet structurally the term applies: most of the professionals (of which we see a plethora) will eventually be stymied or destroyed through some internal character flaw, flaws which dictate the actions of those characters as surely as do the omnipresent regulations enforced by the Gestapo. The *Hindenburg* is ordered to travel despite threats against it because the government would have to admit the existence of a resistance were it to delay the airship's schedule. The ship's captain is so confident of the security measures that he cannot imagine them failing, and he ignores the pleas of the ship's designer to cancel the voyage. Martin Vogel (Roy Thinnes), the brutal Gestapo officer aiding in the security work, in fact undermines his own efforts through his methods. Rigger Karl Boerth (William Atherton) is so determined to make a political statement that he saves the ship from potential disaster due to an equipment malfunction in order to ensure that its later sabotage makes the desired political point, only to have its destruction occur in a manner which vitiates his entire effort.

The most fully developed of these situations is the dilemma faced by the world-weary Colonel Ritter (George C. Scott). Ritter is a highly decorated career military man serving a regime he is growing to despise, yet he cannot commit what to him is treason, despite knowing that he is following his orders ever less enthusiastically. Placed in charge of security aboard the zeppelin, Ritter identifies the saboteur but comes to sympathize with him enough to allow him to carry out his plan, provided the explosion takes place after the passengers have disembarked. Nazism, a mass movement centered on the equation of social structures with a single individual's cult of personality, is incoherent both politically and philosophically. Ritter is the embodiment of the contradictions within which he is attempting to live, a professional whose commitments are irreconcilable, and who therefore is internally incapable of living up to them; he can save the ship and support the regime he loathes or he can act against his sworn duty—duty being at the very core of what his professionalism demands—and allow the ship to be destroyed. His attempt to find a compromise, by giving the saboteur Boerth a schedule which will cost no lives, fails to account for the (already shown) vagaries of travel and timing. Contradictions eventually cancel each other, creating a moral nullity; Ritter's dereliction of his professional duty in the interests of a higher good in which he does not believe especially strongly, will fail, ending only in his own death and the destruction of the ship. There is a grinding conflict here, one reflective of the social tensions which must exist between any conscientious human being and any governmental regime devoted principally to maintaining its own power (which is to say most such, however much their methods may vary). Scott's performance limns the conflict subtly but well; thin-lipped fleeting smiles which leave his eyes untouched suffice for emotional interactions with his fellow travelers, and even the women with whom he has, evidently, some intimate history, are rarely favored with more. Ritter is a man who, like so many, cannot admit, even to himself, the truth about his own role is sustaining the society he despises. Unfortunately, Nelson Gidding's screenplay loses sight of Ritter's dilemma, which is never developed consistently or effectively enough to stand out amidst the rambling plot machinations (diamond smuggling, commercial competition involving coded messages, a pot-smoking countess fleeing the Nazi seizure of her estate, conniving card sharks, and so on).

Wise had wanted to shoot the entire film in black and white but was overruled by the studio. In retrospect the studio's decision can be seen as regrettable; the film would have benefited considerably from Wise's original plan. The opening minutes are a genuine newsreel from the period, and the shift to color as the credits roll is as startling as it is irrelevant; continuing in black and white would have better matched both Wise's documentary-style approach and the rather dated feel of the action (special effects aside, this could have been made decades earlier).[35] Even so, *The Hindenburg* is among the most spectacular demonstrations of technical professionalism in Wise's body of work; the special effects and production design were astonishing when new and remain impressive today. Wise takes full (perhaps a bit too full) advantage of the opportunities provided by the reconstruction of the zeppelin's interior; some of the shots are almost abstract, effectively symbolizing the isolation and entrapped nature of the characters, who are all caught up in historical processes of which many are all too unaware. Unfortunately, the film too often loses its way amidst the effects, coming to life intermittently (often with the aid of David Shire's gently nostalgic score). Only at the climax does the long-delayed return to black and white (to accommodate the actual footage of the explosion and crash), and even tauter editing, provide an effective conclusion, as what virtually any audience member would know must happen finally does so. As it is, this is a good example of Hollywood film production technique at its best, though much less successful as a coherent story. Ritter's dilemma is the central point, and the effort expended on developing minor characters, or even whole subordinate plotlines, to no real purpose serves mainly to deaden the impact of that dilemma.

Audrey Rose (1977)

At several points during his career, Wise directed films which served as tangents to a contemporary trend; although related to the trend, the films were in fact atypical thereof. Thus *The Day the Earth Stood Still* is akin to many '50s alien invasion films, but without the fear-mongering and paranoia common to the sub-genre. *Odds Against Tomorrow* is a caper film but with an explicit political core uncommon to its brethren. *The Hindenburg* is superficially similar to '70s disaster films, but the disaster waits until the final reel to occur. And *Audrey Rose* begins as a film about a stalker, acquires a supernatural aspect, develops into something of a legal drama, one which pits two professional worlds against each other in a fight neither can win, then becomes a kind of medical thriller. The combination of different genres within yet another genre proved baffling to most critics, and the film has had a poor reputation ever since its release. While Wise's final foray into the supernatural is weaker than his earlier films in the genre, it retains considerable interest both as a thriller and as an exemplar of his overall approach to film in general.

Janice and Bill Templeton (Marsha Mason and John Beck) have a daughter, Ivy (Susan Swift), who is troubled by nightmares. They, too, are troubled — by the discovery that a bearded man unknown to either of them (Anthony Hopkins) is apparently stalking Ivy. Eventually they learn that the man, Elliot Hoover, claims to have lost his daughter Audrey Rose in a car accident moments before Ivy's birth and that Ivy is the reincarnation of that daughter. Hoover kidnaps Ivy, for which he is sued by Bill Templeton, though Janice's decision that Hoover is telling the truth threatens to derail the case. Prompted by the prosecuting attorney, Bill authorizes a past life regression experiment, which succeeds all too well; Ivy/Audrey relives the experience of death and ends up dying all over again.

Audrey Rose is something of an intellectual oddity among Wise's films. It will be obvious that it inverts one of Wise's most common tropes: the presence of a child as a guarantor, or at least symbol, of some kind of moral stability or hope. Here the child is the source of the instability, a fact reflected in the disintegration of the Templeton marriage. The film also inverts Wise's otherwise resolute secularity, although in an manner atypical of most Hollywood films. People in Wise's films often express or demonstrate religious beliefs (Barbara Graham in *I Want to Live!* being a prime example), but nowhere else does one of his films in itself convey or endorse a particular religious attitude. *Audrey Rose* is an anomaly in this regard, and is the weaker for it.

Frank De Felitta's screenplay, adapted from his own novel, faces two problems, one of its own making and the other inherent in the situation depicted. The first difficulty is that De Felitta is clearly aiming not merely to create a plausible story, one accepted on its own terms by the audience, but to convince the viewer of the truth of a particular view of reincarnation as it might apply to her or his own life. This requires, and leads to, the second difficulty, the need to explain exactly what is happening in some detail; Hopkins's character is especially burdened by the need for large chunks of expository material lest the plot be otherwise too confusing and the conclusion unconvincing as an argument. The result is that we often feel as if we are being talked, rather than lured, into believing, with a concomitant loss of conviction. In essence, De Felitta (and Wise, as director, though whether he believed any of this is unclear) are attempting, in the space of 113 minutes, to cause a religious conversion among the film's likely viewers. It doesn't work, and the courtroom sequences, in which we hear only the defense's case (that is, the case, albeit a very weak one, for reincarnation) and never the prosecution's, looks and feels like something from a different film altogether, weakening *Audrey Rose*'s impact still further.

This is unfortunate, for there is much good work in the film. As had often been the case in his earlier films, Wise realized that the already sensationalistic material needed two things to succeed: a very calm overall approach and some manner of linking the diverse elements. The film is thus devoid of many of the usual gimmicks associated with supernatural films of the period (*The Exorcist* [1973] and *Burnt Offerings* [1976], for example); there are no garish tricks with make-up or revolving heads, no vomit, no blood, and no overt evil.[36] Much of the film is lensed, and acted, in a manner indistinguishable from a straight drama (say, *Two People*, Wise's last film but one before *Audrey Rose*). The result, as Wise well knew, allows him full play to use appropriate lighting and camerawork to emphasize the supernatural outbreaks (the reincarnative possession) when they do occur. The first part of the film, before Elliot Hoover turns into a veritable metaphysical windbag, is much the best, in its pacing, its acting (particularly that of Susan Swift, whose inexperience shows through less noticeably here than later in the film), and its use of camera movement, color, and light.

The method Wise uses to unify the film, like the manner of presentation, is subtle. Confronted with a story about two personalities in one body, one of whom died in a fiery car crash because she was unable to break through the car windows, Wise found an ideal visual equivalent: throughout the film, but especially at critical moments, we see one or another of the characters through, or in, some transparent material (plastic, glass, mirrors) separating them from someone or something of importance at the moment. Of course Ivy/Audrey is shown frequently in this manner, but so are other characters, stressing their disconnection from what is happening and why. The very opening of the film, showing the initial moments of the accident which sets the plot in motion, is seen through a windshield. Later on, Janice Templeton, having been hit by a car and delayed in reaching Audrey at school, runs to her classroom only to see, through the door window, that the room is empty. A particularly effective example shows us Janice rushing to answer a telephone call from the apartment building concierge. As she answers, she is seen both as herself and as a mirror image, almost splitting the screen. Learning that the outside call is from Hoover, she directs the concierge to say that she is not home; as she does so, the camera dollies forward and to the right until the mirror image occupies the left half of the screen. The right half then fades into a shot of Ivy tossing and turning in bed, seen from outside her window. As Janice's image fades, the camera dollies out from Ivy's window, moving left across a gargoyle building ornament, and over to Janice's window, through which we see her asleep. It is an elegant and haunting way of conveying both the passage of time and the isolation of the two characters.

The use of windows and mirrors climaxes at the film's central crisis, the film's third shift of tone and approach, the regression hypnosis of Ivy. The pompous psychiatrist (Norman Lloyd), almost a caricature of a professional medical man, is seen apparently addressing himself in a mirror, until a reverse shot reveals that the jury in Hoover's trial is sitting behind it watching the proceedings. He drones on and on, putting Ivy into a trance, as the jury, along with Hoover and Bill Templeton, watch, separated by one level of glass; Janice is even worse off, for she, having argued with her husband over the process and stalked away, is watching the process on a closed-circuit television set seen through a glass wall, her contact with her daughter thus doubly mediated. Predictably Audrey/Ivy ends up beating her hands against the mirror as she relives her death, the psychiatrist uselessly chanting his pleas for her to break out of her hypnotic trance, until Hoover shatters the mirror from behind with a chair, a startling image filmed in slightly slow motion. The camera gazes at the shards of glass at some length, cutting at last to a particularly large piece tinged with a mysterious yellow glow, presumably linked with the earlier fiery car crash.

The rest is anticlimactic. Audrey/Ivy does indeed die, as if from burns (though we do not see these), after which the Templetons apparently return home in a state of uneasy truce. Janice gives Ivy's ashes to Hoover, who takes them to India for some arcane ritual, and the last scene consists of a voice-over of Janice's letter to him, read in a peculiarly emotionless, almost zombified, voice, thanking him and explaining that Bill may at last be on the verge of accepting the reality of reincarnation. An intertitle — a quotation from the Bhagavad-Gita — ends the film, apart from the credits.

Audrey Rose is, in a sense, an attempt to do for reincarnation what *The Day the Earth Stood Still* did for the idea of a strong United Nations. The contemporary context, though, was not so receptive as for the earlier film, nor were contemporary Western viewers as well prepared for at least understanding, even if disagreeing with, the central message. Nor is *Audrey Rose* aided by the fact that, structurally, it echoes *I Want to Live!*, in the sense that a highly dramatic first part is followed by a much slower second (and in this case, third) part. In the earlier film, the tension generated was an integral part of the drama; in the later film, the slowness merely drags out what most audience members know has to happen from quite early on, and for no particular reason. The result weakens the film's impact considerably; films such as this need to keep the audience's critical faculties off-balance enough to maintain the necessary suspension of disbelief, whereas here the audience is allowed somewhat too much mental space in which to question the goings-on.

Audrey Rose is intermittently quite striking, but Wise cannot overcome the flaws in his material consistently enough to maintain the film's focus. One has the feeling that at least one of the three major segments of the film could have been omitted, or at least vastly truncated, much to the benefit of what remained. It is neither mysterious enough to sustain a sense of the supernatural nor convincing enough to serve didactically. The point may be that Bill Templeton lacks the imagination to do what is necessary to save his daughter (though whether anything could have done so is decidedly unclear, despite Hoover's insistence that his— Hoover's— presence was necessary to do so), but the viewer's imagination, stultified by Hoover's extensive lectures, as well as the testimony regarding "Indian" beliefs (as if everyone in India held the same beliefs) rather than arguments for those beliefs, has too little here on which to take hold for itself. Wise's other films of the supernatural, in their refusal to explain, retain a much greater hold on the viewer's imagination, which must leap beyond its, and even the film's, own reality to share the work of creation and comprehension. Wise would remember this in making his next, and in some ways greatest, film, *Star Trek: The Motion Picture.*

A Storm in Summer (2000)

Wise's final film, made for television from a thirty-year-old Rod Serling screenplay, schematic but touching nonetheless, answers a question scarcely asked by any of his previous examinations of individuals confronted with a potentially life-changing crisis. The action is set in the summer of 1969. The central figure is Abe Shaddick (portrayed superbly by Peter Falk), a bitter and sarcastic Jewish delicatessen owner. Shaddick fled one war (he arrived in the United States in 1914, presumably ahead of forced service in the army of one of the Central powers) but lost his only son in the next (Benjamin "Benjy" Shaddick was killed while serving in the U.S. Air Force in 1944). Having already lost his wife, Shaddick ekes out a living with his small business and fills the silence by talking to his dead son. In essence, Shaddick is a man who has met the crisis head-on and given in to it; he is what we could imagine Stoker Thompson becoming should his small post-boxing dreams disintegrate along with his marriage. The question Shaddick will face, phrased quietly but insistently by events, is what happens when a man who has surrendered to the past is forced to confront, in someone else's life, the same event which has nearly destroyed him.

Into Shaddick's shop and apartment returns his ne'er-do-well nephew Stanley (Andrew McCarthy), a young man who drifts from rose-colored money-making scheme to rose-colored money-making scheme with equally limited success in each. Drunk while at a party at a country club, Stanley agrees to host a black child from Harlem for two weeks as part of a Fresh Air program. Soon afterward, with the child already on his way, Stanley tells Abe that he has an important interview at a strip club in Atlantic City and has to leave.[37] Heading out, Stanley meets the child, Herman D. Washington (Aaron Meeks, in a remarkably assured performance) at the bus station, greets him with insincere protestations of regret, and sends him on to his uncle's. Abe is at first gruff and unhelpful, but is quickly touched emotionally and soon opens his heart to the young boy. They bond during encounters with racist bikers and country club members ("from the bellicose to the varicose," Abe comments), just in time for Abe to be the one to have to tell Herman that his beloved brother Bill has died in Vietnam. Herman leaves, pledging to come back. Abe, having been forced to confront and share another's grief, finds a kind of redemption.[38]

Bound by strict time requirements of a television film, Wise could not explore the connection between the two main characters at feature-film length. Accordingly, he relied on a high proportion of close-ups, developing the emotional content of the film through reaction shots as much as through dialogue or dramatic images.[39] Thanks to the quality of the performances, this works well enough that he is able to allow the significant dialogue sequences toward the end to stretch out; many television programs have a rushed or choppy quality, especially in their latter scenes, a flaw avoided here. Wise also made use of expressive camerawork uncommon in his films, such as the overhead crane shot of Herman in the Harlem bus station as he prepares to leave, emphasizing his isolation, or the series of carefully composed shots of Shaddick in tears near the end, seen alternately through a rain-streaked window and alongside it, in the latter case with his reflection, most visible during the lightning flashes, standing in symbolically for the ghosts of his own past which he must, and perhaps may, exorcise.

It is the nature of this exorcism which links the film to the central theme found in so many of Wise's films. Shaddick opens the film with a litany of complaints, presented half-humorously but indicative of his general attitude; "Upstairs, in the kingdom of heaven, they got a special department; it's a celestial bureau, it's staffed by a hundred fallen angels, and it's got one job [....]: to harass Abel Shaddick." Shaddick is a man obsessed with his own experiences, his own sorrows, to such an extent that he has lost all empathy for others. His moral imagination shut down the day his son died, and only a similar death, this time of a total stranger, manages to reawaken it. In getting to know Herman, Shaddick extends his personal boundaries step by step, such that, in offering such condolences, he at last recognizes the universal nature of grief, and that his is simply a subset thereof — not unimportant, but not unique either. He rejoins, as it were, humanity.

This is expanded by the awareness, touched upon but left as a subtext rather than a focus, of the grounds behind the deaths of both men, Benjy and Bill. Both men died in wars involving bigotry and hatred; any and all wars are similarly grounded (the desire for advantage which generates wars requires, and feeds upon, the illusion that those of whom the advantage is being taken are in some manner inherently inferior). Shaddick, even in his detachment from the situations of other human beings, retains this awareness, and we see it in action when the two are set upon by the racist bikers. Shaddick speaks up, almost taunting the two men for their mock bravery in attacking a small boy and an old man. Herman actually pulls a knife (which is quickly knocked from his hand). The police arrive and the bikers are ordered out of town, after which Shaddick covers for Herman by telling the officer that the knife is his. He then returns it to Herman, telling him to never let him see it again. The writing here is fairly weak, but at least serves the purpose of allowing Shaddick to state his fundamental philosophy: "If I ever reach the point where I have to cut into another man's stomach, I will have lived too long." Herman is adamant about being willing to use violence, which prompts Shaddick to comment on "the worst thing about prejudice: the haters turn the victims into haters."

Shaddick's lesson, though, is not over; his true epiphany comes when he must tell Herman of the death of Bill Washington. He tells a long story about receiving the telegram announcing his son's death, of the tears which followed, and of his realization that the tears do, someday, end. Herman replies to Abe's efforts at comfort with his own story, one involving his brother Bill's insistence that Herman not cry over a small accident, a lesson Herman has taken too much to heart. "I don't cry, Shaddick, not me," Herman announces stonily. "I ain't never gonna cry." Shaddick mumbles some words of acknowl-edgment, then crosses from the more brightly lit back rooms where he lives into his darkened storefront and suddenly, shockingly, gives way to his grief, sobbing brokenly. In Herman's words he has seen the last 25 years of his own life, how much he had given up, how much he has lost irrecoverably, and how little has changed in the ensuing 25 years socially.

There is a strong echo here of Jake Holman's breakdown in the engine room of the *San Pablo* after the death of Po-Han (which event I examine more closely in Chapter Six), and it occurs for similar reasons. Both men have recognized that the system within which they are living, and which they have accepted or at least stopped questioning, has in some manner failed to live up to its own promises. Both men have confronted deaths which would not have occurred but for the political and military choices made by others utterly unconcerned, yet still intimately connected, with the fates of those who have died. Both men have confronted their isolation as human beings. The simi-larity goes further, though in *A Storm in Summer* there is a touch of optimism missing in the earlier film. After their respective epiphanies, both men, Jake and Abe, understand that the only path out is a path forward, an expansion of one's human sympathies and a concomitant unwillingness to seek violent revenge, but neither will have a long time in which to act upon that under-standing. Jake Holman will be killed even as he attempts to adjust his choices to his understanding; Abe Shaddick is an old man with an indeterminate number of years in which to avoid falling back into his familiar patterns (there is no Ebenezer Scrooge awakening here; as always in Wise, going for-ward will entail hard work and continued affirmations of the initial compre-hension). The lesson the two men have learned, and the lesson Herman is learning, as we see when, at last, he does cry, may seem elementary; yet clearly, considering the circumstances of the deaths of the three young men, friend (Po-Han), son (Benjy), and brother (Bill), and the situation of the world today, it is one which remains to be learned by a substantial portion of human-ity.

A Storm in Summer is an occasional piece, enlivened by some excellent performances. While certainly not Wise's finest film, it does provide a kind of distillation, by no means completely negligible, of his ongoing concerns with expanding the range of human contact, empathy, and moral imagina-tion. As such, it serves effectively as a quiet coda to a 67-year career in the movie industry.

Chapter Two

Warnings

When we remember that in every neurosis there are contradictory tenden-cies which the neurotic is unable to reconcile, the question arises as to whether there are not likewise certain definite contradictions in our cul-ture, which underlie the typical neurotic conflicts. (Karen Horney)[1]

Preface

Even a brief survey of Wise's characters, professionals, amateurs, and minor figures alike, reveals that many among them live and act in tension with, and often because of, the surrounding social and political structure. For the most part, these tensions are side matters, with no explicit conclusions drawn from or about them. Nor should this be surprising. Studio films from the 1940s and 1950s were seldom seen as vehicles for critical social commentary, especially as regards the system within which the studios operated. But there were exceptions, accidental or intentional — films in which the curtain was drawn aside, even if only briefly, and a perceptive audience allowed a disturbing glimpse of the machinery which sustains the power hierarchy. Wise avowedly avoided "message" pictures (with one major exception, noted below), but he was always happy to work with scripts in which a progressive social message was embedded. These films encouraged, and display, some of his best work.

The four films analyzed next epitomize this aspect of Wise's career. They are certainly not the only films which express his progressive social and political views, but each does, I think, suitably encapsulate some major part of that progressivism, of Wise's underlying awareness of serious social and political problems. None of his films is revolutionary, whether in technique or content (though *Odds Against Tomorrow* is, both literally and figuratively, explosive in its development), but many of them, considered with due diligence, contain much that simultaneously expresses dissatisfaction with the current social order and leaves the thoughtful viewer with good reasons to accept, and perhaps to expand upon, that dissatisfaction.

In a sense, dissatisfaction propels art. Works of art, in whatever medium, gain impact by being larger in their implications, and more expansive in their coherence, than the world within which the person experiencing them lives. It is partly this which allows for quite disparate — but not thereby contradictory — reactions to the same work; any two people will bring to their experience of the work different sets of previous experiences, understandings, and emotional, moral, and intellectual commitments. The spectrum of possible reactions is thus virtually infinite. On one side, those whose range of experiences is small will often derive genuine pleasure from works quite limited in perspective and minimal in quality simply because those works, however narrow overall, do extend beyond the horizons previously explored by the person in question. On another, those whose range of experiences is extensive, especially within the art form at hand, may find it hard to enjoy a given work, even quite a good one, because to them it seems merely to echo what they already know. As personal horizons expand, so do expectations regarding works of art. At some point, the questions the work raises become at least as important as the answers it provides, for questions make us reach beyond who we are, whereas answers, all too often, merely reinforce our limitations. The best answers, in the realm of the arts (and sciences), are those which impel us to ask further, deeper, questions. The greatest works of art are those for which no answer, however extensive, exhausts the range of relevant and intriguing questions.

There is a balance needed within each work, though. Too broad a question, and any answer is relevant, or none is; in either case, the work itself is unnecessary. Too narrow a question, and the answer is already contained within it, or is too trivial to sustain interest; again in either case, the work itself is unnecessary. Wise's directorial errors tend to fall into the second category; his weakest films are mechanical applications of excellent technique to trivial material. Technique — an answer to the question, how may I best achieve the desired result? — is important, but cannot carry a major film (or any other work of art) for long on its own; even the handsomest films, if lacking in content, eventually grow wearisome. Neither can pure content easily carry a film; many a film has been abundant with its ideas yet difficult to care about, or to understand, because of incoherent presentation. Nonetheless, intriguing ideas are more likely to sustain our curiosity than even the best applications of pure technique. Emotion provokes interest in ways beyond the reach of intellect; as Alfred North Whitehead commented, "It is more important that a proposition be interesting than that it be true."[2] This suggests the reason why Wise is not, and should not be, on anybody's list of the greatest directors, even though he has given us some very fine films indeed. His lesser films suffer from a kind of insularity, providing neatly wrapped packages of ideas and responses which carry little emotional or intellectual force outside their own boundaries.

The central exceptions to this insularity, themselves highly revealing, are found in films such as those I examine in this chapter and the four which follow, the films constructed around more or less explicit critiques of human social and political interactions. All films, all works of art, partake of the historical circumstances surrounding their creation, but some contain additional layers of emotional, intellectual, and aesthetic meaning which remain valuable even after the topical appeal has diminished or vanished. It is these layers which, in essence, maintain each work's claim to artistic significance, and it is the continual presence and discovery of such additional layers in overall body of works upon which evaluation of the individual as an artist is based. Understanding the nature of these layers, which will vary from work to work and artist to artist, is a key component of that evaluation.

To develop an understanding of Wise's strengths and weaknesses as a creative artist, it may be helpful to briefly compare his work with that of his close contemporary Ingmar Bergman (1918–2007), whose name will certainly be found on any list of the greatest directors. The choice is not arbitrary; the careers of the two men share parallels which make the differences between them, and the reasons therefore, all the more illuminating. Wise was born in 1914 and died in 2005; he directed 39 theatrical feature films, the first in 1944 and the last in 1989. Bergman was born in 1918 and died in 2007; he directed approximately 35 theatrical feature films, the first in 1946 and the last in 1982. Bergman also directed a number of television films of which theatrical versions, usually truncated from the original, were released; Wise directed only one television film, never released theatrically. Both men worked their way up through the film industry, Wise starting in 1933 as a film porter (literally: he carried prints to the screening room for producers), after which he became a sound editor and then film editor; Bergman began in 1943 as a screenwriter (as late as 1961 a script on which he collaborated was filmed by another director).

The differences between the works of the two directors are many, and it is necessary first to acknowledge what might be called contingent elements, things which, however important in the final analysis, are largely a matter of situation and professional luck. Wise worked in a huge industry, Bergman in a small one (the entire population of Sweden is not vastly more numerous than the population of the Los Angeles metropolitan area). Although both men worked for several different production companies during their careers, the comparison is misleading, as by far the vast majority of Bergman's theatrical films were for a single company, Svensk Filmindustri (at least 24 features), whereas Wise made no more than nine for any one company (RKO, at the beginning of his career). The corporate continuity of Bergman's career developed and fostered a continuity with his collaborators, actors and crew alike, a continuity itself further aided by the small casts and intimate conditions of production found on most of his films.[3] An astonishing number of his films, for example, were photographed by either Gunnar Fischer (at least ten films) or Sven Nykvist (at least 16 features, and several of the television films); similarly, actors Gunnar Björnstrand, Liv Ullman, and Max Von Sydow, among others, appear almost as frequently. Nor is this only a matter of repeated work. Each of these contributors is among the finest and most sensitive in their respective fields; as they became familiar with Bergman's demands, and with their own relation to his work, they could refine and expand their contributions, such that each film to some degree built upon the previous ones. Wise, on the other hand, although at times working with some of the best actors and technicians in Hollywood, could rarely count on continuity of personnel from film to film, even within the same production company (in his nine films with RKO, for instance, he worked with seven directors of photography). Bergman once commented that he made each film as if it were his last; one might say, exaggeratedly but with a degree of truth, that Wise was forced to make each film as if it were his first. Finally, it must be noted that Bergman wrote almost all of his own scripts, especially in his later career, allowing him to develop his cinematic ideas throughout the film's gestation period, whereas Wise, though occasionally collaborating with excellent screenwriters, rarely did more than make suggestions for refinements on an already finished piece of writing. This last point was recognized by Wise himself as vital. Pressed to select the central element in making a successful film, Wise avowed that "the most important is the story." Even before the screenplay itself, the story carried within itself the seeds of success or failure; "We never escape the strengths of that original story or its weaknesses." Other elements, technical and personal, are relevant and important, but "none of us, none of those people, the stars as well as the others, can escape the rightness or the wrongness of that original decision of what story to make into a motion picture."[4]

Wise's signal achievements of the 1940s are directly comparable in overall quality to Bergman's of the same time, and in some ways superior; Wise's films of the period are tightly constructed, emotionally judicious, and highly imaginative; Bergman's best, though certainly imaginative, are often loosely constructed and overwrought emotionally. Had both directors died in 1950 neither would be accounted among the greats, yet both would be hailed for the possibilities suggested by their wide-ranging explorations. Nor should the occasional sense of greater maturity of subject matter in Bergman's work be considered a reflection upon Wise; no Hollywood script of that era, or for years to come, could have directly taken up such topics as abortion, and nudity was, of course, simply unacceptable. This is one reason why so much of Hollywood's best work of the period, films which continue to hold the interest of viewers decades later, is found in genre pictures, especially so-called film noir; these scripts often pushed hard against the limitations of conventional drama, and many directors, including Wise, took advantage of the opportunities offered to expand their own stylistic repertoires. Bergman's work of this era may often be more directly personal than Wise's (a major criterion for acclaim within auteurist theory), yet the resultant films are by no means always more interesting; *The Body Snatcher* and *The Set-Up*, for example, are as structurally taut and dramatically rewarding as any of Bergman's films of the period, and more so than most.

By the mid–1950s, though, Bergman was creating some of the finest films of that or any other era, whereas Wise's remained primarily at the level of solid craftsmanship. While there are exceptions, at least to a degree — Wise's 1954 film *Executive Suite* is, I think, better crafted, more tightly constructed, and at least as interesting in cinematic terms as *A Lesson in Love*, Bergman's comedy from the same year, for example — what had changed was not merely the increasing control Bergman had over his films, or the fact that by now he was working almost exclusively with cinematographer Fischer (Nykvist began his tenure with Bergman in the 1960s), but the fact that by this time Bergman had transmuted his own obsessions into dramatic expressions of more widespread fears and concerns, whereas Wise was still mostly bound by generic conventions. Bergman at this point is developing an ever greater emphasis on individuals, and finding ever more striking ways to capture and explore their innermost thoughts and frailties, a development shown by the increasing weight given to extensive close-ups. From the 1950s until the end of his career, Bergman will remain one of the greatest of all directors (which is not to say that every Bergman film is itself great, or even good); during the same period Wise will become increasingly famous, but his best work will rarely be recognized as such precisely because of its apparent lack of personal emotional involvement (probably more people have seen *The Sound of Music* than all of Bergman's films put together, but its far more serious close contemporary *The Sand Pebbles* was, and is, all but ignored).

Yet while Bergman's best films are directly personal in a manner quite alien to Wise, this should not suggest that Wise's work lacks subjective intensity. It is here that his political commitment comes to the fore. Bergman's personal concerns find their expression in his most striking visuals; Wise's political and social concerns likewise elicit some of his most powerful images. Bergman's films are almost expressionistic in their subjective focus, but are often nearly blind to the social situations within which the personal conflicts depicted are being generated and experienced; Wise's films to a degree invert this balance, exploring personal conflicts but emphasizing the underlying social forces which have helped to generate those conflicts. To put it starkly, if somewhat simplistically, Bergman's films explore personal conflicts while Wise's explore the personal impact of societal contradictions. This foundational difference has a powerful impact on the nature of the films created by the two men, one most visible if we consider their specifically political films in relation to their others. While both Wise and Bergman made explicitly political films at various points during their respective careers, Wise's are invariably among his best, whereas Bergman's are rarely more than competent, adding no luster to his reputation. Compare *The Day the Earth Stood Still* (1951) with Bergman's implausible Cold War spy thriller *Such Things Don't Happen Here* (1950).[5] Both films are at heart propaganda, but Wise's film is indubitably better on all levels. *The Day the Earth Stood Still* is, as I shall demonstrate subsequently, tautly constructed, literately scripted, convincingly acted, and filmed with careful attention to visual details which heighten its overall impact as well as reflecting and supporting the central political message, whereas Bergman's film is slickly but lifelessly presented (Bergman himself dismissed the film, a studio assignment, as "rubbish").[6] The same comparison holds true of Wise's *The Sand Pebbles*, a political drama set in the 1920s (the subject of Chapter Five), and Bergman's *The Serpent's Egg* (1977), likewise a political drama set in the 1920s. Again, Wise's film is much better at conveying the political confusions, and the underlying causes of those confusions, than Bergman's. Bergman himself recognized the flaws in his own film, and the reasons therefore; referring to the film's "artistic failure," he decries his decision in favor of historical specificity. "If I had created the City of my dream," he wrote in his autobiography,

> the City that is not, never was and yet manifests itself with acuteness, smells and loud sounds, if I had created *that* City, I would not only have been moving in complete freedom and with an absolute sense of belonging but also, more importantly, I would have taken the audience into an alien but secretly familiar world. Unfortunately I allowed myself to be led astray by my excursion into Berlin in the mid–1930s [sic], that evening when absolutely nothing happened. In *The Serpent's Egg*, I created a Berlin which no one recognized, not even I.[7]

Bergman's self-understanding is accurate; his films are in essence vividly realized dreams, and the specificity required when considering political matters as such is generally alien to them. Wise's more hard-edged approach, on the other hand, is precisely suited to such subjects.[8]

We can see the significance of this for both directors by taking up what is commonly considered to be Bergman's best political film, *Shame* (1968). It is indeed far better than his other political films, in large part because Bergman makes no effort to situate the film specifically; it thus becomes a nightmare about the effects of war upon individuals. Notice that we have no idea what groups are fighting or why; Bergman is making no statement about any particular war, but rather about war in general and its relation to civilians. Bergman reduces the chaos entailed by wartime conditions to chaotic events in the lives of a very small group of individuals, personalizing the situation by largely eliding the broader political elements. In this regard, *Shame* is akin, though vastly superior, to *Two People*, Wise's 1973 film about a Vietnam-era deserter from the United States Army (Peter Fonda) who agrees to return home to face a court martial and then meets a beautiful woman (Lindsay Wagner) with whom he immediately connects but from whom he will be separated by his decision. Wise's film not only lacks the requisite chemistry between its leading players (a fact noted almost instantly by Wise himself, as well as most of the few critics who gave the film much attention), it has dated considerably, both as public awareness of the Vietnam War has faded and because the United States has wisely abandoned the military draft in favor of a volunteer military. The key difference between the two films is evident; Bergman's film draws little of its strength from its historical specificity, whereas Wise's film, carrying an implicit critique of particular attitudes within a specific historical period, requires at least some comprehension of that period to maintain its fullest strength. The moral debates at the heart of Wise's film are too specifically grounded in contemporary issues to retain interest over time, whereas those at the heart of Bergman's film remain vital. As Georg Lukács commented, regarding literature but with equal relevance for cinema, "a perspective that sticks too closely to day-to-day events is rarely successful: concrete and determinate in matters which are of small interest to literature, it fails to produce adequate aesthetic solutions in more important matters. Lasting typologies [studies of human character], based on a perspective of this sort, owe their effectiveness not to the artist's understanding of day-to-day events, but to his unconscious possession of a perspective independent of, and reaching beyond, his understanding of the contemporary scene."[9]

In this regard, it is also illuminating to compare *Shame* with *Odds Against Tomorrow*; Wise's film is again more aware of its political content, and was produced at a time, and in a country, where the issues it confronted were violently present on a daily basis, while Bergman's film has no such rootedness. Also again, the specific political situation which drives *Odds Against Tomorrow* has changed, whereas that evinced in *Shame* has not. Yet while the overall impact of Wise's film has thus lessened to a greater degree than that of *Shame*, *Odds Against Tomorrow* remains compelling for both technical and political/emotional reasons in a way that *Two People* does not; while the Vietnam War, and particularly the draft, are largely dead issues to most viewers, the problems of bigotry and hatred are not, and thus one need not be as fully cognizant of a particular historical situation to appreciate the forces driving the action. Since otherwise *Odds Against Tomorrow* and *Shame* are in many ways at a similar level of cinematic quality (I do not think, for example, that Joseph Brun's cinematography suffers by comparison with Sven Nykvist's), the combination of aesthetic interest and political and emotional content keeps Wise's film alive in ways beyond its purely topical appeal. Wise's political films capture their contemporary situations well, but only the very best transcend them; Bergman's films often all but ignore the contemporary scene, but usually transcend not only it but the specific concerns of their characters, reaching instead deep into much broader human concerns.

This contrast of specificity and generality leads to a further consideration. In the Introduction, I remarked upon the underlying humanism of virtually all of Wise's films; with few exceptions, religious questions as such simply do not exist in Wise's cinema. Quite the reverse is true of Bergman's films, many of which are consumed with questions regarding the non-existence, or at least the utter silence, of a deity. This dimension adds a layer to Bergman's films which is almost entirely unavailable to Wise's, for to speak of deity is inherently to speak vaguely; there will be at least as many meanings attached to the term as there are members of the audience. Vagueness in itself does not create the basis for interesting questions, but it can, if handled carefully, create an atmosphere of uncertainty which challenges the viewer to strive for clarity of understanding within themselves. If that uncertainty is well developed and enticingly presented, it will create a desire for greater certainty which will fix upon and develop the hints of answers the work provides, answers which will almost necessarily generate further questions as those answers are tested against the answers found by others. Few topics are more conducive to this sort of experience than religious ones; deity is presumptively greater than any single consciousness, and therefore to think of it is to think of more than can be comprehended — in short, to think of a god, or of its absence, is to ask questions. Given the centrality of religion in the lives of most human beings (even those who are complete and comfortable atheists cannot be unaware of, and will rarely be unaffected by, the role of religion in the lives of many of those around them), any film which genuinely engages with the subject, at whatever level, will raise important and often moving questions which will connect with most of its viewers, regardless of their own beliefs in the matter. All art of value reaches beyond the purely personal. For Wise the extrapersonal element comes principally at the level of human society; for Bergman it comes at the level of the divine, or, more accurately, the prominent absence of the divine.

This is why Wise's best films of social and political criticism are so strong by comparison with Bergman's, whereas his interior dramas remain generally weaker. Wise's creative emotions are most fully engaged when he is depicting the impact of social constrictions upon individuals and the way those constrictions create damaged or destructive behaviors, while Bergman's are engaged more deeply by considerations of the isolation of human beings from each other, and from the divine, through their own flaws and fears, the source of which is largely unimportant to him. Wise's characters are visibly shaped by the social systems within which they exist, whereas in many cases Bergman's seem almost completely detached from any particular social system at all, allowing the viewer to project her or himself into the situation more intimately. Wise's cinematic energies are stimulated by the underlying questions of human interactions within a given system (and therefore by concerns about the manner in which that system has influenced those interactions), whereas Bergman's energies are driven by questions of individual character, however it has come to be. It is not, of course, that Bergman or his characters are somehow outside of the social system within which he creates, but that his focus as a creator is less upon the "why" of personality and more upon the "who."[10] Bergman's best films have deep personal resonances for audience members extending well beyond the immediate experience; the films raise profound questions, directly implied by the on-screen images and actions, which force the viewer to confront the limits of their own experience and knowledge. This is much less true of Wise's conventional dramas or lesser genre films; *Audrey Rose*, for example, is a far better film when we are uncertain of what is happening than it is when its specific position becomes clear. Bergman's films often raise expansive questions about the meaning of individual actions; Wise's films are more often centered on individual responses to externally imposed situations. Wise's films are thus rarely directly disturbing at the level of personal self-assurance in the manner of the greatest works of art, works which challenge us, by their very existence, to reach beyond our present self-conception (a challenge, it is perhaps needless to say, which many refuse to take up).

Yet the broad social questions Wise's films do raise can be quite disturbing in their own right, for they involve the very nature of how our social conflicts shape and, potentially, control us. His films do, of course, center on individuals rather than groups. But his individuals act, are acted upon, and react within often quite narrow boundaries, boundaries forced upon them by powerful social structures. It is this tension which Wise excels at portraying, in a striking variety of settings and situations. These films deserve close consideration, and to them I now turn.

I. *The Body Snatcher* (1945)

One of the hallmarks of capitalism is the conversion of individuals into commodities, atomistic economic entities who must either market themselves or, more often, be marketed by others. These relations lie at the heart of *The Body Snatcher*, a grim fable about the depths to which those who forget their humanity in the service of their profession can fall.

The opening sequences briskly present several important plot elements without explicating their significance: a blind singer, the dog mourning at a boy's fresh grave and a mother's fear of grave robbers, the ominous presence of Cabman Gray (Boris Karloff), the crippled girl Georgina Marsh and her attachment to Gray's horse, and the problems of Dr. MacFarlane's student Donald Fettes (Russell Wade). All of the shots are at eye level, until Mrs. Marsh and Georgina enter the house of Dr. MacFarlane, at which point a high-angle long shot emphasizes their isolation; it is soon followed by equally unsettling low-angle shots. Already we know that something is wrong, though we do not yet know what.

Mrs. Marsh has come to consult the renowned Dr. MacFarlane (Henry Daniell) about her daughter's paralysis. His examination is conducted in a brusquely patriarchal manner which leaves no doubt of his competence and command, but his questions are unavailing; Georgina refuses to answer, and whispers to her mother that she fears MacFarlane. Fettes enters, and MacFarlane has him interview Georgina, with (predictably) better results. A diagnosis results; for Georgina's cure an extremely delicate operation, one of a type hitherto unperformed, would be necessary. MacFarlane refuses Mrs. Marsh's pleas that he perform it; he is, he tells her, more a teacher than a surgeon. He has, he tells her, "the responsibility of training thirty other doctors to attend a thousand children like your own." His response to her sad comment — "Then there's nothing I can say for one small child" — is rational, utilitarian, and cold: "I'm not heartless, madam. I've every sympathy for you and for the little girl. If I were to consent to every operation brought to me, I'd have no time for teaching. And that's a great responsibility. A *great* responsibility." He has Fettes show her out.

Fettes then returns to say that economic circumstances are forcing him to abandon the study of medicine. MacFarlane will have none of this, and makes Fettes an assistant on the spot, an appointment which both confirms Fettes's standing as a top-rank student and confers new responsibilities, of which MacFarlane proceeds to inform him. As he does so, we see the Portuguese servant Joseph (Bela Lugosi, in one of his typical, superbly sly performances), listening in, a habit which will have fatal consequences. The principal fact which Fettes must now learn involves the bodies used for study. The law prescribes the donation of the bodies of paupers for medical research; those who could not afford to live can hardly expect to be afforded dignity in death, but "There aren't enough of them, Fettes, there aren't enough of them," MacFarlane mutters. Once more utilitarian professional demands require the suspension of moral scruples, and the very next shot shows the source of additional corpses, as the fresh grave we had seen in the film's opening is plundered, with the mourning dog slaughtered on the spot lest its barking alert a passerby.

A direct cut reveals Fettes tossing and turning as if dreaming the sequence we have just seen. Awakened by the sound of knocking, he draws on a robe and heads downstairs, where he admits Gray, carrying a fresh body. The dialogue is detached, clinical in its commerciality. "You'll find the specimen in good condition," Gray assures Fettes, who queasily admits that MacFarlane had told him to pay Gray. "That's the soul of the business, the pay," Gray avers; as he leaves, he expresses the hope that this will "be the first of many profitable meetings." As Gray leaves, MacFarlane enters, amusedly assuring Fettes that this represents "a milestone in your medical career."

It is one, but perhaps not what either Fettes or MacFarlane intended. The next day Fettes discovers the source of the corpse, and witnesses the mother's anguish as she carries the dead dog away from the gravesite. He returns to MacFarlane's office to tender his resignation. MacFarlane deters him with another strongly utilitarian argument:

> Fettes, I was an assistant once. I had to deal with men like Gray. Do you think I did it because I wanted to? Do you think I want to do it now? But I must. And you must. Ignorant men have dammed the stream of medical progress with stupid and unjust laws. And if that dam will not break, the men of medicine have to find other courses[....] I'm sorry for the woman, but her son might be alive if more doctors had been given the opportunity to work with more human specimens. As for me, I let no man stop me when I know I'm right. When I know I need those lifeless subjects for my students' enlightenment and my own knowledge. And if you're a real man, and want to be a good doctor, you'll see it as I see it.

The sequence is carefully staged. As MacFarlane begins his speech, he is alone on screen. At "I had to deal with men like Gray," a cut establishes a two-shot centered on MacFarlane, implicitly subordinating Fettes to a long-established chain of practices. At "And if that dam will not break," MacFarlane is again shown alone, until his assertion that he lets no man stop him, at which point the two-shot returns, again pulling Fettes in. Finally, as MacFarlane applies the conditional "if you're a real man," he grasps Fettes's shoulder and the shot reverses; still a two-shot, it is focused on Fettes now, as if offering him the chance to take control of the situation and withdraw at once from the moral morass into which he is wandering — an offer he does not take.

Shortly afterward circumstances conspire to drag Fettes still further into complicity. Mrs. Marsh returns, asking to see him; she wants him to intercede on Georgina's behalf with MacFarlane. Fettes agrees, and sees his opportunity that evening, as he and MacFarlane encounter Cabman Gray at a tavern. Gray drunkenly menaces MacFarlane with hints of unspoken knowledge about MacFarlane's past, and takes up Georgina's cause, more to assert his own power than out of altruism. Under pressure and the influence of drink, MacFarlane agrees to perform the operation, and Fettes hastens the next day to assure Mrs. Marsh that MacFarlane's god-given powers must surely have been granted to save Georgina. Returning, Fettes is shocked to discover that MacFarlane has changed his mind, apparently for professional reasons; such an operation would require very careful consideration of the spinal column, and they have no available specimen for study.

Fettes now takes the decisive step in his own involvement in MacFarlane's web; he seeks out Gray and insists that a fresh body be found. Gray demurs, but as soon as Fettes leaves he heads out, and within a few moments, in one of the more celebrated sequences in the film, Gray murders the blind singer.[11] When Gray delivers the corpse, Fettes is horrified, but MacFarlane warns him that he is implicated and had best abandon his intention of going to the police. The body is dissected, with MacFarlane reserving the spinal column for his own study preparatory to the operation on Georgina. Medically, this is a success, in that the girl lives and the tumor growing on her spine is removed, yet she still cannot walk, despite MacFarlane's insistence that she do so (his command is given in positively Christ-like terms: "Child I say to you, get up out of that chair and walk"). MacFarlane will have nothing to do with Fettes's gentle approach, one resting on imagining what Georgina will be able to do in the future; rather he simply asserts that if she cannot walk he, MacFarlane, must somehow have failed. Leaving Fettes to usher Mrs. Marsh and Georgina home, he heads to the nearest tavern to drown his sorrows. There he meets Gray and pours out his anger and sorrow at the failure of the operation (and reveals important elements of their prior relations, involving the notorious grave robbers Burke and Hare and their trial, in which Gray covered up for MacFarlane's involvement). Gray forces MacFarlane to look at himself in a mirror and delivers a stark verdict: "There's a lot of knowledge in those eyes, but no understanding." MacFarlane indeed does not understand, and, his temper rising, argues with Gray; the latter threatens MacFarlane with exposure, only to discover that his hold may not be secure as he thought. MacFarlane scoffs and invites Gray to expose him far and wide, but to remember that "They hanged Burke, they mobbed Hare, but Doctor Knox is living like a gentleman in London." The entire confrontation is filmed in tight two-shots; the equation of MacFarlane and Gray is oppressively evident.

The relevance of Dr. Knox, MacFarlane's teacher, quickly becomes clear. Gray returns home, only to be accosted by Joseph, who has heard enough to figure out Gray's activities; he demands money. Gray laughingly complies, plies Joseph with drink, then suggests that the two should be partners, like Burke and Hare. Again the profit motive underlying so much of the film surges to the fore. "Eighteen people they killed and sold the bodies to Dr. Knox, ten pounds for a large, eight for a small; that's good business, Joseph," Gray asserts. Joseph, his senses befuddled by liquor, barely has time to agree before Gray kills him, after which Gray delivers the corpse to MacFarlane's house, as a sort of warning.

It is this fiscally profitless murder — that is to say, one which is not grounded in his illicit "profession" — which seals Gray's own fate. Shocked at Gray's action, MacFarlane decides that Gray must be gotten rid of, and he confronts him back at the stable. He first tries to bribe Gray, only to learn that Gray's motivations are even stronger than money. Gray wants power, and there is only one way he can maintain it in such a society. "I am a small man, a humble man," he says with barely suppressed ferocity (powerfully delivered, this is probably Karloff's best acting in the film; Wise was always a good director of actors), "and being poor I have had to do much that I did not want to do. But so long as the great Doctor MacFarlane jumps to my whistle that long am I a man, and if I have not that, I am nothing." The essence of power relations within capitalist society has seldom been so tersely and compellingly evoked; where power is attained through control and manipulation of things, and where people have themselves become things, even a poor man who can find a way to manipulate a wealthy one can still consider himself important.

Faced with such intransigence, MacFarlane attacks and kills Gray (the climax of the fight scene is filmed with only the shadows of the two men visible; by implication neither is truly human any more, but rather they are merely the effects of the system within which they have struggled to find power and freedom and personal worth). He brings the corpse home, exulting that he is at last free of Gray (despite having been warned by Gray earlier that he would "never get rid of me"). He plans to make Gray's body "serve a good purpose," dissection and demonstration, after which he, MacFarlane, can begin his life anew.

Fettes, unaware of these events, meets Mrs. Marsh and Georgina at an overlook in the city. He tells the mother of his having left Dr. MacFarlane, and his reasons echo much of what we have already seen and heard: "I feel that I've learned nothing from MacFarlane. He taught me the mathematics of anatomy, but he couldn't teach me the poetry of medicine." Yet even as he says this, Georgina, impelled by the hope of seeing Gray's horse, which she imagines passing by below the overlook, manages to stand, revealing that MacFarlane's operation was indeed a success. Fettes is thrilled, and rushes to tell MacFarlane, whom he must follow to an outlying town where MacFarlane has gone to sell Gray's horse and cab. In an illuminating sidelight we overhear the man who bought them boasting of having conned MacFarlane, unaware that it was he who had been taken advantage of; there is virtually no one in the film who is not tainted by the overriding relations of money and power. Informed by Fettes, MacFarlane attributes the delayed success of the operation to his having killed Gray (though he does not tell Fettes of this), and he vows that his teaching, and thereby his students, will benefit. As the two men are speaking, a pair grieving over the burial of their sister enters, and MacFarlane realizes that a fresh corpse has conveniently become available. Offering a reprise of his earlier argument about the stupidity of people and laws opposed to the advancement of knowledge, he concludes that "We can do our own dirty work, and we will," insisting that Fettes join him in stealing the corpse. After a moment's hesitation, Fettes does so.

The two dig up the body (Fettes apparently doing the bulk of the work), and, as a thunderstorm descends, head back to Edinburgh with it. MacFarlane hears Gray's voice taunting him; at last stopping the cart and looking at the corpse, he is horrified to discover that it is Gray's. The horse panics and pulls the cart away from Fettes, standing alongside holding the lamp over the body; as Gray's flaccid pale corpse entwines with MacFarlane's arms the latter loses control, and the cart breaks free and plummets over the edge of the road, killing MacFarlane. Fettes, chasing after the runaway cart, discovers the bodies, but his lamp reveals to him, and to us, that the stolen corpse is indeed that of an older woman. He clambers up the hillside and walks toward Edinburgh as a peculiarly ambiguous intertitle, presenting a quotation attributed to the famous ancient physician Hippocrates of Cos, signals the film's end: "It is through error that man tries and rises. It is through tragedy he learns. All the roads of learning begin in darkness and go out into the light."

Probably unintentionally, the quotation effectively highlights the inescapable social and personal contradictions at the heart of this film. To begin with, the final sentence is denied by what we see; Fettes, the only one to whom the words appear to apply, is walking down a muddy road in darkness amidst pouring rain. Nor is it clear that Fettes has learned anything; he was all too willing to assist MacFarlane in acquiring a fresh corpse, and his disturbance just before the film's climax stems from MacFarlane's behavior, not any moral solicitude. MacFarlane and Gray, being dead, have clearly learned nothing. Mrs. Marsh will still regard MacFarlane as the great man who saved her daughter, and Georgina will be too consumed with learning to walk again to care for any moral lesson at all. In fact, the quotation contradicts the entire visual movement of the film; all of the opening sequences take place in bright sunlight, and all of the major characters are introduced in well-lit settings, after which the film becomes progressively darker. The action which initiates the catastrophic denouement, Joseph's interrupted first bid at blackmail, is virtually the last one to take place in daylight. The ensuing scenes occur either in dim interiors or at night; the sole exception, the moment of Georgina's recovery, which ought to be one of great joy, occurs under heavily clouded skies which suggest the degree to which even her innocence is tainted by the circumstances which have allowed her to recover.

Such implications grow more disturbing the more one considers them, a fact which helps explain the resonance the film maintains even after repeated viewings. *The Body Snatcher* is only tangentially a horror film, or even a thriller.[12] Rather, it is a study of what might be called necessary inhumanity, one in which overweening professionalism leads to disaster just as surely as does any attempt to exceed one's expertise. The film takes few explicit stands regarding its characters. MacFarlane's dedication is in many ways admirable, and his arguments for his transgressions are not without force; they are those which are made, and which must be made, by anyone who defends the utilitarian insistence (itself not without plausibility) upon attaining the greatest good for the greatest number. These arguments are so widely used as a cornerstone of modern liberal capitalism that it is easy to forget their own implication: if attaining the greatest good for the greatest number requires the utter destruction of an individual or small group thereof, then such cost must be borne without demur. Those benefiting usually see no problem with this argument, but they often fail to see its concomitant shadow: that it reduces all human beings (as well as anything else) to a mere potential for instrumental value, to an ability to be used in attaining the putative greatest good. This is true even if the greatest good could be easily identified and agreed upon; there will rarely be a single path to its achievement, and thus any and all human beings become nothing more than potential bricks to be used in constructing that path. Utilitarianism is the principal philosophy of capitalism because capitalism requires that all those who labor under its burdens see themselves as things to be used, even while acting as if this were not true (we will see this even more clearly, and analyze it more deeply, in Chapter Three, on *Born to Kill*). Utilitarianism subsumes the individual to the group, training everyone to think of themselves as something to be sacrificed as necessary, even as they strive to excel in their chosen line of work. Recall

MacFarlane's comment as he strove to convince Fettes of the necessity of grave robbing: "I had to deal with men like Gray. Do you think I did it because I wanted to? Do you think I want to do it now? But I must. And you must." He does not question the system because he cannot question it, because he is too closely caught up in it. Acting as he does achieves good results, personally and professionally; that is all he needs to remember, and all he wants to remember. So MacFarlane dedicates himself to his profession and becomes less and less human in his reactions; at one point Gray asks him, "Could you be a doctor, a healing man with the things those eyes have seen?" Gray is not merely MacFarlane's dark side personified, he is also his conscience, the voice which speaks what MacFarlane cannot admit (hence the plethora of close two-shots when the two men are confronting each other).

But why should MacFarlane think otherwise? He lives and works in a society which is hypocritical regarding the preciousness of both life and death; the poor are of no account, and their bodies can be disposed of as objects, so it is obviously not the bodies themselves which have some innate worth or dignity. Rather, it is the bodies of those who can afford private burials and grave watchers which are of significance. MacFarlane simply takes advantage of a system he finds already in place. It is vital to understand that he is no "mad scientist," but rather one who has crossed a boundary already made vague by the circumstances surrounding him; like Jeremy Stone in *The Andromeda Strain*, he has become compromised by the actions he deemed, probably correctly, necessary to attain his scientific goals. He is no monster, but merely a man in an unscrupulous world who has been given too many opportunities to overcome his own scruples. By his own lights, and probably by those of most of the film's viewers, MacFarlane acts in a generally decent manner for much of the film. He provides fiscal support to Fettes in order that he may continue as a student, and he works hard to provide the best possible instruction to all of his students. He purchases corpses not for personal gain, but in the service of medical progress. Only as he grows desperate as the film progresses does he begin to transgress his own limits, by which time his well-trained ability to rationalize his actions makes it impossible for him to stop his downward spiral. The contradictions of the world in which he lives are mirrored in his actions and attitudes, and doom him even as they make him rich and respectable.

Cabman Gray (equated with his job, he has no other name of any significance)[13] has of course been desperate, and aware of his desperation, for far longer. His obsession with money is, like MacFarlane's with medicine, a reflection of his status within society; a few pence here and there will no doubt make the difference between merely tightening his belt or going to the poorhouse, should he or his horse be taken ill. Gray embodies not merely

MacFarlane's conscience and, in a sense, *alter ego*, but the unexpressed values undergirding the society in which he lives; in a world where the poor have value literally only as objects after their death, Gray follows the logic through to the next stage: acquiring the valuable objects before their death. No one, apart from Fettes, seems to notice their absence. Gray understands the situation of marginal individuals like himself; confronted with Joseph's demand for hush money, Gray comments knowingly, "I don't suppose the great Dr. MacFarlane's overlavish with his pay," but his insight does not lead to empathy or even pity; he simply disposes of Joseph as he would any other socially useless body.[14]

Gray's degradation is, as he acknowledges, all but complete, but even so he has carved out a more or less viable way of life within his society. He cannot, though, accept his constant exclusion from a world which exists because of those like him, and from lives which succeed because of his sacrifice. It is this which will doom him; once he begins to demand what he sees as fairer or better treatment, MacFarlane will eventually have to dispose of him, something which he does with a brutality which nonetheless leaves little emotional evidence in his subsequent behavior. We do not mourn the disposal of a malfunctioning appliance, and MacFarlane does not mourn the murder — his murder — of Gray. He has better things to which to attend, among them the education of his prize pupil Fettes.

In terms of viewer identification, Fettes is the focal point; neither so exalted in status as MacFarlane nor so debased as Gray, he is an earnest and on the whole likable young man seeking to make his way in the world. He, though, represents even more of a problem than do the other two, for in Fettes all of the social contradictions inherent in the utilitarian social structure come to a head. His career is entirely contingent on the will of others; as his name suggests, he is already in metaphoric chains, already fettered. Fettes, like Gray, has few financial resources, and can continue on his chosen path only because of his luck in studying with a wealthy and intermittently generous patron. Fettes, like MacFarlane, is a talented medical man, one with considerably better skills at personal interaction than his mentor, but he must compromise his own morals to remain such; even his one success, getting MacFarlane to operate on, and save, Georgina Marsh, occurs only at the cost of the blind singer's life, a death for which he is directly responsible (MacFarlane does not know of Fettes's errand, while Gray had no plans to go out that night, and on some later night the wandering singer would presumably have been elsewhere). Fettes knows all, or certainly most, of this, yet in the end he continues to follow MacFarlane, for there is no other path toward the goal he seeks. This is why Fettes's fate remains uncertain at the film's end; just as the contradictions within and under which he struggles continue after the conclusion of the action, so too he cannot simply escape them. Yet it would appear that his career is doomed, for even should he escape implication in the robbery which preceded MacFarlane's death, his sole source of income and education has now been cut off. We are perhaps invited to take pity on Fettes, yet even a moment's thought will suggest that, to the degree that we do so, we ourselves become embroiled in condoning his earlier actions and supporting the system which required them. Given what we have seen, we can neither completely condemn nor completely support Fettes, yet we recognize also that, if any favorable outcome for Georgina was to occur, sheer passivity would be just as unacceptable.

And here we find the film's final grim recognition, the reason why Georgina's recovery took place under lowering clouds rather than in bright sunlight: by extension Georgina and her mother are implicated as well, not in the murder itself but through benefiting thereby. Capitalism is a total system; even those who are nominally innocent cannot entirely escape its taint if they wish to survive at all. It is this, more than anything else, which keeps most of us willfully blind to the costs of maintaining our own places in society; there being apparently little we could do to counter the evils which exist to sustain us, we choose instead to ignore their existence. But until we do acknowledge — indeed, confront — those costs we remain in darkness, morally and humanly, as did MacFarlane and Gray, and as does Fettes.

The Body Snatcher, the last of Wise's films for producer Val Lewton, is an excellent film, with striking production values (especially given its minimal budget of $125,000), but it is also a remarkably bleak one in its honesty regarding capitalism and its innate strictures on human needs and freedoms. There are more beautifully filmed Lewton productions, but none, I think, as profound in their undercurrents as this one. It is unsurprising that within two years Wise would give contemporary society an even harsher examination, in *Born to Kill*. Nor is it surprising that he would grapple with the implications raised here for much of the rest of his career, seeking some kind of progressive resolution.

II. *The Day the Earth Stood Still* (1951)

Wise knew that many of his films carried implicit social and political messages, but he rarely drew attention to the fact. "I always want my films to have a comment to make," he said, adding that he preferred that "the comment should be made by the story itself, the development of the plot and the interplay of the characters, without having the actors say it in so many words." *The Day the Earth Stood Still* is a significant exception to this rule; as Wise pointed out, "The whole purpose of it was for Klaatu to deliver that warning at the end."[15] The film is, in essence, superb propaganda for a strong United Nations and against international rivalry and warfare. As such, it challenges some very basic principles of modern global politics. It also challenged the assumptions underlying most of the science fiction films of the 1950s, as well as several conventions of Hollywood cinematic storytelling. As the historian of science fiction John Clute said, "Nobody who saw it in 1951 ever forgot it, and it is still a film one returns to with nostalgia and fright."[16]

The paranoia which engulfed American culture in the years after World War II is amply reflected in the films of the era, and has been the subject of much comment. Nowhere were the fears corroding social cohesion more visible than in the science fiction films which proliferated after 1949. Invaders—humanoid, insectoid, amoeboid, and otherwise—threatened America, small town and big city alike, again and again. Most of these films were quickly made, briefly exhibited, and soon forgotten, but some transcended their context enough to remain worth watching today. The more of them one sees, the more one appreciates the character of Wise's first science fiction film. There is no paranoia here; if anything, the reverse is true. But there is indeed fear, of a deep and abiding nature, a fear which was shared by many people around the world in 1951: the fear of unrestricted atomic warfare.

When *The Day the Earth Stood Still* was released, the Korean War was ongoing and the nuclear destruction of Hiroshima and Nagasaki lay only six years in the past. Prominent in the public memory would also have been a postwar attempt to regulate atomic power, to turn it to international, rather than national, purposes: the so-called Baruch Plan, an American plan which got its name from Bernard M. Baruch, the advisor to U.S. president Harry S Truman who presented it in the United Nations in June of 1946. His introductory words would find their echo in Edmund H. North's screenplay for *The Day the Earth Stood Still*. "Behind the black portent of the new atomic age lies a hope which, seized upon with faith, can work our salvation," Baruch intoned. "If we fail, then we have damned every man to be the slave of Fear. Let us not deceive ourselves: We must elect World Peace or World Destruction." Following hard upon Baruch's invocation came a set of proposals for the internationalization of atomic energy and the eventual destruction of atomic weapons (at that time possessed only by the United States). An international agency with full regulatory and enforcement powers was to be created to control all activities, anywhere in the world, related to atomic energy, to license atomic energy facilities, and to supervise or conduct research regarding the peaceful use of atomic energy. Any attempts to defeat the agency's purpose, or to produce weapons-grade nuclear material, would result in "immediate, swift and sure punishment."[17] Some of Baruch's contemporaries, and many later historians, recognized a central flaw in the proposal: that the nuclear disarmament of the United States would come only after all other aspects of the plan were in place and fully functional. "A suspected violation of the control plan by the Russians at any time in the intervening stages," comments one Cold War specialist, "held the prospect — implied though not stated in the plan — of a devastating atomic attack upon the Soviet Union. Thus the Baruch plan did not differ in substance from an ultimatum the United States might have given Russia to forswear nuclear weapons or be destroyed."[18] Mutual distrust, along with other legitimate worries regarding the plan's practical aspects, doomed it, a fact punctuated dramatically when the Soviet Union detonated its own atomic bomb in 1949, years ahead of what American planners had expected, another event all too familiar to contemporary viewers of the film.

Given the historical circumstances, a useful yardstick against which to measure Wise's achievement in *The Day the Earth Stood Still* is one of the first, and best, of the alien invasion films — *The Thing from Another World* — released the same year but strikingly different in attitude and outcome. Credited to director Christian Nyby but produced by, and very much bearing the stamp of, Howard Hawks, *The Thing*, as it is familiarly known, set the template for much of what was to come. Here there is no room for doubt; the alien being — which in any case appears to have no means of communication save inarticulate howls— is on a mission of conquest, not diplomacy.

The plot is archetypal. An object of unparalleled weight and speed crashes in the Arctic; upon investigation it proves to be a space ship. The ship is destroyed, but one of its crew is discovered encased in the polar ice and is brought back to the scientific research installation nearby. The alien revives and demonstrates its brute strength and vicious nature by killing members of the station's complement, stringing up their bodies to attain blood for the purpose of reproduction. Gunshots and kerosene are of no avail, but just before catastrophe strikes the creature is electrocuted and destroyed. The film ends with a famous warning to "Keep watching the skies!"

The underlying message of *The Thing* is a suspicion of scientists, who are seen as fundamentally naïve, clever within their own world but hopelessly out of touch with political and, most importantly, military reality. Wise will present a parallel vision in *The Andromeda Strain*, save that there he offers a warning about overspecialization and the loss of balance between the moral and intellectual components of personal and public life. Hawks's production takes a simpler line, dismissing the overall character of science and its practitioners in favor of more traditionally masculine activities. Referring to the attitude of the scientists regarding the creature, the Air Force captain Hendry

(Kenneth Tobey) sums up the film's stance regarding such men: "Ah, they're kids, most of 'em, like nine-year-olds drooling over a new fire engine." His assessment is reinforced soon afterwards, even as it is putatively countered, by Nikki (Margaret Sheridan), the secretarial assistant to the researchers; defending Carrington, the chief scientist, she describes him as being different from such ordinary people as herself and the captain. "I know him," she tells Hendry, "and — he doesn't think the way we do anyway. But he's found something that no one can understand, and until he can solve it he'll — you know, like a kid with a new toy he'll just — ." Hendry, having learned that Carrington is using blood plasma to feed seedlings taken from the alien killer, interrupts her: "Only this toy is liable to bite him."

Carrington (Robert Cornthwaite) is indeed as cold-blooded as Hendry imagines. He is something of a caricature, enthusing, though in a clipped and restrained voice, over the emotionless nature of the vegetal entity; "Its development was not handicapped by emotional or sexual factors." Clearly having no personal life himself, he sees little value in conventional methods of human reproduction as compared to the seeding method of the alien, "The neat and unconfused reproductive technique of vegetation. No pain or pleasure as we know it. No emotions. No heart. Our superior. Our superior in every way." The unjustified inferential leap concluding his rhapsody warrants no confidence in his judgment elsewhere, a lack of confidence only reinforced by his paean to knowledge toward the end of the film. The entire sequence is illuminating: "Knowledge is more important than life, Captain," Carrington insists. "We've only one excuse for existing, to think, to find out, to learn[....] It doesn't matter what happens to us, nothing counts except our thinking. We've thought our way into nature, we've split the atom — ." At this point a crew member interrupts sarcastically, "Yes, and that made the world happy, didn't it?" Amid general laughter Carrington perseveres, his argument collapsing into complete incoherence; "We owe it to the brain of our species to stand here and die, without destroying a source of wisdom. Civilization has given us orders— ." Hendry, having heard more than enough, orders one of his crew to "Get him out of here." Complaining, Carrington is hustled away. He will attempt to sabotage the plan to kill the alien and then make one futile attempt at communication before being brushed aside violently. Carrington, and by implication, the scientific community in general, is irrelevant to the entire situation.

It is not merely the case that Carrington is naïve; he is shown as being consistently wrong about the situation faced by the small band of humans. Hendry, on the other hand, is either right in his concerns and actions or, when wrong, is wrong in a manner which works out for the best anyway. Thus, for example, he gives orders which result in the accidental destruction of the alien spacecraft, but learns later that the orders he gave were those the Air Force would have recommended. He consistently overrides Carrington, the man nominally in charge of the station, a civilian installation, even at times in contravention of direct orders from superior officers, yet it always turns out that those officers, once apprised of the situation (and sometimes even beforehand) have reconsidered their position and arrived at one akin to Hendry's. This, it might be worth pointing out, is consistent with military practice, which recognizes that it may be necessary for superior officers behind the lines to defer to the judgment of those on the scene during combat operations. *The Thing* is in many ways a conventional war movie, save that the war is against an alien being, and Hendry embodies the conventional military virtues of strength, decisiveness, and calm self-control. Action takes precedence over theory, and military necessity over scientific woollyheadedness; as Robin Wood puts it, "In the scenes between the soldiers there is a continual sense of living human beings responding to one another with an intuitive awareness the scientists largely lack."[19] While the fruits of science are, on the whole, useful and welcome, this is true only so long as they are in the proper hands— those of upright military men such as Hendry.

The Thing depicts, and celebrates, a world of masculine action, cooperation, and camaraderie. It is easy to forget that Nikki is not the only woman on the Arctic base, because, whereas Nikki acts in ways culturally masculine (she can outdrink the hero, for example), the other woman (Sally Creighton, credited as playing only "Mrs. Chapman") is restricted purely to more conventional roles, such as making coffee and succoring the wounded, and receives no accolades from anyone for performing these tasks, however well she does so. Only those who are part of this world, or who can behave in the manner it demands, are accorded full status as individuals (even Scotty, the newspaper reporter, is largely a figure of fun, always missing his photo ops and, after the creature has been destroyed, passing out from shock — this despite his having apparently been present during some of the bloodiest fighting during the Pacific campaign in World War II). Humanity, in the film's view, is a fairly narrow group of active individuals.

The Day the Earth Stood Still inverts both of the main positions suggested by *The Thing from Another World*, an inversion apparent from the opening moments. In *The Thing*, after the opening studio fanfare, the title, accompanied by Dmitri Tiomkin's thundering score, burns its way out of a black background, which gives way to a scene of ice and blowing snow; this shifts to a shot of a sign revealing the first location: the Officers' Club at a base in Anchorage, Alaska. The camera pulls back to reveal a solitary figure, and the action begins. *The Day the Earth Stood Still* likewise starts with the title card (and an even more compelling score, one of Bernard Herrmann's best), but the underlying images are, at first, paintings of sidereal images of no immediately obvious relevance; as the credits unfold, the images grow more detailed, until at last the planet Earth is seen, and then clouds. Without a word being said, it is evident that whatever is about to unfold will have extensive implications, reaching far beyond any particular geographical locale.

This is confirmed by what follows. In quick sequence we see the crew of an American radar station, that of a British radar station, a Calcutta newscaster, a small group of people listening to a French news report, a BBC newscaster, and Elmer Davis, a once well-known American newscaster. As the last-named speaks, further quick shots show various calm but intent listeners: a cab driver and his passenger, a gas station attendant and his customer, and so on. Finally, another then-renowned broadcaster, H.V. Kaltenborn, is seen, assuring his listeners that there are many signs of normality "here in the nation's capital." As he speaks, shots establish the location to which he is referring, and we see at last the flying saucer, which lands (in a sequence still impeccable from an effects standpoint) near the Smithsonian. The first person to actually announce the arrival of the space ship in Washington, as opposed to fleeing from it, is a single man who runs through a busy street bellowing that "They're here!" It's a risible moment, deliberately so, foreshadowing the fact that only genuine collective action on the part of humanity will answer the question, and address the promise, the visitor will provide.

Almost at once the police and military mobilize, and shortly the saucer is surrounded. These sequences are typical of the genre, and appropriate to the situation; faced with an unknown incursion, it is the job of the military to organize the best defense they can in the time available. This they do. Unfortunately, the situation is precisely such that these men, keyed up by their confrontation with the unknown but conditioned to regard suspicious situations as potentially threatening, are in fact ill-equipped to best handle it. Drew Pearson, an early television commentator, is seen analyzing the situation. Reporting military and governmental concerns over panic in several Atlantic seaboard cities, he declares, "I am authorized to assure you that so far there is no reasonable cause for alarm." The film here subtly undercuts expectations; many viewers (both of Pearson's broadcast and of the film itself) would have recalled Orson Welles's famous 1938 radio adaptation of H.G. Wells's *War of the Worlds*, and perhaps expected something similar, or worse. There will, though, be few pyrotechnics here. With Pearson's didactic commentary providing a bridge, the scene shifts to the Washington ballpark where the saucer has landed. The ship's side opens and a thin being (yclept Klaatu, as we will learn, played by Michael Rennie), helmeted and clad in a silver uniform, strides out to face the massed and trained rifles, howitzers, and tanks. Pausing and raising a hand, he declares that "we have come to visit you in peace, and with good will." He then continues forward, slowly, reaching into a slit in the front of his uniform to pull out an object of unknown import. As he moves forward, he extends the object, and it flicks open. This at last is too much for one of the soldiers, who fires twice, shattering the object and wounding the alien.

This entire sequence is impressively constructed and presented. The alien is seen principally in medium shots usually from in front and thus alone, while the soldiers are seen in group shots. Amidst these are interspersed shots of the spectators, careful to emphasize the multifarious nature of the crowd, old and young, black and white, and so on (the significance of this will become amply evident at the film's climax and conclusion). Apart from the few words of the alien and the occasional click of a gun being cocked, there are no sounds save Bernard Herrmann's score, itself consisting mainly of sustained chords. The sound of the shot, startling and loud, is the cue for general crowd sounds, shouts and screams and a hubbub of conversation, as the soldiers approach the wounded alien.

But this sequence has tricked us; it is only the prelude to something yet greater and more ominous: the apparition of the robot Gort (Lock Martin). The crowd and the soldiers understand immediately that this is another order of being altogether; the former flee, the latter back away from the wounded alien, again raising their weapons. These prove irrelevant; Gort trundles forward, opens the visor on the front of its head, and disintegrates several weapons, ranging from rifles to a tank. Two key points are made here, although neither of them is stressed. The first is that Gort destroys weapons, not persons; a hierarchy of values is implicitly present even as the robot acts in an apparently violent manner. The second is that the soldiers, despite what could be described fairly as provocation, do not open fire in return. Professional discipline holds; having received no orders to attack they do not do so (thus, as we will soon realize, saving at least the city of Washington, D.C., from annihilation). Klaatu, satisfied that the assault upon his person was the result of fear, not vicious intent, convinces Gort to stop (his exact words are "deglento brosko"; whether these are a request, a command, or something in between is unknown). The commanding officer arrives and orders the wounded person to be taken to an Army hospital, as much for observation as for care. This fitting in with Klaatu's intentions, he makes no objections.

The film thus far has been, as the presence of so many widely known figures from the news world suggests, visually akin to a documentary, though the music ensures that the viewer is involved emotionally from the very beginning. Wise recognized that such material could only gain from a visually detached, though by no means bland, introduction (the same is true of Nyby's approach to *The Thing from Another World*, which is likewise documentarian in its visual style). But once the introduction is over, the style gradually grows more varied, taking on at times an appearance akin to Wise's films noir, as he expands upon Klaatu's mission. Having gotten the audience to accept the plausibility of an alien visitor, he now uses a wider range of cinematic techniques to encourage our identification with said visitor, and thus implicitly with the message he had come to deliver.

The tonal shift is evident immediately. Recuperating in a hospital bed, Klaatu is visited by Mr. Harley (Frank Conroy; we never learn the character's first name), "secretary to the president." The first 30 seconds of the scene are a single shot of Harley from over Klaatu's left shoulder; the principal light comes from a single bulb over Klaatu's head, harshening contrasts already pointed up by Harley's dark suit and throwing Klaatu's profile into sharp shadowy relief, such that Klaatu's actual appearance remains a mystery. Harley expresses the president's apologies for Klaatu's shooting, and comments on the surprise caused by Klaatu's arrival. Only when he asks how long Klaatu has been traveling (that is, at the point in which the dialogue will most emphasize Klaatu's alien origins) does a reverse shot reveal Klaatu's face, which is, we discover, gauntly handsome.[20] Klaatu evades the question of his planetary origin; "Let's just say that we're neighbors," he says. "Rather difficult for us to think of another planet as a neighbor," Harley replies, his expression almost comic in its incredulity. Klaatu does not smile. "I'm afraid in the present situation you will have to learn to think that way," he says. His tone is somber, even slightly minatory, and there is no suggestion of doubt regarding his, as yet unstated, purpose; the composition of the two-shots which carry much of the dialogue forward suggests the true balance of power, with Harley always being lower on the screen, even, indeed especially, when he is the object of the shot, than Klaatu. The preliminaries established, Klaatu and *The Day the Earth Stood Still* can now begin their true missions.

Klaatu has no interest in meeting with the president or any other individual. "This is not a personal matter, Mr. Harley. It concerns all the people on your planet," he declares. He has learned English from radio broadcasts his people have monitored, but he has only a sketchy idea of Earthly politics, and his request for a meeting with "representatives from all the nations of the Earth" is dismissed as utterly unrealistic by Harley. "Our world, at the moment," he tells Klaatu, "is full of tensions and suspicions[....] I'm sure you, you recognize [...] the evil forces that have produced the trouble in our world." Klaatu interrupts him; "I'm not concerned, Mr. Harley, with the internal affairs of your planet. My mission here is not to solve your petty squabbles. It concerns the existence of every last creature on Earth." Clearly growing frustrated with Harley's explanations, Klaatu warns him that "the future of your planet is at stake." He extracts from Harley a pledge to present this message to the president and various world leaders, and to attempt to assemble them to hear what he, Klaatu, has to say.

Harley is true to his word, but returns the next day with bad news, and a host of telegrams to back it up: the world leaders are opposed to meeting with Klaatu as a group for this, that, or the other specious political reason.[21] A brief but important exchange on the larger situation follows, the dialogue being carried by a series of two-shots which maintain Klaatu's visual dominance (he is both taller than Harley and filmed so as to emphasize his greater height).

> *Klaatu:* I will not speak with any one nation or group of nations. I don't intend to add my contribution to your childish jealousies and suspicions.
> *Harley:* Our problems are very complex, Klaatu; you mustn't judge us too harshly.
> *Klaatu:* I can judge only by what I see.
> *Harley:* Your impatience is quite understandable.
> *Klaatu:* I'm impatient with stupidity. My people have learned to live without it.
> *Harley:* I'm afraid my people haven't. I'm very sorry. I wish it were otherwise.

This is not merely an advance peek at the central propaganda line to be taken at the climax. Klaatu is an alien who must learn more about what he is encountering, and his interactions with Harley, a representative of a major authority figure on the planet, are part of this education. As the two men speak, Klaatu's expression undergoes a complex evolution, growing more tender as he grapples with the contrast with Harley's evident desire to work with him and his inability to make anything happen. Looking out a window, he declares that he should not make any decision without meeting ordinary people in order to "become familiar with the basis for these strange, unreasoning attitudes." Harley quashes this idea, and requests that Klaatu make no effort to leave, as the military people think this isolation necessary. He leaves, and a soldier locks the door from outside; hearing the key turn, Klaatu smiles for the first time.

Thus ends the first act of the film, in which the professionals— military, medical, and political — demonstrate their irrelevance and ineffectiveness.[22] The second act, which opens with the discovery of Klaatu's escape, develops his efforts to investigate matters on his own. Taking the name Carpenter from the dry-cleaning receipt on a suit he has stolen from the hospital, Klaatu wanders the streets of Washington, listening to a variety of radio and television broadcasts offering different, and often contradictory, perspectives on the nature of the alien visitor.[23] He finds a rooming house and enters to ask for accommodation. The residents are gathered about the television set watching Drew Pearson describing the situation, to which description Pearson adds his own reminder that the evidence is not yet conclusive; "though this man may be our bitter enemy, he may be also a newfound friend." Klaatu stands in the entrance hall in deep shadow, his face invisible (visually echoing Pearson's on-screen comment that the only photographs available are of Klaatu in his helmet). The shot is striking, and symbolically significant; Klaatu represents Earth's future, and the future is always at least partly in shadow, leaving it up to human beings to decide whether or not, and how, to greet it or fight it.

In the rooming house Klaatu meets the several boarders, including Helen Benson (Patricia Neal), a young widow, and her son Bobby (Billy Gray). Over breakfast soon afterward he encounters a small sample of the "strange, unreasoning attitudes" he is investigating. A rabidly xenophobic radio denunciation of the "monster," who must be "tracked down like a wild animal" and "destroyed," catches his ear, as does the banter among the residents. "Why doesn't the government do something?" asks one. "What can they do?" counters another; "they're only people, just like us." The first will have none of it; "People my foot," he huffs, "they're Democrats." Only Helen is somewhat sympathetic, offering the possibility that, having been shot as soon as he arrived, the spaceman might himself be afraid. Another of the residents, Mrs. Barley (Frances Bavier), thinks the whole matter is something of a hoax; "Well if you want my opinion," she declares, "he comes from right here on Earth. And," she adds with a significant glance around the room, "you know where I mean."

As often in Wise's films, the presence of a child indicates the direction in which our sympathies will be urged; children represent the future and the possibility of applying education and training so as to enhance, or warp, it. In this case, Klaatu and Bobby Benson hit it off promptly, a process aided when Helen goes on a daylong date with her boyfriend Tom Stevens (Hugh Marlowe) and leaves Bobby in Klaatu's care (that Tom's relationship with Helen will go nowhere is indicated almost as soon as we meet him by his evident disinterest in Bobby). Bobby and Klaatu go to Arlington National Cemetery, burial site of Bobby's father (killed in action during World War II), where Klaatu is startled by the vast number of war deaths and Bobby is startled by Klaatu's ignorance of the cemetery's reason for existing. Klaatu allows that he has been very far away, and Bobby asks whether they have cemeteries where he is from. Cemeteries, yes, but not this sort, Klaatu replies, adding that "they don't have any wars." Bobby's response is naïvely enthusiastic; "Gee, that's a good idea." His naïveté is quickly surpassed by Klaatu's regarding finances; offering to take Bobby to a movie, he asks whether money is necessary to do so. It is, but Bobby politely offers to pay, using the two dollars his mother had given him. Klaatu demurs, asking instead whether the theater would take the diamonds he carries ("in some places those are what people use for money," he explains). He offers to exchange two of them for the two dollars

Bobby has; Bobby cagily agrees, but requests that Klaatu say nothing to Helen, "She doesn't like me to steal from people."

This little scene is easy to overlook, yet it contains material of vital import. Bobby's attitude displays within it the seeds of corruption; by his own moral code he is acting wrongly, and knows himself to be acting wrongly, yet he does so in pursuit of easy gain at the expense of another (that Klaatu does not appear to understand, or to care, that he is being taken advantage of, is irrelevant, since it is on Bobby's, not Klaatu's, moral grounds that Bobby's act is wrong). This is not moral error, an act performed in ignorance, but a conscious choice to cheat another, to choose wronging someone else in order to attain a personal advantage. That we so easily miss its significance is itself part of that significance; possibly every one of us has acted in a similar fashion at some point, though probably self-generating a greater fog of justification than Bobby bothers to. Such acts, though, are simply the causes of war writ small; all wars begin as the result of some group having attempted to obtain an advantage for itself over, and at the expense of, another group or groups (whether the group is a tribe or a clan or a nation is of no significance, save as regards the size of the eventual conflict). It is no accident that the transaction takes place in a cemetery dedicated to the war dead.

We excuse Bobby's greed partly because we recognize that it is without malice and partly because of his youth, which we presume to be relatively free of adult understandings. Another instance of this, again used to point up common misunderstandings among adults, comes soon afterwards, as Klaatu takes Bobby, at the latter's request, to see the space ship. Bobby expresses curiosity regarding the ship's propulsion; Klaatu tells him it is driven by "a highly developed form of atomic power." Bobby is surprised; "I thought that was only for bombs," he says. "No," Klaatu replies, "no, it's for lots of other things, too." His educated tone catches the ear of some nearby yokels, who mock the explanations he is giving Bobby. Soon afterward, a roving reporter asks "Mr. Carpenter" for his opinion on the spaceman, expecting him to express the same fear that so many others have expressed. Klaatu's thoughtful response, "I am fearful when I see people substituting fear for reason," is not to the reporter's taste, and he cuts him off and moves on. Klaatu's education is continuing apace, and he is becoming increasingly aware that he has been mistaken in expecting his message to resonate with, or even be understood by, the peoples of the various nations, most of whom, based on the samples he has seen thus far, live in a mental world shaped by ignorance, greed, fear, and selfishness, their political circumstances guided by a plethora of conflicting, but equally ignorant, authorities. If the message is to be heard at all, another path will need to be chosen.

Klaatu decides to make his appeal to the scientist described by Bobby as "the smartest man in the world," Professor Barnhardt (Sam Jaffe). Barnhardt is recognizably based on Albert Einstein, who in 1951 occupied a unique place in the eyes of much of the world, a place of honor for his scientific researches and their results and of respect for his great humanitarianism. Einstein's political views, including a consistent advocacy of a world government, were well known. As he wrote in 1946, for example, regarding the increasing linkage between the economic and military fates of nations,

> The only hope for protection lies in the securing of peace in a supranational way. A world government must be created which is able to solve conflicts between nations by judicial decision. This government must be based on a clear-cut constitution which is approved by the governments and the nations and which gives it the sole disposition of offensive weapons. A person or a nation can be considered peace loving only if it is ready to cede its military force to the international authorities and to renounce every attempt or even the means, of achieving its interests abroad by the use of force.[24]

Einstein recognized the connection between war and nationalism. "So long as the individual state, despite its official condemnation of war, has to consider the possibility of engaging in war," he wrote, "it must influence and educate its citizens—and its youth in particular — in such a way that they can easily be converted into efficient soldiers in the event of war. Therefore it is compelled not only to cultivate a technical-military training and type of thinking but also to implant a spirit of national vanity in its people in order to secure their inner readiness for the outbreak of war."[25] He, like many people then and later, looked to the spirit of science as a pathfinder toward internationalism, for science itself, as a method, is not subject to any boundaries but those of the natural world it is investigating. It is this approach to which Klaatu now looks, counting on Barnhardt to see beyond the fears dominant in so much of the population.

Barnhardt does not fail. Klaatu comments on Barnhardt's faith in him, and Barnhardt counters with a straightforward assessment of his, Barnhardt's, own motives: "It isn't faith that makes good science, Mr. Klaatu, it's curiosity." Scientific curiosity is a kind of imagination, but a very special one, for it requires not merely envisioning what we do not know but inventing ways to learn more. Barnhardt is extremely curious, and to him Klaatu, though still reluctant to speak only to one person regarding matters of such significance to all persons, reveals more of his mission than to anyone else thus far. The people of the other planets are aware of Earth's researches in atomic energy and rocketry. "So long as you were limited to fighting among yourselves with your primitive tanks and aircraft," he tells Barnhardt," we were unconcerned. But soon one of your nations will apply atomic energy to space ships. That will create a threat to the peace and security of other planets. That of course we cannot tolerate." The people of Earth must become aware of this, for the process, if unchecked, will end in disaster; "by threatening danger your planet faces danger. Very grave danger." As always in this film, the staging reflects the situation; despite Barnhardt's invitation to be seated, Klaatu remains standing, towering over the scientist as he delivers his warning (Klaatu is taller than every other significant character save Gort). Yet the camera set-ups soften the impact of this imbalance through predominance of close-ups rather than wider two-shots; Klaatu's words are ominous, but he is treating Barnhardt as something of an equal. This becomes even more evident after Klaatu tells Barnhardt that his message is too important to be delivered to only one man. Barnhardt now takes the initiative, verbally and visually. He stands and walks around his desk; in a single smooth shot the camera dollies forward, and Klaatu turns his back on the screen, to follow him, such that Barnhardt's next line, "I gather that your efforts on the official level were not entirely successful," is given maximum weight within the power relations between the two men. Klaatu expresses frustration, and suggests that violent action — "leveling New York City, perhaps, or sinking the rock of Gibraltar" are the examples he gives— may be the only thing to which people will respond. Barnhardt anticipates Klaatu's intentions; "Would you be willing to meet with a group of scientists I'm calling together?" He could explain to them, and they could explain to their people and governments. Nor is Barnhardt politically naïve; "It is not enough to have men of science. We scientists are too often ignored or misunderstood." The best people from a wide range of disciplines are needed. Smiling, Klaatu leaves the arrangement of this meeting to Barnhardt.

Barnhardt, aware of the terrible consequences should even these intellectual leaders fail to accept Klaatu's message, recognizes also that some sort of demonstration of the power behind Klaatu's words is indeed necessary. "I wouldn't want you to harm anybody or destroy anything," Barnhardt says, but a dramatic lesson affecting the entire planet would be helpful. Klaatu agrees; the results of this agreement inaugurate the final act of the film, as well as providing its title.

It will be evident that Barnhardt is poles apart from Carrington in *The Thing from Another World*. His method is scientific but the underlying attitude remains deeply humanistic; that is, he understands the facts of the matter but sees their context as well.[26] Carrington would sacrifice all of humanity to a "superior" being, apparently simply because it knows more about technology. Barnhardt works with a superior being in an effort to save humanity from the consequences of its own ignorance and its consequent misapplications of its own technology.

Klaatu gets back into his ship and arranges the demonstration. Unfortunately, he is followed by Bobby (the noir lighting and Herrmann's broodingly minimalist score here creating a marvelous sense of tension out of very simple elements), who afterwards tells his mother and Tom Stevens. Stevens finds one of Klaatu's diamonds, and Klaatu's disguise begins to unravel. The next day Klaatu learns from Bobby what the latter has seen, and visits Helen Benson at her office to ascertain her intentions. The two are trapped together in an elevator when the power shuts down, for the demonstration arranged involves the neutralization of all electricity around the planet, save those involving "hospitals, planes in flight, that sort of thing," for a half an hour. Accompanied by some of Herrmann's most original music, dissonantly shifting chords played against reversed recordings of the same material, we see scenes of paralysis, from farms to factories, laundry rooms to ice cream shops, motorcars to railroad engines, in city and country after city and country. "It's that spaceman," one onlooker observes.

Framing the scenes of inert chaos are two segments involving Klaatu and Helen in the elevator, segments which subtly but unmistakably underline their respective situations. By now the viewer should have realized that Helen stands in for the best of ordinary people; she is unexceptional in her position, her education, or her intellect, but she has the one thing without which these other aspects of human personality are crippled: she is capable of genuine empathy, of exercising moral imagination. When she and Klaatu are first trapped in the elevator she is, as might be expected, initially unconcerned; she will press another button and move them onward. Klaatu tells her about the electricity, and she gazes at him in growing fear. The slatted lighting, suggestive of prison cell window bars, combines with the two-shots, familiar in their emphasis on Klaatu's superior position, to add punch to Helen's apprehension. "Bobby was telling the truth, wasn't he?" she murmurs. "Yes," he replies softly. When we return to them, the balance has shifted. Klaatu has revealed the truth of his mission, telling her more than he has told even Professor Barnhardt. The camera set-up reveals this even before Klaatu speaks; for the first time we see Klaatu and Helen in a straightforward two-shot, facing each other in profile. From now on, all shots of the two will be such as to stress their visual equivalence.

Events conspire against Klaatu. The military steps up its manhunt, and Stevens, having figured out who "Mr. Carpenter" must be, and expecting to be "the biggest man in the country" for doing so, passes the information on to the military, over the protests of Helen. "It isn't just you and Mr. Carpenter," she says, "the rest of the world is involved." His dismissal is bluntly honest: "I don't care about the rest of the world." He may win his reward, but he has lost Helen, who leaves to attempt to save Klaatu. A chase sequence right out of a film noir follows, with Helen and Klaatu in a cab, trying to reach

Professor Barnhardt, with the military forces closing in.[27] Realizing that he is unlikely to escape, Klaatu gives Helen the three vital words that remain the best known component of the film — "Klaatu barada nikto" — and warns her of Gort's destructive power. The cab is stopped, and Klaatu, fleeing, is shot down in the street. Again the camera set-up and lighting convey very much the manner of a noir murder, still further humanizing Klaatu. The emotional connection is intensified as Helen cradles his head for a moment and he tells her to "Get that message to Gort"; the camera is almost at street level, angled up at her, crouching by Klaatu's side, as she looks around the gathering crowd as if trying to find just one sympathetic face. In the ensuing confusion Helen sidles away and soon confronts Gort, who receives the message, deposits her in the space ship, and retrieves Klaatu's body, which, using special machinery, he restores to life.

Professor Barnhardt having arranged for his experts to assemble at the space ship, they are already present when Klaatu exits the space ship and at last delivers the message at which the entire film has been aiming. "I am leaving soon," he tells the assembled luminaries.

> And you will forgive me if I speak bluntly. The universe grows smaller every day. And the threat of aggression by any group, anywhere, can no longer be tolerated. There must be security for all or no one is secure. Now this does not mean giving up any freedom, except the freedom to act irresponsibly[....] We of the other planets have long accepted this principle. We have an organization for the mutual protection of all planets, and for the complete elimination of aggression[....] In matters of aggression we have given them absolute power over us. This power cannot be revoked. At the first sign of violence they act automatically against the aggressor. The penalty for provoking their action is too terrible to risk. The result is, we live in peace, without arms or armies, secure in the knowledge that we are free from aggression and war. Free to pursue more profitable enterprises. Now we do not pretend to have achieved perfection. But we do have a system, and it works[....] It is no concern of ours how you run your own planet. But if you threaten to extend your violence, this Earth of yours will be reduced to a burned-out cinder. Your choice is simple: join us and live in peace, or pursue your present course and face obliteration[....] The decision rests with you.

Klaatu and Gort then step into the space ship and depart; as the opening music is heard one last time, the words "The End" appear to approach us from the glowing dot that is all we can see of the ship.

The filming of Klaatu's two-and-a-half minute speech is filled with telling details. It occupies 22 shots, roughly even in length; there are no jump cuts or unusual angles, and the camera does not move until the final shot. Gone are the noir effects; we are once again in the realm of a kind of naturalism. Wise recognizes that this sort of propaganda requires that one find it powerful even after the film's initial impact has faded; the fewer tricks we can dismiss as meretricious the harder it will be to escape the involvement into which we have been enticed throughout the film. The first medium shot is of Klaatu, with Gort in the background; it is followed, and balanced, by a medium shot of Barnhardt, with Helen standing beside, but lower than, him. A new Klaatu/Gort shot, as he warns that aggression cannot be tolerated, links quickly to a series of medium shots, seen as he refers to the need for "security for all," of various individuals in the crowd, always with members of several different ethnic groups prominent, reminding us of the mixture in the earlier scenes of the crowds gawking at the space ship. Two more medium shots of Klaatu and Gort, the second closer than the first, re-establish his dominance of the sequence, and set up the ensuing long shot of the crowd from behind, with the soldiers prominent among them, as Klaatu refers to the "complete elimination of aggression." We see Klaatu in a half-body medium shot, then a close-up of Barnhardt, intent upon his words, with the crowd murmuring behind him, as he makes the point about the "absolute power" given to the robotic police force, a point strongly underlined by a low-angle close-up of Gort. The next shot is essentially from Gort's point of view, from behind Klaatu's back, of the crowd's reactions as Klaatu announces that the enforcers react "at the first sign of violence." Representatives of each of the opposing approaches to the situation — that is, of the possible human choices of response — are simultaneously visible, Barnhardt and Helen in the center, the group of infantrymen screen left. Another multi-ethnic group shot (including an obviously Soviet military type, one of the film's few nods to the actual Cold War situation) moves us into the warning regarding the terrible penalty awaiting an aggressor. Four further shots balance the Klaatu/Gort duo with the Barnhardt/Helen duo, after which a close-up of Klaatu pulls us into his words even more closely as he comments on the Earth's fate should it export its violence. A crowd shot, once more revealing multiple ethnicities, gives us the human reaction, after which a shot of Gort and Klaatu turns, by way of a dolly shot, the first in the sequence, into a close-up of Klaatu's face as he utters the fateful words, "The decision rests with you."

Silence ensues, in which there are several shots of the various groups, clearly representing many races and nations, gazing somberly at Klaatu. He sends Gort back into the ship, then turns and, with a small smile, his first since beginning the speech, crossing his face, makes a gesture of acknowledgment toward Helen, who likewise smiles tentatively. There is hope, though not certainty; the music played under these last few moments of emotional contact between Klaatu and Helen is that which was played as Bobby Benson and Klaatu toured the Arlington National Cemetery. Whether that hope is real depends, the music implies, on whether or not we have heard, and respond properly, to Klaatu's message.

But what, exactly, is that message? It may not bode well for the future of our species that a surprising number of commentators seem to have missed it altogether.

It is not religious. Carlos Clarens, in his influential study of horror films, criticizes the film along precisely these lines: "The film trips on its own long seriousness and the religious parallel becomes embarrassing after a while." It is not entirely clear what parallels he is objecting to, for his brief discussion of the plot, which is itself filled with errors, suggests that he sees an Old, rather than New, Testament approach. In any case he is unimpressed with Klaatu's efforts. "If Klaatu is God's angel on earth," Clarens writes, "his rather conservative display of power simply is not enough to convince humanity of the power at the source of his words. And if he is a man, better than our men, the product of a civilization beyond ours, why does he not bring with him the formula for peaceful living that has supposedly succeeded so well in the cultures of other planets instead of an awfully earth-sounding ultimatum?"[28] Whether or not the demonstration Klaatu arranges is effective is open to question, but its "conservatism" (which presumably refers to its lack of destructive force) is both deliberate and necessary, for Klaatu is, after all, bringing a message of peace (even Gort kills only after Klaatu is killed, and then only, thanks to Helen's timely message, the two soldiers standing guard at the saucer). Nor does he fail to bring the answer Clarens seeks, albeit without demanding that it be applied to planetary political conflicts; the other planets "do have a system, and it works." The ultimatum, more of which follows below, refers only to aggression beyond Earth's boundaries. But Clarens's objections already suggest that his principle assumption—the religious underpinning of the film—is inaccurate. Klaatu does not do what Clarens demands in the manner Clarens demands because Klaatu is not supernatural in his powers. His appeal is to rationality, even if only the human desire to remain alive, and his methods are those of science and technology, not magic and divinity.

The film does not advocate or support the imposition of its solution on any given nation by any given nation. Variants of this charge, often expressed in excessively heated terms, are most commonly found in the sequential statements of opinion which pass for discussion on internet chat boards, where they are presumably triggered by attacks on, or defenses of, recent military actions by the United States of America. Klaatu is quite specific in his denial of any interest in exalting one nation over the others, or in interfering with the internal affairs of any one nation or group of nations. In a certain sense, Klaatu's approach is classical liberalism written on the scale of a planet; liberalism in its purest form holds that restraints on actions which hurt only oneself are illegitimate, and Klaatu's message includes the assertion that what earth does to itself is its own business ("It is no concern of ours how you run your own planet"). It is only when the violence so common to Earth is exported that swift and conclusive action will be taken.

The film is not fascistic. The charge is understandable, but it, like the others, rests on a misunderstanding of Klaatu's message. He is quite clear in his references to a "police force" (robots such as Gort), existing as an agency with one task and great powers applicable thereto but not otherwise. His people have recognized that a separation of the executive (enforcement) branch from the legislative (law-creating) branches of government is vital. Where the enforcers have no legislative authority, no control of the mechanisms of government and communication, the possibility of fascism, which is in effect the maintenance of political power for its own sake, is mitigated. As Klaatu says, the robotic executive branch exists to allow the people of the other planets greater freedoms in their personal lives.

Klaatu's message may be frightening, but it is not in fact especially alien. It is largely in line with the ideas of Albert Einstein and Bernard M. Baruch. Simply put, what is being demanded of the Earth's people is that they either confine their warlike activities to their own planet or that they agree to supervision by the external police force attuned to detecting and eliminating aggression. By extension, then, what is being called for in real terms is that the power of production, manufacture, and use of what we now call weapons of mass destruction be removed from the purview of any given nation and placed in the control of an external, supranational, force — the United Nations, but with a military force of its own. In one sense this is radical, yet in another — the preservation of the increasingly outmoded concept of national sovereignty — it is quite conservative. What is being presented here begins with the idea that what any given nation does to its own people is a matter outside the purview of the supranational agency and its police force. This is not to preclude, say, economic sanctions, but only the application of violence, of military force. Should that nation export its violence, however, should it attempt to conquer or occupy another nation, the response would be overwhelming, a fact which would have a powerfully cooling effect on the taste for military adventurism among the citizenry. It is a simple concept and political structure, yet one vastly difficult of achievement.

Hence the overall depiction of characters in *The Day the Earth Stood Still*; the individuals, although quite distinct on their own, also form a representational structure intended to engage the viewer with an idea and to leave them with a sense of its possibility. Klaatu and his message are the focus of the film, and Professor Barnhardt the avatar of its method, but Helen Benson is its heart. In one sense, Klaatu is concerned with policy while Helen and Bobby represent those who would be affected by the policy. There is a triple identification operant here. Klaatu's warning would have been especially resonant with the film's contemporary audiences, for whom whole-scale slaughter was a matter of recent daily headlines, and who were vividly aware of the power of atomic weaponry. The film is careful to engage us with Klaatu, to make him comprehensible and attractive, such that we listen to his words with sympathy, and regret his putative death. Thus presented, Klaatu serves as an effective symbol for the danger humanity faces from its own warlike behaviors.

This is not enough; we need some sense that there are those whose allegiance to violence is minimal, who might be able to lead humanity away from the abyss of self-destruction. Enter Professor Barnhardt. Einstein's renown as a scientist and humanitarian has become more generalized since the film's release, but some of the power his image held in 1951 still comes through, as does the promise of applying scientific method to international relations, of encouraging reason to govern politics. Barnhardt and Einstein, the fictional and factual avatars of a different society, point away from the contemporary fixation on increasing national or tribal power. They know that modern weaponry makes traditional wars increasingly dangerous to all of humanity. As Einstein wrote in 1951, the same year *The Day the Earth Stood Still* was released, "The devastation wrought by the wars of the last half century [has] brought home the fact to everybody that, with the present-day level of technical achievement, the security of nations [can] be based only on supranational institutions and rules of conduct. It is understood that, in the long run, an all-destroying conflict can be avoided only by the setting up of a world federation of nations."[29] Where national interests are backed by independent armies and common interests of humanity are subsumed in the political ambitions of a few powerful individuals, peace cannot be secure.

This, though, is still not enough; intellectual realizations are vital components of the human campaign for peace and social balance, but they cannot come until ordinary human beings feel, as well as cognize, the circumstances compelling destructive behavior and the actions necessary to change them. This is the role of Helen Benson; in her very ordinariness, she brings home to the viewer the possibility of personal change in the face of apparently overwhelming forces. Helen is not involved with politics, save perhaps as a voter; she is concerned principally with taking care of her son, of bringing him up to be as good a person as possible. It is Helen's willingness to think empathetically of others which allows her to understand Klaatu's mission and its importance, for she, even more than Barnhardt, has an emotional response both to Klaatu as a person and the plight of humanity as a whole. Helen is our key into the film's world, for, the film strongly implies, if she can achieve such an understanding then so can we. Helen does something we see no one else doing in the film: she loves. Love, in its emphasis on individual connection, counters the tendency toward abstraction in political calculation. A good political system, therefore, is one which fosters and encourages love between individuals; one which does not do so, or which does so in a warped or restricted manner, is one which does not support peace and the expansion of human potential.

The Day the Earth Stood Still is, as I have noted, excellent propaganda. It is also unusual propaganda, for it stems from Wise's personal commitment to an internationalist outlook rather than to a given national or political system. Its formal structure reflects this, as does its structure of character relations. There is no happy ending in the conventional sense; indeed, there is not so much an ending as simply a momentary cessation of the action. Helen's romance with Tom Stevens has been terminated, and her attraction to Klaatu is not, and cannot be, consummated emotionally. The Earth has been warned, but the political outcome of the warning is not so much as hinted at. Wise has here carefully balanced two of his chief concerns—the dangers inherent in human greed and ignorance and their concomitant aggressiveness, starkly developed in *The Body Snatcher* and *Odds Against Tomorrow*, and the possibility of finding a way forward in the face of such patterns of behavior, hinted at in *The Captive City* and *A Storm in Summer* but most fully developed in *Star Trek: The Motion Picture*—yet left the conclusions to his audience. *The Day the Earth Stood Still* is a chilling film but at base an optimistic one (for an author does not preach progress where they believe none is possible), and remains among Wise's, and science fiction cinema's, finer achievements.

III. *Odds Against Tomorrow* (1959)

Wise's most visually striking black-and-white film, *Odds Against Tomorrow*, is also one of his most somber, a film that even Wise's detractor David Thomson describes as "exceptionally tough and bleak."[30] Although the cinematography (by Joseph Brun) is often more shadowy than dark, beautifully exploring a vast range of greys, the grim outlook of the screenplay (by Abraham Polonsky and Nelson Gidding) has earned the film a reputation as being the last of the true films noir.[31] Whatever term one applies, it is a landmark in Wise's career.

Odds Against Tomorrow operates on two levels simultaneously. The first level is that of a caper film; as is traditional in such films we see the meticulous plotting of a robbery and watch it all come to naught, a process which amply provides the requisite dramatic tension. The second level, though, is much more complex and compelling; it is the slow unveiling of the forces driving the plotters to their various decisions, actions, and fates. To concentrate on the first level while ignoring the second is to miss the point of the film altogether; individual actions do not take place in a social and political vacuum, and much of what we see is driven by forces of which the characters themselves are only partly aware. It is not enough simply to note the presence of the film's anti-racist element, for this itself is only a part, albeit an important one, of the larger picture. Racism itself is driven, or fueled, by other, broader, social factors, and it is these which underlie the film and give it much of its power.

Decades after the release of *Odds Against Tomorrow*, when overt expressions of bigotry are for the most part both less common and less acceptable, some of the film's original impact is inevitably lost. It is worth remembering the original context here. The late 1950s saw many changes, large and small, in the political and legal treatment of African Americans, changes which were accompanied by a disturbing upsurge in racist rhetoric and actions. Among the events involved are ones which resonate to this day. In December of 1955, for example, Rosa Parks, a middle-aged working woman, refused to leave the "whites only" section of a public bus in Montgomery, Alabama; she was duly arrested, prompting a boycott of the bus system by the black community. Despite violence against the boycotters, including Martin Luther King, Jr., the protesters held their ground. Revenues for the bus line dropped precipitously, and a year later, under both legal and financial pressure, the company capitulated, fully integrating the bus lines. On a larger scale, in 1954 the unanimous Supreme Court decision *Brown v. Board of Education of Topeka* (usually called simply *Brown v. Board of Education*) overturned decades of legally sanctioned segregation in schools. The Court, still speaking unanimously, strongly reaffirmed and reinforced the original decision in 1955 in a second *Brown v. Board of Education* and in 1958 in *Cooper v. Aaron*. The latter case stemmed from one of the most notorious events of the period, the attempt by Arkansas governor Orval Faubus to use the Arkansas National Guard to override an earlier court order requiring integration, an attempt quashed by President Dwight D. Eisenhower's use of U.S. Army troops to enforce the order. The civil rights struggles which would transform the country were, of course, only just beginning; Faubus and similar demagogues spoke for many in the white community with their rejection of change and their invocations of violence. It is this atmosphere in which *Odds Against Tomorrow*'s message was first received.

Contained within the first *Brown* decision was an acknowledgment, based on careful research done by the plaintiffs' lawyers (including future Supreme Court Justice Thurgood Marshall) that segregation, of whatever sort, was inherently harmful; it generates within the minds of those who are segregated a deep sense of being second-class citizens, creating a sense of futility regarding the future, a sense with baleful effects both personally and, potentially, socially. These causes and effects are systemic, indicative of deep social conflicts which will, inevitably, have an influence extending well beyond the obvious victims. It is one of the signal achievements of *Odds Against Tomorrow* that it manages, without turning into a sociological tract, to capture the systemic devastation of which racism is as much an effect as a cause. The two levels—crime thriller and social commentary—are tightly imbricated, such that our response to the first points us forcefully toward a consideration of the second.

The two levels are audible in John Lewis's score even as the film begins. Under the HarBel logo (for *Harry Belafonte*, whose company's first film this was) we hear bright brassy swinging jazz, as if the score will repeat the approach in *I Want to Live!* This gives way, as the credits proper begin, to something much more melancholy and bittersweet, the mood which will in fact dominate the film. We feel the emptiness of the lives of the characters before we so much as see one of them. Wise visually limns the racial tensions underlying the film right from the choice to film in black and white; even the stark white of the title against a black background foreshadows the complications to come. The very first shot divides the screen between a white sidewalk and a refuse-strewn pool of water in the dark street, the distinction made more severe through the use of infrared film. The same holds true of the first shot of Earl Slater walking down the deserted sidewalk, the infrared film and bright lighting harshly overemphasizing the whiteness of his skin (yet note also that this technique already subtly indicates the artificiality of distinctions made on such a basis). Earl's animosity and racial epithets will come as no surprise later on.

Following the credits we meet, in quick succession, the three principal figures in the caper: Earl Slater (Robert Ryan), Dave Burke (Ed Begley), and Johnny Ingram (Harry Belafonte). Burke, a former cop who was jailed for refusing to testify against other police officers in a crime probe, is the instigator. He has discovered a bank in Melton, a small town upstate from New York City, where security is lax enough that a simple operation will secure an easy $150,000 in small bills. Every Thursday night at six a drugstore delivery man drops off coffee and sandwiches for bank employees preparing the next day's payroll; substitute your own man for him, and you're in. Burke needs accomplices, and has selected Slater and Ingram because each is, or has been, in some trouble; Slater has served two terms in prison, one of them for manslaughter, and cannot hold a job, and Ingram is deeply in debt to a local mobster. The problem with his choices is evident almost immediately; Slater is a violent racist and Ingram is black (his participation is necessary because the delivery man is also black, a fact of which Burke does not inform Slater). Tensions between Slater and Ingram mount, climaxing at the actual robbery. Slater refuses to give Ingram the keys to the getaway car; as Richard Keenan notes, "in his demented panic, he knows only that he, gun in hand, is in charge and that white men do not give *keys*— symbols of authority and control — to black men."[32] Burke, to whom he has given them instead, is mortally wounded by the police and then commits suicide, leaving the keys a few inches from his dead hand — and several feet from Ingram and Slater. The hatred between the two men, who are now unable to escape, boils over; shooting at each other, they run into a refinery, where their last two shots, fired simultaneously, ignite an oil tank. Both die, their charred corpses indistinguishable from each other.

Each of the three central characters has in some manner been damaged personally by his profession, or at least his understanding of that profession, past or present. Burke lost his through misplaced loyalty; having bought into the culture of silence so often found in law enforcement organizations regarding internal corruption, he covered up for someone and was removed from his job. Without that, he discovered that he was no longer accepted as a member by the larger police community, and he has been living on the edge of poverty ever since. Slater was trained, and served, as a combat soldier, growing used to a rigidity of expectation and duty (and, implicitly, to a segregated environment, as the armed forces were not integrated until after 1948, when President Harry S Truman issued an Executive Order requiring integration in the military). Having served his country, Slater is now confronted with changes beyond his comprehension and reacts violently at the personal level, as Faubus and his followers were doing at the political level. Johnny Ingram is a nightclub entertainer; his job entails getting audiences to like him, an approach he has carried over into his personal life with considerably less success. He has internalized the prevailing social idea that the appurtenances of wealth (flashy clothes, a nice car, a free and easy attitude toward money, etc.) are indicators of the quality of the person, but he has, like so many others, discovered that maintaining such appearances requires the expenditure of more than he earns, which has led him into racetrack gambling and debt.

The twinned depictions of Slater and Ingram are the heart of the film. We meet the two men sequentially, their actions seen as two sides of a coin, so to speak (they even enter Burke's seedy residential hotel from different sides of the awning over the front door). Slater, walking to his rendezvous, is bumped into by a little black girl playing with a group of other children. He lifts her up and cautions her to watch where she is going, his tone humorous but his words racist (he calls her a "pickaninny"). Ingram, not long afterward, parks his car (a sassy little convertible) and hands out quarters to the same children, who are clearly enthralled by the car.[33] Slater refuses all conversation with the black elevator operator; Ingram jokes with him. Slater's barely controlled rage is evident, as is Ingram's easygoing geniality.

Slater is a racist, but he is no cardboard caricature. He is a man who has lost himself, who is unable to live up to social expectations which he has internalized. His relationship with his girlfriend Lorry (Shelley Winters) suggests this; it is she who earns the money, she in whose apartment he lives. An early scene shows him preparing to leave with Burke to case the bank; Lorry asks how much money Slater has. The question triggers some very revealing dialogue.

> *Lorry:* You got enough money, sweetie?
> *Earl:* Plenty.
> *Lorry:* How much is plenty?
> *Earl:* About —fifteen dollars.[34]
> *Lorrie:* You better take some more.
> *Earl:* Burke is paying.
> *Lorry:* What do I care if he's paying? You take some money, and then if you feel like paying you just pay.
> [Here the music enters for the first time, subdued and pensive; it will continue in a like manner throughout the remainder of the scene. Earl half smiles, then goes to Lorry's purse and takes money, though he is careful not to take all she has.]
> *Lorry:* Earl, you don't have to take this deal if you don't like it. If this isn't what you want, just don't take it, there's no hurry.
> *Earl:* There is a hurry. I have to make it, Lorry, and I have to make it now. It wasn't too bad when I was grubbing along by myself —[*Lorry:* I know, but —] It was always too tough, too greedy, but now, because of you, I have to make it on my own, Lorry, because of you, and I have to make it any way I can.
> *Lorry:* No you don't, not just any way. And you mustn't even try.
> *Earl:* I have to.
> *Lorry:* Earl, listen. I have you, right? You have me. What difference does it make where the money comes from?
> *Earl:* They're not gonna junk me like an old car.

Living in a society in which men are supposed to be the breadwinners, and having accepted that arbitrary definition, Earl sees himself as diminished by Lorry's concern and generosity (notice his repeated assertions that he has to make it "because of you"). The casting of Robert Ryan combines with the situation to remind us of *The Set-Up*; Earl Slater could easily be Stoker Thompson twelve years later, still looking for a break but increasingly conscious of his own age. Stoker would have been 47 by the time of *Odds Against Tomorrow*; although Earl's age is never given it is not unreasonable to see him as of a similar age, an age by which, especially in the late 1950s, a man was expected to have made his mark in the world, or at least to have taken the place from which he would make it. Earl recognizes the way the world will see a man such as himself; he is unproductive, unable to perform in accordance with social expectations, and undeserving of anyone's sympathy. His concluding *non sequitur* makes the point clearly; in a society in which being economically productive — being useful — is the primary function of a human being, the fate which awaits one who is not is that of any useless piece of equipment. The pronoun ("they're") shows his understanding; it is not in fact Lorry's reaction which is deepest in his fears, but that of the social structure under which he lives, which will reject him far more brutally.

There is a choice here, though one which Earl is unable to take, a choice indicated by the staging of the scene. There are few single shots; most of the dialogue is spoken in two-shots, and virtually the entire segment in which Lorry dismisses the importance of money and Earl reveals his sense of being pressured by time is filmed in a single close-up of the two together, Earl pressing himself against Lorry such that he is lower on screen than she — a close-up, moreover, set up by a shot of Earl taking the money from Lorry's purse in which the camera moves to make her visible in the mirror of the vanity on which the purse stands. Only when Earl stands on his last line does the closeness break, and we see him alone (we'd seen him alone earlier as well, at the point where he asserted that Burke will pay; both shots stress his isolation in matters involving money and self-respect). Earl cannot accept the idea that Lorry's love is not conditioned on his ability to sustain a traditionally masculine role; he must act lest he fail to live up to his (mis)understanding of her expectations, expectations which are in fact purely social in nature.

This misunderstanding carries over, this time more damagingly, into their next scene together, following his return from scouting the robbery location. Earl, having picked up a dress from a dry-cleaning shop for Lorry, stopped in at a bar where, confronted by a cocky soldier who dismissed him as an "old veteran" and goaded him into a fight, he disabled the man with one blow. But the words rankle, and he returns to Lorry's in a foul mood (his brooding presence stressed as he enters by a very low angle pan accompanying his passage toward the bedroom). He is inattentive to, perhaps even annoyed by, her announcement that she has an opportunity to advance in the company where she works and make even more money. She notices, but doesn't understand the reasons for, his surly mood; the encounter between the two is much more choppily filmed than the earlier one, with more frequent use of mutually exclusive shot-reverse shots and less of two-shots. Lorry tries, and fails, to encourage him. "Earl, you know I knew you were in trouble when I fell in love with you," she reminds him. "But I didn't care. You don't have to be the great big man with me, Earl. I don't care about things like that. There's only one thing I care about, sweetie." But Earl, mired in self-pity, opts to deliberately misunderstand her. "I know," he says. "But what happens when I get old?" This is too much even for Lorry's tolerance; provoked, she lashes out. "You are old now," she snarls as she grabs her coat. Earl, too late recognizing his mistake, calls out, but her answer is angrily savage: "You can go straight to hell!" She leaves, slamming the door behind her. Earl, seeing no further option, calls Burke and agrees to take part in the crime.

It is important to understand what is happening here. Slater's decision is grounded in his need to act in self-assertion as over against a world he perceives as indifferent at best and hostile at worst. Nor is he entirely wrong, for the world within which he sees himself as acting is a Hobbesian one, a world in which the individual exists for his or her self, acting only on his or her own interests (I shall examine this attitude in greater detail when considering *Born to Kill*). But Slater's perceptions, though not wholly erroneous as to the character of the system within which he exists, are deeply flawed, indeed self-contradictory, at the individual level. To define yourself in opposition to someone or something is to surrender the possibility of genuine self-definition; you must become what they are not rather than what you could be. It is not merely a failure of imagination (though it is also that), but a failure of self-understanding, for the limitations on self-development to which one has surrendered through the initial opposition are not in fact externally imposed but self-administered. Defining oneself through hatred is to negate oneself as a free agent. This negation, being internal, will be experienced as a personal lack, an emptiness, leading in turn to ever greater efforts to fill the emptiness, efforts doomed by their disconnection from the actual problem.

This we see soon after Lorry's departure. Helen (Gloria Grahame), an upstairs neighbor of Lorry's, stops by. Slater had earlier insulted her (an insult for which Lorry has already apologized on his behalf), but now he sees her as a means to an end, a way to prove to himself his potency as a man. He flirts with her, and she, coincidentally angry with her husband, not only flirts back but proves just as willing to use him for her own purposes. Helen is another empty person, living her life vicariously.[35] "How did it feel when you killed that man?" she asks Slater. He understands her unspoken desire: "you want me to make your flesh creep"; she wants him to arouse her and to make love to her. "I enjoyed it," he says, closing in on her. "It scared me, but I enjoyed it." The entire sequence, question and developing answers, is filmed in increasingly tight two-shots as the sexual tension builds; each is getting what they want, but each is paying a disturbing personal price as they confront their own desires made flesh. "What did he do?" Helen asks. "He dared me," Slater replies, as an extreme close-up of Helen's eyes fills the screen, followed by one of his. "Like you are now." We see her eyes again, then a low shot of their two torsos, hers from neck to thighs, his a dark mass on the left forefront, as pure desire takes over. Slater closes the door, and Helen, barely nodding, murmurs "just this once" as they embrace. Having figuratively embraced Burke's criminal plans as a means for asserting his virility, Slater now literally embraces Helen for the same purpose.

There is no love here, nor even a genuine, if temporary, escape from loneliness, for Slater is attempting to overcome himself, his own insecurities and fears, through actions based entirely upon those insecurities and fears. "But once we have ventured along the path of sensuous disorder," as Georges Bataille notes,

> it takes a good deal to satisfy us. Destruction and betrayal will sometimes go hand in hand with the rising tide of genetic excess[....] Brutality and murder are further steps in the same direction[....] Our only real pleasure is to squander our resources to no purpose, just as if a wound were bleeding away inside us; we always want to be sure of the uselessness or the ruinousness of our extravagance. We want to feel as remote from the world where thrift is the rule as we can. As remote as we can: — that is hardly strong enough; we want a world turned upside down and inside out. The truth of eroticism is treason.[36]

Slater has betrayed Lorry based on a misunderstanding of his own making. What Lorry wants in return for her love of Slater is not sex, but that *he love her in return*. It is precisely this which his warped self-understanding will not allow him to do.

Earl's self-destructive spiral now accelerates. He leaves Helen to meet with Burke about the robbery (apologizing to Burke for his lateness with an ambiguously dismissive reference to "girly trouble"). Ingram is already there, but Slater pointedly ignores him. As George Meredith wrote, "Silence is commonly the slow poison used by those who mean to murder love. There is nothing violent about it; no shock is given; Hope is not abruptly strangled, but merely dreams of evil, and fights with gradually stifling shadows."[37] The love Slater is murdering is that of his fellow human beings; we have already seen him respond to Lorry's importunings with silence, a silence broken only by vicious words, and the pattern is repeated here; when he at last acknowledges Ingram's presence he is sarcastically condescending, even referring to Ingram as "boy," then as now a particularly offensive term when applied to African American men. Burke, fearing for the success of the plan, intervenes, but by now anyone rational could have seen the central problem, one not involving bank security or the police.

Slater will be offered one last chance at redemption. He returns to Lorry's apartment and finds her waiting, in tears. Struck by her distress, he embraces her as she offers an apology: "Earl, I'm — I'm like all the rest of them. I keep telling you how to live, and not letting you be what you are." Earl is conciliatory. "I spoil everything," he admits; "I can't help it, I just have to spoil everything." Lorry attempts to show the changes in her understanding, her willingness to give him even more leeway in his actions, but ends by showing her own terror of loneliness, the true driving force behind her love for Earl; "Only don't leave me, Earl. Please, darling, don't leave me." Her words, or perhaps more the raw emotions behind them, prompt something of an attempt at an honest self-assessment on Earl's part, though one which, due to his lack of genuine understanding, can go only so far; he knows the facts of his life but cannot imagine the reasons behind them. He won't leave her, he says (though we know that he already has, in more ways than one). "I've been leaving all my life. Since when I can first remember." His plaint builds to a self-contradictory climax:

> When the wind blew us off the land in Oklahoma, we left. After that I never stayed. Not in the Army, not in Detroit, not anyplace. I'd start something, if it didn't work right away I'd blow it. And it was always something. A lousy captain, a polack foreman in the auto works, or it'd be too slow. Well, I'm getting too old to take things slow. If I don't make it now, I never will.

The contradiction is dramatized visually when he stands and walks away from Lorry on "I'd start something," ending up in a darkened corner of the room. Yet Earl is not utterly without glimmers of insight. Lorry, looking for an opening to some solution of the problem, asks if things are ever easy for him. "Only when I get mad," he admits. "Then they get too easy. I think that's why I get mad, to make it easy." The moment of self-revelation is immediately erased; "But I've got something now," he tells Lorry. "And I'm gonna stick with it." A jump cut to the destination sign on the Melton bus elides any closing tenderness; Lorry will never see Earl again. His destiny now lies with Johnny Ingram, a man he hates.

If *Odds Against Tomorrow* has a protagonist in any conventional sense, it is Johnny Ingram, though he is just as trapped by his situation and lack of imagination as is Earl Slater. Nor is he free of his own prejudices, though they are subtler than Earl's because the reasons for them are more plausible. Johnny is not self-pitying and has a degree more self-knowledge (he describes himself as "just a bonepicker in a four-man graveyard"), but he is, in his own way, as self-destructive as Earl, and for much the same reason: he has internalized warped definitions, of himself and of others, derived from a system which is itself warped.

Ingram's first reaction to Burke's proposal is dismissive. "That's not your line, Dave," he says. "That's the firing squad for you. That's for junkies and joyboys. We're people." The encounter is filmed in balanced close-ups and two-shots giving Ingram predominance, as for the moment he has the moral high ground. He quickly regains his easygoing attitude and suggests that Dave find a hobby to get his mind off such dramatic remedies for what ails him. Ingram gives Burke a ride downtown and repeats his reluctance to get involved in such an affair.[38] But Burke knows that Ingram is deep in debt, and Burke knows the man to whom Ingram owes the money; he arranges for the gangster Bacco (Will Kuluva) to put the pressure on Ingram. Bacco does.

He shows up at Connoy's, the nightclub where Johnny performs, and tells him to pay the entire $7,500 by the next day, a demand he knows Johnny can't possibly meet. Johnny pulls a gun, allowing Bacco to explode in righteous outrage, at the climax of which he threatens to take the debt out of Johnny's ex-wife and child (Bacco's tantrum is exaggerated by his close-ups, in which he leans into the center of the screen, his jowly face and wide mouth almost distorted in their proximity to the viewer).

Thus far, Ingram has been presented as something of a self-satisfied lightweight. The threat to his wife and child, though, sets into motion a reconsideration of his moral standing, one which will deepen his character considerably. We first get a sense of his helpless rage immediately after his confrontation with Bacco. Some time has passed, and he is quite drunk. He steps up to the stage where another performer is singing, and half joins her, half distracts her, eventually making nonsense sounds and beating furiously at the vibraphone, an instrument on which one cannot, with soft mallets, make a very loud sound at all, however much one flails away. The visual and aural metaphor is striking; Johnny Ingram is a person who wants to make a big noise in the world but is, because of his own choices, unable to do so.

The next day Ingram visits his ex-wife Ruth (Kim Hamilton) and daughter Eadie (Lois Thorne) for his "once a week Fathers' Day"; he arrives late, presumably because he is hung over from the night before. The contrast between the two adults is obvious, both to audience and Johnny. Where his life is one of easy money and even easier expenditures, of cards and horses, hers is one of PTA meetings and interracial middle-class stability. Ingram, introduced to the members of the PTA Steering Committee, white and black together, standing in his wife's living room, can only make an awkward joke. Yet it is absolutely clear that he loves his daughter without reservation, and she him; she runs eagerly into his arms, and their interactions are unreservedly good-natured and relaxed. When he asks Ruth, who is reluctant to let him so much as kiss her, what he ever saw in her, she responds, nodding her head toward the off-screen child, "That."

Ingram takes Eadie to Central Park. A series of close-ups of the heads of merry-go-round horses, visually echoing the earlier close-ups of Bacco's tirade, ironically underline Ingram's situation; his losses at the track have trapped him in a cycle of debt and danger which now threatens the most important thing in his life. These are interspersed with shots of Johnny nuzzling a laughing Eadie, both of them caught up in enjoying the moment. All of the scenes with Eadie only gain poignancy on repeated viewing, for her innocence contrasts sharply with Johnny's situation and eventual fate. Ingram sees two of Bacco's thugs standing nearby, watching him and Eadie; he hands her another ride ticket and moves to confront them, explaining to her that the merry-go-round "makes me dizzy." Her response is that he is "too old," creating a small but telling link with the situation, and feeling, of Earl Slater. Ingram confronts the thugs, yet the implicit message has been received; after the hoodlums leave he calls Burke and agrees to take part in the robbery. Ingram sees no cause for celebration, but sees no other way forward; "I know I got rid of a headache," he tells Burke. "Now I've got cancer."

Returning from her meeting, Ruth finds him asleep on Eadie's bed, his arm curled protectively above her head. She wakes him, and they embrace for a moment before she breaks away. In the living room, Ingram gives her the keys to his car, saying he is going away for a couple of days, and, upon her thanking him, attempts once more to hold her. "No," she says, breaking away yet again, though it is clear that she still feels strongly attracted to him. Ingram wonders what happened between the two of them, and Ruth's reply is blunt: she left him not for her sake, but for Eadie's; "The child can't have a father who lives your life," she tells him. "You're tough," Johnny says. "Not tough enough to change you," Ruth replies. At this Ingram's frustrations boil over, leading to a pointed argument.

Johnny: For what? To hold hands with those ofay friends of yours?
Ruth: I'm trying to make a world fit for Eadie to live in. It's a cinch you're not going to do it with a deck of cards and a racing form.
Johnny: But you are, huh? You and your big white brothers. Drink enough tea with them and stay out of the watermelon patch — and maybe our little colored girl'll grow up to be Miss America, is that it?
Ruth: I won't listen when you talk like that. You'd better go.
Johnny: Why don't you wise up, Ruth? It's their world and we're just living in it.

There is much to consider in this. Neither character is wholly right or wholly wrong, a balance signaled by the filming; after two close-ups, the rest of the argument is seen in a single fluid pan from just below shoulder level, until a cut motivated by Eadie's coming out from the bedroom complaining of being awakened. Ruth's efforts are indeed appropriate (they foreshadow the coalitions which would propel the civil rights movement so successfully in the succeeding decade), but they are also slightly naïve; many blacks won acceptance by the majority white world of local politics through "proper behavior," with improper behavior defined as anything which made whites both uncomfortable and aware of the person's race (by contrast, Bacco's criminal activities are illegal, but not, in this sense, improper, as they are driven by an accepted motive, the desire for material gain). Johnny's reaction to Ruth's conciliatory approach is overstrong, but not without justice; to this day civil rights advances (and not only for blacks) are too often grudging concessions from those in control. Johnny's own words provide a clue to the political realities underlying the situation, realities which will have an impact on Ruth and Eadie whether they will it or not. He uses the term "ofay," an insult applicable to whites which is akin to, but far less devastating than, "nigger" (which word Slater uses). There is, though, none of the violent resonance of the latter word, for there is no power behind the former one, no social and political structure which can enforce the hatred behind the word.[39]

Having been interrupted, Ingram tells both Eadie and Ruth how much he loves them, then leaves. His next appointment is in Melton.

Like Earl, though, Ingram will be given a last chance to turn away from the path he has chosen. The three men meet in Melton, make their final plans, then split up so as to remain inconspicuous. Ingram sits by the edge of the river, gazing at the detritus nestled against the breakwater, staring at a ruined doll. The moment is stunning, subtle yet strong, rightly singled out for praise by Richard Keenan: "Ingram's wasted life, the daughter he loves, the current impasses in which he finds himself as he searches hopelessly for alternatives; the entire range of his introspection is there for the viewer to see."[40] Even the river adds to the mood, its endless unstoppable passage reminding us of the flow of events in which these three men are caught up. Ingram sees this, but fails to see that he could still say no, still seek assistance (perhaps by turning to the police for protection of his wife and daughter, if not himself, an option against which we have seen him brush in scaring off the hoodlums near the merry-go-round). But he cannot bring himself to do so.

The film's denouement is now inevitable; *Odds Against Tomorrow* is indeed a tragedy, not merely politically but formally as well, with each of the central characters being destroyed by their own flaws. That denouement, though, will not come swiftly; Wise daringly draws out the wait, cutting between the three men biding their time and various images of the town and its surroundings. Ingram contemplates the river, Slater loads a shotgun and takes aim at a rabbit, but does not fire until it has already hopped unsuspectingly away; his shot impotently turning, through a jump cut on the sound, to the plink of a pebble against a tin can tossed by a sitting Burke. It is as if the world itself is holding its breath.

Just before the actual crime begins, there is a last gruesome reminder that whatever these men have become, whoever they are, is not a process isolated from the society and its accepted behaviors. Burke is waiting in front of the drug store to intercept the delivery man and arrange an "accident" which will necessitate his return to pick up more coffee and allow Ingram the time to pose as the delivery man. A mother enters, telling her two children to wait outside, "and no nonsense with those guns." No sooner has she left them than they are squirting each other vigorously, exchanging lists of hits as they do: "There, I got you right in the mouth. I got you in the eye. Right in the nose." As they run about, they confuse the situation just enough that Burke's intentional collision with the delivery man seems quite genuinely a matter of trying to avoid them, and they thus become his accomplices, however unwitting. The violence which underlies adult crime is not something for which there have been no preparations.

The climax of *Odds Against Tomorrow* is often compared with that of *White Heat* (Raoul Walsh, 1949), but the similarity is purely visual in that both films end with oil tank explosions. Otherwise there is no point of comparison. Cody Jarrett in the earlier film chooses his immolation, and it has an air of maniacal triumphalism; Slater and Ingram are barely aware of the danger, and both are destroyed unknowingly. The police in *White Heat* are given only a couple of moments to savor Jarrett's death before the closing logo; the police and firefighters in *Odds Against Tomorrow* have time to contemplate the burned bodies, and for a brief exchange pointing up the irony: "Which is which?" asks a medic. "Take your pick," a police officer comments with a shrug.[41] But most importantly, *White Heat*'s conclusion leaves no echoes behind, whereas that of *Odds Against Tomorrow* leaves many, for we have met those who care about, and whose lives will be hurt by the deaths of, Johnny Ingram and Earl Slater.

The greatest strength of *Odds Against Tomorrow* comes not from its action, or even its firm anti-racist stance. It comes from our awareness, as audience members, of the shattering impact of these deaths upon the survivors. As I began by noting, there are two levels to this film, which is only secondarily about crime; Richard Keenan sees only the first level when he criticizes the apparent conclusion: "Since the robbery fails, it would seem that in an odd fashion racial disharmony has acted in the service of society, thwarting the robbery. Surely Wise does not wish to say that if only the psychotic redneck bigot and the happy-go-lucky black gambler can solve their differences and work in harmony, the beneficial result would be a more efficiently executed bank robbery?"[42] By now it should be evident that Wise is playing off two different aspects of the same situation: first, the tendency of audiences to identify with, or at least root for, the criminals in heist films (I examine the reasons for this in greater detail in my discussion of *Born to Kill*, Wise's other great film noir, in Chapter Four); second, and far more significantly, the personal situation within which each of the men has chosen to take part in the robbery. Earl Slater and Johnny Ingram are bound by anger and hatred; what they cannot see is that their hatreds are not only irrelevant to their true situations, but distractions from the greater forces playing upon them; oppressive systems always thrive upon, and therefore foster, externally focused hatreds as a means of avoiding scrutiny from those living under them. Thus these two men are not simply bad people, not just a "psychotic redneck bigot" and a "happy-go-lucky black gambler." More than most noir films, *Odds Against Tomorrow* admits, indeed insists upon, the complexity of its characters; it has neither a hero nor a villain in any conventional sense. To understand these complexities is to understand the film's true message.

What emerges as we consider the film's events is, at least potentially, a sense of the very strong societal forces driving people, and men especially, toward an emphasis on power and acquisition, whether it be of money, things, or other people. Slater lacks money, and sees himself as lacking true masculinity because of it. Ingram has affairs, and affairs cost money, so he attempts to acquire too much too quickly; hence his gambling. Burke lacks the money to escape his tiny apartment, and thinks having it will restore his pride ("They sure changed your color when they rehabilitated you at Sing-Sing," Johnny comments to him; "Fifty grand can change it back," Burke expostulates). Bacco has money, and wants more, as he can always get people in his power by lending it out at ruinous rates of interest — and, besides, paying the salaries of his gang of hoodlums is no doubt expensive. These men are not wrong in their understanding; money is key in modern society. Without it, a person is seen as being of little account, of little value — even the common terms suggest the economic emphasis.

Yet, and this is the vital point which emerges alongside the other, Earl and Johnny are not wholly isolated, despite their irresponsibility, their flaws, their relative poverty. The focus of the film is on Slater and Ingram, but they stand out against a background of women: Lorry, Ruth, and Eadie.[43] It is their voices which lend depth to our understanding of the two men. For the fact is that, even though Slater and Ingram are both deeply flawed, *they each are also deeply loved*, in ways which make it harder to justify the audience in disliking them, even as they dislike their behaviors and actions. What we have here, then, is essentially a plea, and a very powerful plea, for mercy as well as for change, for us, as active responders to the film, to help break the cycle of greed and insecurity which has led, and which will continue to lead, to such destructive behaviors, in whatever form. The portrayal of characters such as these, neither wholly good nor wholly evil (for the former would be unbearable if not unbelievable, and the latter would be at best uninteresting and probably completely alienating), invites us to consider the mixture of motives and actions in our own lives, to criticize ourselves and our circumstances along with those we are watching, with the difference being that we can do something about our situations. It is not, of course, that most of us are gamblers or violent bigots in exactly the same manner as Ingram or Slater, but that some parallel between the imperfection of their lives and that of our lives almost certainly exists, perhaps even a closer parallel than we would like (after all, gambling is not, in most jurisdictions, even illegal, and it is very popular). As Martha Nussbaum puts it, "To perceive the particular really accurately, one must not simply be concerned with retribution. One must, in addition, 'judge *with*' the agent who has done the alleged wrong. One must, that is, see things from that person's point of view—for only then will one begin to comprehend what obstacles that person faced as he or she tried to act."[44] The final appeal here, as so often in Wise's films, is to our imaginations, to our ability to envision the situations of others. In comprehending the places and choices of others, we open ourselves to a deeper understanding of those others, of still further others, and of ourselves. It is this which impels *Odds Against Tomorrow*, and which gives it the strong impact it retains.

IV. *The Andromeda Strain* (1971)

Wise's documentary approach reaches its climax in his second science fiction film, which purports to be a record of "the four-day history of a major American scientific crisis." Or so the printed acknowledgment which appears before the credits asserts, an acknowledgment which assures the viewer that much assistance in establishing the facts was obtained from participants in the events recorded, who "encouraged us to tell the story accurately and in detail." Lest one be worried that government secrets have been improperly revealed, though, the acknowledgments conclude with the comforting claim that the relevant documents are soon to be published, and that "they do not in any way jeopardize the national security." As will be discovered, it is precisely such secrets which helped create the crisis in the first place.[45]

The plot is minimal. A satellite, part of a secret military project known as Scoop, has returned to Earth bearing a sub-microscopically small alien organism which wipes out Piedmont, a tiny town in New Mexico. A team of scientists is mobilized to determine the nature of the organism and find a means of neutralizing it. They are taken to a secret biological research facility, known as Wildfire, where they achieve their goal, but only after the organism has mutated into something already far less deadly—though in the process the research station itself is nearly destroyed by an atomic self-destruct mechanism, which is stopped, with only eight seconds to spare, by one of the scientists.

The initial point is not the unfolding of the plot, though Nelson Gidding's carefully constructed screenplay is so tautly directed that one can forget how little actually happens. Despite the obvious differences in style and subject matter between the two films, *The Andromeda Strain* shares with *Star!* a concern about professionalism run amok, although here the potential consequences are far graver. The central tension is between pure science—or, more accurately, a kind of scientism, a worship of method at the expense of reality — and humanism, an approach in which the human relevance of the facts at hand forms an integral part of any assessment of the actions to be taken. Thus *The Andromeda Strain* is, like *Star!*, a glamorous film tinged with failure, but here the glamour is that of science and technology, gleaming, efficient, and sterile, and the failure is political: the technology has been created in the service of biological warfare, and nearly destroys its creators. *The Andromeda Strain* is certainly not anti-scientific, yet it does implicitly recognize what many among its characters do not: that while facts may be necessary foundations for values, facts in themselves have importance only within a particular structure of valuation.

This disjunction is suggested throughout the film, particularly through a striking visual technique used here and nowhere else in Wise's body of work: several times we are shown simultaneous images locked off from each other in rectangular boxes of various sizes — not a conventional split screen, but one in which there is no direct contact between what are supposed to be concurrent events. Likewise, a considerable portion of what people see and do is literally mediated; because of the fear of contamination, much of the work must be done with mechanical devices, and much communication carried on through television monitors. Apart from a few handshakes, almost no one directly touches anyone else during the central portion of the film because almost no one *can* directly touch anyone else. Human contact is minimized in every way; the tests performed on the members of the scientific team as they move through the increasingly sterile levels of the research facility are done by machines, with part of the process involving the reduction of the "outer epithelial layers of your skin" to a "fine white ash," as a disembodied voice informs the scientists. Communications between individuals are terse, sometimes almost to the point of risibility (Dr. Stone, the chief scientist, learns of the crisis by being told, "There's a fire, sir."), or are cut off altogether (Dr. Stone's wife attempts to call her father, a senator, about the mysterious behavior of the military men with whom her husband has abruptly departed, only to have the call interrupted by a coldly efficient voice which informs her, "This connection has been broken for reasons of national security. You will be briefed at the appropriate time."). On several occasions we see shots of people speaking, but the camera is on the wrong side of the glass walls, and we cannot hear what is being said. Even the film's structure is disjointed, with abrupt flashes forward and backward in time, and imagery that is both alienating and impersonal (the first shot after the skin-removal, for example, is of a piece of machinery so abstract as to be unintelligible visually, while the weird colors and wavering images which accompany the sterilization process make the scientists resemble alien creatures themselves).

Central to this tension is Dr. Jeremy Stone (Arthur Hill), instigator and designer of the Wildfire containment facility, itself intended by Stone for research on possible extraterrestrial organisms. He serves as head of the emergency team, and is the only one among them to have Top Secret clearance. The name is appropriate; Stone is a man of few emotions and a granitic sense of purpose. Nor is his self-confidence without justification; he is a Nobel laureate and has twice served as president of the National Academy of Sciences. These honors, though, have generated a hubristic certainty in his own knowledge and methods which verges on the obsessive. In this regard, Stone is comparable with Dr. Markway from *The Haunting*, albeit with vastly superior credentials and much greater scientific credibility.

Stone's obsession is all the more problematic in that he has neglected to consider the context within which he has thus far succeeded. He is a quintessential establishment man ("Stick to established procedure," he admonishes one of his colleagues who suggests speeding up the investigation), he is "well known in Washington" and is married to a senator's daughter, and he is evidently accustomed to being listened to attentively. Like many such persons, he fails to understand that his usefulness does not imply that he is being told everything, which means that his decisions, the further they stray from his areas of immediate expertise, are less and less likely to be appropriate. Stone treats the world as if it were a scientific problem to be solved, or a technological tool to be manipulated, an attitude drawn out forcefully in a confrontation with Dr. Mark Hall (James Olson), another of the scientists, who is concerned for the lives of the only two survivors of the original catastrophe. Impatient with abstract theoretical responses, Hall urges prompt action, reminding the others, "I've got two patients down there." Stone corrects him with cold-blooded specificity: "The *team* has two subjects." Hall will have none of this; "They're not guinea pigs, Stone," he insists.

Stone's view, which, as we shall see in greater detail later, is akin to that of Dr. MacFarlane in *The Body Snatcher*, is harsh but not without merit, limited not so much by error as by omission. Scientific facts may be difficult to ascertain, but they await discovery by anyone with patience, skill, and the proper equipment; the application of those facts, however, is another matter entirely, one with social and political ramifications of which Dr. Stone is not fully aware. We learn this quite early on; in a flash forward to a closed Senate hearing held after the crisis has passed, General Sparks (Peter Hobbs), head of Scoop, the military project which brought the satellite back to Earth, assures the assembled committee that, prior to the emergency, Dr. Stone "didn't know Scoop existed." A senator expresses astonishment, but is assured that keeping Stone ignorant was necessary: "Reasons of national security." An acerbic second senator approves: "Very smart. We've had experiences with scientists before." An ironic point is made without calling undue attention to itself, but it is an important one. All of the individuals involved in the various sets of decisions are specialists, presumably quite competent in their own field, with limited knowledge of others, yet all base the totality of their choices on the assumption that they know everything that is necessary. All are wrong.

The small irony points up a deeper one: in a film suffused with scientific, military, and technical expertise, the central component is ignorance. Everyone in the film displays some measure of ignorance, with those who admit their ignorance, or at least who hesitate in their actions because of their own uncertainty regarding the facts, being more likely to avoid making errors. Stone is largely unaware of the military purposes to which Wildfire has been turned, though his behavior suggests that he has some idea that his pet project is being used for simulations fundamental to carrying out biological warfare and that he has accepted this as part of the price for attaining his original goal. He was also unaware of the nature and progress of Scoop. General Sparks is unwilling to admit the potency of the alien organism, deeming its disintegrating effect on plastic merely a coincidence. Dr. Ruth Leavitt (Kate Reid), a member of the scientific team, refuses to acknowledge her own susceptibility to epileptic seizures; she misses important data through a minor one (triggered, in another poignant irony, by the flashing red light informing her of the very thing for which she is seeking), and almost causes a panic by having a major one at the height of the crisis. The "highly trained" electronics technicians at Wildfire closely examine their equipment for malfunctions but fail to notice a sliver of paper which interferes with transmissions; as the president's science advisor Dr. Robertson (Kermit Murdoch) testifies in a voice-over, coming from a later inquiry but accompanying the scene of the men poking and prodding at various circuit boards, "For them, it was like trying to see an elephant through a microscope."

The principal exceptions to the parade of errors are the other two scientists on the team, Dr. Hall and Dr. Charles Dutton (David Wayne). It is not that they do not make mistakes (they are no more in the know about Scoop and Wildfire than anyone else, at least at first), but they are quicker to admit ignorance, and thus in a better position to learn from their errors.

Dutton is the most imaginative of the four, and the most aware of the social implications of scientific research. It is no coincidence that he is the only one with a full family life (in Wise's films, a visible family is often a marker for broader humanity, for shared moral and emotional interests; we saw this as a major component in *The Day the Earth Stood Still* and will again in *Executive Suite*). Stone has a wife, but the brief interaction we see does not suggest connubial bliss; Leavitt wears a wedding band, but makes no reference whatsoever to her husband; Hall is established as a single man, and makes no mention of a partner of any sort. Dutton, by contrast, has not only a wife (clearly long-suffering but loving, and retaining a sense of humor withal) but a daughter and grandson as well; he, unlike the others, remains solidly connected to the personal network within which the scenario is unfolding. Nor is his family entirely uninformed; his daughter bluntly asks him if the mysterious late-night summons is connected with "the germ warfare people." Evidently he keeps his family at least somewhat in the know, unlike Stone, who appears to have told his wife nothing at all.

Dutton served as colleague and advisor to Stone in Wildfire's early stages, but his take on the matter has been less rigid from the beginning. He openly considers the possibility that life forms encountered in space may be no larger than a flea or a microbe, and wants to be careful in exterminating the newfound organism in case it might be intelligent but unaware of its effect on human beings. He acknowledges the dangers of hubris regarding new discoveries; "Don't encourage the president to think scientists are wizards," Dutton cautions Stone apropos of Stone's original letter advising the creation of a facility prepared to handle potential extraterrestrial organisms or diseases; "If things get out of control, and they might, even you can't work miracles." Stone's response is flippant, though it indicates his respect for Dutton; "I'll expect to have your help, Charlie." Soon enough he does, but he will find Dutton's probing questions increasingly uncomfortable.

Dutton himself is increasingly uncomfortable with what he has helped to create. Wise captures his sense of alienation with another divided screen; as Dutton and Leavitt take a hidden elevator into the underground recesses of the facility, their images are divided by a representation of the facility, the elevator, and the shaft — the image foreshadowing the separations they will increasingly feel as they become more involved in the crisis. As they descend, Dutton gives voice to his discouragement: "What a world we're making. I can see why the kids are dropping out. *We* should have." Leavitt, remembering the photographs of the dead village, reminds him of the emergency. Dutton's response is ambiguous: "They brought it on themselves." Leavitt is properly outraged; "Who — the people in Piedmont?" she asks angrily. But an immediate seamless wipe to another elevator suggests who Dutton has in mind, as we see Stone and Hall, still in their biohazard suits, descending in another elevator. Dutton knows, or at least suspects, that Stone has compromised the ideals of science more than Stone will admit. The difference between the two men is limned by their greeting as they first meet at Wildfire. Even as he shakes hands with Stone his first question is, "How's Piedmont?" Stone's response is brusque; "Had to order up a seven-twelve," the code name for a nuclear strike to utterly sterilize the area. Dutton utters a groan of regret, but Stone, having answered the question, thinks no more of the matter.[46]

The scientific façade begins to crack, though in a manner at first unnoticed by the scientists, when Stone files for a code name for the project following the decisive breakthrough in comprehending the organism. The response is immediate, almost as if someone were waiting with code name in hand. Soon afterward, the team realizes (in a chillingly effective scene) that the organism multiplies whenever energy is applied to it — and that the nuclear strike called for by Stone and at last authorized by the president (presumably Nixon), would be the worst possible action, as it would provide the Andromeda Strain, the code name for the organism, with unlimited energy for replication and expansion, what science advisor Robertson sums up as "a fantastically rich growth medium." In short, if the military solution is applied, Andromeda would be out of control. Exactly how out of control is seen immediately afterward, when a computer simulation of the growth process ends in a "601" error message, indicating an overload of the processing capacity of the central computer (Wise allows the computer image of crystalline growth to occupy the entire screen, rather than showing the scientists reacting, thus pulling the audience even more directly into the threat).

The bomb drop is canceled, but an even more worrisome discovery remains to be made. Stone resets the computer in order to call up a "bio-math mapping of its new growth potential and spread." The map appears instantaneously, already labeled:

SCENARIO > WILDFIRE BIOWAR MAP <
SIMULATED TOXIC EXCHANGE >
WEAPONRY > ANDROMEDA

Stone, as is his wont, begins an analysis of the data in respect to the project at hand. Dutton and Leavitt see the larger picture, and the political confrontation in outlooks lurking under the film's action explodes at last.

> *Dutton:* Jeremy, these are biological warfare maps.
> *Stone:* Why, yes, so they are. Oh, but simulations, Charlie. Defensive. It's just a scenario.
> *Leavitt:* That's not the point, for God's sake! Wildfire was built for germ warfare! Wildfire *and* Scoop. And you knew, Stone. You knew it.
> *Stone:* That's not true, Ruth. I learned about Scoop the same time you did.
> *Dutton:* They already have Andromeda programmed. The purpose of Scoop was to find new biological weapons in outer space and then use Wildfire to develop them. [...]
> *Stone:* We have no proof.
> *Dutton:* The map!
> *Stone:* Don't be an ass. That map only shows what Andromeda *could* do in the hands of an enemy.

Dutton: Enemy? We did it to ourselves.
Stone: Perhaps, but this is hardly the time to organize a protest.
Leavitt: Another giant leap for mankind.

At which point Stone switches off the images, declaring that all that matters is the research at hand. He angrily orders them to resume work; after a moment Dutton accedes. Leavitt sits at the computer, commenting that, as Andromeda has mutated before their very eyes, "its effect might be radically different." Stone, framed in an open doorway with darkness to either side, looks dismissive but remains silent, perhaps realizing that his credibility is minimal, then leaves.

Leavitt is right, and Stone has already passed up a chance to see the change about which she is speculating. In his earlier haste to insist upon a directive seven-twelve he had dismissed mention of a crashed jet; had he then listened, he might have realized that Andromeda was unstable, and that its effects were unstable as well. The change, to a form which disintegrates rubber and plastic, leads to the action climax of the film. A gasket crumbles, and Andromeda is released into the station's air, leading to an automatic activation of the atomic self-destruct mechanism. Hall must evade the security mechanisms and deactivate the device.

Dr. Mark Hall is Dutton's counterpart, but his skepticism is more focused; as we have already seen he is more heedful regarding specific human needs than theoretical problems, however much he is aware of the relation between properly diagnosing those needs and understanding the larger picture.[47] He is the most willing of the four scientists to admit ignorance; even as he and Stone begin their investigation of Piedmont he admits to not having read all the materials regarding Wildfire sent to him by Stone over the months. ("I never went in much for science fiction," he comments.) Stone rebukes him, but Hall is more nearly right than Stone, as Stone's materials, reflecting as they do his own ignorance of the true purpose of Wildfire, have left out some of the most vital information. Hall has an eye for tangential but important details which Stone lacks; during their search for the satellite in Piedmont it is he, not Stone, who notices the actual medical condition of the corpses (as opposed to their simply being dead bodies), who thinks to examine the body of the doctor who found and opened the satellite, and who hears the squalling infant who has somehow survived the catastrophe, and who will provide a vital clue later on.

Hall's first thoughts are for his patients, and his first question when he meets his assistant Karen Anson (Paula Kelly) is whether anything has been done for them. Ascertaining the situation, and her name, he comments briefly, "I couldn't cope with two machines." It is his first statement, as opposed to question, in the scene, and it is immediately followed by another question.

Learning the nature of the complex medical technology at his disposal, he is dismissive; "I prefer the personal touch," he assures Anson, who responds dryly, "It's hard to come by in those suits," referring to the bodysuits which isolate patients from doctors. Hall asks about her experience, and learning that she's had three months of training with the equipment, says, with apparent sincerity, "Thank God for an expert. This whole sort of thing's new to me." He, unlike Stone, is willing to learn from anyone he can; during the entire scene he makes only six statements—and asks five questions. His effort to make a personal connection will pay off in an unexpected way; when Leavitt has her major seizure, it is Karen who, trusting Hall, will overcome her fear and obtain the necessary medication.

Hall, committed to human complexity, seeks connections where Stone, constrained by his unwillingness to see the deeper political connections, seeks isolated facts. "I'll know the answer," he asserts, "when I know why a sixty-nine-year-old sterno drinker with an ulcer is like a normal six-month-old baby." He does indeed find the answer (an acidic imbalance in the blood), only to discover, along with Stone and Dutton, that Andromeda has mutated into a form which has compromised station sterility and triggered the atomic self-destruct. At last Stone snaps; "When the bomb goes off there'll be a thousand mutations! Andromeda will spread everywhere! They'll never be rid of it!" One chance remains; Hall must clamber through the central core (reversing the process of arrival not only in direction but in content; this journey is made without the aid of any machines), avoiding security lasers, to reach a level not yet closed off to insert the key which will shut down the process. This he does, and Wildfire and the station staff are saved. The clouds bearing the Andromeda organism are seeded with silver iodide to provoke rainfall into the Pacific Ocean, where the organism will be destroyed by the salt water.

Or so Jeremy Stone assures the acidulous senator from Vermont (Eric Christmas) at yet another hearing. The senator, having ascertained that the cloud seeding worked, seems inclined to dismiss the entire affair as a "so-called biological crisis," though he is forced to admit that there is now conclusive knowledge of extraterrestrial life. Stone reminds him that "with this new knowledge, there's no guarantee that another 'so-called biological crisis' won't occur again." The senator is disturbed; "Hm. What do we do about that?" Stone's response is to repeat the question: "Precisely, Senator, What do we do?" A concluding image shows the Andromeda molecule replicating again and again, ending with another 601 message, suggesting that perhaps the surviving strain, still under study at Wildfire, is not so secure as one might hope.

The Andromeda Strain is a complex film, the realism of which is not grounded in any particular scientific fact; rather, its power comes from its unwillingness to demonize any given person even as it makes clear its allegiance to a balance between humanism and science. Expertise is, as we see again and again throughout the film, vital to achieving understanding. Yet expertise must not blind itself to the much larger zone of ignorance which surrounds even the greatest knowledge. To do so is, all too often, to undercut or vitiate the contribution the expertise genuinely offers. Where the expertise involves matters such as national security, it is even more vital that it be open to new understandings and different perspectives, for the consequences of remaining closed to them are potentially very grim indeed. Wise would revisit the vital nature of this openness to new perspectives in his last, and greatest, science fiction film, *Star Trek: The Motion Picture.*

Chapter Three

The Social Contract Disintegrates: *Born to Kill* (1947)

For the love of money is the root of all evil....[1]

Film noir is commonly held to present a critique of American culture, albeit a critique veiled by the exigencies of the Production Code. "Not all film noir works were concerned with criticizing society," film historian Robert Sklar writes. "But in most of them, something was amiss; the individual was out of step with the social order and doomed to pay the consequences."[2] The characters, as Raymond Chandler said of those in the hard-boiled detective stories which prefigured the noir vision, live "in a world gone wrong, a world in which, long before the atom bomb, civilization had created the machinery for its own destruction, and was learning to use it with all the moronic delight of a gangster trying out his first machine gun."[3] Nor were the shadows commonly associated with film noir only visual; as Robert G. Porfirio notes, the term applies as much to outlook as style. What makes these films "noir," he says, "is the underlying mood of pessimism which undercuts any attempted happy endings and prevents the films from being the typical Hollywood escapist fare many were originally intended to be."[4] *Born to Kill* is among the bleakest and most pessimistic of films noir, portraying no wholly sympathetic characters and avoiding even a hint of a happy or redemptive ending. Only the Production Code requirement that its protagonist be punished for her transgressions against law and morality is honored in the closing moments, and in a manner designedly less than satisfactory emotionally.

The bleakness of *Born to Kill* is indeed undeniable. But the film goes further than mere bleakness; the screenplay by Eve Greene and Richard Macaulay is in fact an extremely precise depiction of the underlying nature of human relations under patriarchal capitalism; for all its hyperkinetic melodrama, it is at heart realistic. The problem faced by the dual protagonists of the film, Sam Wild (Lawrence Tierney) and Helen Brent (Claire Trevor), is not that they are "out of step with the social order," but rather that they are too closely in step with it. Neither has a profession, yet the very lack of profession is key to understanding each, for it is the attempts to develop the equivalent of a professional position — a place from which to operate successfully as an individual within the normal bounds of society — which will doom both. Helen and Sam are unwitting players in a zero sum game in which the rules change in invisible ways even as each player attempts to operate within those rules. They have internalized the message of capitalism but failed to understand the methods of capitalism. They are two poles of a field of energy from which neither can escape; with one partial exception, to be discussed in due course, all of the other characters are defined by their relation to them.

Sam Wild

We discover Sam sequentially. First we hear about him; the flirtatious Laury Palmer (Isabell Jewel), who is dating him, is fascinated by his evident strength and forceful attitude. "He's the quiet sort," she says. "And yet you get a feeling if you stepped out of line he'd kick your teeth down your throat." (I will examine this lighthearted yet disturbing scene in much greater detail when considering Helen Brent.) Later that night we, and Helen, see him for the first time, at a gambling club, where Sam is shooting dice and, evidently, doing well. Significant glances abound, suffused with Sam's ever-present cigarette smoke (where would noir films be without cigarettes?), often exhaled through his nostrils like a blast of steam from a locomotive. Laury passes by, intent on Sam's seeing her with Danny, a potential rival (Tony Barrett); he does indeed notice, and his expression does not bode well. Only at the end of the scene, in a passing call from the man running the dice table, do we hear Sam's first name.

Laury returns home with Danny, but Sam is already there, waiting in the darkened kitchen; he is discovered by Danny, who has gone in to mix drinks. Sam's emotional coldness is captured in a striking visual pun; half the screen is covered by the open refrigerator door, such that even though Sam is some distance away he dominates the room as if he were an icy emanation from the machinery. Sam's first words are a peremptory command: "Get out." Danny temporizes humorously, but Sam will have none of it; "I say, get out." This is now a matter of honor for him; "There's no man big enough to cut me out," he tells Danny. "Maybe so," Danny says with a sneer, flicking open a switchblade, "and maybe not." Maybe not indeed; a few moments later he is dead, bludgeoned by Sam. Laury, who has heard the fight and discovered the body, joins him almost immediately afterward.

Sam returns to his friend Mart Waterman (Elisha Cook, Jr.) in their room somewhere in Reno. The single bed suggests a comfort with intimacy, perhaps from shared prison time (nothing in the script or performances suggests a homosexual relationship between the two, a point I will take up again later), and it will become clear that Mart is indeed Sam's only friend, one who has evidently spent much time looking out for Sam's interests. Told that Sam has murdered two people, Mart is unsurprised. "Why'd you do it?" he asks with much the same sort of vague concern one might show over an unexpected romantic break-up. "They were making a monkey out of me," Sam tells him. Mart admits that he'd been worried about this sort of trouble, especially since Sam had some sort of "nervous crack-up last summer," but it is clear that his interest is in Sam, not the victims. "You go nuts about nothin', nothin' at all," he says like an indulgent parent cautioning a mischievous child. "You gotta watch that." He casually accepts Sam's reason for the killings; "He was cutting in on me," Sam says, and this, Mart agrees, was a worry. Not that Laury ("the Palmer dame") mattered; rather, it was the principle of the affair: "It's just that I never let anybody cut in on me on anything."

Mart Waterman, as his name implies, is weak where Sam is strong,[5] but has accordingly learned to think quickly rather than relying on brute force; it is he who directs Sam's exodus from Reno. He knows the schedule of trains and tells Sam to board the one for San Francisco in an hour, and to buy his ticket after he boards. He asks if Sam needs any money, to which Sam replies in the negative. Telling Sam that he, Mart, will stick behind and keep tabs on what leads may turn up, he sends Sam off with a final warning: "No dames, understand?" Sam agrees; "I've got a dame on my mind, and she's dead. And that's plenty for me." It won't be, but for the moment an ominous balance has been reached.

We now know nearly everything factual we will ever learn about Sam (only his last name remains to be heard; it will be announced by a servant later). What we know doesn't amount to much. Sam's background remains a mystery; though he will suggest that he is from a lower-class background, this may or may not be true. Sam's source of income is uncertain; he may have been in the military (he's of the right age, and clearly able-bodied), but never makes any reference to the service one way or another. He must have had a family, but makes no reference, admiring or disparaging, to either a mother or a father, or to siblings. Georgia Staples will later comment that his experience is limited to having "been a fighter and managed a cattle ranch or two," but the equivocal nature of her recollection suggests that his account may have been vague, misleading, or an outright lie; in any case, we have no way of ascertaining the truth of the matter. Sam is literally, as his name suggests, wild; he is unconnected with, and largely unbound by, the external conventions of civil society. Sam is presented as a force of nature, the embodiment of the American will to power, the drive to succeed; he is, literally, the title character. "I could have anything I want," he declares, calmly but without reservation, "anything at all if I put my mind to it."

The words are similar to those spoken by a hundred heroes in a hundred celebrations of American perseverance, here set in a context which transforms their meaning dramatically. In Sam we see unfettered the dark side of the arch individualist celebrated in American lore and writing, a man responsible to no one but himself. After the first two murders (or at least the first two of which we know), Mart warns him, in an almost conversational tone, that he "can't just go around killing people whenever the notion strikes you, it's just not feasible." Sam's response is a curt question: "Why isn't it?" If he read books, which it is difficult to imagine him doing, he would be devouring the works of Ayn Rand, a virulent revenant of social Darwinism enjoying her first great successes in the mid–1940s, who dismissed the validity of any claims to consideration of others in the actions of the individual. Rand inverts Hobbes, seeing only virtue in rampant selfishness (one of her later books is in fact entitled *The Virtue of Selfishness*). "There is only *one* fundamental right (all the others are its consequences or corollaries)," she asserts: "A man's right to his own life. Life is a process of self-sustaining and self-generated action; the right to life means the right to engage in self-sustaining and self-generating action — which means: the freedom to take all the actions required by the nature of a rational being for the support, the furtherance, the fulfillment and the enjoyment of his own life." This gives him (considering Rand's demeaning portrayals of women throughout her career, the masculine pronoun is no doubt appropriate) "freedom to act on his own judgment, for his own goals, by his own *voluntary, uncoerced* choice."[6] Rand is quite serious about this; for her there is nothing about any other person's needs or desires which should influence the private decisions of an individual. The consequences are vividly brought to life in King Vidor's 1949 film, to Rand's own screenplay, of Rand's novel *The Fountainhead*. Displeased at changes made to his design for a building, the architect Howard Roark, Rand's mouthpiece, dynamites the almost completed structure. Put on trial for this act of terrorism, he does not so much defend himself as offer a turgid and naïvely ahistorical sermon espousing Rand's philosophy; his conclusion is, as his positions have been throughout the film, bluntly uncompromising: "I wanted to state my terms. I do not care to work or live on any others. My terms are: a man's *right* to exist for his own sake." He is of course acquitted, and soon after rewarded with the commission to build the tallest building in the world (conveniently, the man commissioning the building then commits suicide, allowing Roark to inherit his wife as well). Rand makes it clear that, should unauthorized changes to this structure be made, Roark would be perfectly happy to, say, fly an airplane into it in service of his, and her, ideals. Rand's screenplay and Vidor's film combine in the service of a vividly phallocentric celebration of what in *Born to Kill*, and many other noir films, is understood as diseased and deadly.

Using Rand as a foil here may seem unfair; after all, it might be argued, few take her writings seriously any more, save insecure adolescents and discredited economists (Allan Greenspan, one of the chief architects of the deregulation which helped lead to the great financial crisis of the early twenty-first century, was a devoted Randian), with even otherwise ardent capitalists seeing her as too extreme.[7] But it is precisely that extremism which is relevant here. Modern capitalism has found many ways to compromise its ideals in order to retain its centrality (a process which Karl Marx failed completely to predict, so eager was he to see the revolution occur, a failure which has allowed his critics to casually dismiss many other, more accurate, insights), compromises which often obscure the unchanging aspects of its inner structure of human relations. Rand is far more honest than her critics within the ranks of free marketers, though often less aware of the consequences of what she purports to defend. Rand, and Sam Wild, are true and unbending atomistic egoists, people for whom all that matters is individual desire and self-definition, will to power. Sam, having no philosophical bent, is unaware of the contradictions his views, which are generally identical with his actions, contain, and will simply and uncomprehendingly be destroyed by those contradictions. Rand and Howard Roark, putatively more philosophical, choose to ignore identical contradictions, but the result is the same; their own claims, followed through to their logical consequences, likewise end in destruction.[8]

Sam, of course, does not see his career this way at all. His trajectory will be upward and onward, with each flight from a disaster simply a move toward the next success, a success which he does not doubt. He has no conception of the forces which operate on, and through, him. Wise limns this subtly but strikingly; as Mart warns Sam about "dames" and Sam assures him that the one on his mind is dead, the cross-fade to the next scene, at the train station, is already beginning, with the engine's headlight centered in Sam's forehead, indicating that his desires are already moving on. On the train he meets Helen, involvement with whom will determine both his greatest success and final catastrophe; their scene together ends with a jump cut to the engine speeding through the night. Framed by symbols of the mechanical operations of destiny, Sam, whatever he may think, is as much subject to forces beyond his control as anyone else.

That this is so, and the reason why, becomes clear through the scene with Helen in the train's club car. Informed by the porter (Napoleon Whiting) that the club car is closed, Sam simply declares, "Well right now it's opening again." Helen is impressed, though at first a bit sarcastic; "What an assured man," she comments. Sam misses the sarcasm, taking it as tribute to his decisiveness. "You've gotta know what you want in life, be sure you're gonna get it, and you can't miss. I found that out early," Sam tells her. The ensuing dialogue is enlightening.

> *Helen:* Most people don't know what they want out of life in the first place.
> *Sam:* I'll bet you do.
> *Helen:* Do I?
> *Sam:* Yes.
> *Helen:* Yes, I do. Exactly. Don't you?
> *Sam:* I know what I want when I see it.

The last phrase is key: "when I see it." Sam is a creature of impulse, driven by desire, an ideal customer — except that he has never internalized the compromises between desire and attainment which keep capitalism both moving and from self-destruction. For him everything exists to be consumed, to be used.

This is a contradiction which can end only in disaster, but it is one built into the social structure within which he operates, and which has trained him. Without ever-expanding desire the capitalist economy would contract and disintegrate; a shrinking economy equals job losses, which lead to a diminution of the money available to purchase the things (their nature and quality being irrelevant) the sale of which drives the economy. Hence the increasing proliferation of advertising, the function of which is to create desires for things which no one needs. An expanding economy geared toward production requires an ever-increasing number of acquisitions by the individuals connected to that economy in order to survive, so the desire to consume, or at least to own, must itself always be increased; as the economist John Kenneth Galbraith succinctly described the process, "If production is to increase, the wants must be effectively contrived. In the absence of the contrivance the increase would not occur."[9] Ever more emphasis is placed on ownership, on the possession of objects, whether or not these are of any actual use to the possessor (the most famous cinematic example of this is the colossal warehouse full of unrelated and unremembered items seen at the end of *Citizen Kane*). Unfortunately, the inevitable corollary to this process is the increasing tendency for individuals to think of others, and eventually of themselves, as commodities, things to be bought and sold (consider all the modern self-help books explaining how to "market" yourself)— and controlled. Here we find the heart of the contradiction: this increasing lust for possession, a necessary element in capitalist economic structures, is also that which must in some measure be checked, for its logical climax would come in chaos, as each individual strove mightily to subordinate every other to their desires. The result, the fear of which lurks at the heart of so many noir films, would be a collapse into Hobbes's terrifying vision of humanity in a state of nature, a vision directly applicable to Sam's existence and its greater implications:

> Whatsoever therefore is consequent to a time of Warre, where every man is Enemy to every man; the same is consequent to the time, wherein men live without other security, than what their own strength, and their own invention shall furnish them withall. In such condition, there is no place for Industry; because the fruit thereof is uncertain: and consequently no Culture of the Earth; no Navigation, nor use of the commodities that may be imported by Sea; no commodious Building; no Instruments of moving, and removing such things as require much force; no Knowledge of the face of the Earth; no account of Time; no Arts; no Letters; no Society; and which is worst of all, continuall feare, and danger of violent death; And the life of man, solitary, poore, nasty, brutish, and short.[10]

Erich Fromm underlines the point; consumption as an end in itself creates classes and, inevitably, class conflicts. "As long as everybody wants to have more, there must be formations of classes, there must be class war, and, in global terms, there must be international war. *Greed and peace preclude each other.*"[11] The artificially created drive toward consumption creates inequalities, which create resentment, which leads to violence, both by those looking to protect what they possess and by those who desire to acquire more things or the power which comes from possession. It becomes a question of control:

> To control other living human beings we need to use power to break their resistance. To maintain control over private property we need to use power to protect it from those who would take it from us because they, like us, can never have enough; the desire to have private property produces the desire to use violence in order to rob others in overt or covert ways.[12]

On the one hand those without power seek it; as they can strike only at individuals, their actions tend to be personalized (robbery, rape, murder, and so on). Those with power, on the other hand, seek to preserve it by institutionalizing it, entrenching their power in systems to which others, most of whom are quite unknown, and of no personal interest, to the powerholder, will be subject. The more successful they are, the more those without power are shaped systematically in the interests of the power structure itself. We have already touched upon this problem in a variety of ways, but here we can see it in a fuller setting and greater detail:

The growing person is forced to give up most of his or her autonomous, genuine desires and interests, and his or her own will, and to adopt a will and desires and feelings that are not autonomous but superimposed by the social patterns of thought and feeling. Society, and the family as its psychosocial agent, has to solve a difficult problem: *How to break a person's will without his being aware of it?* Yet by a complicated process of indoctrination, rewards, punishments, and fitting ideology, it solves this task by and large so well that most people believe they are following their own will and are unaware that their will itself is conditioned and manipulated.[13]

But the tension between the training of individuals to desire ever more and the restraints which must be placed on their actions in the service of those desires cannot wholly be erased, and the possibility of dangerous or damaging actions remains omnipresent. Sam Wild is the avatar of this danger; for him all things, including people, are simply tools to be used to assuage his desires of the moment, desires which he has not chosen and cannot explain, even to himself. He must be controlled, or he must be destroyed. *Born to Kill*, like most films noir, acknowledges the fact that desire, once past a certain point, cannot be controlled but must simply be eradicated; the question, which in effect provides the plot, is how many other individuals will be destroyed along with Sam.

Sam embodies contradictions most individuals confront, at some level, in ordinary life: the tension between individual desire and social awareness. We want what we want when we want it, yet also realize that this attitude cannot be universalized without destroying the shared foundations which allow us to obtain whatever it is we have. Hence the appeal of characters like Sam, and of dark and often brutal films such as many films noir or horror films, then and now. Most of those watching these films have little power, minimal control over the major aspects of their lives, and in such circumstances there is a great appeal to seeing, without danger to ourselves, the possibility that the system which surrounds them (and all of us) can at least be challenged. The villainous characters allow us to vicariously act out the rage inherent in life under capitalism, the wish to strike out at those who represent, or are taken to represent, the forces which keep us under control even as they encourage ever more desire for what we do not, and in most cases cannot, have.[14] The police in films noir are seldom central or especially appealing as characters, and are sometimes seen as even worse than those from whom they are ostensibly protecting society (as with Richard Boone's brutal Ed Cornell in *Vicki* [Harry Horner, 1953], who has few if any redeeming qualities), whereas the antagonists are usually much more interesting, even as we acknowledge their criminality. Detective Mark MacPherson (Dana Andrews) wins Laura (Gene Tierney) in Otto Preminger's 1944 film, but Waldo Lydecker (Clifton Webb) is by far a more intriguing, complex, and memorable character. Everyone recalls the murderous Raven (Alan Ladd), for example, in *This Gun for Hire* (Frank Tuttle, 1942), while few remember, or care that they have forgotten, Michael Crane (Robert Preston), putatively the hero. What audiences appreciate is the momentary taste of freedom, however corrupt that freedom may be, glimpsed in the actions of the criminal. As Gary Collins noted in his discussion of the career of Bela Lugosi, perhaps the most celebrated portrayer of screen villains,

> Whereas the actions of the hero are governed by a fairly rigid standard of conduct, the villain has been limited only by the range of his own resourcefulness. Whether motivated by the prospect of ill-gotten gains, unlimited power, revenge, or the simple joy of perpetrating a misdeed, the genuinely inspired bad guy, like any creative spirit, earns the admiration of everyone who appreciates a sense of dedicated professionalism.[15]

The criminal acts out the urges we must suppress, thus allowing a sense of liberation. At the same time, though, such films can be read as essentially conservative, in that the conclusion provides the audience member with an example of the awful consequences of acting out those urges, an example which implicitly (and sometimes explicitly, as in *The Captive City*) justifies the systemic measures taken against such freedoms.[16]

The danger, of course, is that one takes illusory glimpses of potential freedoms for reality and acts upon them. It is this which Sam does constantly, enticed onward by his apparent successes, successes which give him the confidence which attracts others (a "confidence man" is not merely someone we mistakenly trust, but one whose attitude projects the self-belief — the personal confidence — which fools us to begin with). People tend to admire action, even when its results are less than optimal; the politician who takes time to ponder choices, for example, is often perceived as weak or indecisive, while the one who plunges ahead garners plaudits and votes — at least until the unreflexive action ends in disaster.

So it is with Sam, who is nothing if not quick to convert desire into motion. The night after arriving in San Francisco he shows up at the home of Helen, arriving in the parlor simultaneously with the newspaper announcing the murders in Las Vegas. There he meets Helen's bland fiancé Fred Grover (Philip Terry) and sister, Georgia Staples (Audrey Long). Helen is less than pleased, but despite her attempts to steer him away Sam is invited by Georgia to join the three of them for dinner. At the restaurant Sam gives vent to his feelings: "Why him?" he bluntly asks Helen about her fiancé; he is frankly nonplused that she could be attracted to such a milquetoast. Sparring with her, he reveals his underlying conviction that human relations are at best matters of mutual convenience, dismissing Helen's comment about loving Fred with the brio of a used car dealer arguing against buying from a competitor: "I think I could change your mind about this marriage deal if I decided to." Underlying his comments are class resentments; when Helen laughs at his presumption, he attacks her directly: "Oh I see. You'll cross the tracks on Tuesdays and May Day with a basket of goodies for the poor slum kid. But back you scoot, and fast, to your own high-toned neck of the woods." Helen's demurral, "I wouldn't say that," is flipped aside: "No, you wouldn't say it, but that's the way it is."

But Sam is wrong, as he and we quickly learn. Helen is Georgia's foster sister, and has little or no money of her own. As soon as Sam realizes this, he changes direction; within moments he is dancing with Georgia, making verbal love with her. Before the evening is over he has arranged to have lunch with her the next day, and is already planning to get married. His motives have nothing to do with love, as we see soon afterward in a single long take. He is lying on the bed in his hotel room; as the camera, positioned directly above him, draws slowly closer, he takes a call from Mart back in Reno. "I'm getting married," he tells Mart, but "I don't know when. I just decided." Asked about the woman, he gives the important elements: her name, her status as "an orphan," and the fact that "her old man died and left her San Francisco's biggest newspaper." Mart is impressed; this sounds like the big league, he comments. Sam is unfazed; "Sure, it's the big league," he says. "Isn't it about time I was up there?" He expects great things of this marriage, none of them having to do with Georgia or romance; "We'll not only be rolling in dough but — marrying into this crowd'll fix it so's I can — so's I can spit in anybody's eye." Money is power over others, something we know to be vital to Sam's self-identity. Wise rarely uses such overhead shots, reserving them as a means of emphasizing the character's isolation. A similar shot appears in *I Want to Live!*, where the point is less subtly made than here; in that film we already know how isolated Barbara Graham is, whereas here Sam is at least talking about one of the most intimate of shared human experiences. The camera set-up reveals the truth of the matter.

Having seen what he wants, Sam does indeed take it; the next time we see him is at his wedding to Georgia, held at Georgia's house, some weeks later. His passion is evident, surprising to Fred Grover and infuriating to Helen Brent (as inserts of their respective reactions make clear). Soon after accepting congratulations from all the men present, Sam seeks out Helen to bid farewell and finds her brooding in the library. She speaks to him sarcastically, but soon enough her feelings become clear; she is indeed very attracted to him, and believes that his interest in Georgia is purely monetary, that Sam is simply a very attractive — and successful — social climber. Sam does not entirely disagree. "I'm nobody much," he says, more as a boast than an admission, as his next words indicate. "But I'll make myself a lot more than I am.

I can do it, too. You don't think I can, do you?" As he speaks the camera dollies away from him into a two-shot, as if afraid of his barely repressed violence. Helen, already implicated by the camera movement but still unaware of her coming role, shrugs off the question — "I haven't given it much thought," she claims — but a brief negative shake of her head reveals the lie as she speaks it. Nor is Sam unduly disturbed; having obtained Helen's admission of her feelings for him (and even a kiss), he is convinced that he holds the whip hand, and that she will, soon enough, come around. He leaves, unaware of two things: first, that there is a detective in the kitchen asking questions about him, and, second, that he has underestimated Helen's emotions.

Helen Brent

Helen Brent is more complex than Sam, and in the end more interesting, more nearly tragic. We know almost as little about her as about him, but whereas Sam is the embodiment of will, Helen, being a woman, and a woman without wealth at that, in a society dominated by men and money, is far less free to develop herself. This fact is apparent in the film's brief opening scene between Helen and her divorce lawyer. He makes a strained joke about how the "bonds of matrimony can weigh heavily on one's soul," adding quickly that, of course, his own marriage is secure. Helen indicates, with a hint of sarcasm, her understanding that his wife is "a very fortunate woman." The lawyer concurs; "Oh, I often tell her that." Men assert; women accept — or so the conventional roles would have it. Those roles are difficult to escape for both genders, but especially so for women; Helen, despite her divorce, is not in fact free, and we are reminded of this throughout the film, as Helen is referred to as "Mrs. Brent" by almost everyone, including her divorce lawyer and the (female) owner of the rooming house where Helen stayed while waiting for the divorce to come through. She is defined by simply having been married, and we must accept this starting point even though we know nothing whatsoever about her ex-husband.

The same kind of male-defined places are occupied by all of the other women in the film. Mrs. Kraft (Esther Howard), the rooming house owner, herself twice-divorced, retains the name of her last husband. Laury Palmer is enthralled, as we have already seen, at the brute strength of Sam. Georgia Staples longs for excitement, in the form of a man in her life (soon after meeting Sam she complains to Helen about never having any experiences; Helen's comment that she is "just about to have one" provokes a cross-fade to the aforementioned high-angle shot of Sam on the bed). Even two of the female Staples servants watch the wedding with expressions of envy while commenting on Sam's attractiveness: "Isn't that Mr. Wild the *cutest* thing?" asks one rhetorically. "Mmm," agrees the other. "His eyes get me. They run up and down you like a searchlight." "Yeah," breathes the first.

These reactions are typical responses of both cinematic and actual women to strong men, but they are reflections of social structures rather than inherent realities. "The fact is that we have nothing to do here with laws of nature," as Simone de Beauvoir recognized in *The Second Sex*, coincidentally published soon after the release of *Born to Kill*.

> It is the difference in their situations that is reflected in the difference men and women show in their conceptions of love. The individual who is a subject, who is himself, if he has the courageous inclination toward transcendence, endeavors to extend his grasp on the world: he is ambitious, he acts. But an inessential creature is incapable of sensing the absolute at the heart of her subjectivity; a being doomed to immanence cannot find self-realization in acts. Shut up in the sphere of the relative, destined to the male from childhood, habituated to seeing in him a superb being whom she cannot possibly equal, the woman who has not repressed her claim to humanity will dream of transcending her being toward one of these superior beings, of amalgamating herself with the sovereign subject.[17]

Women, even quite competent, forceful, and intelligent ones, have internalized a self-conception which values abnegation over assertion. In a masculine society they see the only way to act for themselves as, paradoxically and ultimately contradictorily, acting through another; supporting the male in his actions becomes a means of being important as a woman. Hence Laury Palmer's thrilled description of Sam's incipient brutality, "You get a feeling if you stepped out of line he'd kick your teeth down your throat," and Mrs. Kraft's response, "My, ain't that wonderful." To have such force applied to one allows the illusion that one's existence is worthy of such force, that one is important enough to warrant such violence. It is, as we saw in considering *The Haunting*, a version of this fallacy which keeps many an abused woman linked to her abuser.

This is not all. Such relations are part of a process of exchange. Men offer strength, will, action; women, too often, have only their sexuality with which to bargain. Laury knows this; it's why she's going out with Danny that night, adding that Sam "knows I'm crazy about him. He knows he's got me all wrapped up. So I've got to start him worrying. It's a bore, but that's the way you have to handle men." Mrs. Kraft laughingly describes Laury's approach as "cold-blooded," but Helen thinks it's merely "practical." Women are not stupid; they often understand their situations and, amongst themselves, mock them even as they conform to them.[18] But, all too often, they do conform. Men like Sam Wild will continue to get what they want, or at least most of it, as long as there are women like Laury Palmer or Helen Brent to give it to them; it is, therefore, in the interests of such men to maintain the social and personal structures which keep women from asserting themselves as truly independent individuals.

For all her apparent confidence, Helen, too, is caught up in this male world, although she does not yet know the extent of her entrapment. The first clue is provided when she meets Sam in the gambling parlor. We see her losing, changing tables, placing a new bet in accordance with his (a fact acknowledged silently by both), winning, placing a second bet in opposition to his (rather to his startlement), and losing. The exchange is portrayed in purely visual terms; no words are said, yet the situation which will shadow the rest of the film is already eminently clear. If it were not, any doubts are quickly resolved, for it is Helen who discovers the bodies of Laury and Danny. She has no idea as to the killer's identity, but decides not to call the police, seeing no purpose in involving herself—yet her decision in fact involves her all the more closely with Sam, for it is her hasty departure which ensures that they will meet at the train station.

Helen's problem is in some ways worse than that of Laury or Mrs. Kraft, for she is a strong-willed woman, clearly ambitious—which means that she will face tremendous pressures to act through an even stronger man. There are no women with whom she can even potentially explore and develop her own possibilities (save, and only in a limited sense which I will consider shortly, her step-sister). As Robin Morgan has commented regarding the similar situations of countless ambitious women throughout history, "*She may not rise with her people. She must abandon them, abandon her own experience, and, more important, her own intuited, envisioned possible transformation. If she wants power, she must learn that power is synonymous with his power—and his means of seizing it. If she wants freedom she must learn that this too is synonymous with his definition of it and his struggle for it. Neither will save her. Both will destroy her.*"[19] Helen will indeed be destroyed by her own, increasingly desperate, attempts to assert herself against a world in which what and who she is carries little weight or meaning.

Thus Helen's frustration at the wedding of Sam and Georgia. She is attracted to Sam, but he has neither money nor power, and thus has, in blunt economic terms, no exchange value to offer in return for her sexuality. She cannot rise through him, nor can she, having no money of her own, finance such a rise and derive vicarious fulfillment thereby (the old saying, "Behind every successful man stands a strong woman," reveals more than at first appears; the strong women traditionally stand behind the men because those women would rarely be allowed to succeed on similar terms *as women*). Helen has virtually no external identity as such (the newspaper headline revealing her death at the film's end will refer to her simply as a "socialite," as vacuous a term as any for describing a human being), and is seeking some means of making an impact, of creating some meaning for herself. But all of her efforts thus far have been through others, whether her adoptive father or her former husband or her step-sister, and have left her with little true freedom of her own. Understandably, she resents this, even as she acknowledges it. From this comes her challenge to Sam regarding Georgia.

The entire scene, understood from Helen's perspective, is rife with complexities unavailable to Sam. After the preliminary sparring, half flirtatious and half sarcastic, all filmed in half-body two-shots and medium close-ups, Helen shows her hand, a hand she doesn't yet know she holds. Standing so as to bring herself on a level with Sam, she jabs questions at him. "I think you've got a secret of some kind, haven't you?" [A tight close-up of Sam shows her words hitting home.] "Well, haven't you? Why does your face go tight all of a sudden sometimes, and — and what about this friend of yours, this — this plug-ugly you've brought to the house?" She is on dangerous ground, but both she and Sam are quickly distracted by other matters. "Anything else you'd like to know?" he snaps. "Yes," Helen says, her voice softer as she moves closer to him within an already tight close-up. "Why do you stay away from me?" Sam's slow smile as he realizes the import of this question is among the most chilling moments in the film. His oddly irrelevant response — "Vanity of vanities, all is vanity"— provokes an outburst from Helen about his "phony intellectual patter" and social climbing which leads to his comments about himself described above.

Sam has made his point and, to his mind, received his due in Helen's admitted attraction to him. He misses the import of what follows. Helen comments on his ardency, provoking another slow sly smile, but she is intent upon warning him about harming her sister. The ensuing exchange uncovers layers of class-based tensions barely suspected by most of the characters, Georgia included.

Helen: Georgia's my sister and I love her very much.
Sam: After all she's done for you, you'd be crazy if you didn't.
Helen: You don't know anything, do you? You're talking about her money. I hate her for her money. [As she says this, the camera dollies away and backwards into another two shot, mirroring its movement away from Sam earlier, and for much the same reason.] Every time she pays a bill, every time I see something I — I don't own, I'm only borrowing I — hate her for her money. That's nice of me, isn't it, after all she's given me without even thinking.
Sam: I know how you feel.
Helen: There's more to it than that. Her money has made her something I'll never be. She's completely innocent. She has a perfect faith that if she asks someone a question, they'll — they'll give her the right answer.

A cut to Sam's slow sly smile shows that he is reveling in having won over such an innocent, and missing Helen's real point altogether. She continues as if unaware of Sam's look; "Anyhow, I love Georgia, and if you hurt her, I'm your enemy. And I make a very bad enemy, too." It is a measure of the corruption depicted here that even expressions of love come attached to bitter avowals of the power of hatred. Sam's response is to kiss Helen. He then leaves, smugly saying, "Good-bye, sister," returning to Georgia to depart for the honeymoon.

Thus it is that Sam misses the entrance of the head maid Grace (Kathryn Card), who informs Helen that "there's a man in the kitchen asking an awful lot of questions about Mister Wild." Helen heads to the kitchen, where she confronts a private detective who is indeed prying into Sam's background. He drops ominous hints about the dangers of involving the police, and Helen drops a hint of her own about Sam's lack of connections with the household, a hint acknowledged by the detective with a small smile and slight bow. Helen then returns to the reception, being met by Sam and Georgia as they prepare to leave. Now it is she who kisses Sam, saying, "Good-bye, brother" (leaving him puzzled and perhaps even slightly vexed at the idea of her suddenly taking the initiative). Taking a glass of champagne, she assures a dubious Grace, "His [the detective's] coming made me feel wonderful, with the keys to the city right in my hand." Helen, like Sam earlier, believes herself to be in control of the situation.

Like Sam, she is not.

Albert Arnett

Nemesis comes to Sam and Helen in an unlikely form: that of a dumpy, cynical, Bible-quoting, and thoroughly corrupt private detective named Albert Arnett (Walter Slezak). Arnett occupies a peculiar space within the film. There is no doubt that Sam and Helen are the protagonists, in the sense that their story is central to our attention; but, as Sam is a murderer and Helen is presented as at best largely amoral, and eventually murderous in intent if not in act, they could hardly be described as the heroes of the film. Nor could Helen's fiancé or step-sister, neither of whom has enough screen time or weight as persons to engage our sympathies. In fact there is no genuine hero; nor, given the society which Born to Kill depicts, and within which its characters function, could there be one in any conventional sense. Yet if we take the hero as the person who consciously maintains social order against chaos, whose deliberate actions serve as a balance to the actions of those who would destroy that order, then Arnett plays the role of hero, for it is he who, against great odds, tracks down the criminal and sets in motion the forces of law and order which will stop him. In some ways, then, it is Arnett who most embodies the stark understanding of capitalism which undergirds *Born to Kill*, for the incentive for his putative heroism is entirely a matter of money.

His impecuniousness is made evident almost as soon as we meet him, as are his pompousness and profession. His "office" is a coffee shop, his "secretary" the proprietor, Mrs. Perth (Netta Packer). To a comment by a laundryman that coffee smells better than it tastes, Arnett offers a sententious apophthegm: "As you grow older you'll discover that life is very much like coffee: the aroma is always better than the actuality." This not being enough, he patronizes the man as well: "May that be your thought for the day." Arnett is clearly an autodidact whose knowledge is spotty (he refers to those to whom he owes money as "debtors," for example), but he has a certain oily charm and a high degree of cunning. Reminded by Mrs. Perth (she, like so many of the other women in the film, is identified only by her married name) that he owes back payments on the telephone, he dismisses the comment airily with the promise that he will soon "extract a sizeable retainer" from a client he is meeting presently.[20] The client is Mrs. Kraft, who has found his name in the telephone book, and who commissions him to find Laury Palmer's killer. Arnett enumerates the difficulties he faces, and sets his retainer at five hundred dollars (a very large amount in 1947; recall that Stoker Thompson, two years later, sees this as the upper range of his financial dreams). Mrs. Kraft expresses outrage, but Arnett has already investigated her and knows she can afford it despite her protests; "I'm a detective, remember."

Thus it is that Arnett shows up at the Staples mansion, smooth talks his way into the kitchen as an extra dishwasher, asks questions and encounters Helen, and sets in motion the catastrophe which will leave everyone but himself distraught or dead.

Helen and Sam

Helen's situation becomes increasingly clear as we consider the camera movements in the next eight scenes, which form a sequence. The first is a meeting between Helen and Mart in which she attempts, fruitlessly, to pump him for information regarding Sam. Of the twelve shots here, the camera moves in only one, a minor adjustment at the beginning of the scene. The second, an argument between Helen and her fiancé Fred Grover over Helen's decision to invite Mart to live at the Staples mansion, is covered in two lengthy two-shots, in both of which the camera moves substantially. This argument is interrupted by the unexpected return of Sam and Georgia, who have had an argument over Georgia's refusal to give him control over the newspaper, a stance backed by both Fred and Helen. The ensuing scene contains twelve shots, the camera moving in only two, and moving substantially only in the last, by which time both Sam and Georgia have left the scene. Sam's agitation over Helen's apparent betrayal of him is covered in seven shots, the camera moving in all but one; the last shot is a pan which brings Helen, whom Sam has sought out, into the image. The scene between Helen and Sam, during which their strong mutual attraction and Helen's realization that he is the murderer are both revealed, and the interruption of their respective passions by the entrance of Mart, is covered in 25 shots, most of them close-ups, of which six involve camera movement. The subsequent scene between Sam and Mart, in which Mart tries to warn Sam not to wreck his present ideal situation over Helen, takes 17 shots, and is split almost evenly between still and moving frames (nine and eight, respectively). Helen's confrontation with her own feelings and her newfound awareness of Sam's murderous past is likewise evenly split (ten shots, six still and four moving, but with the latter occupying much more time, and including motion in close-up, a technique not used in the preceding scenes). Helen's subsequent attempt to buy off Albert Arnett is simply a series of static medium close-ups, the sole camera movement coming at the end of the lengthy shot which ends the scene. The confrontation between Helen and Sam, mediated by Mart, which concludes the sequence, is likewise rigid, consisting of five shots, only one with a moving camera.

These are not simply statistics; they reveal how carefully the camera demonstrates the underlying situations. Helen is caught between two options, each answering one vital aspect of her personality and denying another. Fred Grover represents "peace and security," as Helen later tells Sam; Fred provides the kind of freedom that only money can buy. But his world is that of utter respectability, and is, as we see in all of his interactions with Helen, completely without passion. Indeed, this is part of his attraction; he deadens Helen's own passions, passions of which she is afraid. "Without him," Helen admits, "I'm afraid of the things I'll do, afraid of what I might become. Fred is goodness and — and safety." Helen is not, at this point, speaking of criminal activity; apart from not reporting her discovery of the bodies in Reno she has done nothing even remotely illegal thus far, nor does she yet suspect Sam of anything particularly untoward. She fears what she has repressed: her own powerful sexual urges, her own physical desires. Money is important (it is, in a capitalist society, the source of life itself, since everything one needs in order to live costs money), and she hesitates to give it up, but self-expression is vital in an even more fundamental manner, for it is the only thing which distinguishes the person from the objects which surround them. Helen has financial security with Fred, but no passion, no love. She knows this, yet sees no way out, for she has no voice that is truly hers. "All my life I've lived on other people's money," she admits. She mirrors in microcosm the conflicted structure of a society built upon the equation of material acquisition with freedom and self-expression. Herbert Marcuse acutely summed up the social situation of which Helen is but one expression:

> Eros creates culture in his struggle against the death instinct: he strives to preserve being on an ever larger and richer scale in order to satisfy the life instincts, to protect them from the threat of non-fulfillment, extinction. It is the *failure* of Eros, lack of fulfillment in life, which enhances the instinctual value of death. The manifold forms of regression are unconscious protest against the insufficiency of civilization: against the prevalence of toil over pleasure, performance over gratification.[21]

Helen cannot *create* anything, even herself; she will follow her heart, but a heart trained by a selfish society is unlikely to be offered, let alone be able to make, ideal choices.

All of this is demonstrated visually. The dialogue is important, yet it adds details rather than fundamentals; the camera and the staging tell the underlying, and far more important, emotional story. Freedom, actual or potential, is indicated by camera movement; entrapment by a steady series of medium shots. Yet Fred Grover's freedom is different from that of Sam; Fred need do nothing but reap the benefits of having money, whereas Sam must strive for whatever he will get (that his striving is in the end destructive and futile is a reflection on the system which has corrupted him, not on the nature of freedom itself). Fred offers Helen stability, but along with it a suffocating kind of propriety, indicated in the length of the two-shots involving them, in which Helen is never out of his sight; Fred himself recognizes that his attitude could appear "completely mid–Victorian." Sam's freedom is choppier, less stable but more exciting — too much so; where Fred represents stagnation, Sam represents chaos. The climax of this, along with the most direct use of the camera to make thoughts visible, comes in Helen's struggle with her own conscience and desires after the clinch with Sam. The camera centers on Helen as she enters her bedroom, pans to follow her as she moves erratically around the room, then tilts down and dollies in as she hurls herself into a chair. An insert of a wedding photograph of Georgia, Sam, and Helen fragments the shot, which then resumes as an upward tilt and tracking shot as Helen crosses to the wedding photograph. Close-ups of her and the photograph alternate, with the camera following her thoughts as it closes in so as first to exclude Georgia from the image and then to center on Sam as Helen's internal allegiance (driven by the desire for passion and freedom) shifts and she subsumes herself in Sam's will to power.[22] "If, then, transgression for a woman is made into an unthinkable act, or at least one for which she knows she will pull down much more opprobrium than a male," as Robin Morgan reminds us, "*she must transgress via a man.*"[23]

The sexual element of such a transgression comes to the fore in the preceding scene with Sam, one which surely pushed hard at the limits of the Production Code. It is not merely the words, disturbing as these are, which impel the scene, but the pacing of close-ups, used here more frequently and more intensely than in any other scene. The scene begins with the aforementioned pan as Sam walks into the kitchen, bringing Helen into the medium shot, which remains centered on Sam, who is standing beside a refrigerator (much in this scene echoes the earlier murder of Danny and Laury, including, as we shall see, the climactic moment). A cut to a slightly closer medium shot of Sam cues his first line: "Why were you against me tonight?" Helen's reaction, given in another medium shot, is one of indifference. Sam reasserts his ability to run the newspaper; Helen, brushing past him into the pantry as the camera pans to follow her, agrees that he probably could. It is the last camera movement motivated by Helen for some time; her moment of freedom, of being able to walk away from Sam and all that he promises and represents, is quickly past. Ostensibly her reason for opposing Sam was that Fred did, and she loves Fred. Sam sarcastically echoes her claim, more as a rhetorical question than an agreement, but Helen, already clearly uncomfortable, changes the subject, only to discover that she has stumbled onto the real subject of Sam's feelings.

> *Helen:* Why this sudden passion to run the paper?
> *Sam:* I'd be on top. I could make people, or break them. *I* could do that. You
>   understand?
> *Helen:* Yes, I think I do.
> *Sam:* Sure you do. 'Cause your roots are down where mine are. I knew that the
>   first time I saw you.
> *Helen:* Soul mates, eh?
> *Sam:* Stop laughing.

The first three lines are given in medium close-ups, almost medium shots, of the speakers. The cut to Sam on "Sure you do" is closer, and the camera moves to follow him toward Helen; she may not yet recognize it, but her destiny is now entwined with, and controlled by, his. The remainder of the dialogue above is given in the head and shoulders close-up, a continuation of Sam's, into which he draws Helen as he kisses her after telling her to stop laughing.

Helen spars with Sam, more from confusion than flirtation, but the ensuing shots are never less than medium close-ups, until Sam says that Georgia means no more to him than Fred does to her. He grabs her again, demanding she admit how little she cares about Fred, pulling her into the closest shot yet, angled down from over his shoulder toward Helen's face. The remainder of the scene between the two is carried out either from this angle toward

Helen or from behind her shoulder toward Sam; in both shots, it is Sam's presence which dominates visually, such that Helen's attempts to define herself separately from Sam's will are clearly doomed.

Sam understands Helen's feelings toward him, but not her feelings about Fred. Hearing her defend Fred as providing "peace and security," Sam stabs at the heart of the matter; "It's his money then." Helen's response begins by mirroring her earlier comments about Georgia's money, at the same time revealing her inability to escape the situation which most galls her. "Yes, partly," she admits. "All my life I've lived on other people's money. Now I want some of my own." That such money as she would get from Fred would come with thick strings attached she does not mention, for another element of her feelings obtrudes immediately. It is then that she expresses her fears about what she might do in the absence of Fred's stable respectability. Sam presses his advantage (remember that this entire dialogue is spoken with Sam holding Helen tightly against him). "And what am I?" Helen looks into his eyes; "You —," she says; "you're strength; and excitement; and depravity." At this point, for the first time, her hand slides along his shoulder, cementing the mutuality of their passion. "There's a kind of corruptness inside of you, Sam." Sam is darkly amused; most women would flee such a man, but not Helen; she's made of tougher material.

Sam: Georgia told me how you found those two in Reno. [...] You didn't yell or faint.
Helen: No.
Sam: And it wasn't only finding them dead. It was the way they were dead. The kid jammed in the doorway. The Palmer dame lying there under the sink.
Helen: Blood on her hair.
Sam: Blood all over the place, and you didn't yell.
Helen: No, I didn't.
Sam: Helen...

Accompanied by surging strings in the best tradition of romantic scene-painting tradition, they embrace and kiss, until Helen pulls away, her face revealing her horrified realization that Sam is the murderer, there being no other way he could have known about the crime scene in such detail. The shot of Helen's dawning awareness visually refers to an earlier shot of Laury Palmer, who, having discovered Danny's body and spotted Sam, has unthinkingly embraced him in relief, only to realize almost instantly that his presence can mean only one thing, a realization which impels a similar, but briefer and less successful, movement away from Sam. In both cases the lives of the women are subordinate to the desires and actions of the man, and their fates are ultimately the same.

With this scene the underlying nature of *Born to Kill* comes clearly into view. The entire film is something of a parody of conventional romantic comedies, and through them of normal social life altogether. Absent the opening credits (the title, after all, does suggest something other than a romantic comedy), it would not be until the actual murder of Danny and Laury that anyone would be certain that Helen's now ex-husband would not come back into the picture in the manner of, say, Cary Grant in *The Philadelphia Story*. Even afterwards, the film is structurally similar to romantic comedies, in that the wayward male (Sam) must find ways to impress the female (Helen) despite the doubts of his best pal (Mart). Sam makes errors along the path (in this case getting married), but finally achieves what he and she have both desired all along. Clinch, kiss, and cut to the credits: a happy ending all around.

What is elided in such endings, particularly in films of this era, is what follows for the women. Having joined their destinies (and, as the frequent references to "Mrs." Brent, "Mrs. Kraft," and even, now, "Mrs. Wild" [Georgia] remind us, their very identities) to a particular man, each woman is expected to follow him wherever his star leads. Helen, although not married to Sam in a legal sense, is certainly now committed to him, as her next action, and the way it is filmed, tells us. She arranges to meet with Arnett to find out what he knows. The encounter is filmed entirely in static medium close-up two shots (a minor camera adjustment at the end scarcely counts as movement, and is barely noticeable), indicating the degree of Helen's entrapment and, coincidentally, her moral equation with Arnett; neither, for their own reasons, is in fact interested in justice. She probes, hesitating at first, to make an offer for his silence in order to protect Sam. He is unembarrassed by the situation: "I am a man of integrity, but I'm always willing to listen to an interesting offer." Helen indicates her willingness to pay "handsomely," although her idea of what this means and his are quite different. "Obstructing the wheels of justice is a costly affair," Arnett observes; he demands $15,000 to keep silent. Helen fences, but Arnett is adamant; having done his research, he knows how wealthy both Georgia and Fred are, and he anticipates that Helen will be able to raise the money, especially as he has recognized Helen's attraction to Sam. Parting, he has one final comment: "Neither of us looks like a scoundrel. Do we?"

This latter is the true point of the scene. In a world in which everything is for sale there are no external indications of trustworthiness, since appearances are merely another form of marketing. Just as Sam sold himself to Georgia, through his handsome visage and virile confidence, Arnett sold himself to Mrs. Kraft with a lie (he told her his office was being redecorated and he couldn't abide the smell of paint as an excuse for having to meet her in a public park), and Helen is selling herself, albeit less successfully, as a loyal sister protecting the interests of a brother-in-law.

The inverse lesson is brought home presently. Helen returns to the

Staples mansion; the cross-fade, with a medium shot of her entrance through the gated front door superimposed on a close-up of her face as Arnett leaves, momentarily leaves her visually caged by the gate's bars. She is confronted by Sam, who demands to know where she has been. Under duress she explains, further covering for Sam even as she does so (Mart is present, and Helen evidently does not know the extent of his knowledge). The next day Mart tracks down Arnett and follows him to find out the client's name, and thus Mrs. Kraft, who has followed Arnett to San Francisco, reappears.[24]

Mrs. Kraft is the only person in the entire film who could be described as positively good (Georgia is at best neutral and, later, will compromise herself considerably; Fred, while not actively bad, is utterly without empathy and will directly contribute to the film's final catastrophe), but her goodness is anything but conventional. She cheats at cards, dresses gaudily, is physically unattractive, loud, alcoholic, and bossy. She also loved Laury, and wants to do right by her simply for the sake of her memory. Hence her hiring of Arnett and her willingness to fork over quite large sums of money almost without demur (though being who she is, she is quite willing also to make sarcastic comments as she does so). She is good, in part, because for her power is unimportant and money is irrelevant save as a means to an end; she is thus, as much as possible, untainted, though hardly unaffected, by the system surrounding her. Her failure will be one of the most powerful indictments of the destructive nature of human relations in a fundamentally competitive, as opposed to cooperative, society.

Mrs. Kraft's failure is all the more shocking in that we are led to expect that she will succeed. At Sam's behest Mart follows Arnett and discovers Mrs. Kraft's location. Playing on her naïveté he lures her to an isolated spot and pulls a switchblade, but she proves feistier than expected and manages to evade Mart long enough for Sam to kill him while she escapes (I will discuss this killing at greater length shortly). The next day the police visit the Wild mansion, where Helen is compelled by a lie of Sam's to lie as well to cover for him. She is coldly furious, as much for the clumsy murder attempt as for being forced to lie, and gives Sam a dressing down before promising to handle Mrs. Kraft on her own: "I can do better than you did; and I won't need any knives or blunt instruments either." She then visits Mrs. Kraft to apply her own pressure, less overtly violent but far more cruel. The first shot of Mrs. Kraft is a shocker; she is drab, unkempt, shriveled, and almost devoid of energy. She suspects Helen's reason for appearing, for the morning paper has already revealed Mart's connection with Sam, Georgia, and Helen (the headline and description making certain to emphasize the important point here: "Wealthy Friends Unable to Shed Light on Tragedy" and "Sam Wild who recently married the wealthy Georgia Staples"). She is morally certain that Sam killed Laury, and is planning to tell the police. "If you go to the police, you'll see Laury sooner than you think," Helen warns her. A series of shot-reverse shot close-ups intensify as Helen's emotional battering of Mrs. Kraft reaches an appalling climax:

> *Helen:* Perhaps you don't realize — it's painful to die. A piece of metal sliding into your body, finding its way into your heart, or a bullet tearing through your skin, crashing into a bone. It takes a while to die, too; sometimes a long while."
> *Mrs. Kraft:* But I won't die!
> *Helen:* I tell you you will.
> *Mrs. Kraft:* I'm so tired. Can't you leave me alone?
> *Helen:* Does it matter very much if this man isn't caught? [...] Do you want to live or die?
> *Mrs. Kraft:* Laury, Laury, I've failed you.

The camera's movements have been limited to small tilts to follow the two women as they stand or sit, leaving the question of the imbalance between them momentarily in abeyance; between the last two lines cited, Mrs. Kraft attempts once more to stand, but is blocked, as it were, by the camera, itself now acknowledging Helen's greater power by refusing to allow any further freedom on Mrs. Kraft's part. Her admission of failure is painfully poignant (Esther Howard's performance here is excellent); it is also the only moment of untainted love in the entire film — and it comes at, and as a result of, an indisputable moment of catastrophe.[25]

Mrs. Kraft's initial escape was made possible by another catastrophe, this one driven by Sam's possessiveness. Sam, having arranged with Mart to lure Mrs. Kraft out to be killed, takes advantage of the desolate site to kill Mart himself, acting purely out of anger at what he takes to be Mart's intention to woo Helen. Mart had indeed attempted to turn Helen away from Sam, but only in order to protect Sam's larger interests in Georgia and her wealth. Mart's entrance into Helen's room was witnessed, and misunderstood, by Sam (Mart couldn't say he wasn't warned; earlier he had described Helen to Sam as "a creamy dish," to Sam's evident jealous displeasure).[26] The main point is evident; all of Sam's murders have taken place as a direct result of jealousy, the quintessential capitalist emotion. Where people are seen as things to be controlled — in essence, as property — and where a perceived right to property is foundational, jealousy is not merely likely, it is inevitable, as are all of its consequences (the jealousy of husbands remains the single-most common cause of murders among spouses to this day). Possessiveness leads to jealousy, and jealousy to catastrophe.

Self-contradiction, whether systemic or individual, cannot be sustained forever, and further catastrophes now follow swiftly. The first is tangential, though not unpredictable; Fred Grover breaks his engagement with Helen. His reasons are revealing, as is the way he expresses them. He takes a total of

15 sentences to break the engagement, 13 of which include some reference to "I" or "me" (usually the former), sometimes in a quite stilted or repetitious manner. "It seems to me," he tells Helen, "that since I've known you you've become lovelier, more mentally assured. But it also seems to me that when I first knew you, you had a heart. I don't think you have any more." Acrimony ensues, and Fred walks away. Helen rushes after him, prompting the single-most rapid camera movement ever associated with her, pleading with him to stay. "If you leave me I haven't a chance," she cries, clinging desperately to him. "Stay and help me. The person who said I was cold also said I was rotten inside. Well, part of me is, but — I'm not — I'm not clear through, not yet Fred. I'll fight it. I'll fight it off and I'll be all right, if you'll help me." Fred remains unmoved and unmoving; he flatly dismisses her feelings, the camera remaining locked into a two-shot in profile as he does so. "I'm afraid I can't help you." One would think she was a stranger supplicating for undeserved charity. Again he condemns her, declaring that the changes he has observed all date from after Sam's arrival (in other words, he is throwing over his engagement for a shift in mood which has lasted only a few weeks). Still cold, he leaves.

Fred's break with Helen is not, and cannot be, based on any real evidence at all, since he is privy to none of what the audience has seen. He is responding, in his own words, to Helen's increased self-assurance; as she has become more able to assert her own priorities she has become less attractive to him. He claims still to be in love with her, but his manner, here and before, implies very strongly that he never has been in love with her and indeed hasn't the faintest conception of what truly loving someone would entail. Certainly his actions display no sign of empathy or even compassion.

Helen, left alone, struggles to find some secure ground on which to stand; she sees clearly that her attraction to Sam is resulting only in problems, but less clearly how to break with him or where to turn to replace him. Informed by Grace that Arnett is on the telephone asking for her, she grabs the opportunity (her cross to the telephone extension is covered in a single extended tracking shot, indicative of her attempt to create the conditions for her own freedom). Arnett has been called off the case by Mrs. Kraft (and is pretty certain why), but has no intention of backing off his blackmail demands on Helen. Go ahead, she tells him; "The gentleman in question has cost me much too much already." Arnett probes, but Helen remains adamant. He concludes with a misquotation from the Bible: "I find more bitter than death the woman whose heart is snares and nets, and he who falls beneath her spell has need of God's mercy."[27] Arnett's misuse of scripture is apposite, though not in the manner he thinks; it serves as a reminder of the many ways in which the male wielders of power have been quite happy to warp the situations surrounding women in order to keep them in line.

Helen is all too aware of her own entrapment, but still thinks to alert Georgia of the impending catastrophe (again the camera moves with her, toward the stairs and then back toward the library where Georgia is doing some work; Helen is striving for freedom, a freedom she will ultimately be unable to attain). She tells Georgia that Fred has broken the engagement, then attempts to warn her that Sam is going to be arrested for the murders of Mart, Laury, and Danny. Georgia is not merely dubious, she is dismissive. "Oh, really, Helen," she expostulates; "Sam killed Mart. Sam killed some people in Reno." But Helen reveals that there were fingerprints, and Georgia begins to believe. This, though, does not have the effect which Helen anticipated, although it mirrors her own efforts on Sam's behalf; Georgia starts toward Sam's room, "To put some of his things together, he's got to get out of here." She, too, has attached her will to that of a man; like many such women she will make excuses for her man, little realizing that she is speaking not with her own voice but with his. "Do you think I'm going to let my own husband walk into a trap?" she demands of Helen, not seeing that it is she who is in the trap.

The climax of *Born to Kill* develops so swiftly that it is easy to miss its complexity. Two elements implicit in all that has preceded now become explicit, their contradictions grinding against each other. The first is embodied in Helen's situation as a woman (and to some extent in Georgia's as well). Where the quest for power is the dominant factor in society, and where power is defined and largely controlled by men, women must perforce, as we have seen, act through and with those men if they are to act at all. Love becomes a means to an end, not an end in itself; "And so, instead of the union sought for, the woman in love knows the most bitter solitude there is; instead of cooperation, she knows struggles and not seldom hate. For woman, love is a supreme effort to survive by accepting the dependence to which she is condemned; but even with consent a life of dependency can be lived only in fear and servility."[28] To submit one's will to the will of another, even if one thinks to do so in the service of one's own presumed desires, is to contradict the nature of selfhood. To will not to will, to choose not to choose: each of these stances undercuts, even as it asserts, itself. Helen — Mrs. Brent — is attempting, quite rationally within the context in which she is acting, to use herself as a means to an end, to convert herself to a thing in the service of the will of another. She is discovering that this cannot be done successfully; as she has no other options, however, she is discovering as well that the framework within which she is acting is itself unstable.

Here we find the climactic development of the second contradictory element which has driven the film. Helen's immediate situation is personal, but it expresses a larger social contradiction. What she is striving for — wealth and power — is itself a desideratum only within a certain set of beliefs and practices, beliefs and practices which she has internalized as part of the process of making herself into an instrumental object. Helen is not free because she embodies an unfree social structure; "Psychological categories become political categories to the degree to which the private, individual psyche becomes the more or less willing receptacle of socially desirable and socially necessary aspirations, feelings, drives, and satisfactions."[29] Where gender, wealth, and power are the defining categories of a social hierarchy, an individual whose consciousness has been developed within, and by means of, the political structures demanded by that hierarchy will reflect, and all too often enact, those definitions in their daily activities as they endeavor to live up to their own expectations regarding what it means to be successful within that hierarchy. This is why it is possible for one person to hold apparently contradictory beliefs simultaneously; the structure of their consciousness, grounded as it is in a self-contradictory social structure, will necessarily be conflicted.

This all plays out in the last minutes of *Born to Kill*. Helen recognizes the shock the news about Sam must be to Georgia, and diagnoses its cause correctly, but fails to understand how Georgia will react. "You've never had to take any jolts," she tells Georgia, echoing Georgia's own earlier comment about never having any experiences. "Your money has always protected you."[30] Georgia is immediately suspicious, and accuses Helen of having delayed calling the police for personal reasons. "Fred was through with you tonight, wasn't he, Helen? You were willing to let my money go when you had Fred's, but not when Fred walked out on you. Then you suddenly realized you weren't going to get his money or mine. Well you were right, you're not." Helen is startled by this new assault, and attempts to deny it; "Georgia, listen. Whatever else I've done, I've — I've loved you." But Georgia will have none of it; "All you've ever loved is my money, that's all you've ever hung around me for."

Notice what is happening here: *both sets of claims are accurate*. This is what it means to act from contradictory motivations simultaneously; Helen does love Georgia, as we have seen, and hate her money, yet she also needs that money, or its equivalent, as part of her self-definition. Her motivations are unclear even to her, because clarity requires the absence of contradiction; hence her equivocation regarding her own desires and choices throughout much of the film. Yet Georgia is only marginally better off, even with the ostensible protection afforded by her wealth; she has attempted to live ("have an experience") through the virile passion of Sam as much as has Helen, and with less self-awareness. All she can see now is the money question; she vows that Helen will never see another nickel from her, prompting Helen, who thus far seems genuinely puzzled by Georgia's vehemence, to call her "crazy."

Georgia accepts the charge, but "at least I'm crazy with love for a man; all you're crazy about is money and yourself." This much is nonsense, and Helen says so; then, hearing Sam entering the house, she decides to demonstrate just how little Sam cares about Georgia. She pushes Georgia into a high-backed chair, then calls to Sam as he passes. They embrace, and Helen warns him that trouble is afoot. Georgia breaks into the conversation, ordering them both to get out. Helen now throws the dice one last time; appealing to Sam's violent side: "Sam, she'd never let us be happy, never while she's alive. Do you hear me, Sam — she doesn't want us to go away, we can never be together, never till she's dead." Sam pulls his gun, but at precisely that moment the police, called by Arnett, start pounding on the front door. Georgia tearfully tells him, "I loved you so, Sam, that I would have saved you no matter what," revealing her own self-willed detachment from social morality, but also mentions that it was Helen who called the police (Georgia does not know, and presumably never learns, about Arnett).

Sam believes her rather than Helen's protestations otherwise, and shoots at Helen as she runs up the stairs and into her bedroom. He gives chase as she runs to her bedroom and into the bathroom, locking the door behind her (the camera moves to follow her but covers Sam without motion; Helen still has at least the possibility of freedom, whereas Sam is already doomed). Yet the possibility is illusory, as Sam shoots through the locked door, mortally wounding Helen, just before the police gun him down. Helen is walked to a chair, next to which, almost unnoticeable, is the same wedding picture at which she had gazed so intently earlier, to await an ambulance, but knows this is the end. Her final moments are ironically framed by the camera, which closes in on her in such a manner that all we can see of the wedding picture is Georgia, the sole survivor of the family.

There is, of course, one other survivor, completely indifferent to the outcome: Arnett. The film closes with his purchasing a newspaper which makes it clear that Helen is dead ("SOCIALITE SLAIN!" is emblazoned across the top of the article, with the large-print lede being sure to mention that she was the foster daughter of "the late Thomas Staples, wealthy publisher"). Arnett reads a bit of the article, then intones yet another biblical motto: "The way of the transgressor is hard."[31] His conclusion is oily in its insincerity, and is accompanied by a supercilious smile: "More's the pity. More's the pity." He then makes dismissive sounds, tosses the newspaper down (apparently into the street, but perhaps into a trash can), and strides obliviously away, unpunished for his own transgressions which, after all, involved only money and deceit.

Born to Kill was not well received on its first release; perhaps it struck too close to the bone politically. I began by noting the need to work within the Production Code; *Born to Kill* does so, barely, yet also subverts virtually every aspect of the Code. "The basic principles can be put quite simply," as Robin Wood notes:

> capitalism, the right to ownership; the home, the family, the monogamous couple; patriarchy, with man as adventurer/pioneer/builder/breadwinner, woman as wife/mother/educator/centre of civilisation (the "feminine" sensibility); the "decent" containment of sexuality/love within this structure, its permitted manifestations governed by the foregoing principles and deviation from them punished; the general sense that all problems can be resolved within the system — that, although it may be in need of a bit of reform and improvement here and there, the system is fundamentally good (natural, true) and radical change inappropriate.[32]

Consider how many of these categories are battered by *Born to Kill*: the evident unhealthiness of an obsession with money (the very heart of capitalism); the insecurity of the home; the absence of anything like a functional family; the complete disinterest in portraying a successful monogamous relationship (we do not see even the faintest hint of a single one in the entire film); the inversion of conventional patriarchal values featuring a handsome leading man who is a maniac and killer; a beautiful woman who educates no one, serves in no family capacity, and clearly has a strong sex drive of her own; a criminal couple who are foiled, yes, but by a representative of law and order who is a mercenary crook. This was uncomfortable viewing in 1947, and remains effective today, its reputation having grown as its uncompromising stance, complex psychological underpinnings, and underlying truthfulness have become better understood. It holds up well, better than some of its more celebrated companions in the noir filmography, in part because of its content, in part because of its very tight construction, and in part because of Wise's decision to film it largely naturalistically. That it *was* a choice is evident by comparison with *The Body Snatcher* and *The Set-Up*, films made a couple of years on either side of this one, in which chiaroscuro plays a substantial role in setting and maintaining the mood. Not so in *Born to Kill*; Wise's approach here is the visual equivalent of the underlying contradictions, in that it subverts our expectations of film noir. Contrasts abound, in script and in visuals alike (not always, strictly speaking, contradictions, but as clues indicative of the contradictory pulls faced by the characters), contrasts large — the conflicts between character appearances and their actions (not only the good looking ones who act badly, but the fact that the only genuinely good person is a decrepit alcoholic) — and small — the visual disjunction between Helen and Georgia in their final scene, Georgia the blonde in white, Helen the brunette in dark. Even the music, in noir films often simply a thunderous presence demanding that the audience surrender to the film's will, helps indicate the conflicts, as when its most Romantic violin scoring throbs forth precisely at moments of gravest immorality. And so on. The bleakness of *Born to Kill* is a moral bleakness which comes from contemplating a world — our world — in which everything is for sale and nothing has value. It is a vision against which Wise would fight, with varying degrees of success, in later films, but it is a vision to which honesty would compel him to return again and again.

Chapter Four

Manufacturing Optimism:
Executive Suite (1954)

Those who lack the capacity to achieve much in an atmosphere of freedom will clamor for power. (Eric Hoffer)[1]

With *Executive Suite*, Wise and screenwriter Ernest Lehman, in the first of four scripts he would write for Wise, invented a new sub-genre, the business drama. Appropriately, the central message of the film is delivered in the climactic boardroom confrontation, a *tour-de-force* of acting, camera placement, and editing. The keys to the film, however, are found much earlier, in the opening sequences, although it is not until after the climax that we fully understand their significance.

The film begins with a series of shots of skyscrapers, the camera always tilted upward, accompanied by a curious prologue narrated by Edward R. Murrow, perhaps the most celebrated news broadcaster of the period, whose voice, and authority as a commentator, would have been instantly recognizable to audiences of the day. I quote it in its entirety:

It is always up there close to the clouds, on the topmost floors of the sky-reaching towers of big business. And because it is high in the sky, you may think that those who work there are somehow above and beyond the tensions and temptations of the lower floors. This is to say that it isn't so.

The opening credits follow immediately, to the deep sound of a tolling bell, with the nature of the narrative "it" revealed by the title itself: the Executive Suite.

After the credits a second curiosity appears: for several minutes the camera takes a first-person viewpoint. This is a rare technique, most notoriously used by Robert Montgomery throughout *The Lady in the Lake* (1946), widely

151

regarded as a failure. Wise himself had already used a subjective camera briefly and effectively in his early and very minor film *Mystery in Mexico* (1948), although essentially as a dramatic flourish. Here the use is somewhat more extensive and vastly more important, though for reasons not immediately apparent; at first we simply learn that we are seeing the world from the viewpoint of someone named Avery Bullard, who concludes some sort of business deal, sends a telegram, hails a taxi, has a stroke, drops to the sidewalk, and dies.[2]

Motion pictures are complex creations, a complexity which generates a need for careful control; very little happens by accident, especially in Hollywood studio productions. The reasons for directorial choices are not always clear (sometimes not even to the directors themselves), and the choices are not always right, but they are choices, and it behooves a careful viewer to consider the import of any given choice, especially large scale ones such as script content and camera use. Wise has, therefore, presented us with a conundrum: why was Avery Bullard shown (or, properly speaking, not shown) in such a manner? The answer will be of great significance for our understanding of the rest of the film, but only in retrospect.

The objective camera now returns us to the office which Bullard has just exited, where Julius Steigel (Edgar Stheli) and George Caswell (Louis Calhern), executives of a company affiliated with the New York Stock Exchange, are discussing the purpose of Bullard's visit. Caswell comments on the fact that Bullard, president of Tredway Furniture, has yet to appoint a new executive vice president, the last one, a man named Fitzpatrick, having died some months ago at age fifty, leaving the company at risk should something happen to Bullard. Caswell dismisses the ability of the board of directors, of which he is a member, to act, as they serve merely as a "rubber stamp" for Bullard's plans. As he speaks, he glances out the window, sees the ambulance below, notices the body on the sidewalk, and realizes that Bullard has died. "A one man company without its one man," he muses in a chortling tone as he calls one of the Steigel company's agents and directs him to sell short on Tredway stock, as much as possible before the market closes (that is, to sell stock Caswell doesn't actually own on the assumption that, when the news of Bullard's death drives Tredway share prices down, Caswell will be able to buy the stock—eventually some 3,700 shares—with which to make good the sale at a reduced price and make thereby a hefty profit). Although Caswell's transaction is completely legal, Julius, who seems genuinely moved at Bullard's death, is disgusted, commenting somberly, his words emphasized by a half-body close-up from slightly below eye level, "There are some ways that don't seem right to make money."[3] In case we miss the point, an immediate cut reveals Bullard's wallet being stripped of its money by an anonymous figure and buried in a trash can even as a police officer phones in the report on the death of an unidentified man. Morally, if not legally, theft is theft, at whatever level. Also being made is the link between money and identity; in this world, we are worth what we have, and absent possessions we are close to nothing at all.

Bullard having called a meeting, it is the province of Erica Martin (Nina Foch), his secretary, to pass on the message. Her attitude toward Bullard is all but worshipful, and her interactions with each of the vice-presidents, or their secretaries, brisk and terse. As she passes on the message we learn, in quick succession, of the possible candidates for executive vice president, each man's name and title emblazoned on the door to his office: the company treasurer Frederick W. Alderson (Walter Pidgeon); the absent Jesse Q. Grimm, in charge of manufacturing (his absence is symbolic, as he is already planning to retire and has largely abandoned interest in the company); Loren P. Shaw (Fredric March), the controller (overseer of expenditures); J. Walter Dudley (Paul Douglas), in charge of sales; and McDonald Walling (William Holden), in charge of design and development.

The names and titles suggest already the limitations and potentials of each man. In their own fiefdoms they reign supreme, but their vision is limited by their lengthy devotion to their specific sets of professional tasks (the exception being of course Walling, whose task is, by definition, to look beyond the present — though he, too, has things to learn before he can become president). It is evident that each man lacks imagination, and that each thus lacks the ability to reach beyond their own circumstances in whatever manner is most necessary to the survival of the company. Yet Lehman's screenplay, one of the most layered and intelligent of the 1950s, is very complex, and what at first seems so evident will turn out to be only part of the problem; in fact, each man does not so much lack imagination as have the wrong sort of imagination, or apply it inappropriately. Imagination might here be said to have two poles of attraction, one to change and one to stability; too heavy a reliance on either will strand the individual, for both aspects are vital to any constructive developments, whether personal or corporate. Much of the film is devoted to developing an understanding of this point, both in the minds of the characters and for the consideration of the audience.

Of the men, the presumptive heir is Alderson; he has been with the company for 29 years and grown grey in Bullard's shadow, despite a putative closeness. Moments after the two have heard the news of Bullard's death, his wife Edith (Virginia Brissac) is urging him on, her voice and expression increasingly harsh: "Dear — There's nothing you can do for him now. You've got to think of yourself. You've worked for it, Fred[....] You've earned it, you have a right. And so have I. You gave your whole life, lived in his shadow[....]

We've waited a long time. I want something for those years, I want us to be *paid back*!" In the trailer, she is presented as simply greedy for power and prestige, but the bitterness runs more deeply than mere social climbing; she has had to share her husband with Bullard for decades, watching his confidence and self-assertiveness — his masculinity, in a certain all-too-common sense — dwindle, to no avail save the acquisition of money (of which they do appear to have a great deal). As we shall see, Edith is giving voice to the central concern of the film in precisely the manner and for exactly the reasons against which it will warn us, herself half-knowingly warped by the process of which she has been a subsidiary part for so long. Her situation is suggested by a subtle detail of Brissac's performance; as she crosses from the living room through the foyer to the study where Alderson is brooding after hearing the news report announcing Bullard's death she clutches her stomach, her womb, as if acknowledging the barrenness of those 29 years and its cause (we see no sign of there ever having been Alderson children, and it is unlikely that there are any).

Alderson fails the test almost immediately. Walling arrives, suggesting that Alderson will want to get back to the Tower, as the company headquarters is known. Alderson agrees; "I guess I'll have to get on top of things right away." They arrive only to find that Shaw is already there and has the situation well in hand; he greets them calmly, as if they were subordinates: "Fred, Don, good you came down. Perhaps you can make some suggestions here." He enumerates his decisions. The waiting reporters are being given appropriate stories, and Shaw has released the earnings report, nominally the province of the treasurer. "I didn't authorize that," expostulates Alderson, but Shaw has a quick and sensible response. "Served up cold the news of Mr. Bullard's death would hit Tredway stock pretty hard at Monday's opening. By countering with the good news of our increased earnings, we'll not only check the decline but send Tredway stock up quite handsomely. It's not a bad way to start a new management, is it?" His voice rolls on, smoothly detailing further plans, all carefully organized for maximum efficiency, concluding with a rhetorical question, "Anything I've missed?" Alderson's only response is a grunt and a tentative gesture.

Alderson is clearly not in charge, and his growing frustration leads him into a tactical error. Shaw announces that Bullard's funeral will be at four-thirty on Monday, to which Alderson objects; two o'clock, he says, allowing Shaw to roll out a veritable panoply of counterarguments. Perhaps there's been an error, he comments, but "when I checked the church calendar I found a wedding scheduled for two," he informs Alderson. Nor is this all; "The highest proportion of older factory workers, those who might want to attend the funeral, are found on the seven to three shift." Alderson's subsequent comments are expressed with increasing heat, while Shaw's voice remains level, dripping with assurance and fiscal rectitude. "What difference does it make?" Alderson asks "The factories will be closed anyway." Shaw is dubious—"For the day?"—as is Walling, who starts to intervene against the idea but thinks better of it. "Yes, for the day," Alderson continues, clearly frustrated; "I suppose all you're thinking of is the money it'll cost." Shaw is unapologetic, and plays his trump card, a reference to the dead man himself. "Not as a first consideration," he claims, "but I did happen to recall Mr. Bullard pointing out at the time of Fitzgerald's death that a paid holiday would represent a loss to the company of approximately $87,000. And that figure of course was before the last wage raise. Be somewhat more at the current rates." A few moments later Alderson explodes impotently. "Even Mr. Bullard's death has to fit into one of your charts!" Still Shaw remains calm; "I don't rate that, Alderson, I don't rate that at all. I have only one interest: the good of this company." Alderson, stymied in every way, storms out.

He knows he has failed; what is more, he knows why, and the realization is painful. Soon afterward Walling finds him sitting in the dark in his office. Switching on a lamp, Walling attempts to succor him, but Alderson will have none of it (the lighting parallels that of the earlier scene between Alderson and his wife, emphasizing the other-directed nature of his life).

> Sorry Don, made a mess of it. [...] You were disappointed in me; I was disappointed in myself. Thought I could do it, but I can't. [...]'Twasn't Shaw, 'twasn't Shaw at all. That was my mistake, thinking I was fighting him. [...]'Twas Avery Bullard I was fighting. Can't you see that? I could have coped with Shaw, it's easy to fight somebody you hate. But I couldn't fight Avery Bullard, never could. [...] Avery Bullard doesn't want me to be president. He never wanted me to be anything but what I am: a number two man. Never more, never less.[4]

The momentary shift into the present tense toward the end of his self-flagellation is significant; Alderson remains trapped by the past, by his own sense of mediocrity. On his own, he will achieve nothing more.

There comes a time in the life of many an individual when they must face what they have become, and to acknowledge that they have not lived up to the dreams, perhaps even the promises, of earlier years. With great luck, there will yet be an opportunity not merely to accept but to embrace that discovery in a manner which still allows creativity and dignity. Alderson's moment does arrive, and in an unexpected manner. He and Walling, desperate to stop Shaw, decide to recruit Dudley to stand for the presidency. Walling soon realizes that this would be, if anything, worse than having Shaw run the company (Shaw has too much spine, and of the wrong sort, but Dudley has none at all) and rushes to the airport, where Alderson is awaiting Dudley's arrival. The encounter is an important stage in the development of both men.

If not Dudley, then who? asks Alderson. "Me," replies Walling. Alderson strides away, a half smile on his face; he had suggested the idea earlier, but has had time to reconsider. "You haven't got a chance," he tells Walling; the latter, who until quite recently had claimed to not want the position, gives vent to an angry outburst which suggests that he has not been entirely honest with himself. "You've had a chance to change your mind, is that it? I'm not ready yet. Five more years to be properly seasoned while the company goes down the drain. I've never had my picture in *Fortune*, I get my hands dirty once in a while. I don't know the rules. I'm not old and tired or — or weak and afraid." The hesitation shows his awareness that he is hitting Alderson below the belt, and Alderson rightly upbraids him for it, comparing him directly with Bullard: "One thing Bullard always had was respect." Walling acknowledges his transgression, apologizing promptly. Yet the passion, the list of ostensible disqualifications which are really qualifications, and the apology itself have their effect; Alderson knows that the company needs a dynamic leader, and after a few more arguments he offers only a weak objection: "But how do you expect me —." Walling interrupts vehemently, "I don't care, it's got to be done." There is a pause as Alderson considers; then, with a slight but unmistakable smile framing his eyes, he looks straight at Walling. "Is that an order?" he asks softly. "Yes," replies Walling, smiling back more broadly, "that's an order." The exchange, filmed in a series of full two-shots with the camera alternating position between the sides of the two men, is beautifully played, such that there is no hint of humiliation for Alderson, no shadow of arrogance from Walling; rather, Alderson has understood that even as a number two man he still has vital choices to make and an important role to play in ensuring that the proper number one man is strongly supported. Alderson's role will henceforth be subsidiary, but proudly so, for it is a role he has at last chosen for himself.

The minor candidates are easily disqualified. Dudley is a glad-hander of a sales rep, good at what he does but with no real vision past the next sale. In addition, he is having an affair with his secretary, disclosure of which would ruin his marriage and career (the film takes place in 1953, when such matters were given more weight than nowadays). Shaw is well aware of the affair, and Dudley, perforce, will act at Shaw's bidding. George Caswell was, as Julius Steigel opined, disqualified by Bullard at the beginning of the film (though we will hear more of him later). Jesse Grimm (Dean Jagger) is too wrapped in bitterness over the changes at the plant and the decline of his once-close relation with Bullard to care, or at least thinks so.

Two serious candidates are left: Walling and Loren P. Shaw. Keeping in mind the imaginative poles I mentioned earlier, the positive (change-oriented) and negative (stability-oriented), it's easy to see that Walling, the researcher, represents the positive pole, the pole of imagination and possibility, and Loren Shaw, the accountant, the negative, the pole of numbers and facts. Shaw, as a character, foreshadows the way American business practices have developed in the decades since *Executive Suite* was released, and in some ways seems more contemporary now than he did more than a half century ago. His regard is entirely for fiscal expansion; he is the embodiment of the economist Milton Friedman's famous (and later) dictum that the sole social function of business is maximization of profits. When first seen he is listening to the playback of a dictaphone message he is preparing for Avery Bullard complaining about cost overruns on experimental work. "In view of the consistent high profit curve achieved by our budget KF line," he wishes to meet with Bullard to discuss "the economic soundness of Mr. Walling's experimental program." It is clear what his recommendations will be. Shaw was not born into money, and he has the intense regard for it that is so often seen among those who have been without; as the novelist Arnold Bennett, who knew both early poverty and later great wealth, said, "If you've ever really been poor you remain poor at heart all your life."[5]

Like most people whose lives revolve around profit/loss balance sheets, Shaw overvalues efficiency, and he is a model thereof, always attempting to anticipate the needs of Avery Bullard and to outmaneuver the others—his competition—in the company hierarchy.[6] His first question to Erica Martin on being informed of the intended meeting is, "Was there any information Mr. Bullard might want at this meeting, anything you suggest I have ready for him?" It is by continually asking such questions that Shaw has been making inroads into each of the other departments in his quest for the executive vice-presidency and, eventually, the presidency. His suggestions are rarely well-received by the others; Dudley, on being given "a volume and price chart for each major item" in which the intersection of the two curves reveals "your relative net profit," says sarcastically, "Maybe you oughta go to Chicago and try pushing the KF line, Shaw. See how far you get with the boys with your kind of intersecting curves." It is clear that Alderson and Dudley detest him; as Alderson will say later, whoever becomes president, "It's not going to be him," gesturing in the direction of the recently departed Shaw.

Yet Shaw's qualifications are many, nor is he merely a simpering toady; his efficiency extends to keeping very close tabs on exactly what each board member has been doing, both inside and outside the company. As we have seen, he knows about Dudley's affair. He learns within a very short time about Caswell's short sale of Tredway stock, and takes measures that will ensure that the expected decline in share cost does not happen, leaving Caswell facing a potentially crippling financial situation on Monday; Caswell will have to work with Shaw. To be elected president will require the affirmative vote of four board members, and Shaw knows he can count on three of these: his own, Dudley's, and Caswell's. One more will be sufficient, and he turns for that purpose to Julia Tredway, daughter of the company's founder.

Probing Erica Martin about Avery Bullard's relationship with Julia Tredway, Loren Shaw elicits a stark response: "Mr. Bullard saved the company after the death of Miss Tredway's father. He helped her regain her health when she broke down. They became good friends[....] Those are the facts, Mr. Shaw. *All* the facts." They are not, and Shaw knows so, but he has failed to recognize one very human fact that makes Erica Martin the last person he should have asked: she herself was desperately in love with Bullard. So was Julia Tredway (Barbara Stanwyck), who is thus intimately connected with the central metaphor of *Executive Suite*, but has only half recognized the fact, and lives in misery because of her inability, or unwillingness, to see further. Julia is pivotal here. Not only is she related to the company's founder, she had been Avery Bullard's lover for ten years—and she holds a considerable amount of Tredway stock, enough that, should she sell, Bullard would lose control of a company he saved from disaster during the Depression. Depressed at her father's suicide, and bitter at Bullard's having distanced himself as he grew more wedded to controlling the company, she is immured in the past, increasingly indifferent to anything but somehow regaining Bullard's love. His death having made this impossible, she alternates between making gestures toward getting rid of her connections with the Tredway Corporation and contemplating suicide.

Yet it is she who asks the central question, and embeds within it already half of the answer. Confronting Alderson in Bullard's office, before either of them is aware of Bullard's death, she bursts out in anger that her constant threats of selling her stock are the only way she has of retaining Bullard's interest. Almost immediately, she apologizes, wearily pondering the hold Bullard has on those around him: "How does he do it to us? Your devotion; my imagination." She expands on the role of the latter, missing in the process a key point; "It does take imagination, you know, to think up reasons for coming here because — he won't come to me any more." She is too wrapped up in her own loneliness, and Alderson too wrapped up in his dedication to the company, or at least to his image thereof, to see that this absence is precisely the issue. It is here that we begin to understand the significance of the first-person camera in the Bullard scenes.[7]

Avery Bullard is an idol, and like most such he occupies the space he does not because of innate qualities of his own but because of the power others have assigned to his image. Julia Tredway admires and loves him, but cannot admit that he is no longer the man she once loved. McDonald Walling considers him "a great man; the greatest man I've ever known." Alderson has been faithful to the point of almost losing his own soul. Jesse Grimm was once very close to him, inviting him to dinner and sitting up "half the night talking"; much of his present bitterness stems from the loss of that contact. Erica Martin considers him virtually a god, and Luigi the elevator operator (Charles Wagenheim) positively oozes deference, stating categorically that he'll stay late on his shift because "I don't mind waiting for him."

Yet the warning signs against idolatry are many, and there are those who recognize the problem, though not always in a constructive manner. Even as Bullard is dropping dead, Caswell is dismissing the "rubber stamp" board of directors; later, Caswell will refer to the necessity of replacing "that kind of dictatorial leadership." Jesse Grimm acknowledges that his best conversations with Bullard took place "a long time ago." Eva (Shelley Winters), Dudley's secretary, refers sarcastically, if privately, to "Mr. Bullard's orders" before passing them on to her boss. Mary Walling, McDonald's wife, has evidently been pressuring her husband for some time to acknowledge that the situation is not as it was when Bullard hired him with rosy promises of strong and enthusiastic support for research into product improvements; "He's changed, Don," she reminds him during the course of an argument, evidently one they've had before, "and — you're dying a slow death here because you refuse to admit the truth, the truth about Bullard." Loren Shaw sums it up to Walling after the confrontation with Alderson: "We know things haven't been run too perfectly around here."

We as audience members are involved in these estimations of Bullard as well, and the subjective camera is a vital part of so engaging us. Having seen no one, we must form our own understanding of Bullard's looks, Bullard's attitudes, Bullard's significance; everything we know of Avery Bullard comes through someone else's descriptions, with or without ulterior motivations guiding them. We must judge Bullard, for only in doing so will we be able to affirm or reject the conclusions the film will draw at the end, but in the absence of objective evidence (that is, in the world of the film, of actually witnessing Bullard's interactions with the men and women around whom the corporation functions rather than hearing about them) each of us will reveal our own character in the judgment we reach. The deeper significance of this will become clearer as the film progresses.

It is ironic that only Loren Shaw, of the insiders, sees Bullard's feet of clay directly, for it is in part Bullard's increasing reliance on Shaw's fiscal judgment which has led him astray. Yet Shaw will be unable to make use of his knowledge, for he lacks a vital quality, already mentioned by Julia Tredway: imagination. Shaw is reactive, not creative. He is very good at taking advantage of a situation, but only within very narrow parameters. Outside of those lines, he is lost, as we saw in his interaction with Erica Martin

regarding Avery Bullard and Julia Tredway. He will come close to winning
Julia Tredway's support for the presidency, but only while she is still trapped
within her own past — that is, while she, too, is failing to open her imagination beyond the limits of her own immediate situation. He controls Dudley
on the level of fact, but his control slips as soon as a higher level of possibility is revealed. His true opposition is therefore not Alderson but Walling.
Shaw recognizes this (hence his refusals to approve the necessary funding for
Walling's experiments in improving the furniture, experiments of which only
the cost, and not the value, can be known in advance), but there is little he
can do.

    The casting ensured that few audience members could have been in any
doubt that McDonald Walling would become the new leader of the Tredway
corporation, but his path is not an easy one; he must first overcome his own
veneration of Avery Bullard and develop his own vision. This comes in several stages, but the central fact about each of them is that always his development is aided by the presence of others and his willingness to listen to
them. Walling succeeds not because of his economic or political qualifications;
he has fewer of either than almost any of the other characters. Rather, his success comes because he, alone among the others, understands the necessity of
change and growth, both personal and professional. He not only recognizes
his errors, he acts upon that recognition. In so doing, he makes connections
at a much deeper level than any of the others.

    This centrality of human connections is limned by the depictions of the
family lives and personal connections of each of the main characters, depictions which clearly have been thought through very carefully. Erica Martin,
the consummate executive secretary, is never seen outside of the Tredway
headquarters. Julia Tredway is seen only in Bullard's office and the board
conference room, save for one brief scene in her own living room as she learns
about Bullard's death. This latter is filmed in two shots, first with the camera dollying toward the telephone from behind the chair in which she is sitting, the other with it dollying toward her face as she reacts; her isolation
amidst the press of external events, emotional and physical, is thus silently
reinforced visually. We meet Alderson's wife, but only in a narrow context,
and only inside their house; there is no exterior to connect that house with
the larger world; although the Aldersons are hosting guests, we see no interactions therewith. Jesse Grimm's wife, Sarah (Mary Adams), appears in one
brief scene in a car; their marriage, though on her part supportive, is not
explored. Caswell is emotionally distant from his unnamed trophy wife
(Lucille Knoch); their life together apparently wanders incessantly from pent-
house to nightclub to racetrack and back (one suspects that following his
incipient bankruptcy and disgrace she will divorce him and move on, a cir-

cumstance regretted by neither). Caswell does interact briefly with several other minor characters, but never on a personal level, with the partial, and for Caswell unsatisfactory, exception of Julius Steigel. Shaw wears a wedding ring, but never so much as mentions his wife or any family; we never see his home either. His interactions are all at the level of power; where he is in control he is smooth and ingratiating, and where he is not, or thinks he is not, he is edgy and nervous, his tension signaled by his constant wiping of his sweaty palms on a handkerchief (aware of the problem, he keeps fresh handkerchiefs in his desk drawer). Dudley's external connections are almost all at the level of sales camaraderie. His wife is experienced only through his half of an angry telephone conversation; their marriage, if it ever genuinely existed, is assuredly over in all but name. His affair with Eva is as much a matter of comfort as of sex, and he gives little in return; "She lets me say what I want, be myself," he fumblingly explains to Loren Shaw, who is more bothered by the spittle in "the corner of your mouth, the right side" than interested in Dudley's words. Eva will break off the affair soon afterwards, dismayed at Dudley's inability to take an interest in her emotions and needs; "I'm not helping you — and you're certainly not helping me," she tells him, dismissing any possibility that he can change. "You've never faced an unpleasant situation in your whole life; you never will. You're too busy being popular." Dudley here confronts his own character as had Alderson earlier, with less successful results (the camera set-ups, which alternate between two-shots of him and Eva and close-ups of her, never of him, subtly stress Eva's newfound resolve and independence and his dependence); his promise that "a guy can change" sounds hollow, and is not backed up by subsequent action until he has in effect no other choice.

Walling's personal and family connections are the only ones we see in detail. His professional life is not centered on the boardroom but on the Pike Street plant where the research facilities are located, and he has strong links to many of the employees there, researchers and line workers alike (on several occasions we see him speaking with, and (far more importantly) listening to factory staff, at least some of whom he knows by name. In line with this, his is the only residence of which we see both interior and exterior rooms (the whole domestic suite: living room, bedroom, study, kitchen, and bathroom). Here he lives with a son, whose baseball game he attends, albeit distractedly, and a loving wife.

Mary Walling (June Allyson) occupies the place in Walling's life that Julia Tredway should have occupied in Bullard's. She is still very much in love with him, but she understands that this neither guarantees happiness nor allows overconfidence. Their marriage is not flawless. They fight, evidently repeatedly ("Why do we do this to each other?" she asks him at one point) and evidently over Avery Bullard. But Mary's commitment is strong, and expressed in terms which will inform Walling's later transformation; "I'm only interested in loving you," she tells him; "I'll fight anything, anyone — even you — I think will make you into someone I can't go on loving." The interjected phrase is vital; Mary is not, like Edith Alderson, wedded to the idea of aiding her husband's climb up the corporate ladder at any cost, but to the idea of aiding her husband's development of all of his capacities as a human being. Waking very early the morning after Bullard's death to discover her husband brooding over a design in his study, she expresses concern ("you'll be a wreck"), asks after his meeting with Alderson, then expresses appreciation of what he is sketching ("Oh, I like that"). As the conversation progresses, she probes his feelings before offering a suggestion quite the contrary, one feels, of what any of the other wives would have offered under similar circumstances. "Don," she says gently, "maybe this is the time for you to leave Tredway." He demurs, but she presses the case, *his* case: "But you could do what you always wanted to do, be on your own, design what you want, build what you want." His loyalty to Bullard triumphs, but the greater point stands out; Mary is willing, indeed even eager, to accept whatever sacrifices in income and position might be necessary to allow the creative side of her husband fuller play. Her willingness, however expressed, is not that of servility; she listens to Walling's reasons for not seeking the presidency himself and agrees with them, so much so that when he decides that he must put himself forward she is able to use his own words against him. "I've got to try," he asserts; "Why?" she asks. His response is not exactly helpful: "Why not?" She has reasons, and good ones; "For one thing because I love you, and I wouldn't enjoy seeing you crack that handsome head of yours against a stone wall trying to do the impossible." Again his response is terse: "Nothing's impossible." Mary recognizes the source of Walling's passion and his words; "Bullard's line, not yours," she reminds him. Again they argue, Mary reminding him of his lengthy frustration within Bullard's company (Wise showing their distance, and Walling's inner ambivalence about his choice, by filming a substantial portion of the scene with him standing in front of a mirror, such that Mary is arguing with two versions of her husband). He rushes out to attempt to meet with Julia Tredway and obtain her vote, leaving Mary angry and hurt. Almost immediately comes a call from Alderson, asking her to call the company and leave a message for Walling to delay the vote; Mary begins to call, then changes her mind, hanging up without speaking.

Walling does not find Julia Tredway at home; she is in Avery Bullard's office weeding through personal papers and tossing them into the fireplace (figuratively burning her bridges with him, the company, and the past; "The funeral pyre of nothing at all," as she describes it). The confrontation between the two is not pretty. Walling is too obsessed with his own situation to have much empathy for hers, and she is too angry and bitter to see beyond her own emotions. "I hate to bother you," Walling begins, "but this is important." Julia is quietly dismissive; she knows why he has come. "Important?" Walling, oblivious to the emotional tenor of the room, explains: "It has to do with the company." Julia is dismissive. "The company," she intones with subdued sarcasm. "I don't want to hear another word about it. I've said all I'm ever going to say to Mr. Shaw." Walling is appalled; this is not what he expected, and certainly not what he wants to hear. "Shaw?" He presses his case, evoking a drifting response, half in the present and half in the past, half in Julia's voice and half in her memory of Bullard's. "You mustn't be unreasonable, we wouldn't want that, would we? There, there, my dear, you'll be all right, that's a good girl. You've got everything in the world to live for. Money, brains, beauty. So you just sit here and wait. And if you wait long enough, say ten or twenty years, maybe something else will happen. Because you know, Julia, no matter how horrible things are — they can always get worse." This is Julia Tredway's moment of self-recognition; it is not Avery Bullard who is to blame for what happened to her but her own decision to rest her self-worth upon his love. She has sacrificed her individuality in the service of a man who may never have cared, and who did not, and who could not, have cared enough to provide what she has needed. Her life has been a waste.

Walling still misses her point, and stupidly presses his case. Learning that not only is she selling her large holdings but that Shaw is handling the transaction, he becomes aggressive. "You can't do that!" he asseverates; "You're selling out the company, Bullard's company, your own father's." Julia, her understanding expanding to include her own family history, replies with increasing emphasis; "What did I ever get out of it except loneliness and sudden death? What did I ever get out of them but the sight of their backs?" Walling's anger overflows; "Bullard gave you everything you have," he shouts. "There wouldn't be any stock if it hadn't been for him. You wouldn't be here at all." Julia's answer, all but screamed, is ferociously poignant: "I gave him ten years of my life and all my love. Isn't that enough?!" Not for Walling, who is being almost willfully obtuse, and who continues to troll for her vote. Finally, devastatingly, it comes home to him; she has given Shaw her proxy. He snaps, eventually bellowing out his unjustified rage. "If you want to stab a dead man why don't you do it yourself instead of having someone else do it for you? [...] Go on, sell out, smash everything he lived for. That's what you want to do, isn't it? Pay him back for loving the company more than he loved you." Julia yells at him to leave, they tussle briefly, and Walling storms out. Julia, sobbing, hurls the last of the papers toward the fireplace and turns to the window, at once willing and fearing her own death. The booming of the great bell in the Tower, announcing six o'clock and the decisive meeting, intervenes; Julia throws herself against a parapet, pressing her hands against her ears and screaming.

The rightly celebrated climax of *Executive Suite* is the fight for the presidency, which forms an extensive drama within the larger picture. It has several acts. The first begins with maneuvers by Shaw, who believes himself securely in control of matters, to hasten the process. He summarily overrides objections by Walling, his responses always in accordance, and careful to be recorded in the minutes as being in accordance, with the corporate bylaws. Even so, not quite all proceeds according to plan; unexpectedly, Julia Tredway enters and takes her seat, her first-ever attendance at a board meeting (Bullard had always held her proxy). "This won't be necessary, Mr. Shaw," she tells him as she tears up her proxy and glances at Walling; "I'll do it myself." Shaw of course does not fully understand her point, yet remains confident of eventual victory. Following instructions, Dudley nominates Shaw for the office, with Caswell seconding. There is no debate, nor, despite Erica Martin's hopeful request, is there another nomination. The vote proceeds; as Erica Martin collects the envelopes Shaw stands nervously by the window, the camera unmovingly contemplating his profile as he listens to the vote tally, cutting away only to show Erica Martin's obvious pleasure as she announces a hitch in Shaw's plans; someone has abstained, and Shaw remains one vote shy of the necessary majority.

The someone is quickly identified. George Caswell, needing to make certain that Shaw would, as president, cover his 3,700 shares, abstained as a means of ensuring the transaction in advance. The two have a quick tête-a-tête in the executive washroom, where Caswell flaunts his bargaining power. "It's not just that my 'no' keeps you out, my 'yes' puts you in," he gleefully reminds Shaw. Shaw, authorized by Julia Tredway to sell her stock, exasperatedly shows Caswell the letter of transfer, signed in advance of the vote by him (Shaw) as president, and Caswell grins and is ready to do as needed.

But, as is so often the case in Wise's films, the tide has turned on this small matter and the few minutes it added to an onrushing process. Several events will now conjoin to lead directly to Walling's actual election. The first is Walling's recognition of his own unjustified treatment of Julia Tredway. He approaches her while Shaw and Caswell are conferring. "Miss Tredway, I don't know how you just voted but — I wanted to tell you how sorry I am for what I said. No matter how I feel about the company I had no right to do that." She does not respond, but the point has been made: there are personal matters far greater in value than the interests of a corporation, and Walling has recognized the fact. It is a vital moment in his one development, one which will, so to speak, presently pay handsome dividends. The second event is the arrival of Mary Walling at the Tower. Mary, having reconsidered her decision not to transmit Alderson's message, but unable to contact her husband or Alderson, has had to drive to the headquarters to speak with Don personally. Even as Shaw calls for the meeting to resume, Walling steps out to meet Mary, who explains, apologizes, and passes on Alderson's request. She is distraught, convinced that she has acted wrongly, but even so she makes a core assertion; "If it's what you want, *really* want, it's all that should matter to either of us." Her concern is not with Walling's power or prestige or fiscal reward, but with his innermost convictions; it is these, and nothing else, which matter. "Is there still a chance in there?" she asks him, then reminds him, in the best possible way, that he should not give up the fight: "Nothing's impossible, remember." Walling's response is surprisingly tender — he, too, is coming to grips with what is most important, both in his personal life and in his relations with Bullard and the company. He had indeed all but given up, sitting and sketching numbly and silently as Shaw rolled toward what should have been an inevitable victory. Now, refreshed and with a new perspective, he returns to the boardroom ready to do proper battle, to begin his final showdown with Shaw.

Walling begins with a challenge. Even as Caswell seconds Dudley's renomination of Shaw, Walling interrupts, asking Shaw just what kind of vision he has for the company. Shaw takes the bait, partly because he is still not certain of Julia Tredway's vote and wants to nail it down by explaining his dedication to maximizing profits. His case is calmly presented, solidly buttressed, and, from a certain perspective, eminently reasonable (it is, after all, the one which dominates conventional business outlooks to this day). "I believe," he begins, "that a company is answerable first and last to its stockholders. To fulfill that obligation, primary emphasis must be placed upon return on investment." He is interrupted by the arrival, at last, of Alderson and Jesse Grimm. Mary, waiting outside, takes the opportunity to push the boardroom door open slightly after they enter; she is thus implicitly present for Walling's fight, as suggested by the camera movement toward her as she edges open the door. Walling is not alone.

Shaw continues, stressing the monetary aspect of his credo. "When the average stockholder buys Tredway stock," he asserts, "he makes an investment. Now the only reason he makes it is to get a return. That's why I believe that a corporation today must be governed to be what its owners want it to be and have paid for it to be: a financial institution yielding the highest and safest return on investment." Manufacturing and selling are not exactly irrelevant (you have to have something to sell), but neither should they be the focus; they are among the means to the end of maximizing profits, and must be treated as such rather than as having intrinsic value in themselves. Shaw contrasts the profitability of "a new tax-econ procedure I got the government to approve" with the return on investment from the factory floor and the research wings, the latter two losing by the comparison. A few genuflections to Avery Bullard's memory aside (these because he does not understand Julia Tredway's true feelings about Bullard and is attempting to ameliorate what he assumes she will take as criticisms of Bullard), Shaw's smoothly delivered speeches are designed entirely to exalt the wonders of increasing profitability and expanded dividend payments.

Alderson interrupts, as he had done the night before, but this time his interruptions are in the service of a specific goal, peeling away potential votes for Shaw, and his interjections have a deliberately theatrical quality. At last he manages to pierce Shaw's calm façade with a sarcastic charge: "While Jesse and Don are turning out product you figure jugglers and chart men are busy flyspecking it with decimal points." Shaw bursts out angrily, defending his actions and arguing that, if protecting profits requires stepping on toes and hurting feelings, so be it. He stands on his record.

"*Your* record, Shaw?" Walling has seen his opening and takes the offensive. After a few preliminary questions clarifying the issues at hand, he stands and the emotional and moral balance of the scene shifts decisively to his side, a shift indicated by two small but telling details. During Shaw's dominance of the meeting, every single shot is either slightly above the level of the tabletop or considerably higher, metaphorically and physically looking down upon him. Simultaneously, apart from one or two barely noticeable adjustments to accommodate motion, the camera remains still; the scene is broken up with quick cuts from face to face or two-shot to two-shot. As Walling at last stands and bears down on Shaw, the camera, located behind Shaw and to his right, moves away and slightly downward; from then on the preponderance of shots will be at or even below the level of the table, looking upward at Walling, and the camera will move more freely, as if released by Walling's energy.

Walling's first interrogative is personal. He directs his questions to Shaw, but their import extends to everyone in the room, and to the audience members as well. The exchange powerfully captures the tension between Walling's as yet unexpressed outlook and Shaw's:

Walling: The president of a company like Tredway would have to be [...] prepared to make a good many personal sacrifices, willing to devote himself to the company mind and heart, body and soul?
Shaw: If you had the right man there'd be no worry on that score.
Walling: Why? Why would he do it? What would be his incentive?
Shaw: Y'mean outside of salary? There's such a thing as success, isn't there? A sense of accomplishment.
Walling: Exactly. [It is at this point that he stands and the above-mentioned camera movement occurs]. Now let's assume, Shaw, that you're the man, running

the Tredway Corporation your way. Would you be satisfied to measure your life's work by how much you raised the dividend? Would you regard your life as a success just because you managed to get the dividend to three dollars or four dollars or five or six or seven? Would that be enough? Is that what you want engraved on your tombstone when you die, the dividend record of the Tredway Corporation?

Shaw objects that Walling is dismissing the obvious need for profits, but Walling is brusquely dismissive of this weak rhetorical move, using it to pivot into his larger point.

He begins with a rhetorical move of his own, seeming to acknowledge the correctness of Shaw's central point. "Shaw is right when he says that we have an obligation to our stockholders. But it's a bigger obligation than raising the dividend. We have an obligation to keep this company alive." As Walling expands on the point, a third small detail, this time of staging, increasingly affirms his words; apart from close-ups, the previous sequences had all focused on the right side of the table (right side from the perspective of Avery Bullard's seat, the putative center of control) and the end where Shaw is sitting, facing the set of large stone-framed stained-glass windows behind Bullard's place at the head of the table. Now we begin to get glimpses of the windows, Bullard's windows, the largest source of diegetic light in the room, as Walling moves about. Walling turns Shaw's own concerns against him. "There's your waste, Shaw," he all but shouts, "there's your inefficiency. Stop growing and you die. Turn your back on experimentation and planning for tomorrow because they don't contribute to dividends today and you won't have a tomorrow. Because there won't be any company."

Shaw has one more bolt to shoot, and it is with this that the film reaches its moral turning point. "Avery Bullard," he says, grinning at being able to call to his aid the man so central to everyone's understanding of the company, "didn't seem to think my policies were exactly destroying this company." Walling turns away thoughtfully, admitting the truth of Shaw's claim. "No," he says, "no he didn't." Walling pauses in his words, but his motion carries him forward, such that his next line, in which his growing enlightenment at last reaches fruition, is delivered as he stands directly beneath the big windows. "And he was wrong." Nor is it solely Bullard who stands now under indictment; Walling understands that errors of such magnitude do not occur in isolation: "The way a lot of people are wrong these days. Grabbing for the quick and easy, the sure thing. That's just a lack of faith in the future. Something that's in the air today, the — the groping of a lot of men who know they've lost their faith but aren't sure of what it is or how they happened to lose it." Faith is imagination combined with certainty; without the certainty decisive action is difficult, but without the imagination all that remains is dogmatic authoritarianism. Bullard, his counterparts, and by expansion many others, not merely in business but across the scope of society, have sacrificed their imaginations — their ability to envision a more expansive future, emotionally and morally, individually and collectively — to the quotidian dullness of immediate profit.

The result, as Walling avows with increasing fervor, is potentially catastrophic, even for the ones who think themselves best able to benefit from the shift in focus. Bullard, in losing his sense of the genuine purpose behind the company he had saved, lost himself, lost sight of "why he was the man he was — if he ever really knew." This catches Julia Tredway's attention, and she speaks for the first time since the beginning of the meeting; "Do *you* know, Mr. Walling?" He does, or thinks so; pride, he claims, drove Avery Bullard, pride which became hubris. Bullard became "the man at the top of the Tower, needing no one, wanting no one, only himself. That's what it took to satisfy his pride," Walling claims. "That was his strength," he concludes. "And that was his weakness, too." Living in emotional isolation, unaware of, unconcerned with, and unable to imagine the needs of others, Bullard began to exist solely for himself, a self increasingly crabbed and corrupted by the very power he was exercising. Caswell's reference to dictatorial practices was truer to the mark than he knew; Bullard, having colossal power no longer guided by human concerns, was, albeit in a minor way, on the road to a kind of fascism, an unchecked exertion of control for the sake of control.

As so often happens, the corruption at the apex of the power pyramid worked its way downward. Some of the effects, on the assembled vice presidents, we have already seen. But Walling's position regarding such corruption goes further. Jesse Grimm asks why a man shouldn't have pride "if he's earned it." Walling, knowing from the question that Grimm is now at least genuinely listening to him, acknowledges the point but, as he had done with Shaw's concern about earnings, moves beyond it to a greater one. "All right. But why should that set him apart from the people he's working with?" Yes, there is a hierarchy of responsibility; there could hardly be otherwise in any complex organization requiring varied skills applied at different times in different ways. But hierarchy of responsibility need not, indeed must not, depend on or generate a hierarchy of worth, for if it does so it is destroying the base upon which it rests, the willing exertions of those many skills. "The force behind a great company has to be more than the pride of one man," Walling insists. "It has to be the pride of thousands. You can't make men work for money alone, you starve their souls when you try it. And you can starve a company to death the same way." Again the staging reflects the message; Jesse Grimm's question — his first involvement in the discussion — has opened up a further side of the room, and Walling (and perforce the camera) will move more and more extensively as he expresses a vision which includes more and more people. There are accordingly fewer close-ups now and more wide-shots, ones including most or all of the people around the conference table.

Walling resumes his case against a purely fiscal approach to manufacturing, now with a specific target: the KF Line of cheap furniture, Shaw's innovation. Grabbing a side table, Walling savages its shoddy manufacture.[8] Shaw's brief attempt at a defense of the need for the product line as a part of the "profit structure" of the company is brushed aside almost contemptuously. "We're not cheating anyone," Shaw insists. "Ourselves," Walling replies. As he says this, the shot is of him holding the table at an angle in the exact position of Bullard's chair, looking similarly like a tombstone, linking the two visually. Snarling, Walling rips a leg off the table, hurling both to one side. "And what do you suppose the people think of us when they buy it?" he roars. "How do you suppose the men in the factories feel when they make it? What must they think of a management that's willing to stoop to selling this kind of junk in order to add a dime a year to the dividend?"

Walling here is arguing, perhaps consciously, within a great though often ignored tradition. His words echo those, for example, of the 19th century painter, writer, and furniture designer William Morris, who argued similarly against the shoddy goods of his time. "There is a great deal of sham work in the world," Morris wrote,

> hurtful to the buyer, more hurtful to the seller, if he only knew it, most hurtful to the maker: how good a foundation it would be toward getting good Decorative Art, that is ornamental workmanship, if we craftsmen were to resolve to turn out nothing but excellent workmanship in all things, instead of having, as we too often have now, a very low average standard of work, which we often fall below.[9]

Morris and Walling both understand that cheap goods are responding to a genuine demand, though Morris sees more clearly the warped nature of that demand. Walling simply asserts that quality will triumph. "We're going to give the people what they need," he declares, "at prices they can afford to pay." Morris is less confident, though not without hope. "I know that the public in general are set on having things cheap," he argues,

> being so ignorant that they do not know when they get them nasty also; so ignorant that they neither know nor care whether they give a man his due: I know that the manufacturers (so called) are so set on carrying out competition to its utmost, competition of cheapness, not of excellence, that they meet the bargain-hunters half way, and cheerfully furnish them with nasty wares at the cheap rate they are asked for, by means of what can be called by no prettier name than fraud. England has of late been too much busied with the counting-house and not enough with the workshop: with the result that the counting-house at the present moment is rather barren of orders.[10]

Walling's interest in the aesthetic health of workers and management alike is similar; having pledged to drop the KF Line (in his first explicit statement of the "if I am elected" variety) he vows that "we'll never again ask a man to do anything that will poison his pride in himself or his work." Walling now evokes his entire vision, one comprehending all departments and all individuals, in detail. In a single shot watched by a fluidly shifting camera, he makes his way entirely around the conference table, explaining the significance of a quality, rather than profit, based approach.

> We'll have a line of low-priced furniture, a new and different line, as different from anything we're making today as a modern automobile is different from a covered wagon. That's what you want, Walt, isn't it? What you've always wanted? Merchandise that will sell because it has beauty and function and value — not because the buyers like your Scotch or think you're a good egg. The kind of stuff that you, Jesse, will be able to feel in your *guts* when you know it's coming off your production line. A product that you'll be able to budget to the nearest hundredth of a cent, Shaw, because it'll be scientifically and efficiently designed. And something you'll be proud to have your name on, Miss Tredway.

This will take widespread cooperation, and here Walling reaches his peroration. "We're not going to die, we're going to live! And it's going to take every bit of business judgment and creative energy in this company — from the mills and the factories right to the top of the Tower. And we're going to do it together. Every one of us. Right here at Tredway."

Of course the assembled board members are swept up in the excitement. Walter Dudley leaps up to nominate Walling for the presidency, in words identical to those he had used earlier in nominating Shaw but ringing with a sincerity missing in his earlier half-zombified demeanor. Jesse Grimm forcefully seconds, and Alderson moves to make it unanimous. Julia Tredway agrees, smiling; after hesitating, so does Shaw, with a curt nod of his head, echoed by Caswell's, still following Shaw's lead. "So voted," declares Erica Martin, clearly pleased at the outcome. Walling himself knows the proper acknowledgment; he crosses to Shaw and offers his hand. Shaw, looking diminished and humbled, nonetheless shows grace in defeat; "Congratulations," he says. "Thank you, Loren," replies Walling, using Shaw's first name for the first time in the film.[11]

There is something of a coda to this triumphal progression to industrial enlightenment, one which reminds us that promises are not yet accomplishments, and that there must always be some counterbalancing force to the temptation to take power for achievement. Mary Walling is waiting outside the door, her expression a study in ambivalence. Julia Tredway approaches her. "You must be very proud of him," she says. "I am," replies Mary, admitting, "I'm a little frightened too." Julia knows how she feels, because she has been in a similar situation, but understands the vital difference. "Because you don't understand him? We never do. Not completely. Not men like that."

That is, men with such an intense vision. Julia indicates the danger of being linked to someone caught up in such passion. "It will make you very lonely at times when he shuts you out of his life. But then he'll always come back to you." (Stanwyck emphasizes the "you" ever so slightly, indicating that she has still much thinking to do as she rebuilds herself after Bullard; this is not a film in which solutions are reached with implausible ease.) "And you'll know how fortunate you are to—," Julia hesitates "—to be his wife." She then asks Mary to pass on a message to Walling, a message of gratitude for saving her, Julia's, life. The passion for life and genuine interpersonal involvement can communicate itself even between people with no other obvious connections.

Walling and Alderson now exit the conference room, Alderson congratulating Mary as he passes by. Walling and Mary embrace, but before leaving, Walling makes certain to have Erica Martin call a committee meeting for Monday morning to select an executive vice-president. At the very least he will not begin his tenure as president by repeating Bullard's mistakes. As he and Mary leave, Walling thinks to ask after the results of his son's baseball game. "Who won?" he asks. "We did," Mary replies.

My interlaced descriptions of Wise's camera set-ups and stagings will already have indicated the care which went into the filming of *Executive Suite*. It is quite possible to watch the film for the first time, and perhaps repeatedly, without quite being aware of how mobile the camera is, or of the careful use of fragmented scenes as opposed to long takes, so solidly motivated are the various techniques. Consider, for example, a short scene in which George Caswell, by now aware that the released Tredway earnings report poses a serious threat to him financially, contacts Loren Shaw to begin maneuvering for the favor he needs. The camera paces back and forth with Caswell, he behind the sofa on which his wife is lounging, the camera in front of it, underscoring Caswell's entrapment, as he arranges for his call to be placed and argues with his wife. As the phone rings, indicating that his call is ready, the camera dollies in for a close-up. After some choppy conversation of which we hear only Caswell's side, he at last manages to get in his request: "It's very important that I see you." This motivates a cut to a close-up of Shaw, who wraps up the conversation. The camera then dollies out to reveal a waiting secretary. There is nothing flashy or flamboyant here, yet with the greatest economy of means Wise has indicated the salient point: power, once belonging to Caswell (he was the man who brought Shaw into the company), has shifted to Shaw. Contrast this with the final sequence involving Julia Tredway and Mary Walling, another long take. The camera dollies toward Mary from one side as Julia approaches from the other. The two women stand face-to-face, Julia ever so slightly further away from the camera, de-emphasizing Stanwyck's greater height. The dialogue unfolds without so much as a movement from the camera, as befits a conversation between two women who are, through the nature of their experiences, past and yet to come, of equal moral weight. The camera moves only when Julia does, turning to watch her leave. Emotionally, this is what the situation requests, for it is neither deeply unsettled nor completely free; Walling is secure in the presidency, yet Mary remains uncertain of the nature of her future as the president's wife.[12] Noticeable camerawork here would only call attention to itself at the expense of the underlying impact of the scene.

Wise's camera rarely dictates an audience's response; rather, he is punctilious, nowhere more than in *Executive Suite*, in allowing the viewer to explore and develop the implications, emotional and intellectual, of the material under consideration. By refusing to end with a bang (Mary's final words being at most a gentle fillip echoing the results of the greater drama), Wise encourages reflection regarding not only the statements and actions of the various characters but of their resonance beyond the scope of the film. So it is that we can reconsider at last the opening narration, the conjoined claims that, that because the executive suite "is high in the sky, you may think that those who work there are somehow above and beyond the tensions and temptations of the lower floors" and "that it isn't so." What, exactly, we may fairly ask, are the "tensions and temptations" to which we, or at least the vast majority of us who are not corporate executives and never will be, are presumed to be subject? There can be only one serious answer, at least in the context of the film: the temptation to surrender or deny love in the quest for power. This is an option open to any member of the audience at almost any time, for it takes many forms, and need not involve job status or earning capacity; it can be done in the smallest matters involving another. Power, at whatever level of intensity, is both a means to an end and an end in itself. The former is neutral; judgment awaits the exercise of the power, the goal toward which it is directed. The latter is inherently corrupting, for the exercise of power exists only in relation to some thing or situation, and power sought solely in itself inevitably urges its holder to use it to acquire yet more, and thus sooner or later to treat others as means to ends. In this sense, on whatever scale, the acquisition of power means the denial of love and the isolation of the person, for it is only through love that we connect most intimately with others.

Love more than implies, it positively requires, a balance of concern and involvement between two individuals; as the psychologist Erich Fromm wisely describes it in his famous book *The Art of Loving*, published only two years after the release of *Executive Suite*, "Mature love is union under the condition of preserving one's integrity, one's individuality."[13] Love is inherently individualistic, for it is always between consciousnesses, however it may be expressed, and can never be subsumed into group behavior. But love is not simply mutual passion; it must be grounded in an entire structure of personality and the choices which stem therefrom. Again Fromm: "Love is not primarily a relationship to a specific person; it is an attitude, an orientation of character which determines the relatedness of a person to the world as a whole, not toward one 'object' of love."[14] There are many forms of love — erotic, familial, parental, social, and so on —, and we see at least some suggestion of each in Walling's character, although the focus is on his relationship with Mary, for it is through the balance of desires and interests in our closest connections that we most clearly indicate who and what we are. This balance does not require absolute equality of ability or expression or knowledge (difficult to attain even at best), but rather that each person in the loving relationship share of themselves as fully as possible and be fully open to the sharing of the other. Love is not something which happens; it is an ongoing choice. Hence the importance, and nature, of the depiction of the family life of Mary and McDonald Walling. They are not perfect beings who have attained a state of wedded bliss; they are individuals who, having committed to love and transmuted that commitment to one between each other, must therefore constantly adjust to each other's flaws and errors and uncertainties. This they do, and we see them do so. Mary is not simply an adjunct to McDonald's life, the way Caswell's wife is; she is a full partner, as we see when he is called to the research facility while helping his son practice his pitches for the upcoming game. No sooner has he left when Mary takes over, urging her son to "never mind Mom, you just burn 'em in."

So the opening narration points us toward the idea that, despite appearances, the rich and powerful do not automatically attain love (even though they may easily purchase sex), and indeed may have lost it in the service of their own wealth and power, and lost thereby a vital component of their own humanity. Still more follows. There is a trade-off as one climbs the ladder of authority; not only do the temptations grow greater, so does the opportunity for self-destruction. Among the problems of power is its tendency to undercut the purposes for which it is ostensibly being exercised. Politicians confront this always, too often unsuccessfully; having been elected on one set of promises, they grow afraid that carrying out those promises may result in their later defeat, so they cling to office by the simple expedient of doing little or nothing. The holding of power becomes its own justification, and the application of that power increasingly serves the purpose of acquiring more, as much and as quickly as possible. This attitude and the concomitant processes apply throughout the system of power relations, hastening individuals into a kind of lockstep in which their own genuine needs and desires become ever less relevant. These relations further take form in and from the means through which they are executed, through the relations of individuals to the economic and industrial processes which begin by serving, and end by controlling, their lives. In modern mechanized society, the machinery which propels the economy, and which is meant to make life easier, to leave more time for the more important aspects of life, takes its own toll on the lives around it. Love takes time to nurture and develop; it moves at its own pace, not a mechanical one. Yet, as Fromm comments, "Our whole industrial system fosters exactly the opposite: quickness." Too often, we are adjusting our lives to our tools rather than using those tools at the pace a balanced life demands.

> All our machines are designed for quickness: the car and the airplane bring us quickly to our destination — and the quicker the better. The machine which can produce the same quantity in half the time is twice as good as the older and slower one. Of course, there are important economic reasons for this. But, as in so many other aspects, human values have become determined by economic values. What is good for machines must be good for man — so goes the logic. Modern man thinks he loses something — time — when he does not do things quickly; yet he does not know what to do with the time he gains — except kill it.[15]

Love is flexible in its demands on time and energy, for the lover recognizes that the loved one(s) will have ebbs and flows of mood, need, and capability. Machinery, and any system grounded thereupon, will be less flexible, for machines, and too often their minders, know naught of any need but their own.

The question which follows next has to do with our relation, as viewers, to the particular temptations found, figuratively speaking, in the Tower. After all, as I have already noted, few of us will ever hold positions of even remotely comparable authority and power. Yet, again within the context of the film, all is not as it seems as regards the viewer's relation to the on-screen events. While it is certainly true that we cannot influence those, it is much truer that we can influence quite similar ones in reality, a reality which parallels that of the film. Walling inadvertently provides a clue while he is brooding over the succession but before he has decided to try for the presidency himself. "It's going to be Jesse Grimm," he tells Mary, who innocently asks, "Don't the stockholders have anything to say?" Walling's response is uncharacteristically condescending in tone, and probably not entirely accurate factually; "The stockholders had their say when they elected the board." We know that at least one board member (Caswell) was brought on by Bullard, and that the Tredway Corporation itself holds 50,000 shares itself (the fictional company mirroring a standard practice in reality); while the exact number of outstanding shares is unknown, the fact that Julia Tredway, with 39,500 shares, is a "major stockholder" implies that it is not vast, and therefore that Bullard and the company have considerable influence, if not control, over elections to the board. Nonetheless, Walling's point attaches to a far more serious question, one relevant, directly or indirectly, to a considerable portion of the audience. Exactly how much knowledge of the qualifications and aspirations of each board member does any given stockholder have? The answer is, probably, very little; they may not even know the names of the board members. How much, then, can any given stockholder be said to have a voice in the affairs of the board, and therefore of the company? How much control over this organization, one which in turn exercises tremendous control over the fortunes of the town wherein its plant is located, do the stockholders really have? Would they approve of Shaw's penny-pinching, and the concomitant cost in jobs and social stability? "You don't know how it was in Millburgh when Tredway shut down" during the Depression, one worker reminds Walling when expressing alarm about the impact of Bullard's death on the company. This is true — and it may well be asked how much the typical board member, whether of Tredway of any other corporation, knows about such impacts.

Here the final significance of the subjective camera in the opening section of the film becomes clear. It is not merely used to indicate that Bullard is an enigma, though this is certainly part of the story. It is also a means of suggesting to the audience its own absence from the control of the corporations which have such control over their own lives. The subjective camera is rarely used precisely because in film, as opposed to narrative literature, the first-person viewpoint alienates the viewer. "The driving tension of the novel is the relationship between the materials of the story [...] and the narration of it in language," as film theorist James Monaco has noted, "between the tale and the teller, in other words." Film is less able to play with such potential ambiguities. "The driving tension of a film [...] is between the materials of the story and the objective nature of the image."[16] We identify with on-screen characters because we see them act and imaginatively infer their thoughts; where we cannot see them we find it much harder to achieve such identification, ironically, because in seeing everything from their viewpoint we see too little; having no external clues our imaginations have nothing upon which to build as regards motivations. Seeing from Bullard's viewpoint stresses not his presence but ours, our involvement in something which we do not understand because it is not our thoughts and emotions which motivate the actions of which we see the consequences. The subjective camera as used here is a superlative metaphor for the lack of control we have over so much of what surrounds our jobs and our lives.

This realization may lead to a further and deeper dissatisfaction with the events of the film. Walling's victory may ring hollow, both because it strikes the viewer as improbable (fine words rarely sway individuals with their noses pressed to the economic grindstone) and as historically dated (globalization, in which products are increasingly made by the lowest paid workers possible — say prisoners in a Chinese labor camp — has erased all possibility of fine work done by caring individuals sold at prices affordable to those who are not themselves wealthy). There is truth in this charge, but it is neither a universal truth nor a necessary one. The structure of material manufacture and distribution is a human creation as much as any of the companies within it, and therefore it is as subject to control and re-invention as any other aspect of human society. The very existence of the film *Executive Suite*, a complex creation requiring the participation of many individuals, indicates, on a small scale, the scope and nature of the possibility of change. Likewise does the plot point outward to much larger projects to assuage our dissatisfaction. Just as a corporation may, and should, be run for the benefit of all within its ambit, the equivalent of the board of directors of society must be controlled and reshaped, such that the actions they approve and take more accurately reflect the wishes of the stockholders, in this case the whole of human society. As Wise suggested through *The Day the Earth Stood Still*, if the problem is global so too must be the solution. If we are not to destroy ourselves, or to be destroyed, we must take control of the forces militating against us. It is a slow process, and a long one, with many false starts and dead ends (consider Walling's repeated attempts to achieve a new veneering process, spotted throughout *Executive Suite*), and the possibility of success exists only to the degree that we pursue the project.

From loss of control comes the desire to regain it. Perhaps we can do so, at least partially, through the actions of others. Perhaps we can count on the appearance of a McDonald Walling, passionate yet balanced, to make the choices we wish to see made. But the assumption that those above us, with power over us whether figuratively or socio-economically, will always, or often, or even occasionally, consider our needs is a risky one. *Executive Suite*, as the narrator states, is here to say that it isn't so.

Chapter Five

Colonizing Death:
The Sand Pebbles (1966)

War is a racket. It always has been. (Major General Smedley D. Butler, USMC, ret.)[1]

1.

On the face of it, *The Sand Pebbles* is a conventional war movie, with the usual mix of disparate personalities coming together in the melting pot of combat. Jake Holman, the central character, is the misfit outsider who must earn his way in, coming to peace with himself while understanding and accepting his place within the system, doing so in part thanks to the civilizing effect of a woman. Heroism abounds, and personal sacrifice, all accompanied with a good deal of stirring rhetoric.

There is truth in this description, but not the whole truth. Certainly the conventional *form* is present, but the *content* is rather different, and the tension generated thereby is central to the film. *The Sand Pebbles* is a rarity; it is not so much an antiwar film as an assessment of the social and political structures which not only do, but *must*, produce wars. The pointlessness of military adventurism is canvassed in depth, yet what is ultimately condemned is not the actions of the sailors and soldiers, on whatever side, but rather the corruptions inherent in nationalism and political division. Thus neither the sailors aboard the *San Pablo* nor their Chinese opponents are presented, nor should they be seen, as villains, but rather as unwitting victims of a political structure which is— and not metaphorically — at war with their natural desires for true freedom and individualism. This is the tragedy at the heart of *The Sand Pebbles*: the individuals do what they are supposed to do, in the way they are supposed to do it, but the result is not at all what it is supposed to be. Using a historical drama about American involvement in China during the 1920s, Wise captures the contradictions which drive, and which will eventually destroy, any system which professionalizes power hierarchies—which is to say any system of divisive international politics, and therefore the system of political and economic relations under which we live today. *The Sand Pebbles* is thus in one way Wise's most Hobbesian film — almost literally depicting a war of all against all — and in another a forceful critique of the Hobbesian assumptions in which much of modern military action is grounded, a critique also offering a glimpse of a way forward.

Wise was no supporter of American involvement in Vietnam, and he welcomed the opportunity to challenge it cinematically. As a warning about American involvement in Asian politics, *The Sand Pebbles* was made at an apposite historical moment; preproduction started in 1964, not long after the Tonkin Gulf Resolution gave U.S. President Lyndon Johnson the authority to take "all necessary measures" against "further aggression" in Vietnam.[2] By the time the eight-month filming schedule began in October of 1965, military escalation was accelerating, and U.S. troops were involved in extensive combat operations. As filming wrapped up, Representative Melvin Laird famously commented on the growing "credibility gap" between government claims and public beliefs. When the movie was released in December of 1966, the war was fully underway, and the first major domestic protests had taken place. Yet the reaction was muted; the film received generally positive but rarely enthusiastic reviews, and did only moderate business at the box office. Perhaps it was too far ahead of its time; the quagmire of the Vietnam War remained to be fully explored, and the bleak conclusion did not fit well with the current overall optimism of much of the public.

Decades later, the immediate relevance of the film to contemporary politics remains undimmed; indeed, in many ways the situation depicted in *The Sand Pebbles* is more pertinent to the early 21st century catastrophe in Iraq than it was to the situation in Vietnam in 1966. In each of the three cases (a fictional story and two real wars), arrogant and erroneous assumptions combined with illicit assertions of power to produce disaster, destruction, and death. But specific historical confluences are not the focus here. Rather, the crippling effect of exploitation, on exploiters and the exploited alike, is the true subject of *The Sand Pebbles*. A system based on violence will continue to produce further violence, regardless of the intentions of the professionals on whose actions the system appears to rest. Unless and until the hierarchical nationalism which governs modern political relations is foundationally changed, there can be only a further descent into the maelstrom of war and exploitation. It is this descent — and, tentatively, the hope of change — which

Wise and screenwriter Robert Anderson explore in a variety of ways and through numerous characters, and which gives, and will continue to give, the film its compelling force.

There are six main characters in *The Sand Pebbles*. Five of them will be dead by the end of the film, along with several subsidiary figures and a considerable number of extras. This proliferation of characters, and the several interlocking stories involving them, suggests another reason for the film's relative obscurity: it is difficult for an audience member to be sure of where their sympathies are meant to lie. Protagonist Jake Holman is complex enough to make identification difficult, and in any case he dies at the end. Although there are two serious heterosexual love relationships (in Hollywood films usually a clue regarding presumed identification), one ends with both partners dead and the other ends with Holman dead. The heroic Captain Collins dies pointlessly. The semi-comic bilge coolie Po-Han dies pointlessly. The missionary Jameson, who appears to have the clearest grasp of the political situation, dies pointlessly. Shirley Eckert, the teacher who offers the film's few moments of hope, is forced to flee, her ultimate escape uncertain.

But to describe the putative problem is in fact to indicate the depth of the critique of competitive nationalism offered in *The Sand Pebbles*. This is not a film in which stouthearted men and gracious women overcome external forces to win a well-deserved triumph (and each other). Rather, it is an indictment of power relations, not merely in China or Vietnam (or, albeit anachronistically, Iraq or Afghanistan), but wherever nationalism or tribalism are found. Hence the atypical nature of this ostensible war film (a war film in which the only battle comes well over two hours into the action, it may be noted). Heroism is not enough. Duty is not enough. But neither is love enough, nor separatism, nor apolitical indifference. The system of competitive international interests has so tainted the situation that *no* assertion of power can be fully successful, and most will fail altogether. Engine room "boss coolie" Chien is crushed by the machinery over which he attempts to assert power.[3] Jameson, a missionary who, for all his fine words about respecting Chinese law and nationhood, is attempting to convert the Chinese to Christianity, asserts his independence of nationalism only to be killed by people for whom the assertion has no meaning. *San Pablo* crew member Frenchy Burgoyne and his Asian romantic partner Maily attempt, both separately and together, to withdraw from the system only to discover that this is impossible; individual actions cannot avail against a structure which cannot allow genuine individualism lest its authority crumble. Po-Han, who unwittingly becomes an accomplice (or tool) of the imperialists, is tortured by the Communists and shot, as a mercy-killing, by Holman. The brilliant student Cho-jen joins the Nationalists and is part of the force attempting to stop the *San*

Pablo at a river boom, where he and many of his cohorts, as well as many of the Sand Pebbles, are killed.[4] And though the *San Pablo* achieves its aim, it has been so weakened that it has not the strength to break through again should the boom be replaced.

One can thus join *The Sand Pebbles* at a number of junctures, but the destination remains the same regardless of its point of origin (with one vital, though only partial, exception, with which I will conclude). This being a film, not a philosophical treatise, not all of the aspects of power relations are equally presented; nor shall I examine each one in equal depth. While the film unfolds in a linear fashion, zig-zagging among each of the several stories, allowing each to resonate with the others, I shall treat them thematically, trading a loss of some complexity for a degree of analytic clarity.

2.

The action of *The Sand Pebbles*, actual and implied, emotional and physical, begins with the opening credits.[5] Jerry Goldsmith's music immediately takes a key place in the proceedings as an eerie and gloomy motif, redolent of sorrow and menace, replaces the standard Fox fanfare. Under the credits we see the gunboat U.S.S. *San Pablo* (the "Sand Pebble" which gives the crew, and the film, a name), behind which, in silhouette, is an enormous junk. Toward the end of the credits the camera begins to move slowly toward the two ships. The *San Pablo* drops below the line of vision and the camera eventually comes to rest on the sails of the junk. These act both as a literal screen, blocking all vision, and a metaphoric one; the viewer is warned both that the future is a blank screen and that whatever happens to the characters will be driven by no force within their control but rather by the political equivalent of the wind. Until the fundamental situation (the direction of the wind, to maintain the metaphor) changes, then, no permanent social or political change can be foreseen or even expected. This conflict will play out for the rest of the film.

The emotional tone having been set by the credits, the character of the film is indicated in the opening intertitles. They are choppy: "China 1926..." appears first, beneath which appear the rest:

> Ravaged from within by corrupt warlords ... oppressed from without by the great world powers who had beaten China to her knees a century before ... China ... a country of factions trying to unite to become a nation ... through revolution....

The punctuation reveals the situation as much as the words; there is, at least as yet, no coherent vision comprehending the situation. The narrative structure of the film will reflect these tensions.

The tone and character of the film having been suggested by music and written words, what might be called its governing idea is given in the first spoken words. Jake Holman (Steve McQueen), having landed in Shanghai, approaches an MP standing guard over entry to the city. "You got orders?" the MP queries. "Yeah," Holman grunts, and he hands over his paperwork. "Check in on the double, stay off the streets. There's no liberty," the MP tells Holman. The truth of those final three words will be amply demonstrated throughout the rest of the film.

Jake Holman is the flawed protagonist; his name ("whole man") is ironic, as it quickly becomes clear that he is anything but. He is ignorant of, and indifferent to, the political situation in which he finds himself ("I run the engine. All this other [by which he means political matters] is just look-see pidgin ... to make a show, something for the officers. I don't fool with it"). He is casually racist (he refers to the Chinese as "slopeheads"). He is prone to belligerence and insubordination (his first action, immediately after being told "there's no liberty," is to patronize a brothel). He is, as he says, an engineer, evidently with wide experience (seven posts in nine years), and has requested a transfer to the *San Pablo* in the hopes of avoiding engine room interference from officers and fellow sailors ("too many guys trying to tell you how to run it," he declares); his life is limited to making machinery function as smoothly as possible. He is, in short, a professional with little interest in, or experience of, the human world outside his mechanical work (the first time he provides his whole name is when he first sees the engine of the *San Pablo*; a tender expression suffuses his face, and he introduces himself: "Hello, engine. I'm Jake Holman"). Thus it is that the driving force, literally and symbolically, of the film's structure is introduced.

3.

Holman is the center of the film, and all five of the other main characters are in some manner connected to, and their fates influenced by, him. It is no accident that he is an engineer, for it is the engine of the *San Pablo* which is the central metaphor of the film as well as the primary force which allows the plot to unfold. Holman is, of course, unaware of his central role; indeed, none of the characters fully comprehend their place in the story or the ways in which their lives have been shaped by the political context in which they are playing out.

Chronologically the first theme, which we might call rectitude, or perhaps self-righteousness, is sounded even before Holman reaches the *San Pablo*. On the trip upriver to the *San Pablo*, Holman meets Jameson (Larry Gates), a missionary heading to the mission at China Light, and Shirley Eckert (of whom more later). Jameson is the embodiment of "enlightened" Western opinion; "China will be unable to put her own house in order until she is free of your enslaving and unequal treaties," he admonishes a particularly arrogant Englishman. "Foreigners collecting her taxes, placed in charge of her customs, postal system, foreigners enjoying immunity from her laws." But Jameson, in his own way, is almost as detached as Holman; he may sympathize with the Chinese, but he has only limited understanding of the situation. He expresses disdain for the presence of foreign gunboats, but when reminded by the Englishman that "you missionaries are only tolerated here because we *have* the gunboats," his response — "I dare trust God rather than guns." — implicitly acknowledges that he has no response, as does his shamefaced admission that he has fled to their protection twice, though he vows never to do so again.

Jameson is a man of some insight, though, and he later makes a key comment on Holman, and by extension the crew of the *San Pablo*. "I can't help feeling a sort of sadness about his life," Shirley comments as she watches Holman leaving for his posting. "Yes," says Jameson, "it would be sad if he wanted something else. They don't. They reduce life to a very simple point, or no point at all. As long as they obey orders the Navy takes care of them. It's a way of life that appeals to a certain kind of man." This will play out later in the film in unexpected ways.

Jameson is consistent in his self-righteousness, and not entirely wrong to be so, though this leads directly to his own death. Opium is found growing on mission property, and Jameson, held responsible as mission head, agrees to face a Chinese court, which sentences him to die. He is not imprisoned, but rather placed under the supervision of Cho-jen, a student leader of the Nationalist militia, while he appeals the verdict. He returns to China Light, from which, following a major anti–Western uprising, Captain Collins determines to rescue him at the film's climax. Collins arrives only to find Jameson unwilling to be rescued, and unsympathetic to his ostensible countrymen. "Our militia of students went to fight you at the boom," he says; "I was hoping to see them come back victorious instead of you." Even Jameson is tainted by the need for force, a fact of which he seems utterly unaware. For the moment he is strong in his refusal to accept rescue by compulsion. "You alone endanger us," he warns Collins; "I must ask you to leave, now." To Collins's insistence that his duty is to protect them, Jameson replies by announcing that he and Shirley have declared themselves "stateless persons," neither owing allegiance to, nor demanding protection from, any government, a claim Collins dismisses as "romantic nonsense." Jameson and Collins argue, provoking a bitter outburst from Collins: "This afternoon my ship fought its way through down there at the boom. People were killed on both sides. You are not going to make that a futile and meaningless battle." Jameson's response is in line with his overall position: "We will not serve to give meaning to your heroics. Our lives have their own meaning." Changing tactics, Collins warns Shirley Eckert that the troops who are coming will "strip and rape" her; "you don't know them," she replies with a subdued intensity. Jameson counters politically: "What have you ever cared for the Chinese women raped and butchered by the warlord troops you favor with your unequal treaties?" Collins, having no response, and probably not comprehending the point, resorts to commanding them to get ready to leave.

But events are already ahead of both Jameson and Collins; killed at the boom was Jameson's legal guardian and political protector Cho-jen (of whom more below). Troops are already on their way to arrest, or perhaps simply to kill, the remaining missionaries, now inextricably associated with the gunboat. "Damn your flag," Jameson cries out as he sees all for which he has worked collapsing. "Damn all flags. It's too late in the world for flags." A few moments later, as he attempts to show the soldiers the paper declaring himself a stateless person, he is shot down.

Jameson is right, but so is Collins, because each is still operating within the self-contradictory competitive national political structure, and therefore each can represent a conflicting, yet wholly legitimate, aspect of that structure. Jameson has seen its destructive nature, but fails to recognize that he cannot rely upon someone within it for security without becoming tainted thereby. The guarantee is contingent upon the presence of a particular individual, but individuals within a system which gives precedence to nations are themselves essentially contingent, wielding their power only so long as it serves the portion of the system which requires that they do so. Collins is himself an example of this, as his desperate combination of plea and command to Jameson and Shirley — "You are not going to make that a futile and meaningless battle" — suggests. In one of the film's many ironies, Collins comes to embody Jameson's assessment of the military mind, but in so doing he is acting up to what he, Collins, sees as a genuine higher duty. "As long as they obey orders the Navy takes care of them," Jameson had said of a certain type of man; it is Jameson's refusal to obey orders, his refusal to allow the Navy to take care of him, that counters Collins's entire justification for his actions and even his career. Yet it is also Jameson's refusal to accept rescue that leads to his own meaningless death; having denied the authority of the flag-waving gunboats by appealing to another expression of nationalism, he finds that mere words of withdrawal, however well meant, are not enough. It is not simply that the road to hell is paved with good intentions, but that on the road to hell good intentions are irrelevant.

4.

Early in the film the arrogant Englishman, Outscout by name (Ben Wright), confronts Jameson with the hatred many Chinese feel for the occupying foreigners. "I dare love them in return," Jameson replies, sounding another major theme of the film. Apart from some political slogans, the nature of his love is left unclear; Jameson is too dogmatic a person, however justified in at least some of his particular claims, to properly showcase love here. This is left to a subplot involving *San Pablo* crew member Frenchy Burgoyne (Richard Attenborough) and Maily (Marayat Andriane), an Asian woman affiliated with Mama Chunk's, a bordello popular with the sailors.

Frenchy is gentler than most of the crew, Holman and Collins included.[6] He is easygoing and rather complacent; "We got it good here," he tells Holman shortly before advising him to "relax." It is thus no surprise that he should attract Maily, whom we meet under less than happy circumstances. The sailors are patronizing Mama Chunk's. A loutish machinist's mate named Stawski (Simon Oakland) is headed up the stairs with two women when he sees Maily on the landing. A stationary crane shot from Maily's POV shows Mama Chunk pointing her out to Frenchy who, like everyone else, is obviously smitten. The camera cuts to her, smiling hesitantly, then to Stawski. As she walks down, Stawski, a woman on either arm, backs down in front of her. A further cut places the retreating camera behind him, the effect being to suggest a pulling away; Maily is untouchable, morally if not physically.[7] Not that Stawski doesn't make the attempt; he paws at her importuningly, his expression and behavior growing ever more coarse and bestial.

As the scene unfolds, Frenchy and Maily make frequent eye contact, and Frenchy grows steadily angrier at Stawski, eventually making several unsuccessful attempts to intervene, each being stopped by a Shore Patrol officer, whose comments are edifying. The first time he reminds Frenchy that "this little girl's got duties, just like sailors"; the second time he warns him that "you know better than to mess around with another man's girl—till he's through with her."[8] But Stawski is foiled by money, not compassion; on the verge of forcibly obtaining her services, he discovers that she is a virgin, with the price for sex with her set at $200 by Victor Shu, a local gangster to whom she owes the money, which is far beyond a sailor's ability to pay. At this point Mama Chunk intervenes, calming the situation by pulling Maily away and introducing her to Frenchy. Maily is struck by his gentleness, and he by her beauty and situation. She tells him she would be "free" if she had the two hundred dollars. "I wish I had two hundred," he tells her, but not for sex; "I mean, just to give you." In fact he has neither money nor time, and Maily is soon swept up by another sailor.

The sequel is predictable; Frenchy falls in love with Maily. A fight (which I will examine in greater detail later) is arranged between Stawski and Po-Han, a bilge coolie, with the winnings to pay Victor Shu's fee. Maily reveals a fatalistic streak; if Stawski wins, she tells Frenchy, "It will only mean that I'm being punished." He presses, and she admits that she was a foundling brought up by American missionaries from whom she stole two hundred dollars. "Why did you steal it?" Frenchy asks; "To get away," Maily replies. "They wanted me to be a missionary too." Here is the dark side of Jameson's self-righteous appeal to god; religious certainty follows national backgrounds, and with that certainty comes the drive to convert, with all its attendant cultural subversions. Note that it is not the cultural values associated with a particular religious outlook which are being preached, but the necessity of avowing that specific religion. It is not enough to believe that certain behaviors are better or more ethical than others, or even to act upon those beliefs; one must accept the framework imposed around those beliefs. This is, of course, simply another form of imperialism.

To Frenchy's glee, Stawski fails to win the fight, but the crew is summoned back to the ship as a result of a battle between the English and the Chinese elsewhere which is stirring up trouble in Changsha, where the *San Pablo* is anchored, and Frenchy is separated from Maily for some time. In the interim he decides to rent a room where she can be secure when he is able to pay off Shu. When the *San Pablo* returns to Changsha, he and Holman meet at Mama Chunk's to pay off Shu. The attempt brings the problem of money to the fore.

Several kinds of power manifest themselves in *The Sand Pebbles*. There is the power of the ship's engine. There is pure corporeal power, evinced in several fights. There is power of will, evinced in stand-offs between various characters. And there is the power of money. It is unlike the other powers in that the physical objects associated with the word (coinage, bills, or whatever medium is in use at a given time) have only conventional power. Whereas the engine will move the ship, or the muscles will move the fists, regardless of the beliefs or attitudes of those operating them, money functions only as a medium of exchange within a particular society. Paradoxically, it is this which gives it its power. An engine is useful only if one wants to move, fists are useful mainly if one wants to fight, even will is useful only in relation to a particular goal; money, on the other hand, shifts its usefulness as its social setting shifts, and thus its desirability has no specific nature. Money requires belief in order to have meaning at all; it is, on its own, quite literally meaningless. Those who have money are thus already being impelled toward supporting the social system whence that money derives its meaning. Money is, therefore, a powerful incentive to conservatism, to accepting the status quo.

And the status quo of *The Sand Pebbles* (and of the world in which it was made and is being seen) includes the subordination of individuals to the quest for ever more money, money being a prime element of social power.

Nowhere is the potency of money more visible than in the auction of Maily. Holman approaches Victor Shu with the two hundred dollars, and Shu approaches the men with whom she is sitting. "Two hundred and ten," offers one of them. Frenchy matches, and the man raises his offer to two-twenty. "Auction! Auction!" shouts a third man, an idea echoed by the crowd and accepted by Shu. Maily is hoisted onto a table and the third man, an anonymous dirty-looking civilian, begins acting as auctioneer. His words indicate the nature of the exchange: "Now just look at this merchandise," he declaims, gesturing toward the agonized and humiliated Maily. "Now what am I bid for this clean delicious piece of girl-flesh?" (Why is she clean? Because she has remained unsullied by such as him, a fact of which he is, of course, unaware.) He eggs on the ugly crowd, though in fact only Frenchy and the other man are bidding.[9] He offers "Brand fresh new goods untouched by human hands" as he caresses Maily's arms (throughout the scene there are repeated close-ups of Maily, emphasizing her isolation). As the amounts rise, the auctioneer raises the stakes; "Who'll say three hundred and we see it all?" Frenchy, now in the appalling situation of having to bid for what he does not want, takes money proffered by Holman and ups his offer, only to hear a third stranger demand that the auctioneer's offer be taken literally. "Strip her!" he shouts, and the crowd, men and women alike (the women here all already being compromised by being whores and therefore literally subject to the money system) takes it up as a chant. "Strip her! Strip her! Strip her!" As the civilian prepares to do so, Holman has had enough, and he assaults the auctioneer, precipitating a general donnybrook. Holman's action temporarily breaks down the social structure in which money has the dominant meaning, and he and Frenchy are able to rescue Maily.

Maily is rushed to the room Frenchy has found for her, and he stammeringly expresses both his concern for her and his nascent understanding of the true situation. "I sure as hell apologize. I — I don't know what to say about those guys." It seems an odd thing for him to say, as he neither knew nor encouraged the men in the brothel, until we realize what he is surely awakening to: that the *San Pablo*, in protecting so-called American interests in China, is helping to make possible exactly this sort of behavior. Maily is one of the Chinese women to whose fate the foreigners are largely indifferent, save that now she is, to Frenchy, a person. Maily herself does not at first comprehend the change in her situation; "I'll do what you want. You bought me," she says to Frenchy. No, he tells her; money may have changed hands, but I have not bought you. He wants a genuine relationship, one based on mutuality rather than power. He wants, in fact and in contravention of the laws forbidding sailors to marry Chinese women, to marry her.[10]

The two pledge themselves to each other in a chapel (no one will actually perform a ceremony), with Holman and Shirley Eckert as witnesses. But the relationship is doomed. Frenchy jumps ship, swimming ashore in the middle of winter to be with her, only to contract pneumonia and die. Holman discovers Maily huddled beside the body and, unaware of her aversion to missionaries, attempts to convince her to join him at China Light. Corpse snatchers attempt to plunder Frenchy's body, and while they are beating up Holman, Maily, pregnant by Frenchy, flees. Later we are told that she is dead, presumably killed by Chinese soldiers, but no evidence of this is ever shown; her fate remains a mystery.

The failure of love is different from that of righteous political rectitude, though it shares a basis therewith. Both cases take the form of an attempted withdrawal from an all-encompassing system. But successful separatism would in itself be proof that the system from which one has withdrawn is itself otiose, and thus cannot be allowed, save under rigorously controlled circumstances. Barriers, legal and physical, must be thrown up to make separatism as difficult as possible, so that its failure can then be used as proof of the necessity of the encompassing system. In the political instance, separatism will be perceived as a direct threat to the operation of the system being denied, and thus it may be challenged equally directly (and, it must be admitted, sometimes with genuine reason; the withdrawal of the slave states from the United States, for example, was in direct support of a system far worse than that whence the withdrawal occurred). Jameson attempts to deny nationality, and is shot by representatives of a nation being reborn. In the personal instance, the perceived threat is harder to justify, and the response must therefore be less direct; it consists in a removal of vital protections rather than a direct assault. Thus the political system simply denies validity to disapproved love, and thereby ensures the likely failure of that love, for love, like any human activity, rests upon the fulfillment of basic needs. Maily and Frenchy attempt to ignore the social strictures against their love (so different from the officially sanctioned sexual encounters between the sailors and the whores, yclept "pigs" by the men — even Frenchy's realization of his true feelings for Maily is expressed to Holman in the same manner: "I don't know what I've been doing. Years with them dumb pigs.") and discover that not one of the traditional supports given to married couples exists for them.[11] Love fails because love itself is a social construction, and there is no room for expressions of love which simultaneously confute the necessity of the social structure within which they take place.

5.

The failures of rectitude and love are failures of withdrawal, and as such are not typical of personal entanglement with a social system, whatever its nature. Far more common are attempts to work within the system, to use individual effort as a lever by which to attain some form of acceptable success. This requires a corresponding degree of individual subordination to the system, and if the system is inherently contradictory then one will, as we have seen again and again, inevitably contain within oneself similar contradictory elements. One's attempt to advance within the system ultimately ends in one's self-willed self-contradiction. This we see in the tale of Po-Han, who may be taken to represent ambition.

We learn early on that the reason the *San Pablo* can run at all is largely due to the presence of a sizeable contingent of coolie labor, Chinese men not officially aboard but by now indispensable to the lives of the crew. The coolies are organized by their place on the ship, below or above deck, each with a boss, and all under the supervision of Lop-Eye Shing ("He's kind of captain of the coolies like Collins is with the crew"), who handles the "squeeze," the money paid under the table to keep the system functioning. The system can function only on the backs of those it ostensibly controls, and the system must do so surreptitiously.

Chien, the engine room "boss coolie," is crushed by the machinery when a gear slips. Holman, ordered by Collins to train a new coolie, selects Po-Han (Mako) almost at random, only to discover that he, Po-Han, has a strong desire to learn and a much quicker mind than Holman had anticipated. Holman teaches Po-Han, and comes in the process to think of him as something more than just a "slopehead." This leads to a conflict with other members of the crew, in particular the bellicose Stawski; he attacks Po-Han for stepping out of place, only himself to be beaten nearly senseless by Holman.[12] To save face, Stawski spreads the story that Po-Han attacked him. The crew accepts this, and they demand that Lop-Eye dismiss Po-Han. Holman approaches Collins and gets him to agree that, if the crew will retract their demand that Po-Han leave, Po-Han can stay. Leaving Collins, Holman encounters Lop-Eye; "Looks like you ain't running this ship after all, Lop-Eye," he says as he passes. An immediate cut to a high-angle shot of Collins and his executive officer Ensign Bordelles allows us to hear a brief colloquy of great significance. "Lop-Eye's the one who fired Po-Han; he'll lose face if Holman makes the crew change their mind," comments Bordelles. Collins responds pragmatically: "Unlikely as that is, it might serve a purpose. Lop-Eye has a tendency to forget his place from time to time."

Professional hierarchies are inevitable and necessary; after all, we would not want even the world's best pianist supervising our brain surgery. But when created within a competitive system which assigns individual worth, and therefore individual reward, in accord with the individual's place within the hierarchy, the hierarchy itself becomes reified; pride of position overrides pride in actual achievement to demand acknowledgment simply for existing. With self-worth defined by one's place within the hierarchy, one is constantly pressed to extend hierarchization throughout one's life and interactions. The system becomes self-perpetuating, yet another mechanism by which individuals are controlled and ordered. Thus aboard the *San Pablo* we have multiple levels of power: the officers command the men, who command the coolies, who are also commanded by their respective boss coolies. In each case the imbalance of power leads to a tendency to see those of lesser power as also being of lesser worth. Genuine cooperation, as opposed to a false camaraderie grounded on shared prejudices, is all but precluded. In such a system a victory for one requires a defeat for another.[13]

Within the system, therefore, power struggles are inevitable, a fact of which Holman now takes advantage. He engineers a wager: Po-Han will fight Stawski, and if Po-Han wins he stays aboard as the new engine room boss coolie. Stawski, who expects to win, is not simply fighting for the pleasure of beating up a Chinese man. Holman has wagered a great deal of money on Po-Han's success, and Stawski wants that money to purchase the virginal Maily, as seen above.

There's a great deal packed into this situation and its outcome. For one, notice that Po-Han is never consulted as Holman arranges the fight; his acquiescence is taken for granted. Thus even when Po-Han's worth as a human being is ostensibly at issue, the manner of establishing that worth is externally imposed. For another, he is largely unskilled in fisticuffs, and ought to be an easy mark even for the overweight Stawski; that he is not, and that he ultimately defeats Stawski, is in large part due to encouragement from Holman, who stands on the sidelines shouting "Hammer! Hammer!"—suggesting that Po-Han is being used as something of a tool by Holman, who dislikes Stawski.[14]

The fight is a pivotal moment in the film, and it bears a correspondingly significant weight ideologically. In one sense it is simply about the naked exercise of power (almost literally, as both Stawski and Po-Han are stripped down to their shorts). Stawski, here the emblem of white imperialism, is bloated and overconfident, yet understands the weapons at hand (boxing gloves) far better than his weaker opponent. Po-Han, the avatar of Chinese oppression, is less confident and still requires external motivation, but is beginning to assert his own right to participate in the operations of his own society (in this case, the crew of the *San Pablo*, of which he is a *de facto*, if not *de jure*, member). But the assertion itself rests upon violence, and requires, as noted, that Po-Han himself becomes an extension of the machinery (Holman encourages him by telling him that Stawski is running out of steam, another reference to Po-Han's training with the ship's machinery). At the same time the fight is about mediated relations, as the money factor comes prominently into play. Not only is Holman's gamble relevant here, but we see also Chinese wagering against Po-Han. One of the worst aspects of oppression is the way it divides the oppressed against themselves; it is quite rational to identify oneself with superior forces, yet doing so is ultimately self-defeating, for the price of such identification is self-denial, and thus one undercuts the very reason for the identification. Money supplies both the medium of power exchange and a potent symbol of power; those who have it are already able to influence those who do not, for it is money which supports, or even allows, self-expression in a capitalist society.

By "winning," Po-Han has placed his feet firmly upon the ladder of hierarchy inherent in any power-based system, where victories over others are the means of advancement. Po-Han's victory, abetted by Collins, therefore means a defeat for Lop-Eye, who must seek redress (that is, a way of reasserting his own power). This he obtains by sending Po-Han ashore on some errand during one of the periodic uprisings against Western power. Po-Han is attacked by a Communist mob and, in the single-most painful sequence in the film, is strung up with his arms tied behind him and tortured by having his chest repeatedly slashed. Collins's increasingly desperate offers of money to get the Communists to stop are of no avail; the message sent by Po-Han's death is more important to the Communists than is any amount of money; what is vital in one system is meaningless in another. Po-Han is killed, but not by the Communists; Holman seizes a rifle and shoots him, despite express orders from Collins to the contrary. Holman does what Collins could not.

6.

Holman's opposite, rather more traditionally heroic in appearance and action, is Captain Collins (Richard Crenna), commander of the *San Pablo*, and as such the central representative of the system of authority under which all involved are laboring. Collins is something of a martinet, full of patriotic fervor. "For us who wear the uniform," he tells the assembled crew, "every day is Flag Day." But this is not merely regulation bluster on his part; he genuinely believes what he says; "We serve the flag," he continues, and his words have the bite of sincerity.

> The trade we all follow is the give and take of death. It is for that purpose that the people of America maintain us. And any one of us who believes he has a job like any other for which he draws a money wage is a thief of the food he eats and a trespasser in the bunk in which he lies down to sleep.

Wise frames every shot of Collins's speech so as to include the American flag flapping in the breeze. Collins embodies the sense of duty which lies at the core of military professionalism, and without which neither organized aggression nor defense would be possible. Collins quite probably would not recognize the power of money or sex (we never see him involved with either, save for his unsuccessful attempt to buy Po-Han's life); he is thus ill-equipped to function outside the world of the ship, a world pressing ever closer as the film proceeds.

Crisp orders quickly obeyed and clean flags run up smartly make a good show, but it is already evident that the show lacks substance, that Collins is something of a hollow man. The *San Pablo* itself is clearly a tool of a colonial power; it was, we have already learned, acquired from Spain as a result of the Spanish-American War of 1898, the first of America's explicitly imperialist wars. But it is also "something of a painful local joke," as we are both told and see; a large crowd gathers at the ship's berth in Changsha to watch the military drills and imitate them mockingly, with little comprehension of the intended significance of the actions. Collins himself acknowledges this soon after the ship begins a cruise to "show the flag" and Holman informs him that troubles in the engine room require stopping the ship. Collins's response is dismissive; "As long as we move and smoke boils out of our stack, we'll make the impression I want to make on the Chinese." The *San Pablo* itself is "look-see pidgin." The ship functions smoothly because of the coolie system; thus even an American flag-showing expedition can proceed only because of Chinese labor.

Holman tends the engine, but it is Collins who understands one vital aspect of the nature of the system which the engine serves and the irrelevance of individualism. "The crew of this ship is designed just like the machinery that powers the ship," he tells Holman in their first confrontation.

> Captains before me designed the *San Pablo* for a special job that we have here on the backwaters of China. But men will not hold together like brass and steel. We have to refit ourselves into the design every day. That's the purpose of all we do in *San Pablo*. As part of that design you cannot be excused to do what you prefer to do no matter how well you do it.

Collins is absolutely right. The system within which he and Holman and the *San Pablo* exist cannot operate without the repeated subordination of person to function. We have seen this process at work in several of the films already examined, but here we see the nexus of control and obedience by which the system proceeds. Individuals must be kept happy enough not to revolt (hence the whores and drinking allowed to the crew), but kept as unaware as possible that the terms of that happiness are set by the system itself. This is not the result of any conspiracy but simply a necessity of the machinery of power as presently constituted. Without the hierarchy it would be impossible to run the machinery at all, and Holman's occasional independent actions threaten that hierarchy.

This poses a problem, though. In order to control the appetites of individuals there must be those doing the controlling, and they must perform a difficult double purpose: suppressing the desire for genuine freedom on the part of those who serve the system while simultaneously denying their own equivalent desires. They must be both aware of repression and unaware of repression. The representatives of authority must be able to exercise it while avoiding its temptations as a means of individualism. Too little authority, and the system breaks down; too much, and again it breaks down (though less easily, which is why the tendency of those at the top of a political and social structure is always toward the authoritarian). Hence the emphasis placed by Collins on duty and honor; the one is a means of appealing to the men to stay in line, the other a means of self-discipline. Both break down as the system disintegrates.

Despite his symbolic importance as commander, Captain Collins has, as we have seen, surprisingly little effect on events. His battle drills are entertainment. He is berated by Holman for doing nothing as Po-Han is killed, and must watch as Holman takes the only humane action possible, an action forbidden to Collins by virtue of his position (he commands the *San Pablo*, but is otherwise merely a small cog serving the needs of a much larger machine). He spends a considerable portion of the film trapped aboard the *San Pablo* by low water and a Chinese sampan siege, prevented by higher orders from firing or taking any action. His commands to Jameson are ignored. His crew all but mutinies. He is increasingly frustrated by his relative impotence as history unfolds, and his speeches to the crew convey this. Collins is as much a victim of imperialism as any aboard or on shore, in that his importance as a human being is tied to the system, and when the system crumbles his self-worth crumbles with it. The difference is that Collins is in a position to do something about it. Collins needs to justify himself, and Collins has authority; his catastrophic final decision stems directly from the combination of these two facts.

Lop-Eye Shing, having tested the wind, decides to counter Collins's authority directly. He plants opium aboard, leading to a mass exodus of the coolies and an intensification of hatred from the Chinese ashore (no surprise, given the historical use of opium as a means of foreign control). Stawski, ordered to dispose of it, throws it in the furnace, spreading its odors far and wide through the _San Pablo_'s smokestack. There is nothing to be done. "Shall we try to mask the smoke with rubber or something, Captain?" asks Bordelles. "It's too late," Collins replies, an insert shot of thick smoke obscuring the American flag adding punch to his words. The very next shot shows the flag again, this time against a backdrop of Chinese nationalist flags. The camera tilts down as Collins, standing in his accustomed place at the base of the flag-pole, exhorts the crew to stand firm against the state of siege. "There will be no liberty," he warns them, a fact emphasized by his first close-up and each subsequent one; behind him are visible only the Chinese flags. Once a week a military mission will travel to the consulate, with each sailor allowed one opportunity for that brief escape from the ship. He rails against the "new weapons of boycott and propaganda" intended to destroy the _San Pablo_. His words are typical; "They expect in the end to haul down the flag in shame and disgrace. We will not let them do that. When the time comes, we will defend our flag with our life's blood." But his peroration is interrupted by cheers as a large junk, bearing Jameson and Shirley Eckert back to China Light, passes. Jameson is waving and enthusiastic, much to Collins's disgust. "The next incident," he comments to Ensign Bordelles, "they could just as well turn on him and kill him." He is right, but it is he who will provide that incident. It is clear that he wants to take action of some sort. "Pray for an early spring," he continues, "or permission to open fire."

The siege lasts through the winter, with crew discipline growing increasingly slack. Frenchy, despairing of seeing Maily, jumps ship (witnessed by Collins, who does nothing). Holman determines to follow Frenchy on his one trip ashore, and tucks all his money into his pocket (but the Chinese flags fluttering, barely noticeably, outside the window behind him already indicate that he will fail, for he does not belong there and would not be allowed to remain). Hence when Maily is killed, Holman, who was with her last, is blamed by the Chinese (whether for genuine or propagandistic reasons is unimportant, as the outward effect is the same), and the Nationalists demand that he be turned over to justice. Collins refuses, provoking the crew to a near mutiny as they demand loudly and repeatedly that "Holman, come down" off the bridge and turn himself over, thus freeing the ship and allowing the coolies to return to take over the tasks the crew does not wish to perform. The watching Chinese do nothing, even when Collins himself fires a machine gun burst into the water ahead of the sampan bearing the messengers. Collins leaves the bridge, a broken man who has let himself down. In his quarters, he contemplates suicide.

Timing, as so often in Wise's films, is everything. That day the _San Pablo_ is able to clear the channel and escape the siege, and that night the message for which Collins has been hoping arrives: Nationalist troops have taken Nan-king, Westerners are fleeing for their lives, and the Marines have landed at Shanghai.[15] Collins sees his chance for redemption. "What happened this morning has not gone down on paper yet," he tells Bordelles, Holman, and Franks, another officer. "It is not history until it goes down on paper. What *is* going down on paper for the end of *San Pablo* will be quite different." He declares the radio out of order, meaning that he is "not hampered by orders from above." His plan is simple; the *San Pablo* will make for China Light and rescue the missionaries, who will "be desperate for rescue." But this is only part of his goal. "We will make one last savage thrust deep into China," he avers in unconsciously phallic imagery, "and if the *San Pablo* dies she dies clean. It is my responsibility to the ship — and to the men."

The dilemma of power is simple; its very presence invites its exercise. In normal communities there are safeguards to prevent abuses of power, but when community breaks down so do the safeguards. As the imperialist com-munity shatters, so does Collins's restraint. In yet another irony, Collins now acts, for the first time, in contravention of orders, and for the first time such a contravention will be completely wrong.

We at last get the battle that allows *The Sand Pebbles* to be described as a war film. Three points stand out. The first is visual. Collins orders the bat-tle flag raised, and the camera tilts to follow it, revealing that the black smoke from the stack is blowing behind it, in contrast to the opium incident. In the minds of Collins and the crew the stains on the flag are being erased, an idea made explicit by a series of reaction shots of crew and officers looking pride-ful. The second point is linked; at one point during the battle the mast of one of the junks blockading the boom is shattered, eliciting laughter and cheers from the *San Pablo* crew; an insert of the battle flag counterpoints this. (Although we are definitely meant to feel the crew's exultation here, this is not the jingoistic moment for which it can be mistaken. In the longer version of the film, a similar shot of Nationalist fighters cheering a fire on board the *San Pablo*, a result of their shots, establishes the link between the two crews as fighters).

The third point is key. The *San Pablo* grapples with the center junk for boarding. Holman axes the rope barrier, and is attacked by a Chinese fighter whom he kills with an ax blow to the stomach. A sudden close-up reveals the fighter to be Cho-jen, Shirley Eckert's prize student and the personal guar-antor of Jameson. Holman, whose plan to leave the ship had been foiled by events, now finds himself even more entangled in events beyond his compre-hension or control. Holman has for the first time fully lived up to his role as a combatant, and the result will be, as he surely realizes, devastating.

For the moment Collins is riding high on success; "The men performed *brilliantly*," he proudly declares to Ensign Bordelles as he prepares to take a small squad to China Light to rescue the missionaries. They did. It is vital that this battle scene not be read ironically (nor is there any reason to do so); these men have indeed done a superb job of killing (the death toll among the Chinese defendants must be in the dozens; among the Americans perhaps a dozen at most, and probably fewer. Six American deaths are seen clearly, but others are implied). They have carried out their orders, and the mission is, from their perspective, a well-earned success. They are military professionals, and what they have done is what militarism commands be done. The fact that the success is so destructive, and ultimately pointless, is its own condemnation, but it is not the men who are to be condemned; rather, the audience must realize that those men are only living up to the requirements of a system in which each member of the audience is a participant, and therefore in which we are all complicit, whether apparently willingly like Bordelles and Stawski or with inner doubts like Holman (as Jean-Paul Sartre commented, apropos the Vietnam War, "If you say nothing, you are necessarily for the continuation of the war; one is always responsible for what one does not try to prevent"[16]). The more effective the battle sequence, the more strongly we feel the patriotism of the men, the more powerfully we will be moved by Holman's confrontation with the death of Cho-jen and our own involvement in the system which makes deaths like these possible in the thousands.[17]

Collins's redemptive mission has not merely failed; it has made certain that the very result he wished to avoid must occur. He confronts this fact at the mission, both in the refusal of Jameson and Shirley Eckert to be rescued, and in the fact that there would in any case have been only two people to be rescued; more people, indeed more Americans, died in the rescue attempt than would have died had nothing been done. Collins's demand that Jameson accept rescue, whatever the cost — "You are not going to make that a futile and meaningless battle" — reflects his agonized awareness that, in violating orders in the attempt to overcome shame, his and the men's, at being forced to act in a non-military manner (that is, by disobeying military orders not to attack under any provocation but a direct military assault, which never happened), he has failed to achieve even his own goal. There was no real alternative; Collins, as a product of a system which both requires initiative and offers no manner of ascertaining its validity, was bound, sooner or later, to act out the contradictions of the system.

Collins has one further bitter pill to swallow. Holman has at last comprehended the iniquity of imperialism, the error of American presence in China in the first place, and finds the courage to act on his realization. Ordered to "help them get their things together," Holman refuses. "You better get back to the ship, Captain," he says, "because they're staying here. And so am

I." Collins, struggling to control his despair, reminds Holman that this is "desertion in the face of the enemy." Holman is indifferent to the description; "I ain't got no more enemies. Shove off, Captain," he quietly commands Collins. The confrontation between military authority, represented by Collins, and the individual, Jake Holman, lurking beneath the surface of the action for the entire film, has at last come out in the open.

7.

"The men consider you a Jonah," a bringer of bad luck, Collins tells Holman during their confrontation after the death of Po-Han. The men are right, at least in one sense; not only do bad events happen after Holman's arrival, many of them stem in some manner from his presence. Holman represents an anarchic force undercutting the authority of the hierarchical system. At first his resistances are instinctual and stereotyped; he frequents a brothel instead of immediately obeying orders, and he remains cold to the jocular camaraderie of his shipmates. Gradually those resistances become more conscious; in a sense, *The Sand Pebbles* is a cinematic *bildungsroman* about Jake Holman, but with this difference: although Holman does become at least partially aware of the forces which have restrained and crippled him as a human being, he is unable to escape from those forces. It is we, the audience, who must take to heart the lessons learned too late by Jake Holman.

Holman is not romanticized. He joined the Navy because, having assaulted a duplicitous high school principal and "put his eye out," he was given the option of joining the military or being sent to reform school. At first he sees it all as a form of look-see pidgin, a show to which only enough attention need be paid to allow him the freedom of the whorehouses and the engine rooms. With a whore hanging on his arm, he cockily informs the bartender in a Shanghai brothel that the "uniform gets 'em every time." He tells Shirley Eckert that "on a small ship you haven't got any of that military crap." Yet he is not without decency or some degree of self-awareness. In the encounter with Shirley Eckert alone on the deck of the ship taking him to Changsha and the *San Pablo*, he is careful to warn her that "nice American girls don't talk to China sailors." He understands the importance of professionalism, at least at a personal level; "Long as you're good at something they can't bust you down. Like me, you know, with the engine." But his horizons remain severely limited; even after seven years in China he still all but dismisses Shirley's desire to teach the Chinese, clearly an undifferentiated mass in his mind: "Well, those slopeheads could use some teaching."

Holman's education begins with his arrival at the *San Pablo*. He descends into it, quite literally: the road to the dock slants down, the gangway slants down (even his step up onto the deck is elided by a cut), and the engine is, of course, below decks. In fact, downward camera movements will be associated with Holman throughout the film; with one important exception, apart from a very few extremely minor adjustments within scenes, the camera never moves upward while centered on Holman, regardless of his own movements.[18] Unfortunately, Holman's education will, as all of this implies, literally be his downfall, because each step toward true self-awareness is a step away from accepting the status quo, and this cannot be allowed. It is this which makes Holman a Jonah; as he becomes more self-aware he asks questions, to many of which the answers are highly discomforting, and as he asks questions he raises doubts within others less self-aware, doubts which cannot be allowed expression lest they challenge the entire system within which all are operating.

Education is not simply a process of being trained (that would be indoctrination); it begins with, and rests upon, questions. The option of doubt exists for anyone at any level, such that Holman is able to pose questions even before he understands what it is he is really doing. Seeing the coolie system, Holman doubts its validity for racist reasons, but even so he is doubting the status quo. Interrogated as to responsibility for the death of Chien, Holman is blunt; "The system you got on this ship is what killed him. Sir." Holman urges that he be given full authority over the engine, arguing with Collins about the coolie system, leading Collins to give his speech about the crew as part of the machinery, but Collins's thoughtful look after Holman leaves suggests that he is less than convinced by his own certitude.[19]

Unbeknownst to anyone, the die has been cast. Holman begins to expand his horizons, teaching Po-Han, coming to appreciate him as an individual person, and coming thereby into conflict with Lop-Eye Shing, a conflict of which the greater significance can now be seen. Shing sends Po-Han ashore into the arms of the revolutionaries, who use him as an example to the imperialists ("Watch what we do to the running dog"). Holman abandons military discipline out of compassion and shoots Po-Han. Instantly we hear a more impassioned version of the music played under the opening credits, momentarily overwhelming even the sounds of the crowd (though not, interestingly, the splash made by the gun — both the symbol and the mechanism of authority and power — as Holman pitches it overboard). The music continues as Holman leaves the deck for the security of the engine room, the camera sliding downward through the decks as he passes. Holman drops his munitions belt as he enters the boiler room and begins to shovel coal violently, seeking surcease in mindless action and failing to find it. At last he gives way to his grief and hunches over the shovel, sobbing. Holman is confronting his own isolation within a system, one to which he has acquiesced, even if not explicitly, which purposely devalues individual lives. He is starting to reach what can only be an extremely painful new level of self and political understanding, and it will have painful consequences.[20]

The musical motif, now more brooding than anguished, carries through to the next scene, as Shirley Eckert attempts without success to comfort Holman. His responses to her are monotonal and terse; clearly he is confronting thoughts too complex for words. Holman is the first member of the ship's complement to discover that the exercise of his military training (in this case sharpshooting) may in fact be useful only in a context which robs it of all military value. Nor does he escape complicity in the tragedy. Without Holman's well-meant actions in provoking the fight and supporting him before and afterward, Po-Han would be off the ship and still alive. In a self-contradictory social system, what is right can also be what is wrong. Holman knows also that his action will surely have further consequences; he shot Po-Han despite express orders from Collins to do no such thing. For the moment, the entire structure of authority tottered — but in fact it was Collins who was forced to confront the limits of his power and worth.

It is Holman's mercy-killing of Po-Han which sets the rest of the film in motion. Collins dresses him down — "You're opposed to the whole spirit aboard the *San Pablo*," he tells him — and all but orders him to request a transfer, yet Collins also all but admits that he cannot condemn Holman's action, save in his official capacity. It is thus Collins's action which starts a chain of thought in Holman's mind about leaving the ship, while Holman's action has set the stage for Collins's later decision to violate orders for ostensibly humanitarian purposes. The difference is that Holman's action was motivated by genuine anguish for another person's plight, whereas Collins's will be tainted by his desire to obtain redemption for the near-mutiny.

Holman's first attempt to desert is abortive, but the idea of joining Shirley Eckert and Jameson at China Light remains. Having killed Po-Han, a person he respected, it is harder for Holman to rid himself of doubts about killing anyone else. We see this twice during the battle sequence. As the men prepare for combat, Holman raises the sight on his rifle, as he did before shooting Po-Han. A hint of the music heard after Po-Han's death underscores Holman's doubts as he lowers the sight and sets the rifle on a sand bag, an ambiguous expression crossing his face. During the battle itself he hesitates at the carnage before rejoining the fray, but his training will not allow him to do otherwise than fight. And so it is that, as Collins and the boarding parties return to the ship while Holman axes the rope barrier, Holman is left alone to be attacked by, and to kill, Cho-jen. Again we hear what must now be recognized as the music of death as Cho-jen's eyes jerk wide open in shock and he topples to the deck of the junk, his anguished grabbing of his axed gut visually echoing Holman's stance as his grief over Po-Han's death overwhelms him. Holman stands staring as the rope parts; the reaction shot shows Holman surrounded by smoke as had been the American flag when tainted by the burning opium. He is irretrievably tainted by the death, at his hands, of Cho-jen. He has reaped the fruits of the system he had taken for granted for so long.

And thus the great triumphal moment of the film, the *San Pablo*'s hard-won passage through the barrier, is nothing of the sort, but rather a somber smoke-and-flame-shrouded funeral rite. All the forces which have been operating throughout the film have now joined to drive the ship, Holman, and Collins on to the destiny which was implicit from the moment Holman came aboard. There has been valor, there has been sacrifice, honor has been satisfied, and now the price must be paid; the victory dissolves as Collins discovers that force is not enough to overcome the conflicts, whether personal or political, at the heart of imperialism.

Holman's decision to desert stems from this moment, though it is not confirmed until he hears Shirley Eckert declare that she, like Jameson, is staying at China Light. But the brutal reality of self-contradiction cannot be so lightly put off. Even as Holman is refusing Collins's order a refugee from the boom is running into the mission compound with news of the battle. There is a stunning moment of visual ambiguity that is not moral ambiguity at all as Jameson announces the fact. "Shirley, he says Cho-jen is dead," he calls out. "Oh, no," she moans, "no." There is a reaction shot of Holman, then the camera returns to Jameson, but in a position so different from before that his spatial orientation is difficult to discern as he looks up. "You killed him at the boom," he says, apparently directly to Holman. Only the following shot of Collins redirects our attention properly, at least in a visual sense, as Jameson completes his sentence, linking the actions of Holman and Collins: "and now they're coming for me because of you — and your blind pride." Soon Jameson will indeed be dead.

Collins has only one sacrifice left: himself. He orders Holman and the other two men to take Shirley away while he distracts the Nationalists bent on revenge. He does not live long enough after this to achieve his aim, and Holman realizes that, as senior petty officer, it is his duty to do the same; his link with Collins lasts even beyond death. He takes the automatic rifle and bids a brief farewell to Shirley before gesturing for the other men to take her away. For some time he is able to hold off the shadowy soldiers along the roofs and walls, but eventually he, like Collins, is shot. Unable to stand, he sits with his back to a crate of machinery,[21] blood soaking his uniform, a dazed expression glazing his face. "I was home," he murmurs; "what happened?"

And then, in a shout of uncomprehending anguish, "*What the hell happened?!*" A shot cracks out and Holman jerks once, then slumps over dead. As the music of death is heard, quietly this time, a high crane shot slowly pulls up and away to reveal the bodies of Holman, Collins, and Jameson, the only upward motion associated with Holman at all, a motion now of isolation and horror. The tableau invites further consideration: three deaths have evoked the same music, music we heard, in advance of any action at all, under the opening credits. Why there, when no death had yet occurred? It is a subtle point, but a powerful one: death is already implicit in the system we are about to witness, and therefore, since what we see is a reflection of current events, death is already implicit in the system of which we are a part, willingly or otherwise. But the music, though similar, is not identical; we have the option of change, should we wish to take it. Such change, though, will need to be fundamental, akin to rewriting the entire film, if it is to have any lasting impact.

Only two images remain in the film. The first shows Shirley Eckert being urged onward at some distance from the mission compound and the second shows the *San Pablo* steaming away. The outcome of the rescue remains ambiguous, though we are left with some small reason for hope, a hope grounded in Shirley Eckert.[22]

8.

Shirley Eckert (Candice Bergen) offers a genuine counterbalance to the various authority figures, though the nature of this remains unclear for most of the film, and its strength remains ambiguous even after the film is over. Her professed attitude provides the key. "I'm not a missionary, I'm a teacher," she tells Jake in their first conversation; "And if I'm gonna teach I ought to know more." She is the only character who avows either a desire or an intention to understand the entire situation, and one of the few to demonstrate any interest in learning at all. Nor is her interest in learning instrumental; she wants to know simply because knowing is in itself a good thing.

Holman is led to doubt, and thereby to question, the system within which he is living, but he rarely *asks* questions (and most of the ones he does ask are to Shirley). Shirley, on the other hand, asks frequently, and easily avows her lack of knowledge (she probably asks more questions than everyone else in the film put together). Given a chance to make a wish, she is puzzled that Jake expresses no curiosity as to its nature; when he responds to her prompting by asking it turns out to be an implicit question: "I wished that someday you'd feel like telling me more about yourself." He does tell, and still she wants more; "You just keep pulling, don't you?" But her questions are the questions he needs to answer for himself, or at least the bases for those questions. The fact that something of a romantic relationship develops between Jake and Shirley is secondary to Shirley's role in awakening Jake's sense of self.

Shirley is a teacher, and as such takes a different approach to the world than do those who must command or obey; "I hope someday all people can pledge allegiance to something beyond country," she comments to Jake (in the roadshow version of the film), to what they have in common rather than what sets them apart. This is the foundation of education, and thus the wellspring of true teaching. Teaching is a double-ended activity; one must endeavor to find in oneself not merely the joy of making new understandings possible, but a sense of wonder about the events, personalities, ideas, and works being explored. It helps, no doubt, that Shirley is encountering China for the first time, but there is no reason someone revisiting old ideas cannot see them afresh. This does not, however, require a corresponding passivity on the part of the students; in fact, as she notes, "Here [China] there's a real sense of purpose." Unlike the others, with the very partial exception of Jameson, Shirley realizes that she must work *with* the students, instead of *on* them.[23] She must be aware of what motivates them as people, not as cogs within an ideological machine. Her self-awareness, both personal and political, manifests itself, characteristically, in a question to Holman, who has sardonically asserted that the Chinese purpose is simply "to get rid of the U.S. Navy." "Well, wouldn't you feel the same way if the Chinese had gunboats running up and down the Mississippi?" Holman, startled, responds with a quiet question of his own, directed more to himself than to her: "Yeah. How about that?" Shirley's question, even coming, as it does, from within the system of power which will play out so catastrophically, opens the door to answers which have the potential to transform, and perhaps even transcend, an individual caught within that system — and possibly to begin the overthrow of the system itself, for its own contradictions ensure that it can never be completely stable.

It is also this which *The Sand Pebbles* does as a film. I have repeatedly called attention to the refusal of the film to condemn any among its characters, to the fact that, in the various situations, the opposing views are not always genuinely contradictory, and that both may have a modicum of truth because each is an expression of some aspect of a self-contradictory political system. Shirley Eckert, in her insistence upon listening rather than judging, embodies the stance of the film, which is why she allows, and the film provides, the possibility of hope even within the self-contradictory and inhumane system depicted. We are always free to listen, to question, and to act in light of the answers we find. The more we do so, and the more who do so, the greater the possibility of genuine change. But such change cannot be coerced, regardless of the motives, good or ill, behind the coercion, and the film is resolute in its refusal to attempt to coerce or support easy reactions. Acknowledging complexity, though, is not the same thing as refusing to take any stance at all. To "profess" is to speak *for* something, even as one acknowledges the possibility that there is more to that of which one speaks than may at first meet the eye. The honest examination of human conflict is itself already a moral stance, and the exploration of the ways in which such conflict is generated by a crippled political system carries within itself a strong suggestion of how such a system should be judged and changed. In major works of art every element coheres to provide an implicit utopian view of the possibilities of a similarly coherent human personality, *even when the work itself is presenting the most conflicted of human beings or situations.* This is the place of art in encouraging the expansion of human cooperation, but it is a fragile one; no work of art has ever had coercive power, and those which have attempted to attain it have been failures in advance. Shirley Eckert models the role of the teacher, and *The Sand Pebbles* models the role of art, in enhancing human moral and political progress. But they can only suggest; it is we who must act.

It is the nature of these actions which lies at the heart of *Star Trek: The Motion Picture,* to which we turn next.

Chapter Six

Triads of Hope: *Star Trek: The Motion Picture* (1979)

Instead of thinking of removing so-called faults from a work it is wiser, rather, to be favorably predisposed to them, and to treat them as qualities, whose secret we have not so far been able to fathom. (André Bazin)[1]

1.

An individual's reaction to a work of art rests on two elements, separable analytically but rarely in actuality: the emotional and the intellectual. Either element may, for the purposes of a particular analysis, be prioritized, but the other remains always as an unspoken counterpart; if its absence is too noticeable, the analysis itself comes to be seen as significantly flawed. So fundamental are these elements that the nature of their interaction is sometimes forgotten, and it is worth briefly reviewing them.

How we respond to the work of art will often begin with its *emotional* impact; frequently all we remember of a work experienced only once or twice is its effect upon our feelings, or as a purgative for those feelings, whatever they may be (pleasure, boredom, disgust, and so on, whether individually, sequentially, or in combination). Sometimes our emotional response can overwhelm any other aspect of appreciation; a work which disgusts us ethically, say, or one which presents a political vision with which we are in vigorous agreement, may never get a chance to be considered as a work of art at all, being condemned or praised for reasons largely or completely external to its artistic values. The visceral comes in here as well, though it is not the whole of an emotional reaction; it is that which has a direct impact on our physical being (the sheer volume of a large orchestral climax, for example, or the SurroundSound scream of agony as a character dies). Many performances fit in here, but so can something as apparently technical as editing; when we are scared by a horror film, for example, or grow tense during a pursuit sequence, we are often responding principally to the way the scene is edited — and of course we are responding to that which does not really exist in any case.

Emotional responses rarely exist in a vacuum; what we feel connects intimately with what we consciously think, with the *intellectual*, or that which is appreciated principally for the further thoughts it stimulates in us. Obviously relevant here are considerations of structure, but, just as emotions do not exist in a vacuum neither do works of art; thus all sorts of matters which extend beyond the immediate boundaries of the piece at hand come into play as we consider it (as will presumably be evident from the foregoing chapters in this book, for example). Political content, moral content, and informative content: each of these is an aspect of the intellectual, as each involves references, whether implicit or explicit, to something outside the work as an entity in itself. These references can be focused (that is, in the sense that portions of Michael Moore's *Fahrenheit 9/11* may lead us to revile the second Bush administration) or loose (in the way that Alfred Hitchcock's *Vertigo* may lead a viewer to think about the destructive forces inherent in patriarchy, for example). The former is rarely a matter for significant disagreement, save in a debate over its legitimacy (no one with any contextual understanding would deny that *Fahrenheit 9/11* is intended to make us revile the Bush administration, though some might conceivably disagree that such thoughts are either necessary or desirable); the latter is much more open to interpretation and disagreement (it is easy to imagine someone who simply cannot generalize from *Vertigo* to a larger social picture, taking it to be merely a study of an isolated lunatic, say). As with the emotional element, the intellectual can, and in a work of any complexity at all will, operate on multiple levels: sequentially, simultaneously, or both.

Each level acts as something of a corrective to a too stringent or hasty affirmation of the other, warning us against taking a part for the whole. Eventually, these two components of our understanding can connect with and inform a third, much more complex, level of understanding, the evaluative. As with the preceding elements, there can be multiple layers of this, and the more the layers work together the more significant the work is. In a sense, significance begins with uniqueness, but as any work which is not an outright plagiarism will perforce be unique, the more probing question is how far beneath the surface that uniqueness goes. The more deeply it goes, the further one can dig and still find elements, singly or in combination, appreciable on their own, the more the work stands out evaluatively. So, for a fairly simple example, one might admire the beautiful costumes in a film, enjoying them simply as colors in motion. One then sees that the colors always fore-shadow the overall emotional tone of the next scene, and one admires the care with which this was done. Then one notices that certain colors are seen only in conjunction with certain characters, and one realizes that those characters themselves represent certain states of humanity, and that the colors give hints, not immediately obvious, of ways in which those different aspects of human-ity could be reconciled. It was all there to begin with, but required ever deeper ways of seeing and understanding the film.

Clearly these elements work together, and the better the work the more densely imbricated its elements will be, and the more difficult it would be to disentangle them. Nor do we generally attempt to do so while experiencing the work; only later, in thinking over our response, do individual elements tend to become more material. If ever we describe the work to someone who does not know it, these elements will come to the fore, such that what we are describing is in fact something of a re-invention of the work. One of the opening tasks of any commentary is, in fact, to be false to the work as a whole by isolating and discussing the elements which make it function well, or which contribute to its failure. Yet the ideal, even here, is to arrive at a holistic description which enhances the experience, either of the work under discus-sion or of others held to be worthier of attention. Commentaries of any sort, therefore, are always pointing beyond themselves to something to be appre-ciated for and in itself, something greater and more valuable than the com-mentary itself; otherwise, we are not talking about a work of art but something like a guide to assembling a stove; we appreciate a text such as that to the degree that it is useful.[2] But if I ask you why you like X as a work of art, your ultimate answer will have to be something along the lines of, "Because it pleases me" (or, more accurately if less conversationally, "Because these man-ifold elements functioning in concert please me."). If I push further, the ques-tion doesn't even make sense; to ask, "Why do you take pleasure from being pleased?" (or "Why is it good to be pleased?") is simply to restate the first question and to go nowhere.

We reach here one pole of evaluative understanding, which is the sub-jective: how you or I react to what we have seen (or think we have seen). Many people stop here; "I know what I like" is a common response to any debate over art, one meant to shut down any further discussion. Although such a claim is, in fact, essentially incontrovertible, it is neither useful nor interest-ing; all it really does is isolate the speaker from expanding their understand-ing and it conveys no information to another person regarding what might be worth investigating. Nor, despite the assumption often underlying this attitude, does it lead to the desired relativism, because the next step always remains available: analysis: why is this pleasing (or displeasing)? What are the elements which make it work (or fail to work)? At first we respond simply within the context of our own tastes ("I don't like blue costumes," say), but gradually we start extending our understanding beyond the purely personal to a consideration of the work in itself (that is, of the specific but conjoined elements which have led to our various subjective responses), and we can come to understand the idiosyncrasies of our own response and detach them from our overall discussion. That's why it's possible simultaneously to dislike (or at least not positively like) something yet also acknowledge its importance as a work of art.

Out of these subjective processes arises the possibility of objective evaluation. "I don't like X" is not in itself an evaluative statement, but rather a purely subjective psychological report. It may be relevant, or even important, in its own context (when deciding what film to see tonight, for example), but it says nothing at all about X. "X is (or is not) a good work of art" *is* an evaluative statement, though not yet particularly interesting — but it at least opens the door to further discussion. This is the heart of evaluation. It is not enough merely to understand one's own reaction to a work of art, especially one which is complex or difficult; ideally, one should encounter and understand the reactions of others, and understand the way in which those reactions are causally connected with the work at hand. Our response to a work of art is an interaction between two evolving centers of attention: our personal history, conscious and unconscious, and the connections between that history and the thing before us. Two kinds of knowledge are thus equally important here: self-knowledge and a firm grasp on the technical and material means used to attain the emotional and intellectual ends of the work. Without the former, we are merely links in a causal chain of no particular interest or value; without the latter, we have no basis for ascertaining whether the impact of the work stems from its own elements or from quirks within our personality, and thus little basis for sharing our responses with others. Each of these aspects of understanding is fluid and expansive; evaluation, then, is a permanent process rather than a conclusion, although the process includes many intermediate conclusions (this book being one such, for example). Evaluation demands a certain kind of impersonality, an ability to become aware of and then step outside one's prejudices (at least to a degree, as we can never completely escape our preconceptions), because evaluation purports to be a statement about something outside of us, something in the world, not simply about how we feel (although understanding how we feel and why we feel that way is certainly a significant part of analysis). Evaluation is grounded in experience, and experience is subjective, but when enough experiences are explored the result reaches beyond the individual and toward the work itself.[3]

So the first step in evaluating a work of art is to determine its own approach—that is, what elements are most important and why. A mistake here can confuse matters mightily. If one picks up a stick of butter thinking it is a hammer, one's experience in pounding nails will be vastly different than expected. If one watches *The Sound of Music* expecting a documentary on acoustics, one will likely be quite startled. While these sorts of large-scale errors are of course rare, smaller ones are quite common and, if unrecognized, can derail a fair evaluation before it even gets started. One such mistake in particular is frequently made even before people see *Star Trek: The Motion Picture*. The central problem *Star Trek: The Motion Picture* has faced as a film is that many viewers judge it only in relation to a particular vision of a specific television program.

One of the many legends involving the *Star Trek* television series is that the first pilot, "The Cage," was rejected by its intended network as "too cerebral." Although this tale has since been discredited, at least to a degree,[4] something similar did, in fact, happen with regard to the first in the series of the movies based on the characters and ship made famous by the television series. Rushed into release against the wishes of Wise in order to make a rigid holiday deadline, the incomplete film suffered from a lack of focus and finish. Critics and audiences alike generally condemned it as too long, too slow, and too taken up with sequences consisting of little but spectacular special effects; nor did the addition of several deleted scenes in the video release significantly alter the conventional appraisal—although the expressed grounds for this appraisal differed widely among the film's detractors. Fans of the television series generally dismissed (and continue to dismiss) the film as being unlike its progenitor, while critics, on the whole dismissive of the television series, usually attacked the film as being more of the same, only at greater length.[5] For years the film was widely taken as a false start to what later became a highly successful action-adventure franchise.

Although the profitable box office results in some measure preemptively belied the film's reputation, few people in the years since the initial release of *Star Trek: The Motion Picture* were inclined to take it seriously. It remained, even for many of those who enjoyed it, more a promissory note for what should have been than a success on its own; Wise himself expressed disappointment at the initial release version. This is a typical Hollywood story; many directors have cringed at the mangled works attributed, principally or entirely, to them. Atypically, though, Wise was eventually able to revisit, revise, and finish the film some twenty-two years after its first release. The results were striking; with the film's structure and content for the first time unencumbered by irrelevancies or incomplete material, it became at last possible to fully recognize this film as not only a major addition to the slender canon of emotionally, intellectually, and aesthetically complex cinematic science fiction but a remarkably coherent film by any standards, and to understand exactly the significance of just those elements of spectacle which had previously been condemned.[6]

Wise and his collaborators created a profound, subtle, and moving meditation on technology and desire. *Star Trek: The Motion Picture*, unlike most of the horde of cinematic and televised sequels it engendered, operates simultaneously on several levels, such that any discussion which fails to acknowledge that complexity is in effect a discussion of only part of a film. It is perhaps no surprise that those who looked to this film for conventional science fiction action-adventure heroics would fail to see its virtues, for these are present only in a sublimated form, one which places greater emphasis on being than on doing. Thus it was that viewers looking to revive their memories of the earlier television series found themselves confronting something quite different, something perceived as being, one might say, rather too cerebral.

What follows is an essay in analysis and interpretation rather than a history. Apart from the discussion below of the relation of *Star Trek: The Motion Picture* to its two great predecessors in meditative science fiction, Stanley Kubrick's *2001: A Space Odyssey* (1968) and Andrei Tarkovsky's *Solaris* (1972), I shall make no further effort to situate this film in relation either to its television progenitor nor science fiction cinema in general. The production history of the film, and its reputed budget troubles, the latter exaggerated in any case, are of vital importance to accountants but of no relevance to anyone considering the film as a work of art, and I shall ignore them.[7] All films exist within various contexts, but sometimes one or more of those contexts comes to be definitive in trivial or distracting ways; such a fate has befallen this film, and it is my purpose in what follows to attempt to return attention to the film rather than to extraneous considerations. *Star Trek: The Motion Picture* serves as the climax, and in many ways the summation, of Wise's career as a director, and as such, and as a grand experiment in science fiction utopianism, it deserves considerably more attention than it has otherwise received.

2.

Star Trek: The Motion Picture is frequently compared with *2001: A Space Odyssey*. There is some justification for this, at least superficially. Both films have musical overtures and are deliberately paced, with extended sequences apparently celebrating technological imagery. Both films involve the transfiguration of an individual human being into something unknown and largely incomprehensible, a transfiguration nonetheless holding implications for the future of humanity in general. Douglas Trumbull guided the special effects for both films, and some imagery in the later film echoes that of the former. But there the similarities end, and it is worth briefly considering the differences as a means of understanding the intentions and achievements of the two directors and their creative teams.

The principal, and vital, difference between *2001: A Space Odyssey* and *Star Trek: The Motion Picture* may be summed up in a single statement by Stanley Kubrick: "The God concept is at the heart of *2001*."[8] It is from this basis that almost everything else in the film follows, particularly its famous, or notorious, unwillingness to provide answers to the questions it raises. It is almost a matter of necessity that any entity powerful enough to create the monoliths and predict their effects would be seen by human beings as divine. Whether or not the monolith creators still exist is left open, as is the exact nature of the final transfiguration of astronaut Bowman. This is all very much in keeping with the essentially religious approach of *2001*. To postulate a god is to take a religious position, since religion is the formal aspect of our confrontation with the idea of god (or gods). In *2001*, the attitude is, for all of its scientific surroundings, quite traditional; god moves, as the saying goes, in mysterious ways, and our task is simply to accept, rather than to understand, them. Quite the reverse is true of the attitude underlying *Star Trek: The Motion Picture*, and the resultant contrast is clear throughout. In Kubrick's film, virtually every significant development is triggered by the black monoliths; events *happen to* human beings rather than as a result of human choice. There is a very real sense that human beings do not, at least in anything like their present form, belong in outer space; hence the proliferation of disorienting camera angles and images.[9] In Wise's film, conversely, every significant development *happens because of* human action, either directly or indirectly (I shall explore this idea in greater detail later in the discussion). There is an equally real sense that contemporary human beings not only belong in outer space but that it is essentially human values which will transform the significance of space; space is not a terrifying vacuum but an inviting openness. In Kubrick's vision, the audience is left with the disturbing possibility that their own being is purely a matter of external guidance. In Wise's vision, the audience is left with the idea, perhaps equally disturbing but more probably exhilarating, that the future of humanity remains within the control of human beings very much like themselves, even in the (admittedly distant) presence of entities commanding a vastly superior technology. Kubrick's scenario denies human control; Wise's affirms it. Kubrick's film is religious, Wise's is humanistic. Everything else in the two films stems from these disparate starting points.[10]

It has been claimed that Andrei Tarkovsky made *Solaris* as a reaction against *2001: A Space Odyssey*. Certainly his film is far less concerned with technology, and far more concerned with questions of personality: is the Hari with which Kris Kelvin is confronted truly to be identified with his dead wife, is she something else altogether and thus to be abhorred, or is she in fact something in some ways superior to what he has lost? The similar question in *Star Trek: The Motion Picture* will be clear: is Ilia the crew member to be equated with Ilia the fantastically detailed mechanical device with which she is replaced? Likewise, there is a suggestion in both films that the replica develops at least some level of self-consciousness, allowing it to act on its own and in its own interests. The second pseudo–Hari leaves Kris and destroys herself; the Ilia-probe acts so as to make possible the joining with former love Decker that was denied in life. Here there is probably no question of influence, but in any case the foundational differences are essential. Hari's simulacra are grounded in, or at least related to, the memories of Kris Kelvin, whereas Ilia is a reproduction, down to the molecular level, of the person herself. The pseudo–Hari is ultimately destroyed by her inability to reconcile her growing self-awareness with her awareness of her origins; the Ilia-probe, in its moments of self-awareness, reverts to its earlier identity, the basic human[11] self overcoming, and eventually merging with, the external creative power. Kris Kelvin is a man *who does not know what he wants* (hence the bizarre mixture of normality and abnormality at the film's end); practically everyone in *Star Trek: The Motion Picture* knows, indeed at times all too well, what they want. Only V'Ger does not know—and V'Ger is the single-most powerful entity in the film, whose lack of knowledge almost destroys the very thing it is seeking. Most importantly, there is, in Wise's film, none of the nostalgia for an imagined past with which Tarkovsky's film is so profoundly imbued, none of the implied acceptance of quietism. "When man is happy," Snaut tells Kris, "the meaning of life and other eternal themes rarely interest him." It is impossible to imagine any character in Wise's film making the same claim; there, it is precisely when human beings are happiest and most secure that they turn their thoughts toward the most profound questions, for it is only then that those questions can be answered calmly and without fear or despair. Kris Kelvin finds his answers in withdrawing from humanity, though whether by choice or not is unclear; the characters in *Star Trek: The Motion Picture* find their answers in most asserting their humanity, even if in doing so they transcend a particular state of human being.[12]

2001: A Space Odyssey, *Solaris*, and *Star Trek: The Motion Picture* form something of an accidental triad of films, linked by certain external similarities and thematic connections. But the differences among them are greater than their connections. The earlier films have received much analysis and commentary, and their complexities are well known. The same is much less true of *Star Trek: The Motion Picture*, and it is now high time to begin our examination of its complexities, of which there are many more than has commonly been recognized.

3.

The film begins almost motionlessly, with an orchestral prelude and a shot of what are meant to be stars moving away from the viewer; the music we hear, complete for the first and only time, is the music associated with the character of Lieutenant Ilia and, more significantly, with the love and sexual desire between her and another central character, Captain, later Commander, Decker.[13] Musical overtures, whether operatic or cinematic, are traditionally a means of detaching the audience from the world outside the theater and providing a transition from mundane to aesthetic concerns; often the overture adumbrates the essence of the work to follow. Here the overture highlights the absence of an image; the viewer, expecting what the very title proclaims to be a motion picture, is made instead to wait for a considerable time while virtually nothing happens.[14] Thus we ourselves, as members of that audience, have already been caught up in the cycles of desire, eased into an emotional and intellectual pace which encourages rather than overwhelms reflection; the near absence of image, or of movement, in a work explicitly labeled a "motion picture," already invites the spectator to embellish what is on-screen with her or his own imagined possibilities. What André Bazin remarked of Chaplin's *Limelight* is even more deliberately true here: time in *Star Trek: The Motion Picture* is "essentially not that of the drama but the more imaginary duration of music, a time that is more demanding on the mind but also leaves it free of the images that nourish it, a time that can be embroidered."[15] Wise recognized, and called upon, music's ability to convey elements inaccessible through other cinematic means; "A good score, when used in the right way, can add qualities and dimensions that enrich and strengthen your film."[16] The Ilia theme, and Jerry Goldsmith's score as a whole, will play a vital role in organizing and expanding the emotional and intellectual parameters of the film; indeed, the significance of the eight iterations of the main melody will become evident only at the very end of the film.

The credits are accompanied by the most famous of motifs from the film, the march in six-eight time (not only is the tune simple and easily recalled, it served also as the introduction to the first, and most popular, of the several TV spin-offs). The names of the leading players suggest what we will quickly realize: that this music is to be associated with the central human characters. The exuberant music reaches a thumping conclusion, only to disintegrate into something much less clear-cut and focused. Immediately following the credits, we see a vague and amorphous blob of fuzzy colors, a visual cloud of unknowing, accompanied by a single stentorian clap of sound. The cloud is symbolized musically by the "blaster beam," essentially a huge metal string played with a large metal beater (some accounts claim that in this case the beater was, in fact, an artillery shell casing). It is barely capable of producing a recognizable pitch, yet can generate considerable volume; the aural connection to the visuals is immediately obvious. Having first been denied an image, we are now given one without definition; neither size nor shape can be discerned. A reverse shot reveals three space ships approaching (Klingons, in *Star Trek* terminology, but their identity is of little import). The central ship passes under the camera, which tilts and rolls to reveal the cloud, now seen as incomprehensibly enormous. Yet already there is a hint that understanding is possible; along with the clangorous roar of the blaster beam, the score presents, worked into the approach music, an adumbration of the actual V'Ger motif, a figure consisting of triadic quarter-note chords repeated in two groups of three followed by two dotted half-note chords. For the moment, though, understanding is not so much blocked as denied; having scanned the cloud, the Klingons attack without provocation. Desire here is presented in its most brutal aspect: the desire for power, for complete control. The three torpedoes launched by the Klingons have no effect; they simply vanish without explanation.

At precisely the moment the Klingon commander orders evasive action (against an enemy which has, in fact, not yet responded to his attack) the scene changes. A space station is shown, and fragments of transmissions are heard as we eavesdrop on its communications, thus learning its name (Epsilon 9, the number prefiguring the climax of the film, a climax which will be made possible through an understanding gleaned partly from the station's transmissions). Notice how the station is revealed: once more teasingly, delaying our encounter with its actual inhabitants. Time and again, the early sequences of the film prefigure one of its central themes: that true understanding cannot be rushed, but must appear at its own pace.

The command center has intercepted the Klingon transmission and is viewing the battle externally. They, and we, witness a quick catastrophe, as the cloud responds with a vastly more powerful weapon which obliterates, or at least appears to obliterate, the three ships. Desire will not be so easily assuaged. Stunned, the station commander learns that the cloud will pass close by the station "on a precise heading for Earth." He, and we, now know where the cloud is headed, though not as yet why, or what it is. A final shot of the cloud, echoing that with which the sequence began, reminds us of how little information we actually have.[17]

The following scene appears, at first, disconnected from what has gone before. The blue of the cloud gives way to a dark screen, then a reddish sky, as the camera tilts down to reveal a bleak landscape. Only when we see a person, Spock (Leonard Nimoy), one of the principal characters of the *Star Trek* television series, and thus clearly of central importance here, and hear the booming roar of the blaster beam is the connection evident, with the link being reinforced by the tiles upon which Spock is kneeling, which are triangular, and the three huge statues in the landscape; the nature of that link, though, remains vague. Spock stands, and is greeted by three figures: a priestess and two acolytes. The priestess speaks, congratulating him on attaining kolinahr, which is both a state and a process, one "through which all emotion is renounced and shed," as an acolyte helpfully reminds Spock.[18] But Spock is not, in fact, ready; as the priestess presents him with an amulet symbolizing the attainment of kolinahr he stops her, his gesture accompanied by a clang from the blaster beam. Linking with him mentally, she learns of "the consciousness calling to you from space," and announces that "your human blood is touched by it."[19] Spock has failed to reach kolinahr; he has not attained a state of "total logic." He has not achieved complete power over himself and his emotions. He, too, has acted in advance of understanding.

Here, though, two clues as to what he is lacking are provided. The first is the means by which the priestess learns of his connection with the consciousness from space: she touches him, pressing her fingers against his face to facilitate the mental link. The second is the amulet symbolizing the attainment of kolinahr, which she drops to the ground in front of him: a brief insert reveals it to consist of triangle, a rectangle, and a hexagon, arranged in a simple schematic representation of the *Enterprise*, the ship around which the plot will unfold.[20] Both lessons remain to be learned, but the material for learning them is slowly being put in place.

Without warning the scene changes again. After a quick series of establishing shots accompanied by a brisk version of the title march, we see an aircar (number three) arriving at a busy terminal in San Francisco. Aboard is Admiral Kirk (William Shatner),[21] the culminating figure in Wise's line of initially overconfident commanding officers. He asserts his authority immediately; informed that the *Enterprise* requires at least 20 hours more work, he announces that no more than 12 will be permitted, and makes it clear that he will be in command when the ship departs. Admiral Kirk, like Captain Richardson in *Run Silent, Run Deep*, not only has power, he is in a position to use it successfully. Kirk, again like Richardson, will soon learn that the exercise of power is not enough if it is not backed up with imagination.

4.

The three opening sequences of the film have, with great economy of means, established the central tensions which will govern the rest of it. In each instance we have seen someone assert control over an external situation. In the first instance — the Klingon attack on the cloud — the attempt is purely through technological means, a mere matter of force (the Epsilon 9 segment has a further resonance to which I will return shortly). In the second instance, Spock's striving for a state of pure logic, the person controlling and the person controlled are the same, and the result is thus less catastrophic, but the effort likewise ends in failure. In the third case, the most complex, the assertion of control stems from mixed motives, though these have yet to be made clear; accordingly, its success or failure remains in abeyance for the moment, inviting us further onward. In all three cases, an emotional response is in charge while an intellectual one has yet to be attained. The situations, therefore, cannot yet be fully or fairly evaluated, either by the characters or by the audience.

The fundamental structural significance of the number three has by now been deeply embedded in the viewer's experience, even if they are as yet only partly aware of it: three beginnings, three Klingon ships, three torpedoes, three Vulcan attendants, and so on, as well as the fact that most of the music heard thus far has been in three-four or six-eight, the time signature of the music accompanying the opening credits (the Klingon motif, by contrast, is in four-four, as befits their externality to the possibility of understanding and irrelevance to the development of the film). The triadic structure of the film having been secured, its major applications can now be developed. Having seen desire in simple forms, we can now explore it in more complex ones. Desire without understanding of the other will invariably end in failure or worse; what will now be shown are elements of shared desire.

Another sequence of establishing shots moves us into orbit about the Earth. Superb model work, Goldsmith's score, and a series of increasingly lush images once more tease us by delaying gratification yet providing an aural and visual feast. The camera moves toward another space station, aboard which Kirk is transporting. We have moved, literally and symbolically, to a new level of desire, but one fraught with questions (already signaled visually by the fact that the space station itself is seen to be still under construction). "Why aren't the *Enterprise*'s transporters operating?" Kirk asks the ship's chief engineer, Montgomery Scott (James Doohan), in annoyance. Well might he ask; there would appear to be no reason Earth-based matter transporters could not have sent him directly to the *Enterprise*. But the underlying nature (the truth, though not in a purely factual sense) of the situation requires that the

Enterprise be inaccessible by easy means; Kirk must, literally, cross the void to attain his goal. Here, then, is the reverse of the attempt to assert power; rather, power must be attained by sacrifice. Kirk's true sacrifice is yet to come, though, a fact subtly limned by a numerical detail: as Kirk transports aboard the station, we see, between Engineer Scott and the transporter operator, a shuttle pod port door labeled 6, thus implying the step upward from the previous, isolated, triads. Kirk and Scott, though, travel outward on shuttle pod 5. Although neither is aware of the fact, something remains amiss. Some brief expository dialogue clarifies the situation: the *Enterprise* is the only ship close enough to intercept the cloud before it reaches the Earth. "Ready or not, she launches in twelve hours," Kirk informs Scott, who looks dubious. Kirk's words unleash a new musical motif, a simple intervallic pulsation suggestive of tense anticipation. The pod launches, and Kirk gives Scott the background, including the fact Kirk has compelled his superior officers to return him to command; "They gave her back to me, Scotty," he exults, though Scott doubts that it was as easy as Kirk implies. Scott's doubts are accurate; the admiralty did not give the ship back, but rather Kirk, in a sense, took it. And this will make a great difference, as will Kirk's insistence on leaving immediately. Despite his misgivings, Scott pledges that the ship will launch on time and will be ready, after which he grasps Kirk's arm, the second example of touch.

What follows is perhaps the most notorious sequence in the film, a nearly five minute wordless circumnavigation of the space dock and the *Enterprise* within it. Fans and critics alike have complained of the length of the tour, seeing it merely as an exercise in gratuitous special effects, yet they have missed the point. The segment is essential to what follows. Although structurally this scene corresponds to the famous "ballet of the space ships" sequence, set to Johann Strauss's "An die Schönen Blauen Donau," in Kubrick's *2001: A Space Odyssey*, it serves a double purpose not evident in the earlier film.[22] The first aspect is a matter of scale; it is imperative that we understand the massiveness of the *Enterprise*, in order that we experience its relation to the cloud fully (with one minor exception, to be mentioned in due course, the sense of scale is indeed maintained superbly throughout the film). The second, and by far the more important, aspect is that it is here, if anywhere, that we not only understand, but in some measure share, the nature of Kirk's desire. Kirk, chair-bound for over two years despite having the stars in his blood, is seeing, for the first time since leaving command, his old, and truest, love again. Unlike a love between two people, which can be developed through dialogue and gestures, Kirk's love must be demonstrated visually, and it must be shown in such a way as to convey at least some of its intensity. We do not, upon seeing a once and future love for the first time in years, merely glance at them and resume the conversation, and Kirk does nothing of the sort here. Instead, Wise arrived at the idea of teasing Kirk (and the audience) with flashes of the *Enterprise* before the entire ship is shown, deferring gratification once more but this time at much greater length than before, as the nature of the desire is so much the greater and truer than what has gone before. What we see here is pure cinema. As Jerry Goldsmith runs through an extensive, and steadily more excited, series of variations on the opening credit march, we are given the opportunity, visually and aurally, to share the range of emotions running through Kirk's mind. Kirk does indeed desire the *Enterprise*, not simply as a thing but as a symbol of much that is missing from his life, though even *he* does not yet entirely recognize just what it is that he lacks. In case there is any doubt, the link is made explicit by an insert shot through the shuttle pod window in which Kirk's face and the reflection of the *Enterprise* nearly overlap. We and Kirk have now touched upon a vital truth about love and desire: that the requital of either requires that one in some manner enter into the world of that which is desired, rather than simply seeking to compel that which is desired to conform to one's own world. Love must move at its own pace if it is to remain love. This is a truth which must be learned rather than simply assumed, a fact which will be demonstrated repeatedly in what follows.

That Kirk is as yet unaware of the lesson, or even that there is one of which to be aware, is promptly made evident. A young crew member, obviously in awe of Kirk, offers to escort him to—"I think I can find my way, Ensign," Kirk interrupts, after which he boards an elevator to head to the bridge.[23] He would do so; the bridge is the center of control, of power aboard the ship. But the ensign presumably meant instead to take Kirk to meet with Will Decker, the man ostensibly in command of the ship, who is not on the bridge but in Engineering (the literal center of power, as opposed to the metaphorical power of the captaincy). Charging ahead so forcefully, Kirk has lost his way, though it will be some time before he is forced to face the fact.

On the bridge Kirk finds chaos, indicative already of the lack of control he truly has. He is greeted by three former associates, Uhura, Sulu, and Chekov (Nichelle Nichols, George Takei, and Walter Koenig, respectively), who welcome him but reveal that Decker has not yet been apprised of the change of command. Kirk proceeds to the engine room, where he confronts Will Decker (Stephen Collins). Decker, when first seen, is in the midst of repairing the transporter, an intuition he'd had regarding the equipment having proved to be true. He is in control of the technology, every inch a competent officer. Decker, paralleling Bledsoe in *Run Silent, Run Deep*, is unprepared for the news. "I'm taking the center seat," Kirk tells Decker; "I'm replacing you as captain of the *Enterprise*." Decker, who will remain as executive officer, is stunned but perhaps not entirely surprised. "I remember when you recommended me for this command," Decker comments angrily; "you told me how envious you were and how much you hoped you'd be able to find a way to get a starship command again. Well, sir, it looks like you found a way."[24] Kirk merely orders him to report to the bridge.

Kirk's hubris has already been suggested by Decker; "This is an almost totally new *Enterprise*; you don't know her a tenth as well as I do." The point is underlined immediately after Decker's departure. The transporter malfunctions; the technology overrides the control of the technicians, and people die, despite the best efforts of Kirk and Scott. The pattern already established continues; the assertion of power without the presence of the wisdom to use it properly is invariably answered by a reminder of the underlying weakness of the assertion. Without genuine knowledge we may have power, but never true control.

5.

The first of the three overlapping triads of desire which form the structure of *Star Trek: The Motion Picture* is now fully in place: Kirk versus Decker over the *Enterprise*. It is a triangle of *techne*, the desire to control the machinery which allows things to happen. Although this triad, like all situations involving desire, contains within itself the possibility of transcendence, those bound by it must recognize the difference between the will to power and the will to self-overcoming before they can hope to attain what they truly seek. This triad is initially driven by strength, of will or personality or machinery, powers too often mistaken for genuine authority. The potential for disaster within power relations was adumbrated by the Klingon episode, and will shortly be exemplified by the near destruction of the *Enterprise* itself, at which point Kirk, and we, will begin to understand what, exactly, is missing.

At this juncture there is a brief reprise of the opening, as Kirk shows the assembled crew of the *Enterprise* the transmissions from Epsilon 9. Structurally, this serves as a transition to the next stage of understanding, for it provides a reminder that what we are lacking is not simply factual knowledge in itself. The station contacts the *Enterprise*, and the further transmission is shown to the crew. "We're transmitting lingua-code messages on all frequencies," the station commander assures Kirk, but they have received no response. Observing an unusual energy pattern, the commander suddenly realizes that "they could be mistaking our scans as a hostile act." His guess is soon confirmed; within moments the station comes under what is described as an attack, and it soon disappears from the viewscreen. The assertion of power takes many forms; even sensor scans, done in the absence of any knowledge whatsoever, are in fact an attempted form of control (at a personal level, we would describe such a thing as an invasion of privacy, and might well react in a belligerent manner). But for the first time there has been an attempt to communicate with the cloud, and this will provide a vital key later on. Kirk is becoming at least partially aware that he needs more than simple power, or even authority.

The second and third triads of desire now make their appearance in rapid sequence. The second we might call the triad of loneliness and love (*eros*): it will take the form of the struggle between V'Ger and Decker over Ilia. Where the first triad begins with the desires and efforts of individuals largely unconcerned with those of others (the Hobbesian element, though, given the overall course of the film, appropriately subdued), the second already implies personal connections beyond those of strength or power. The force here is an awareness of isolation, experienced initially as a kind of weakness which must be forcibly overcome. Yet loneliness does already point outward, at least in potential, toward another person, one whose openness to the needs of the lonely person carries within it the possibility of a genuine interpersonal duality, a shared selfhood which assuages dual lonelinesses. Such an assuaging, though, cannot be compelled but must develop on its own, lest the duality become the permanent defining division of mutual hatred. Here desire manifests itself in a conventional form, that of heterosexual sexual attraction. The transporter having been repaired (as the result of Decker's actions, it will be recalled), the awaited navigator, Lieutenant Ilia (Persis Khambatta), is transported aboard. It is immediately evident that she and Decker share some emotional connection, one only partially explained by Decker's explanation: "I was stationed on the lieutenant's home planet some years ago." As with Decker's clash with Kirk over the *Enterprise*, there is unfinished business to be attended to, with the difference being that this relationship was, and will eventually be again, mutual.

The third triad, the most complex, the triad of *logos*, of understanding, follows at once. Understanding is broader than mere knowledge or even sexual love; it takes its pattern here from friendship, specifically the mutuality among Kirk, McCoy, and Spock, former crewmates and one-time companions who must rediscover their connections. Friendship comprehends love, but reaches beyond sexual love's tendency for possessive exclusivity; true friendship with one person never requires the cessation of equally true friendships with others. The initial presentation of this triad is tinged with humor (another element often missing in sexual love); just one further crew member is required, one who balks at being transported. "Oh?" says Kirk, heading for the transporter room; "I'll see to it that he beams up." The officer is the chief medical officer, Dr. McCoy (DeForest Kelley), the last of the original stars of the series we encounter.[25] McCoy's appearance signals the end of the centrality of questions of techne and the beginning of the exploration of others. His unwillingness to beam aboard is the last test of the repaired equipment, and it is overcome not through technological means, but as a result of Kirk's need. That need is made clear immediately; McCoy reveals that he has in essence been drafted from retirement for the mission, then realizes that Kirk is behind his having been summoned. Kirk's response is simple: "I need you. Dammit, Bones, I need you. Badly." In acknowledging his need he has taken the first step away from false power toward the conditions of genuine power, power over oneself. He stretches out his hand; McCoy hesitates but accepts it, and Kirk pulls McCoy toward himself as, for the first time since McCoy appeared, the camera moves toward the two as if in approval.

Kirk would appear to have achieved his goals. He has command, his badly needed friend is aboard, and the *Enterprise* is fully ready to depart. Accordingly, for the first time we see Kirk in the Captain's chair, crisply issuing commands. Accompanied by further variations on the march theme and the anticipation motif, the *Enterprise's* departure from orbit is shown in a series of lustrous shots, each more lovely than that which precedes it.[26] Again, to treat these shots in isolation from the film's underlying structure is to miss their point; as we shall see, it is absolutely vital that sequences such as these be embedded deeply within the action. Similarly, to notice their similarity with the planetary alignment sequence in *2001* is to catch a superficial link while missing the more important distinction; in the earlier film, all trace of humanity is rigorously excluded from the sequence, whereas here the images celebrate the existence and beauty of a purely human creation.

The *Enterprise* is impelled forward in three stages: with thrusters, by impulse power, and by warp drive. Each corresponds to a further stage in transcending its initial condition, and each corresponds, thematically, to a deeper level of understanding, a level which can be reached only when the conditions for its fulfillment and comprehension have been reached. At this point, those conditions are still lacking; as a disorientingly angled overhead shot implies, Kirk has not reached the requisite level for advancement. It should be no surprise, therefore, to discover that he nearly destroys the ship through an overhasty command (issued against the advice of Decker and Scott) to move to warp drive, hurtling the ship toward the cloud at faster-than-light speeds.[27] Immediately, as a result of an imbalance in the engines, a wormhole forms, distorting time and energy. A small asteroid posing danger of collision having been drawn into the wormhole ahead of the ship, Kirk orders the phasers (the ship's main weapons) to be armed. "No!" shouts Decker, "Belay that phaser order!" He and Chekov instead use the photon torpedoes to destroy the asteroid. The ship drops to sublight speed, and Kirk, having ascertained that any further attempt to return to the higher speed will create another worm-hole, orders Decker to his quarters for a confrontation, one to which McCoy invites himself.

Kirk now reaches the nadir of his development. Demanding to know why his order was countermanded, he learns that the redesign of the *Enterprise* was such that following his order would have resulted in the destruction of the ship. Decker, who knew of the redesign and knows that his action saved the ship, presses his advantage. The dialogue arrives at a peculiar comment by Kirk, the significance of which will become evident only later.

> *Kirk:* Then you acted properly, of course.
> *Decker:* Thank you, sir. I'm sorry if I embarrassed you.
> *Kirk:* You saved the ship.
> *Decker:* I'm aware of that, sir.
> *Kirk:* Stop —competing with me, Decker.
> [...]
> *Decker:* You haven't logged a single star-hour in two-and-a-half years. That plus your unfamiliarity with the ship's redesign, in my opinion sir, seriously jeopardizes this mission.
> *Kirk:* I trust you will ... nursemaid me through these difficulties, mister?

Kirk dismisses Decker, only to discover that McCoy is not convinced. "He may be right, Jim," the doctor murmurs.

Decker, having exited Kirk's quarters, encounters Ilia leaving an elevator (on Deck 5, the number prominently displayed; their situation, like Kirk's, is as yet unresolved). For the first time since the overture we hear a version of the Ilia theme, and can now make the appropriate association. "Was it difficult?" Ilia asks. "About as difficult as seeing you again," Decker responds. The subsequent dialogue reveals their previous association, one Decker left behind, presumably as a concomitant to his duties, and one now closed to Ilia, who has since then sworn an oath of celibacy (Ilia, it may perhaps be noted, has been established as humanoid but of a non-human species, one which presumably takes such things more seriously than do humans). Decker having placed his hands on Ilia's shoulders, Ilia responds by touching Decker's hand briefly. She then leaves. The contact was limited, but it is real; again, a pathway out of an as-yet-unknown dead end is being indicated.

McCoy, meanwhile, is putting Kirk through a grilling, summing up the indictment against his efforts at control. The scene is very carefully structured visually. The initial two-shot is posed like a showdown in a Western, the two men face to face in full-body profile, as McCoy tells Kirk that it is he, Kirk, who is competing, having "used this emergency to get the *Enterprise* back." As Kirk ponders McCoy's charges, a series of increasingly unbalanced, almost confusing, shots ensues, with the camera angling upward, highlighting the tension between the two men. After a brief interruption as Kirk is informed that a shuttle of some sort wishes to link with the *Enterprise*, Kirk and McCoy are shown, once more, in their "showdown" position. "Your opinion has been noted," Kirk says. "Anything further?" "That depends on you," McCoy replies. Three shots, of McCoy, Kirk, and McCoy again stress the isolation of the captain as McCoy leaves, an isolation emphasized even further as a screen closes between Kirk and the camera, plunging him into darkness.

One advantage of being at the nadir is that the situation must subsequently improve. Although Kirk is as yet unaware of the fact, a corner is being turned even as McCoy is reminding him of his frailties. The shuttle docking with the *Enterprise* bears Spock who, having monitored ship-to-Earth communications, is well aware of the ship's engine difficulties. He enters (through door 3) and heads for the bridge where Kirk is obviously pleased to see him; a brief broad reference to the title music on the strings suggests the identity of Spock's interests with those of Kirk and the *Enterprise*. Spock himself, oblivious to the happy greetings of his former associates and friends (he has, remember, recently come close to purging himself of all emotion), offers his assistance as Science Officer, thus displacing Decker yet again. But the results this time are different; Decker has no objections, as he is "well aware of Mr. Spock's qualifications." No attention is drawn to the fact, but this shift in attitude is symbolic of exactly what will be necessary to achieve the balance toward which the film is striving; Decker willingly surrenders power, and Spock, who receives it, wants it only instrumentally, not intrinsically (though other lessons do remain for him to learn).

Spock's emotional detachment has not gone unnoticed; no sooner has the *Enterprise* achieved hyperlight cruising speed than Kirk summons Spock to meet with him and McCoy in the officers' lounge. The preliminary banter is awkward, with Spock speaking in slow frigid tones. Several times Kirk attempts to get Spock to sit, which is not simply a bit of comic relief; rather, it is when Spock acquiesces to Kirk's request that he is implicitly surrendering some of the control which is keeping him from achieving his own destiny. Spock at last speaks with something akin to enthusiasm, his words coming more rapidly and less monotonously (Nimoy's understated performance is superb throughout the film). As he reveals his emotional connection with the thought patterns emanating from the cloud ("thought patterns of exactingly perfect order"), the scene is fragmented into a series of quick individual shots; there is, as yet, still only limited cohesion among the three men, despite Kirk's reminder to McCoy: "We need him. I need him." McCoy, as always, notes the problem; after pondering Spock's reliability, and thereby eliciting a strong statement of faith from Kirk, he follows the line of thought: "How do we know about any of us?" McCoy has touched upon a vital point, though one which will take time to reach fruition: until one admits uncertainty, until one doubts that one understands, one will never even ask the questions needed to reach truth. That Kirk is still resisting the necessary self-understanding is suggested by another "stand-off" two-shot of him and McCoy.

But understanding awaits and cannot be long denied. The potential personal confrontation is interrupted by a message from the bridge; the *Enterprise* is within minutes of visual contact with the cloud, and Kirk must now act regarding the situation toward which he has been compelling ship and crew. On the bridge, he sees for the first time the extent of what he confronts; as his facial expression makes clear, he now comprehends that this is beyond anything for which he was prepared.[28] Accompanied by agitated versions of the anticipation motif, the bridge crew carries out their investigative tasks, save that when Spock announces that the *Enterprise* is being scanned Kirk orders that no scans be returned, as they might be mistaken for a hostile act. For the first time he is genuinely acting with regard to another rather than his own desires, with the result that the *Enterprise*, unlike every previous vessel encountered by the cloud, will not be destroyed. Kirk opts not to take the *Enterprise* to battle stations, or even to raise the defensive shields, despite Decker's recommendation to do the latter, as these might be misinterpreted as hostile actions. This almost leads to yet another confrontation with Decker, but it is averted in a significant exchange:

> *Decker:* Captain, we've seen what their weapons can do. Shouldn't we take every possible precaution? [...]
> *Kirk:* Mr. Decker, I will not provoke an attack. If that order isn't clear enough for you, I—
> *Decker:* Captain, as your Exec, it's my duty to point out alternatives.
> *Kirk:* Yes it is. I stand corrected.

With those six words Kirk begins to reach the self-understanding which he needs in order to attain his own desires. Thematically, professionalism here asserts its best side; Decker acts up to his duty, and reminds Kirk of the professional relationship between them, regardless of their feelings about their own situations. Kirk, having presumably taken to heart McCoy's warnings, recognizes his own responsibilities, and in so doing begins the process of self-transcendence which will end in a fuller affirmation of that self.

They, and we, have little time to absorb the lesson, though, as the cloud suddenly emits one of its weapons. With nothing to lose, Kirk orders the shields raised; they hold off the destructive force, but only barely, and in the process Chekov, stationed at the weapons console, is injured. As Dr. Chapel (Majel Barrett) and the medics arrive, Ilia, who has rushed to Chekov's side for no apparent reason, reveals that she "can stop his pain." She places her hands on him and, accompanied by quiet fragments derived both from her own motif and from the V'Ger motif, does precisely that (the implicit link between Ilia and V'Ger, later so vital, is adumbrated here with the utmost of economy). Again the importance of touch is suggested, although again the situation is deliberately structured such that we may miss the clue. For the moment it is enough that we have seen human contact (Ilia's touch) take precedence over technology (Dr. Chapel's medikit), without there being any implication that technology is bad or useless, *per se*. We have also been given to understand that Ilia has certain mental and physical abilities which will make her stand out when the *Enterprise* itself is later investigated.

While this action unfolded, Spock has ascertained that the aliens within the cloud have indeed been attempting to communicate, but at a technological level so high that their message was not received properly. With Decker's assistance he reprograms the *Enterprise* computers to transmit a friendship message just in time to avoid the ship's destruction. Nor is this simply a means of ratcheting up the tension; thematically it is vital to what follows. The point is that, for the first time, a true communicative connection between two entities alien to each other has been attained. Mutual communication is, if genuine, inherently egalitarian, and it is only through recognizing the equal claims of another person upon our consciousness that we can make similar claims upon them.[29] But tentative contacts are not enough, and understanding is still lacking. Decker's hopeful comment that the attack was meant merely as a warning is rejected by Spock; such an action would indicate an emotion — compassion — and he senses only "pure logic." Yet behind the logic is puzzlement; the aliens do not appear to understand the nature and purpose of the *Enterprise*. Herein lies a clue to much of what follows, though like most such so far, its significance is presently unclear. With no further threats immediately apparent, Kirk, on the advice of Spock and against that of Decker, orders the *Enterprise* forward into the cloud. As he does so the camera moves slowly toward him, inviting the viewer to join in his clear satisfaction at proceeding into the unknown.

<h1 style="text-align:center">6.</h1>

We now reach the beginning of one of the most magnificent sequences in this or any other science fiction film. The *Enterprise* will move forward in three stages, each corresponding to a stage in the expanding and deepening understanding of self and situation for the characters. The first stage is through the cloud. The second stage will be over the object therein. The third stage will be a voyage into the object itself, at the heart of which all will reach their destiny.

Several elements manifest themselves promptly. The first is Jerry Goldsmith's score, never more evocative than here. An undulating ostinato in the bass, two broken triads (initially D-F-A up followed by C#-A-F down) in six-eight time, the time signature already suggestive of the move toward the second stage of understanding, carries the *Enterprise* deeper and deeper into the cloud, itself presented through a series of abstract multiplanar images of striking beauty. Along with the music and imagery the staging of the sequence limns the necessary points; interior shots of the bridge crew regularly interpose some object between them and the source of illumination, hinting at the gulf which still lies between them and understanding. Yet the reverse shots, after establishing that the images are being seen on the ship's viewscreen, are then allowed to occupy the entire cinema screen, involving the viewer ever more deeply in the implications of the imagery. It is not merely the crew but we the audience who are being carried forward. The point of this will become clear only at the very end of the film.

After a time, Kirk asks Spock for information. Spock's reply is uninformative: "Instruments fluctuating, Captain. Patterns unrecognizable." As he speaks, Spock moves to Kirk's left side; after a moment Decker moves to Kirk's right in a three-shot presenting the triad of the needy, needy who have yet to recognize their true needs, who have not recognized the patterns which will enable them to act appropriately. Yet a new pattern is already unfolding; immediately after this tableau is formed we are given a fresh image of the interior of the cloud, a hexagonal shape comprised of triangular forms, the visual indication that we and the characters have arrived at the next stage of understanding and development. Along with this comes yet another clue: as the *Enterprise* enters into the cloud's new aspect it passes through brightly flaring energy pulses, flares which provoke several reaction shots (Sulu looking frantically here and there at his instruments, Uhura, Kirk, and Spock flinching or squinting against the brightness). Only Ilia and Decker stare straight into the lights without so much as blinking. It is, as we shall discover, they who will find their destiny *inside* the light upon which they so avidly gaze. The cloud parts, and the humans see, for the first time, the structure within it, a six-sided colossus whose scale is all but incomprehensible to them.

Notice also McCoy's apparently irrelevant entrance in the midst of the revelation of the form of the alien. Objectively there is no need for him to be there (he accompanies Chekov, returning to duty, but this would hardly be a priority for the ship's senior medical officer), but emotionally his presence is vital, for it reminds us of the triangle most nearly completed, that of Kirk, Spock, McCoy, and of the internal development of Kirk's character, a development which must come to fruition before the film can find balance. McCoy in effect acts as the embodiment of Kirk's conscience. McCoy says nothing;

his silence further reminding us that even this triangle, in some ways the most obvious, has yet to be closed, an event which will not occur until virtually the end of the film.

Having passed through the cloud, Kirk is ready to take the next step; he orders Sulu to pilot the *Enterprise* over the object at a distance of 500 meters, allowing as close a look as possible without using the forbidden scanners. Sulu complies, albeit with obvious misgivings (providing again the minor motif of the professionalism and competence of the crew even under provocation), and we see, for the first time, a shot establishing the scale of the alien object. The time Wise spent earlier creating a sense of enormity for the *Enterprise* now pays copious dividends; having been lulled into accepting this creation of human will and technology as having tremendous presence and power, we discover that it is virtually insignificant measured against that which its crew hopes to investigate. Virtually, but not completely—in being willing to move slowly, by acknowledging their incomprehension, the crew of the *Enterprise* has facilitated passage beyond what anyone else has reached thus far.

The second stage of understanding is limned by a subtle but striking visual detail. During the cloud sequence, the shots included many of the viewscreen and none of the ship itself save a single establishing shot at the opening of the sequence. Here, external shots of the ship against the background of the alien object are frequent, and the only shot of the viewscreen comes after Kirk has ordered a brief look backwards. All other shots of the alien fill the entire screen, implicating the crew, and the viewer, ever more densely within the ongoing process of comprehension. Accompanying this is another forward-looking clue, as Jerry Goldsmith's score now breaks the six-note ostinato patterns with occasional nine-note measures, the additional beats foreshadowing the climax of the inward voyage, when all three triads come to completion. In addition, the slow somber tune in three-four time heard in the low brass and strings as the sequence opens is derived subtly but directly from Ilia's theme, a matter soon to be of no little significance, as the almost immediately subsequent intrusions of the V'Ger motif indicate.

Understanding must be mutual, at least where consciousness is involved, and it is now the turn of the alien to investigate the *Enterprise*. It does so in the form of an intense pillar of radiant energy, so powerful that it appears to absorb light external to itself, throwing the rest of the bridge into shadow.[30] For all its power and presence, the probe is incapable of touch; its contacts are with the ship's computer banks via tendrils of pure energy. Kirk notes the operations accurately, but does not yet see their significance; "It doesn't seem to be interested in us," he comments, "just the ship." Spock stops the probe's acquisition of secret data ("Earth defenses," etc.) by smashing the computer console with his joined hands (his touch here, though physically weaker than the energy tendrils of the probe, frustrating its operations), bringing the probe's attention to the people standing about helplessly. It singles out Ilia, engulfs her in energy, dematerializes her, and disappears. What exactly has happened is, of course, unclear to the survivors, but the events trigger the next stage in the *Enterprise*'s journey.

The ship is seized by a tractor beam and pulled into the alien ship. For a moment Kirk considers resisting, but upon being informed that the *Enterprise* has only enough strength to fight the tractor beam for fifteen seconds he instantly countermands his own order. Shocked by the evident destruction of Ilia, he is at last coming to recognize that his best efforts will come only when he knows exactly where and why he is applying his own energy. Here and now he is not in charge of events, and by tacitly admitting the fact he has begun to move in the right direction. Thus even the apparent lack of options at the initial moment of the third stage of understanding is contingent upon a personal choice. Kirk could have ordered that the effort to escape continue, even at the cost of the ship, if his goal had been solely to prevent capture or the loss of further information about the ship, its crew, and its origins. To choose passivity is itself a choice, and here it is a vital one.

The three stages of understanding through which ship and crew have been and will be seen as passing are archetypal, as old as Plato and corresponding to common structures of much in Christian mysticism, yet in each case their presence here reveals fully the profoundly humanist reworking of religious thought underlying the film's action. For a direct comparison, consider the three stages of religious awareness evoked by St. Bonaventure in *The Mind's Road to God*, a foundational text of Christian mysticism (it helped shape Dante's *Inferno*, *Purgatorio*, and *Paradiso*, for example). For St. Bonaventure, "There are three successive directions in which the soul's love (or desire) moves in its search for God: *extra nos*, *intra nos*, and *super nos*."[31] The first consists in "the traces which are corporeal and temporal and outside us;" the second comprises our minds; and the third what is "eternal, most spiritual, and above us" (in short, the divine). He extends the idea to the individual, identifying three aspects of the individual human being: "One refers to the external body, wherefore it is called animality or sensuality; the second looks inward and into itself, wherefore it is called spirit; the third looks above itself, wherefore it is called mind."[32] Most important here is the idea of a journey of understanding, of understanding as a process which must pass through several stages rather than coming as a single flash of enlightenment (such as is provided by the monoliths in *2001: A Space Odyssey*). We see this process of comprehension adumbrated in Kirk's voyage to the *Enterprise*, in which he is successively detached from the ship (aboard the space station, complaining about the transporters), outside but in contact with the ship (the long circumnavigation in the travel pod), and within (aboard) the ship. This, of course, merely foreshadows the greater voyage, that of the *Enterprise* itself, a voyage with obvious similarities: first, the ship traveled through the external cloud, with the crew largely in a state of incomprehension. Second, the ship traveled over, physically encountering, the alien construction, speculating as to its origin and purpose. And third, the *Enterprise* is drawn into the alien ship, extending the possibilities of understanding. But notice also the differences here. There is no external guide to the first two stages; they are chosen, directed, and interpreted entirely on human grounds (just how human remains, in fact, to be seen). While the third stage is initially other-directed, it is also incomplete in that direction; enlightenment, literally, must await further human action. The profound metaphysical, or even theological, implications of the relation of human consciousness to these three stages will come to dramatic fruition at the film's climax.

Kirk's passivity is both required and enforced by circumstances. When the *Enterprise* is released from the tractor beam, in front of a complex six-paneled orifice, Kirk orders a full sensor scan. "They can't expect us to look them over now," he says. "Now that we're looking down their throat," comments Decker. "Right," Kirk replies; "now that we've got them just where they want us." He and Decker lock eyes and briefly smile at each other, each for the first time admitting the other as an equal in a situation in which both are equally out of control. Just how out of control soon becomes evident, as Spock reports that all the sensor scans are being reflected back, and no information can be obtained.

Kirk has successfully brought the *Enterprise* this far, but now the initiative passes into other hands. An alert signals an alien presence aboard the ship; Kirk rushes to confront the intruder, giving Decker charge of the bridge and ordering him to hold position. The interaction, though brief, indicates that yet another forward stage in the shared understanding of the two has been reached, as Kirk is now completely able to allow Decker authority, and Decker, who simply nods in response to Kirk's command, is able to accept a command from Kirk without demur. Kirk, Spock, and McCoy reach the room where the intruder has materialized inside a sonic shower, and discover that the intruder is Ilia, or at any rate a robotic probe modeled on Ilia, "programmed by V'Ger," as it/she says, "to observe and record normal functions of the carbon-based units infesting U.S.S. *Enterprise*." A particularly dense security guard queries the descriptive phrase, allowing McCoy to inform equally dense audience members of its point: "Humans, Ensign Perez. Us."

Something of a miniature comedy of misunderstandings now follows. Kirk, called "Kirk-unit" by the Ilia probe, asks whether V'Ger is the name of the alien ship's captain, a question meaningless to the robot. Learning that what appears to be Ilia is a mechanism, he asks where Lieutenant Ilia is; the probe responds (incorrectly, as it will turn out): "That unit no longer functions," indicating that its mission is observation and communication. Kirk asks why the ship is heading to Earth, and receives the startling answer that it does so "to find the creator." Digesting this, he naturally inquires, "What does V'Ger want with the creator?" The reply is no more helpful: "To join with him." Spock, whose mental link with the patterns of total logic has suggested no such apparently irrational purpose, asks how this will be done, and receives an equally circular response: "V'Ger and the creator will become one." He and Kirk attempt to clarify the situation, with no success:

Spock: And who is the creator?
Ilia: The creator is that which created V'Ger.
Kirk: And who is V'Ger?
Ilia: V'Ger is that which seeks the creator.

Frustrated, Spock suggests a medical examination of the mechanism, but McCoy's attempt to take Ilia's arm and guide her to sick bay is unavailing (touch rebuffed, as it were), until Kirk informs the probe that such an examination is a normal part of the carbon based units' functioning. Ilia assents, and the examination proves revelatory, though it raises as many questions as it answers.

During the entirety of the foregoing, quick cuts among the speakers and a total lack of camera movement underlined the situation; mutual incomprehension rules out any expanded understanding. Mutuality returns, and with it camera movement (though both are as yet very restricted) in the subsequent scene. Kirk, Spock, McCoy, and Chapel are standing by an examination bed on which rests Ilia. They are impressed by the incredible detail of the mechanical reproduction; "Even the smallest body functions are exactly duplicated," as Dr. Chapel notes. Decker arrives, accompanied by the Ilia motif, and the camera adjusts position to accommodate his presence, moving for the first time; almost simultaneously Ilia, her motif still playing, looks up at him and addresses him as "Decker," not "Decker-unit." Spock and Kirk summon Decker into the hallway outside the examination room for a quick conference. Again the camera moves to accommodate Decker's departure, almost subliminally indicating that release from the current stand-off will require his involvement.

Spock has already grasped the possibilities inherent in the situation, and he and Kirk develop them. The Ilia-probe "duplicates our navigator in precise detail," Spock says. "Suppose that beneath its programming the real Ilia's memory patterns are duplicated with equal precision." This is not a simulacrum, but an exact replica, one which may have followed its original "too precisely." "Ilia's memory," Kirk realizes; "her feelings of loyalty; obedience;

friendship—might all be there." Intent upon his ideas, Spock rather coldly inquires about Decker's "relationship" with Ilia, provoking an outburst: "That probe in another form is what killed Ilia!" Kirk reaches out, literally. "Commander," he begins; then, more softly, as he grasps Decker's upper arm, "Will—." Here the elements of professionalism and self-understanding intersect; Kirk reminds Decker of the grave danger all are in and the only apparent path out of it, and Decker responds as a trained starship officer. "Our only contact with our captor is that probe," Kirk says. "If we can control it, persuade it, use it—." At this point the Ilia-probe punches its way through the door and announces that Kirk will assist it in its investigations. "The Decker unit can assist you with much greater efficiency," he tells the probe. After a pause, it signals its acceptance with a glance toward Decker. "Carry on with your assignment, Mr. Decker," Kirk says; Decker acknowledges the command with a simple, if subdued, "Aye, sir."

7.

The film now, in its chief connection with *Solaris*, begins to touch upon an extremely complex question: the nature of what it is to be human. In the earlier film Hari is a simulacrum created from the memory of another; here Ilia is an exact physical reproduction which contains the memory of another. The difference is vital. The Hari simulacrum begins as someone other than herself; she must figure out who she is before she can act on her own behalf. The Ilia replica begins by having forgotten who she was; she must rediscover herself before she can act on behalf of another. Notice, though, the implicit assertion underlying Ilia's situation: that human consciousness—the human soul, in other words—is a physical process, one which requires specific kinds of interactions with other human beings to develop fully. We are who we are because of the nature of our human relations, not solely, or even primarily, because of our self-assertion against and over others. *Star Trek: The Motion Picture* inverts the situations, and thus avoids the problems, found in, among others, *Born to Kill* and *Odds Against Tomorrow*; in those films we saw the perils of unrestrained competitive individualism, whereas here the adversarial relationships are subdued in the interests of a greater good (one, incidentally, also benefiting those who have turned away from the antagonistic positions in the first place). Where the overall structure of human relations is such as to emphasize isolation (in fact if not in pretense), competition inevitably turns to conflict, with the result that the surrounding social structure itself becomes threatened. The contradiction ends in destruction, unless ever greater methods of social control are imposed. Where the general structure of social relations is such as to encourage mutuality, the individual will have ever greater opportunities to discover and express his inner potential. *Star Trek: The Motion Picture* uses the foundation of Hobbes's thought against the Hobbesian position; just as Hobbes saw all human thoughts and emotions as physical processes, so does the film. But it recognizes another possibility of social interaction than one based upon fear; it turns, instead, to love and friendship.

This, of course, takes time (another central aspect of the film which, by now, should be evident is its insistence on the gradual nature of the process by which human relations develop; relations which are imposed are never egalitarian, and thus never fully cooperative). Hours pass while Decker, observed on closed-circuit video monitors by Kirk and McCoy, escorts the Ilia-probe around the ship. This set-up allows Wise (in subtle visual terms) to again make the point about Decker's primary role in this matter. We first see Decker and Ilia on a screen, with the on-board camera panning to follow their movements; only after they pause in front of a series of illuminated panels showing various previous vessels bearing the name *Enterprise* does the main camera begin to pull back to show Kirk and McCoy watching Decker and Ilia. Throughout what follows camera movements are associated almost entirely with Decker's efforts, with McCoy and Kirk being shown in unmoving two-shots or brief close-ups.

Decker's approach thus far has evidently been passive, but now he gets a glimmering of what will be necessary to achieve true understanding. He demonstrates games to the Ilia-probe, reaching beyond the level of fact to that of imagination (to *describe* a game is a matter of repeating rules; to properly *play* the game requires an intuitive comprehension of how to transcend them). Among the games is one Ilia formerly enjoyed, and for a moment, signaled by an upsweep of the Ilia motif and an upward movement of both Ilia and Decker's heads, locking gazes briefly, Decker reaches the underlying personality. It is only a moment — the Ilia-probe suddenly declares, unable to comprehend the purpose of play at all, "This game has no meaning." — but it triggers deeper understandings in both of them. For the first time since its appearance aboard the *Enterprise*, the Ilia-probe asks a question instead of making blunt statements: "Why does *Enterprise* require the presence of carbon units?" It couldn't function without them, Decker replies. The probe acknowledges ignorance (as we have seen, a vital step toward attaining knowledge), albeit in a chilling statement: "More data concerning this functioning is necessary before carbon units can be patterned for data storage." Once the investigation is complete, the human beings will be reduced to "data patterns," the ultimate triumph of actuality over potentiality, of fact over imagination. Decker is understandably disturbed, but sees his opportunity. "Within you," he tells the probe, "are the memory patterns of a certain carbon unit. If I can help you to revive those patterns, you could understand our functions better." The probe agrees. "That is logical. You may proceed." It's a peculiar seduction, but it is a seduction; Decker is promising what the probe wants— information — with decidedly ulterior motives, and his methods will of necessity be sensuous.[33] To anticipate later events, he is reaching beyond fact to feeling, for he is beginning to understand that it is not memory itself but the emotional tone accompanying a given memory which provides meaning. In this case, Decker is appealing to his romantic past with Ilia, but not simply as, or for, sexuality. It is not the physicality of love *per se* which matters most, but the way a touch awakens desire for the other and for the expansion and enhancement of our own being they represent. As Iris Murdoch puts it, "Carnal love teaches that what we want is always 'beyond,' and it gives us an energy which can be transformed into creative virtue."[34]

The scene in which Ilia's previous consciousness is brought to the fore is among the most visually complex in the film, and has been misread by more than one commentator. Decker, McCoy, and Chapel are in Ilia's quarters with the Ilia-probe. Chapel drapes a headband, one formerly worn by Ilia, over the Ilia-probe's cranium and turns the probe to face a three-paneled mirror. The camera dollies forward, hinting (along with the almost-constant presence of the Ilia love music) at the intensity of the probe's Ilia-feelings as Chapel switches on a mirror-light. The images proliferate, reminding the viewer of the manifold possibilities inherent within any individual and within the situation at hand, as well as silently reinforcing the questions centering on the true nature of the Ilia-probe (is it, or isn't it, somehow truly human?). "On Delta, remember?" Decker prods gently, as a new angle (not, as one might first assume, a reverse shot) shows him standing by the reflection of Ilia.[35] Again, the visuals reflect the underlying sense of the scene, in this case literally, in that Decker is attempting to reach past a fact (the existence of the Ilia-probe) to reach something imagined (the presence, in the probe, of Ilia's previous state of mind). We see not the actual thing (the probe), but the image of what is sought. We do not know which is the more real.

"Ilia," Dr. Chapel calls out softly, prompting a fresh shot showing both Ilias, framed by Chapel and Decker, as they turn to look toward Chapel, hesitantly speaking her name ("Doc-tor Chapel"). Quick reaction shots, of Chapel and then McCoy, lead to a new angle as Ilia turns to look at Decker, speaking his name as if awakening from a confusing dream —"Will?"— and reaching up to caress his face. This latter shot, and the reverse shots of Decker as Ilia slides her hand down his neck and rests it on his shoulder, exclude the mirror altogether, as if to suggest that Decker has indeed found the true Ilia. He seems to think so, speaking her name quietly but passionately as he stares into her eyes, and he must be reminded by McCoy that "this is a mechanism." Duty recalled, he pleads with Ilia to "help us make direct contact with V'Ger." "I cannot," she avers. Decker tries another tack; "This creator V'Ger is looking for — what is it?" Ilia's reply is a melancholy one: "V'Ger does not know." A few moments later the mechanical aspect retakes control. The Ilia-probe breaks physical and visual contact with Decker and turns back to the mirror as it removes the headband, prompting a repeat of the earlier ambiguous shot, once again posed as a question: what, now, is the real Ilia?[36]

While this has been unfolding, Spock has been demonstrating that he, too, needs to learn patience. Stealing a thruster suit, he exits the *Enterprise*, intent upon penetrating into the sealed inner chamber and confronting V'Ger's perfect logic for himself. His efforts lead directly to the most phantasmagorical sequence in the film, one rife with visual symbols and spectacular imagery. He will fail in his goal, but will attain a more important one in so failing, an attainment which will directly influence the outcome of the encounter with V'Ger for everyone else.

Accompanied by an explosive scherzo prominently featuring a speeded-up version of the ostinato figure which had escorted the *Enterprise* into and through the V'Ger cloud, Spock passes through the orifice and into the inner chamber, where apparently nothing he sees is physically real, even though much of it contains clues to what does in fact lie ahead. Spock observes what he takes to be a record of V'Ger's travels. Since none of what he witnesses will be duplicated, or even visible, during the *Enterprise*'s traversal of the same space later on, we may take it that his experiences are purely imaginative, in that his mind is being directly stimulated by V'Ger in an attempt (only partly successful) at communication. There is something rather Hegelian here, in the sense that Spock's inability to recognize all that V'Ger is offering stems directly from his inability to negate his own conscious control over his reactions (he records a narration of the entire journey as a resource for those back on the *Enterprise*). Later, having had time to think and, more importantly, to feel, he will advance significantly in understanding. We do not gain understanding simply through observation; what we observe must consciously be placed within a larger context, a context which includes our own self-understanding; we must, to speak philosophically, overcome, and thereby negate, our previous self and replace it with a more extensive self, one including both the prior level of understanding *and* the new level. "Importantly, the Hegelian subject is not a self-identical subject who travels smugly from one ontological place to another; it *is* its travels, and *is* every place in which it finds itself."[37] As I have already noted, scenes pointing toward some further level of comprehension often contain a numerical signifier, either one indicating the current triad of understanding (three or six) or one falling just shy of the next step (five, and now eight). Both are the case here. Spock passes through three different sets of eight rings, their putatively factual purpose never explained, before reaching what appears to be a particularly odd arrangement of planets, eight of them around an ovoid object with an opening in the center. Inside this he encounters a huge representation of Ilia, with which he attempts to join minds in the same manner as the Vulcan priestess had done with him earlier. His attempt is only partly successful (his hands are, of course, gloved, and he does not in fact touch anything), but he does obtain enough information to realize the salient fact of the matter: V'Ger is a living machine, apparently coterminous with the entirety of the enormous ship through which the *Enterprise* has been traveling.[38] Spock is then hurtled bodily from the chamber, where his unconscious form is retrieved by Kirk, who had followed him out and waited for just such an eventuality.[39] Kirk takes the body to sickbay, where Spock will awaken, in more ways than one.

The first shot of Spock in sickbay is one of Wise's rare overhead shots. Normally he uses these as a means of isolating the subject, usually with the camera descending in an oppressive intimacy; here the reverse is true, as the camera pulls back to admit Dr. Chapel, in attendance on Spock, revealing thereby Spock's connection with the human world he had momentarily abandoned. As Dr. Chapel scans Spock's nervous system, an insert effortlessly reminds us of the Kirk-Spock-McCoy triad by showing three side-by-side computer images resulting from the scan, with the reflections of McCoy and Kirk superimposed, just visibly, over two of them; acutely missing is Spock himself. McCoy's medical commentary is interrupted, unexpectedly, by laughter from Spock. "Jim," he says, using Kirk's personal name for the first time since boarding, "I should have known." V'Ger is, as Spock suspected, a living machine from a planet of living machines, a purely logical being resting on a basis of extraordinary technology. "V'Ger has knowledge that spans this universe," he tells Kirk. "And yet, with all its pure logic, V'Ger is barren, cold — no mystery, no beauty...." What Spock should have known turns out to be as important for him as for V'Ger; reaching up, he grasps Kirk's arm, then takes his hand, as the motif of touch finds its first climactic use. "This," he murmurs, "simple feeling is beyond V'Ger's comprehension. No meaning, no hope. Jim — no answers. It's asking questions. Is this all that I am? Is there nothing more?" The scene is dominated by three-shots of Kirk, McCoy, and the recumbent Spock, mixed with two-shots of Spock and Kirk, reminding us that the latter has not yet finished his own journey. The three men have little time to explore the moment, though, for V'Ger has arrived at Earth's orbit and the long-anticipated crisis is at hand.[40] "I need Spock on the bridge," Kirk tells McCoy, his admission of his own limitations cueing another step forward.

As Kirk arrives on the bridge, so do Decker and the Ilia-probe. V'Ger transmits a coded radio message toward the Earth. "V'Ger expects an answer," Decker tells Kirk. "I don't know the question," the latter replies. Almost immediately, V'Ger launches orbiting devices which nullify Earth's defenses and proceed to equidistant orbits, where each fragments into three more, preparing to purify the planet of carbon-based parasites which are presumably interfering with the creator's ability to respond. McCoy realizes that V'Ger's creator must be a machine, and Spock makes the necessary connection, completing another thematic link, this time between Kirk's earlier comment to Decker regarding his (Kirk's) need for guidance: "V'Ger is a child. I suggest you treat it as such." McCoy is dubious—"This child is about to wipe out every living thing on Earth. Now what do you suggest we do—spank it?"—but Spock presses his point: V'Ger needs, and knows that it needs, but does not know what it needs. Kirk, taking his cue from the idea of ignorance, makes a desperate gamble; he tells the Ilia-probe that the "carbon units" know why the creator has not responded but will not reveal their information until the destructive devices are withdrawn. He orders the bridge secured and cleared, metaphorically abjuring the exercise of power, the very thing he has sought for so much of the film. V'Ger cuts off the *Enterprise*'s communications with Earth and shakes the ship about ("Your child is having a tantrum," McCoy tells Spock), but Kirk is adamant: the carbon units will disclose their information only to V'Ger itself (Kirk is here partly temporizing and partly acting on Spock's suggestion that a close approach to V'Ger itself might make possible an attempt to control the devices). V'Ger agrees, and the *Enterprise* is drawn into the inner chamber.

Another of the film's subtly great moments now ensues. The camera slowly approaches Kirk and Decker, standing by the captain's chair, as Kirk contacts Engineering and orders Scott to prepare the *Enterprise* for self-destruction on Kirk's order. Scott somberly complies, assuring a concerned but still-composed crew member that there is no doubt that the uncontrolled release of matter and anti-matter will indeed ensure the destruction of V'Ger. After a beautiful insert of the *Enterprise* passing through the interior of V'Ger, one which by its contrast of scale calls into question Scott's certainty, the scene returns to the bridge. The camera dollies forward to hear Chekov's announcement that only 18 minutes remain before the devices are activated, then slowly traverses the bridge, panning and dollying across and then up and then back again, as each of the officers makes, or hears, what may be their final report. Here Wise celebrates true professionalism at its finest, the trained individuals reacting to a dire situation by maintaining their stations and preparation despite having heard Kirk's order and knowing what it potentially means, a far more powerful depiction of courage than would be any amount of rushing about and bellowing meaningless orders. At last the camera comes to rest on Spock, silent and with his back turned. On a cut Kirk begins to ask him a question, only to discover, as Spock turns in response, that Spock is crying, a single tear rolling down his cheek (note, too, that McCoy, still in keeping with his role as Kirk's conscience, appears in the reverse shot as Kirk reacts to the tear). As with so much in this film, the moment is subtle (and wonderfully acted by Nimoy, whose idea this scene apparently was), in full keeping with the film's resistance to overdramatizing the personal development of its characters.

Spock is crying from empathy; "I weep for V'Ger as I would for a brother. As I was when I came aboard, so is V'Ger now: empty, incomplete, and searching. Logic and knowledge are not enough." Spock has developed empathy, the ability to enter emotionally into the needs and feelings of another; he has taken the leap of moral imagination which allows him to feel sadness on behalf of a thinking machine, a truly alien consciousness, to understand it on its own terms. "What would V'Ger need to fulfill itself?" asks Decker. Spock's reply is indirect; "Each of us, at some time in our lives, turns to someone — a father, a brother, a god — and asks, Why am I here? What was I meant to be? V'Ger hopes to touch its creator, to find its answers."[41] As he says this, the *Enterprise* comes to a halt before a small central platform, the source of V'Ger's radio signals, and the film's final act begins.

8.

At first all is in abeyance; the music is little more than percussive taps and indeterminate sustained chords, and the camera restricts itself to cuts without motion. Kirk, Spock, and McCoy start out with the Ilia-probe. Decker indicates his desire to come along, and Kirk, by now having learned his lesson, acquiesces without demur, accompanied immediately and approvingly by the first camera movement since the scene began, following the five as they exit the bridge. They cross a causeway of hexagonal paving stones, accompanied musically by a very slow version of the Ilia theme (here clearly indicating the intense desires underlying and prompting what will follow), into a specially prepared arena, its climactic significance within the film's triadic structure indicated by its own physical structure: it is framed by nine angular columns, the feet of which descend toward a platform on which rests V'Ger, which proves to be an oddly small and battered piece of machinery. As a subdued variation of the anticipation music pulses quietly, Kirk investigates; he espies a name tag covered with soot, and scrapes it away to reveal the entire name: *Voyager 6*, an Earthly probe launched by NASA some 300 years before. And thus the film comes full circle, or nearly so. *V'Ger is in fact a human creation.* It is seeking those who programmed it in order to fulfill the commands it was given centuries before. Having passed through a wormhole and been discovered by the inhabitants of the machine planet, it was given additional technology to allow it to carry out its mission: "Collect all data possible. Learn all that is learnable. Return that information to its creator." As it traveled back across the galaxy, "It amassed so much knowledge it achieved consciousness itself."

Here we see the vital distinction, one I noted above but did not develop, between *Star Trek: The Motion Picture* and *2001: A Space Odyssey.* There the monoliths remain unexplained, and the possibility that they are divine in origin is neither affirmed nor dismissed. Here the solution to the mystery rests entirely on human desires and intentions; V'Ger is, and always was, simply a means to carrying out human plans. Yet those plans, based as they were purely in one side of human existence (the quest for knowledge), inevitably issued in a flawed and imbalanced answer, one which verges now on destroying humanity itself: there is knowledge aplenty but no wisdom, no ability to understand the point of acquiring that knowledge. Knowledge—facts—will not answer any worthwhile questions unless backed by a purpose, and purpose, being grounded in an imaginative leap into the future, cannot itself be based purely upon knowledge. Purpose requires the presence of at least one other person (even a purely selfish purpose requires that the individual driven by it envisions themselves as existing in at least two states: that which desires and that which has acted in fulfillment of that desire). V'Ger has facts, and is striving to develop reason, the ability to assemble purpose regarding those facts. It is a complex relationship, one eloquently outlined by Herbert Marcuse:

> Reason develops through the developing self-consciousness of man who conquers the natural and historical world and makes it the material of his self-realization. When mere consciousness reaches the stage of self-consciousness, it finds itself as *ego,* and the ego is first *desire*: it can become conscious of itself only through satisfying itself in and by an "other." But such satisfaction involves the "negation" of the other, for the ego has to prove itself by truly "being-for-itself" *against* all "otherness." [...] The ego must become *free,* but if the world has the "character of negativity," then the ego's freedom depends on being "recognized," "acknowledged" as master—and such recognition can only be tendered by another ego, another self-conscious subject.[42]

V'Ger has discovered its own desires, but has had no means of acting upon them, for every other being it encountered was negated, "patterned for data storage," reduced to yet another lifeless fact. Only when V'Ger gains the ability to recognize others can it become fully free, but in order to gain that recognition V'Ger must acknowledge and freely interact with the free will of those others, especially those others not yet recognized as subjects in their own right. V'Ger has been following orders blindly, treating them as fundamentals which cannot be questioned, only to discover that this is not enough; as McCoy notes, "The creator does not answer."

Kirk sees the point first. He orders Uhura to find the appropriate codes in the *Enterprise* library, and then boldly declares, "We are the creator," a creator which will prove itself by making it possible "for you to complete your programming. Only the creator could accomplish that." Soon enough the *Enterprise* signals that the codes are ready, and on Kirk's command begins transmitting them. It does not work. V'Ger has at last reached the threshold condition of selfhood and realizes that it must assert itself in contradistinction to its programming; as the coded command arrives, V'Ger's receiver shorts out.

The visuals throughout this sequence are dominated by the *Voyager* spacecraft, but otherwise the unsettled situation finds its expression through an equally unsettled mix of long shots and close-ups, static images and fluid camera movements, odd angles and shifting colors. "The creator must join with V'Ger," the Ilia-probe announces to Kirk, prompting him to order a repeat of the signal. This is an inappropriate response with no emotional resonance, as the torso-level medium shot into which the camera moves subsequent to Kirk's order suggests, and the probe now looks directly at Decker. "The creator must join with V'Ger," it repeats, stepping toward him, as a very unusual low-angle shot of the probe and Decker, bridged visually by the *Voyager* spacecraft's boom arm, indicates the radical shift in its self-understanding now upon V'Ger. Close-ups of the Ilia-probe, its face no longer blank but pleading, and Decker, his face revealing a dawning comprehension regarding just what this might mean, drive home the impending connection between V'Ger's action and its own expanding awareness of the true nature of "joining." The apparent malfunction was deliberate, done in order, as Decker realizes, "To bring the creator here; to finish transmitting the code in person." Or, as he says while staring at the Ilia-probe, "To touch the creator."

The thematic significance of V'Ger's desire should need no further elucidation. Its implications, though, go further. In my comparison of Wise and Ingmar Bergman I noted the contribution Bergman's concern with religious questions made to his films, and suggested that Wise's films had, on the whole, no fully comparable underpinnings. Here, by contrast with so many of Wise's other films, the religious underpinnings form the very structure of the film; in *Star Trek: The Motion Picture*, the absence of a creator occupies the same emotional space for V'Ger as it does, say, for Antonius Block in *The Seventh Seal*, in that each seeks to establish meaning for himself on the basis of the existence of a superior being. The vital difference, though, is that Block's quest demands that the superior being be fixed in its actuality, that there be no further space — mental, moral, or imaginative — left over after the encounter with the deity, whereas V'Ger's search and answers, presented entirely within a humanist viewpoint, require not only the transcendence of its present state of being but that that transcendence be ongoing, always toward what cannot be known but must be imagined. Bergman's films, or at least many among them, are essentially theological, even in their presentation of divine silence or absence, because the inner lives — the self-conceptions — of the central characters, those who provide the focus for audience identification emotionally and intellectually, depend on their relation to, and evaluation of, the god-idea. Wise's films are essentially humanist in that nothing divine matters, because the self-conceptions of his characters depend only on the degree of their own awareness of the social and individual factors driving them; where such awareness is lacking, where others fail to be a part of the self-conception of the person striving to shape the outer world, as with Sam Wild in *Born to Kill*, the characters will be crippled or destroyed; where it is, or becomes, present, where others are an essential part of the self-conception of the striver, as with McDonald Walling in *Executive Suite*, there is room for personal progress and genuine optimism. The climax of this approach occurs here, in that a genuine metaphysical quest, a search for ultimate meaning, finds its resolution through, and only through, decisions taken by human beings acting upon their own moral and metaphysical imaginings. Even V'Ger's desire is a human artifact. What we are seeing here, therefore, is *the replacement of the divine by the human.*

Spock now applies his own hard-won understanding to V'Ger's situation, triggering the dialogue which will lead directly to the film's resolution. "V'Ger must evolve," he tells the others.

> *Spock:* Its knowledge has reached the limits of this universe, and it must evolve. What it requires of its god, Doctor, is the answer to its question: is there nothing more?
> *McCoy:* What more is there than the universe, Spock?
> *Decker:* Other dimensions; higher levels of being.
> *Spock:* The existence of which cannot be proven logically. Therefore, V'Ger is incapable of believing in them.
> *Kirk:* What V'Ger needs in order to evolve is a human quality: our capacity to leap beyond logic.
> *Decker:* And joining with its creator might accomplish that.
> *McCoy:* You mean this machine wants to physically join with a human? Is that possible?

After a long pause during which Decker stares in the direction of both the *Voyager* spacecraft and the Ilia-probe (Wise carefully withholding an answering shot of either, allowing the viewer to ask themselves just what it is that drives Decker here, a love for someone no longer alive or a desire for a hitherto unimagined kind of existence — although either is a fundamental imaginative commitment), Decker declares his intentions: "Let's find out."

He strides to the receiver to manually key in the code; Kirk, attempting to intervene, is casually but forcefully thrust aside by the Ilia-probe. McCoy calls out warningly to Decker, but the latter has already completed the transmission. "Jim, I want this," he declares, an affirmation reinforced by the quick short move of the camera toward him as he speaks. "As much as you wanted the *Enterprise*, I want this." He locks gazes with the Ilia-probe, and we become aware of a two chord motif in three-four time (a quarter note followed by a half note, which latter is held a half-beat into the second measure, followed by the same progression save that the first chord is given as an eighth note midway through the first beat), that of fulfillment, derived from the tail end of the original V'Ger music, various forms of which have been heard at key moments throughout the *Enterprise*'s contact with V'Ger but the significance of which has been obscured until now.

Again the camera moves toward Decker, slowly this time, a movement balanced by a similar reverse shot moving toward the Ilia-probe.[43] At the last, the probe's face, now surely the face of Ilia, shows the merest hint of a smile, the smile of a lover who sees what is missing in their life in the eyes of the one they love. Techne has done its work, and logos and eros can now come together as they have been seeking to do almost since the film began. Again, Herbert Marcuse has expressed the underlying force of the moment:

> The philosophic quest proceeds from the finite world to the construction of a reality which is not subject to the painful difference between potentiality and actuality, which has mastered its negativity and is complete and independent in itself — *free*.
> This discovery is the work of Logos and Eros. The two key terms designate two modes of negation; erotic as well as logical cognition break the hold of the established, contingent reality and strive for a truth incompatible with it. Logos and Eros are subjective and objective in one.... In the exigencies of thought and in the madness of love is the destructive refusal of the established ways of life. Truth transforms the modes of thought and existence. Reason and Freedom converge.[44]

With Decker's transformation the possibility of fact is exceeded by the actuality of imagination; not he, nor V'Ger, nor we know exactly what is happening here. As he transmutes, the Ilia-probe walks toward him, the erotic charge enhanced by the slightly slowed motion. Spock takes Kirk's arm to guide him back to the *Enterprise*, and the flashes and explosions of light seen already during the passage toward V'Ger, the flashes and explosions which made no impression upon Decker and Ilia then, return now, accompanied by a transfiguration of the V'Ger motif, pure and high in the strings, and then, as the two individuals meld fully, by a derivative of the voyaging motif (the ostinato already heard accompanying the *Enterprise* and Spock on their respective journeys into V'Ger), signaling the beginning of their own onward journey. The V'ger ship explodes into scintillations of light and color, accompanied by a very grand statement of the fulfillment motif, the musical signal of joining, the logical (if you will) climax of the efforts made by so many of the characters to make contact, emotional or physical, with others. As this music dissolves, it gives way directly to a new version of the title march, the music of Kirk and the *Enterprise*, which ship duly materializes directly out of the glowing heart of the V'Ger explosion and moves slowly and majestically into its own close-up.

A brief coda follows. Accompanied, notably, by a fresh version of the pulsating music of anticipation, Kirk, Spock, and McCoy return to the *Enterprise* bridge, where they speculate that what they have just seen is "possibly a next step in our evolution," as Spock sagely comments.[45] The triads are evidently complete, or at least their tensions have been resolved. Yet even here there is room for speculation, for further exploration. Each of the central figures has obtained what they sought, whether knowingly or unknowingly, but in each case what has been attained is, and can be seen to be, simply a way-station of some sort. Kirk has obtained the *Enterprise* (in the final shot of him, the camera is moving toward him as it did toward Decker as he obtained his desire), and almost immediately orders the ship out on a new (and deliberately unspecified) direction and mission (Scott's appearance on the bridge at this juncture, like McCoy's various appearances on the bridge earlier, is not objectively necessary but is thematically appropriate, as it serves to link the elements of control and power, the disjunction of which caused so much trouble earlier). Spock has attained the awareness that logical perfection is sterile, that human context (a community of flawed but diverse hearts and minds) is vital, and that his own ambitions require accepting his own imperfections. He has realized that the only possible way to avoid an affirmative answer to the central questions—"Is this all that I am? Is there nothing more?"—is to be forever changing; true life is nothing but change; stasis is the equivalent of death. Decker has regained, and magnified, the love he abandoned, and V'Ger has found purpose. Both events have entailed a shift to a level both inconceivable and ineffable (appropriately enough, as it is their thoughts and actions which have required the greatest degree of faith).

The film concludes with two particular images, ones reflecting both the balance sought and attained and the higher level of instability which is simultaneously a result and a requirement of that balance. The first is a shot of the *Enterprise*, seen from below.[46] As the title music soars out grandly in the full orchestra, the camera pulls back and turns to watch the ship pass, in a deliberate inversion of the shot of the Klingon ship which opened the film's action. The ship disappears into faster-than-light speed, but the camera keeps moving as if wanting to follow it. As the music reaches a cadence and the film ends, the second image appears, an intertitle: "The Human Adventure is Just Beginning." Janus-like, these words apply in two directions simultaneously. On one hand, they refer to the ongoing experiences to be had by each of the characters; on the other, they refer to the challenges given to the audience through the implications of the experiences we have witnessed. *Star Trek: The Motion Picture* is not merely about its own events. As much through its form as through its content, and even through its flaws as well as its successes, the film offers, more subtly and thus in some ways more compellingly than many of its companions among Wise's films, a complex vision of the nature of human hope.

9.

Star Trek: The Motion Picture is not only optimistic but utopian in its implications. Wise's better films tend to be those which are critical of contemporary social and political structures, and even the conventional optimism of a happy ending is thus often denied to them. In comparatively few cases is the ending unambiguously presented as optimistic, definitely pointing toward a better future for the participants; *The Sound of Music* is the obvious example here, along with *Somebody Up There Likes Me*. Somewhat similar in tone is *Tribute to a Bad Man*, in which Jeremy Rodock (James Cagney) wins the woman from the younger man (Don Dubbins) despite his greater age and troubled personality, though Dubbins's narration has a melancholy quality which somewhat belies the mood of the conclusion. *Executive Suite* falls somewhere between these two stools, as McDonald Walling's future is rosy, Mary Walling's fraught with ambiguity, and Julia Tredway's still largely empty. Yet these films are in the minority; far more often the films which end with the protagonist having achieved their goals are at most ambivalent in presenting that achievement; *The Set-Up*, *The Desert Rats*, and *The Andromeda Strain*, as examples, each end positively, in that an explicitly feared catastrophe has been averted, yet none ends triumphantly, as questions extending beyond the ending warn, if they do not promise, that fresh potential catastrophes lurk just over the imaginative horizon. In other films the ending is even more downbeat, with the protagonist, or at least a central figure, achieving the sought-after goal only at the expense of their own death (*Run Silent, Run Deep*, for example, or *The Hindenburg*). Bleakest of all are those in which neither the protagonist nor their goals survive the film; *Born to Kill*, *Odds Against Tomorrow*, and *The Sand Pebbles* are typical examples here.

A comparison among Wise's three science fiction films suggests the unique status of his last. In *The Day the Earth Stood Still* Klaatu is shot down in the street, saved from death only by superior technology; the fate of humanity is very much up in the air at the film's end. In *The Andromeda Strain* the central figures all survive, it is true, but the facts they have uncovered during their fight against the alien microbe have left the ability of those individuals to continue functioning within the current system in doubt, as Jeremy Stone explicitly acknowledges in ending the film with a question directed at the senator already seen as suspicious of science and supportive of the military program which initiated the troubles in the first place. *Star Trek: The Motion Picture*, by contrast, ends with neither failures nor deaths among its principals (Kirk explicitly changes the designation of the fates of Captain Decker and Ilia from that of being "casualties" to "missing" in his report to his commanding officers). Kirk and Spock have achieved their specific goals, and been reunited with each other and with McCoy. Decker has joined Ilia in a greater intimacy than either could have ever imagined, and V'Ger has found, if not meaning, at least a whole new level of questions. One might argue that *Star Trek: The Motion Picture* ends more happily than did even *The Sound of Music*, despite the absence of singing children, for here the characters overcome their problems, whereas in the earlier film they succeed mainly in escaping them.

Yet mere optimism is not enough. Happy endings are all very well, but most involve only the central characters (the "good guys"), leaving the fundamental circumstances against which the ending is measured unchanged. Thus, for instance, *The Sound of Music* ends with the Trapps singing their way to freedom but with the Nazis firmly in control of Austria (and World War II yet to come). It would be unfair to expect every film, or even, perhaps, any particular film, to engage with, let alone to solve, the social or political tensions underlying its depictions of personal conflicts, but such films as do so often take greater emotional and, particularly, intellectual risks, risks occasionally providing unexpectedly powerful rewards. These engagements take two forms, broadly speaking: those which provide or suggest a specific solution to a current problem, and are thus grounded principally on matters of fact, and those which point toward a more general shift in the underlying situation which helped create the problem in the first place, and thus are grounded in matters of faith (that is, of imagination). Art is, and should be, better at diagnosing problems than providing solutions; such works as offer detailed solutions may be potent for a time, but fade quickly once the problem is solved or forgotten, unless they offer other pleasures unrelated to that problem or its overcoming. "A work of art," as Herbert Marcuse reminds us, "is authentic or true not by virtue of its content (i.e. the "correct" represen-

tation of social conditions), nor by its "pure" form, but by the content having form."[47] Yet any work of art, no matter how trivial or bound by its times,
is already, in a sense, also pointing toward the second form of engagement,
for the creation of art itself is already an act of faith in an unknown future.
The next step is for that engagement to reach beyond the simple circumstances of creation, for it to become part of the work's inner necessity; at this
point, the work becomes truly utopian. The person who becomes involved
with it does so, or at least may do so—there can be no compulsion here—
with more than its structure and explicit content. Taking up the work's challenge, they enter into the work's own presuppositions as if they were a part
of them, and experience, even if only intermittently and unconsciously, a
new way of seeing a possible world to come; having had those experiences,
they carry away a residue of desire for that world, an engagement with the
possibility of acting so as to assist at the birth of that world. This engagement
need not have been fully intended by the work's creator(s); indeed, too bla-
tant an intention to reshape the imagination of the viewer can easily topple
over into propaganda, and thus quickly take on the anachronistic flavor of
outdated political debates, of yesterday's news. More interesting are those
works which reveal a deep connection with utopian speculation even while
appearing to address only a particular set of plot components. A work of this
sort is often flawed at the level of conventional artistic expectations, for its
own structure bears and germinates seeds of contradiction already planted
by the situation out of which it came. If, though, it carries those seeds to
fruition, the work is redeemed by the greater consistency between its unconscious contradictions and the higher level resolutions of those contradictions
it implies; "Reading the meanings it unwittingly *enacts* against those it explicitly *intends*, it recovers ever greater dimensions of its own identity."[48] These
resolutions, of course, are neither guaranteed nor final; their value comes
from their faith in the process of extending hope, which is the heart of the
utopian vision.

Although science fiction would seem to be a natural bearer of utopian
hopes, yearnings, expectations, and possibilities, it explores these components
of anticipated futures much less frequently and far less extensively than one
might imagine; the literature of science and technology is too often merely
an amplification of the contemporary uses to which those disciplines are put,
with equally contemporary prejudices and constraints upon imagination carried along without change. Dystopias, requiring merely that some unfavor-
able trend known to the author be inflated to become a permanent fixture of
the half-imagined future, abound; genuine utopias, requiring a much greater
depth of empathy and imagination, are correspondingly rarer. The same is
even more true of science fiction cinema, in part for the simple reason that

blowing things up is both easier and more spectacular than envisioning and presenting a transformed society; the former requires only good special effects, while the latter, being more a matter of changes in consciousness than improvements in technology, requires a careful development of small emotional details and their implications.

It is, in fact, technology which both allows and requires the utopian stance at the heart of *Star Trek: The Motion Picture*. There is here an implicit confrontation between the repressive effects of technology (or, more precisely, what technology represents) and human self-expression and genuine communication. Technology does not exist by itself; technology is always created for a reason, answering to the felt demands of a particular social and political situation; where it is repressive, therefore, it is repressive because the underlying social demands are repressive. A hammer becomes a weapon because someone chooses to use it for the purposes of violence, and that choice itself is not random; it requires already at least the conception of a violent response to a particular relationship, whether with person or thing (the deservedly famous sequence of the ape-man discovering the power of violence in *2001: A Space Odyssey* captures this fact concisely and powerfully). V'Ger in its initial state represents the force of technology without morality or imagination; only its retention of a human desire for understanding allows positive change. That change becomes possible, though, only through an act of love, of a willed supersession of an individual ego (Decker's) in the interests of intersubjectivity. Decker's act, in turn, has become possible only within the context of a community in which conventional responses to imbalances of power can be overcome (Kirk's desire for control of the *Enterprise*, which he must learn to surrender in order to attain). The repressive effects of technology upon sexuality (embodied, literally, in the Ilia-probe) symbolize the repressive effects of a technologically driven society, a society of things and control, upon its members or, as the case may be, subjects. Intellect without emotion, will without compassion, will be sterile and crippling, ultimately destructive of everything truly human (as suggested by the near-eradication of Earth's "carbon units"); sexuality without reciprocity, desire without understanding, are likewise self-sabotaging (as suggested by the initial distance between Ilia and Decker, or Kirk's near-destruction of the *Enterprise*, his fundamental love-object, through hubristically overhasty orders, through an attempt simply to control what he does not fully comprehend). These conflicts can be genuinely resolved only through and within a community in which their resolution is already prioritized as an innate expression of that community. Thus it is that *no one in the film attains a goal individually*; each must, as Spock notes, reach out to others for assistance in becoming who that individual is, in the process providing assistance to others in their ongoing self-comprehension and expression.

Nor is this all; as a great deal throughout, and particularly the conclusion, of the film has already indicated, resolution does not mean completion. Rather the opposite: to be genuinely human is to be always in a state of discovery regarding oneself and others. We see this in a brief exchange between Kirk, McCoy and Spock at the film's end, an exchange easily mistaken for simply a touch of comedic wrap-up. Kirk offers a sort of self-congratulatory summation: "I think we gave it the ability to create its own sense of purpose ... out of our own human weaknesses ... and the drive that compels us to overcome them." McCoy cannot resist the chance to needle Spock; "And a lot of 'foolish human emotions,' right, Mr. Spock?" Spock's reply is dignified but not without its own dry wit: "Quite true, doctor. Unfortunately it will have to deal with them as well." To hear this as trivial banter is to miss a key point implicit throughout the film; there is no necessarily final stage in human development, although any given stage in that development may well be unrecognizable from an earlier stage. Again we see an inversion of a similar point found in *2001: A Space Odyssey*. Bowman's transformation — his rebirth as the star child — is indeed a mystery, isolated not only from our understanding but from his, an act imposed upon his identity by forces unknown, whereas the transformation, not only of Ilia/V'Ger and Decker but of Spock and Kirk as well, is part of an increasingly self-aware process of expanding their ranges of intersubjectivity.

There is no finality; nor is there perfection; there are only stages, and degrees of completion. Kirk's final gesture, a wave of his hand ordering the *Enterprise* to travel "out there — thataway," implicitly removing ship and crew from the realm of Earth's control — is indicative of this open-endedness. This is not at all to deny that any given stage may take on the qualities of perfection as seen from an earlier stage, and may therefore be seen as perfect from the perspective of a consciousness still shaped primarily by that earlier stage. Perfection is itself a conception, not an actuality awaiting discovery.

Strangely enough, and quite unintentionally, the overall presentation of *Star Trek: The Motion Picture*, and its relation to Wise's other major films, echoes this conclusion. Purely technically, this is not Wise's finest film (probably *Executive Suite* deserves that designation, though several other candidates come to mind); there are, for example, some minor but noticeable continuity errors, as well as the weak performances (already mentioned) by certain among the supporting players. By comparison with Wise's other science fiction films, it is looser and less tautly driven by its material. Yet I would argue that it is nonetheless a finer film, for its failures are tangential to its overall integrity, which itself contributes to a much broader and deeper achievement, both implicitly and explicitly. As Alfred North Whitehead observed, "The 'perfection' of subjective form means the absence from it of component feelings which mutually inhibit each other so that neither rises to the strength proper to it."[49] In artistic terms, perfection requires that every single element of the work at hand combine harmoniously with each of the others in support of the whole. Yet there is, as always, more; since a work may be narrow in its range or small in its ambitions, it is possible that perfection may be obtained through the balanced conjunction of only a few elements, individually perhaps quite simple. Even a single tone or color may be perfect in its lack of intrusive elements, yet is not thereby interesting emotionally or intellectually. A movie (a detective thriller, say) may be fully thought out — flawlessly scripted, acted, and filmed — without thereby becoming a significant work of art. It is the scope and complexity of a work's achievement which determines its significance, and thus a film with flaws can be more compelling than one without; "We shall find," Whitehead says, "that always there are imperfect occasions better than occasions which realize some given type of perfection. There are in fact higher and lower perfections, and an imperfection aiming at a higher type stands above lower perfections."[50]

Hence it is that even the flaws in *Star Trek: The Motion Picture* point toward its utopian content. It is quite possible to imagine a better production of a film, a production free of such flaws as aforementioned but otherwise very much like this one, but in order to do so we must imagine overcoming the circumstances which contributed to those imperfections (a male-dominated industry, the rushed production schedule, studio nepotism, etc.). This is, of course, not a unique circumstance; anyone who has seen more than a modicum of cinema can easily bring to mind examples of films which would be much better if only some element(s) could have been different.[51] It is much harder, though, to envision actual circumstances which would have allowed those differences to exist as realities rather than *ex post facto* imaginings. Every flawed work is thus in some manner an invitation to utopianizing. To be flawed, though, is not yet enough (were it, we would be already in utopia); the nature of the work itself must point beyond those flaws. Comparatively few works contain specifically and richly utopian elements within their essential structure, but it is precisely these which can impel both work and experiencer beyond their present state of being, flaws and all. That is the nature of utopia.

A work of art is a combination of elements and events; it comprises its own structure and content along with its implications and the reactions, emotional and intellectual, of those who experience it. These components invite evaluation: first, most commonly and most easily, in and of themselves; second, still commonly but not so easily, as elements, cooperating or conflicting as the case may be, which form, or militate against, a larger entity, itself inviting further evaluation; third, increasingly less commonly and often only with difficulty, as aspects of the consciousnesses, individual and social, of those who encounter the work, aspects which invite still further evaluations, this time not merely of the work itself but of the world in which it came into existence, or of the world in which it has been experienced, or of that world of experiences yet to come, a world which will be shaped by the responses to the first two forms of being, a world which entreats to be born. Art is both real in its application of particular techniques to specific materials and unreal in its application of imagination in the service of bringing into being that which does not exist otherwise. "Art," as Marcuse commented, "breaks open a dimension inaccessible to other experience, a dimension in which human beings, nature, and things no longer stand under the law of the established reality principle."[52] *Star Trek: The Motion Picture*, even more than its great companions in meditative science fiction, *2001: A Space Odyssey* and *Solaris*, even more than any other among Wise's cinematic work, reaches beyond itself, figuratively and factually, toward a new reality, not merely that depicted but that as might be imagined by each of its viewers. Its flaws reflect the problems inherent in present reality. Its development acknowledges the fragility of possibility. Its strengths remind us of the persistence of hope. In it Wise has summed up his cinematic concern with the profession of being human.

Chapter Notes

Introduction

1. Richard C. Keenan, *The Films of Robert Wise* (Lanham, MD: Scarecrow Press, 2007), p. 168.

2. It might also be noted that *The Sound of Music* holds another record: it is apparently the film seen most frequently by a single person. As of 1988, the most recent date for which I could find a tally, Mrs. Myra Franklin of Cardiff, Wales, had seen the film some 940 times; see Susan Sackett, *The Hollywood Reporter Book of Box Office Hits* (New York: Billboard Books, 1990), p. 179.

3. Quoted in Keenan, p. 83.

4. As of this writing, there have been only three books devoted to Wise's overall output. Frank Thompson's *Robert Wise: A Bio-Bibliography* (Westport, CT: Greenwood Press, 1995) is an excellent source of materials for research on Wise's films, especially as regards their critical reception, but is not intended as a piece of critical analysis. Sergio Leemann's *Robert Wise on His Films: From Editing Room to Director's Chair* (Los Angeles: Silman-James Press, 1995) begins with a brief overview of Wise's life and career, then presents a series of comments by Wise on each of the films he had directed to that point (he had not yet made *A Storm in Summer*). While very useful as a source regarding Wise's own experiences, Leemann's book is, like Thompson's, not intended to serve as either a critical or analytic work. Richard C. Keenan's *The Films of Robert Wise* (Lanham, MD: Scarecrow Press, 2007) offers some preliminary evaluations but is concerned more with the production and reception of each of Wise's films rather than extensive discussions of their content, though he does make some thoughtful exceptions to this approach. Keenan describes his book as an essay; I consider my own book to be an essay as well, in that I make no pretenses to having reached a final judgment on Wise's films, but my purpose is broader and more analytic than those of my predecessors.

5. David Thomson, *The New Biographical Dictionary of Film* (New York: Alfred A. Knopf, 2002), p. 942.

6. Quoted in Leemann, *op. cit.*, p. 7.

7. Raymond Durgnat, *Films and Feelings* (Cambridge, MA: MIT Press, 1967), p. 78. Perhaps significantly, Durgnat contrasts Wise with "fake liberals" such as George Stevens and "flabby liberals" such as William Wyler, describing him as belonging among the "younger, tougher more courageous men" (p. 80). What it is that Durgnat has in mind here is never made explicit, though, and he never singles out any details in Wise's films which might support such a claim. Some of what follows is in effect an exploration and expansion of the sort of point Durgnat may have been making.

8. Sidney Lumet, *Making Movies* (New York: Alfred A. Knopf, 1995), pp. 50, 51. Based on this, Lumet draws a distinction between "true stylists" and "decorators." As he says, "The decorators are easy to recognize. That's why the critics love them so" (p. 51).

9. François Truffaut, *The Films in My Life*, trans. Leonard Mayhew (New York: Simon and Schuster, 1978), p. 166.

10. According to Wise himself, he walked off a set only once in his entire career: during an outside location shot made particularly difficult by recalcitrant winds and river currents during the making of *The Sand Pebbles*. See Leemann, pp. 188–190, for Wise's account of the difficult conditions of the shoot.

11. It was not until rather late in the process of writing the first chapter, for example, that I decided that readers would expect to see at least a brief mention of *West Side Story* and *The Sound of Music*, these being by far Wise's best-known films, and that some acknowledgment of each was necessary. While neither is completely detached from Wise's central interests, as my discussion of each should suggest, neither is central to my topic here, and the discussion of each is accordingly not extensive; fortunately for fans of these films (and there are many indeed), there are multitudes of other, far more extensive, examinations of each film available.

Chapter One

1. Herbert Marcuse, *The Aesthetic Dimension: Toward a Critique of Marxist Aesthetics*. Boston: Beacon Press, 1978), pp. 32–33.

2. Thomas Hobbes, *Leviathan* (Harmondsworth: Penguin, 1980), p. 343.

3. Eric Hoffer, *In Our Time* (New York: Harper and Row, 1976), p. 100.

4. Totter's delivery here may strike a modern viewer as perhaps a bit odd, until we realize that she is responding, whether intentionally or not, to the sensibilities of the original source: Art Cohn's screenplay for *The Set-Up* is based on a narrative poem by Joseph Moncure March.

5. The link between violence and consumption is further drawn out through the repeated inserts of a grotesquely obese man (Dwight Martin), stuffing his mouth with all manner of junk food as he beams in delight at the spectacle in front of him.

6. In this regard, Wise's other boxing film, *Somebody Up There Likes Me* (1956), though excellent in its own right, seems more insular. The story is largely true (it's based on Rocky Graziano's life story), but the singularity of Graziano's success, as opposed to the dozens of Stoker Thompsons in any major city, adds a layer of distantiation which lessens its overall impact.

7. Probably we are meant to presume that she is barren, and thus unable to fulfill the societal requirements of womanhood in the 1950s. In any case, her attachment to the child leads to her betrayal of Spencer, for she cannot participate in the child's inevitable murder.

8. A similar situation appears in *Something for the Birds* (1952), one of Wise's few comedies. Edmund Gwenn plays a government printer who uses invitations acquired on the sly from his job to attend high society parties, where he is mistaken for someone of importance. This, naturally, leads to the rest of the plot. Wise thought well of this little-known film, which represents in a nutshell— in both its situation and its environmentally progressive plot — the typological nature of his overall concerns.

9. Wise seems to have taken pleasure in avoiding the famous Fox fanfare, as a surprising number of his films for the studio begin with other music.

10. An earlier, if somewhat less probable, example of this is MacRoberts's escape from captivity (he was taken prisoner while leading a raid on a German encampment): he is freed because an Allied strafing run kills the driver of the truck bearing him and his sergeant, an event on which no one could have counted and for which no one could have planned.

11. That his commanding officer has already said that he would back whatever decision he deemed necessary could help, but would not be determinative; such matters are rarely decided at the field level.

12. All published references to this film include a comma in the title, even though the on-screen credits do not.

13. The film takes some liberties with ship nomenclature here. There was a *Momo* class of destroyers during World War I, but such few of its members as survived were serving as training ships by 1943. Two additional destroyers of a similar vintage, members of the *Momi* class, saw action, but both survived until 1945. A new *Momo*, of the *Matsu* class, was launched in early 1944, too late to have been sunk by the *Nerka*, a fact true of its sister ships as well. The *Akikaze* (actually sunk in November of 1944) was itself a member of the *Minekaze* class, which, despite Kohler's concern, was itself only slightly less outdated militarily than the immediately prior *Momi* class, all of its members being at least 20 years

old by the time *Run Silent, Run Deep* takes place. See Anthony J. Watts, *Japanese Warships of World War Two* (Garden City, CA: Doubleday, 1970), pp. 117–119. It may also be noted that *Nerka* was a name chosen carefully by Edward L. Beach, author of the original novel, as corresponding to no actual U.S. submarine of the period (a ship by that name was authorized but never constructed).

14. Keenan, p. 102.

15. Theodor Adorno, *Prisms*, trans. Samuel and Shierry Weber (Cambridge, MA: MIT Press, 1983), p. 126.

16. The film gains nothing from the occasional interjections of music toward the end, though these at least tend to be quiet, but the major exception, a significant flaw given the overall trajectory of the film, is the ending, in which the louder music of the earlier scenes returns for no good reason. It would have been far more effective to roll the credits in silence.

17. Keenan, p. 115.

18. The chain-link fence will function in a similar manner throughout the film, serving as the central visual metaphor for the emotional and physical cages in which the characters live.

19. I am usually quoting from Ernest Lehman's screenplay, which is included in a booklet as an extra to one of the DVD releases. There the dialect is rather strictly written out; in practice, not all of the elisions indicated were followed by the actors. Occasionally the difference is noticeable enough that I give the words as spoken on screen rather than as written, but I do not call attention to this fact.

20. George Jean Nathan, Section XV in *Living Philosophies* (New York: Simon and Schuster, 1931), pp. 221–233; p. 232.

21. Ernest Lehman's screenplay concludes with a description, unfortunately not fully realizable visually, which indicates his awareness of the problem even then. As the body is borne away, "Nearby, looking across at each other uneasily, and then moving off in opposite directions, are the few Jets and Sharks who have not joined the procession, who are not yet ready, perhaps never will be ready, to give up war as a way of life."

22. Patricia White, "Female Spectator, Lesbian Specter: *The Haunting*." In *Sexuality and Space*, ed. Beatriz Colomina. Princeton Papers on Architecture #1 (New York:

Princeton Architectural Press, 1992), pp. 130–161.

23. This rootedness is shown in a striking series of overlapping dissolves showing the woman's face aging as she lies in her bed.

24. White, p. 150.

25. The link between the emptiness of both Eleanor and Hill House is further suggested by a quick shot of Eleanor glancing toward the highly polished wood floor just after she has entered the house and sees her own reflection quite clearly.

26. The "his" is ambiguous; if in Eleanor's own voice, it presumably refers to Dr. Markway, but it may reflect events involving the second Mrs. Crain, or perhaps the mysterious woman who clambered out the tower window and dropped to her death. Note also that even here it is the concern for a child which motivates Eleanor's strongest resistance to the spirit of the house. When Markway later makes a case to Eleanor that there was, in fact, no child but only a set of sounds, he is unknowingly abetting the agenda of the house.

27. The first shot of Markway is from the far side of a harp which has just sounded on its own; even as he checks his watch and notes the time of the incident, the strings of the harp, like bars on a cell, reveal how trapped he is within his own narrow world. To be right about the facts is not enough; one must also be aware of the moral implications of those facts.

28. Leemann, p. 180.

29. See Keenan, pp. 127–128, for some examples, as well as his own response to the overall critical denigration of *The Sound of Music*. David Thompson, *op. cit.*, is reduced, in his entry on Julie Andrews, to sputtering incoherence in his unexplained loathing for the film.

30. Even a heavily edited and retitled version failed to save the film's fortunes. Audiences wanted Julie Andrews as she was in *The Sound of Music* and *Mary Poppins*, not as an irascible music hall performer.

31. This and all other Kael quotations are from Pauline Kael, *Going Steady* (New York: Bantam, 1971), p. 196.

32. It might be argued that the often very obvious process work fits in here. I'm not convinced by this (hence the relegation of the point to a footnote), but the relevance of similar evident process work to the situations in various Hitchcock films is so commonly de-

fended that it might as well be mentioned here also.

33. Cf. Harlan Ellison's short story "All the Sounds of Fear," in which an actor regresses through his parts until he has none left—and no face either.

34. There is another difficulty faced by *Star!*, also unavoidable under the circumstances but, given the historical ground on which the narrative is built, much harder to overcome: when compared with that of *West Side Story* and *The Sound of Music*, most of the music of *Star!* does not hold up nearly as well. The tunes in Wise's first two musicals are generally more memorable, even after a first hearing, than those here. Given the very high proportion of musical numbers to dialogue scenes in *Star!*, the weakness of the music becomes an unavoidable weakness in the film as a whole.

35. I have tried the, admittedly rather drastic, expedient of watching the film with the color function of my viewer turned off. Although the lighting values are of course not at all what a veteran cinematographer like Robert Surtees (who lensed the film) would have achieved, it is still clear that the color adds little if anything vital to the film as a film, rather than as a box-office draw.

36. I noted above that *West Side Story* has lost some of its plausibility because of our changed perceptions of street gangs; the opening segments of *Audrey Rose*, by contrast, have gained a certain power because of our greater awareness of pedophiles. While we remain uncertain of the direction in which the film is going, the scenes of the parents grappling with the presence of a stalker are chilling in a manner probably unintended by Wise or De Felitta.

37. There is an amusing satirical undercurrent regarding the nature of suburban charities here, in that the boy is already on his way before anyone from the agency thinks to investigate the situation in which he will find himself; to the well meaning but comparatively thoughtless do-gooders, he represents a cause rather than existing as an individual. Toward the end of the film Herman's family's contact person at the agency, Gloria Ross (Nastassja Kinski), announces that she will drive him home; Abe declares that it is Herman's choice to make, a point Gloria comes to recognize, at least to a degree (as with many of Wise's films, the positive reso-

lution is tinged with potential ambiguities, for the future is always open to new understandings—or lack thereof).

38. That Abe has the inner strength necessary to overcome his situation is implicit in his name; a tzaddik, in Hebrew, is a particularly wise and ethically just man.

39. The close-ups are especially important on a small television screen, on which intimacy and intensity are paradoxically more difficult to attain than on a large cinema screen. This is one reason why genuine big-screen films always lose much of their impact on even a comparatively large video screen; it's akin to the difference between a mountaintop vista and a postcard of the same view.

Chapter Two

1. Karen Horney, *The Neurotic Personality of Our Time* (New York: Norton, 1937), pp. 287–288.

2. Alfred North Whitehead, *Adventures of Ideas* (New York: Macmillan, 1954), p. 313. But, as he added, "A true proposition is more apt to be interesting than a false one."

3. The story is told that David Lean, director of such huge-scale films as *Lawrence of Arabia* and *Doctor Zhivago*, once asked Bergman, "What kind of crew do you use?" "I make my films with 18 good friends," Bergman said. "That's interesting," Lean replied. "I make mine with 150 enemies." (Quoted in Irving Singer, *Ingmar Bergman, Cinematic Philosopher: Reflections on His Creativity* (Cambridge, MA: MIT Press, 2007, p. 5.) Wise, the director of some very large-scale films indeed, as well as many smaller-scale ones, would have appreciated the distinction.

4. Keenan, p. 168.

5. Also called *High Tension* or *This Can't Happen Here*.

6. Quoted in Frank Gado, *The Passion of Ingmar Bergman* (Durham, NC: Duke University Press, 1986), p. 139. Most critics agree with Bergman's assessment.

7. Ingmar Bergman, *The Magic Lantern: An Autobiography*, trans. Joan Tate (New York: Viking, 1988), pp. 131–132. Again, most critics agree with Bergman's assessment.

8. As a further point along these lines, consider Bergman's *Port of Call* (1948). A subsidiary plot line develops unexpectedly into a quite poignant critique of the brutal impact of Swedish abortion restrictions, but is then

diffused by an ending which suggests that the loving couple at the film's center need merely stay and fight the forces ranged against them for all to end happily. Given the energy Bergman's plot has put into proving exactly the opposite, the conclusion betrays the bulk of the film; the social message (admittedly not the focus of the screenplay) is undercut by the implausible outcome. Wise's 1949 film *The Set-Up*, by contrast, is at least equally interesting visually, remains tautly concentrated on its situation, and refuses any artificial reassurances throughout. As a drama, therefore, Wise's film is superior, even if Bergman's arguably points toward more important subjects.

9. Georg Lukács, *Realism in Our Time: Literature and the Class Struggle* (New York: Harper Torchbooks, 1971), p. 57. It should be noted that I am an American writing from the perspective of several decades after both films. In fact, *Shame* had a specific impact on Swedish political discourse of the Vietnam War era which has also largely (if not entirely) dissipated over the intervening years. Just as we can still care about the characters in *Odds Against Tomorrow* without remembering the exact details of segregation in the United States, we can care about those in *Shame* without recalling what contemporary Swedes thought of Bergman's underlying intentions.

10. Oddly enough, it is also this which makes Wise's films of the supernatural so compelling; within his humanistic worldview the supernatural is genuinely inexplicable (and therefore leaves open many questions), whereas Bergman's forays into the putatively supernatural generally remain confused and confusing precisely because he himself isn't sure what he's getting at (and therefore the questions raised simply reflect the viewer's puzzlement at just what she or he is supposed to be seeing as opposed to what it means). *The Haunting* remains an effective thriller even upon repeated viewings because, first, the cinematic elements all cooperate in support of the overall impact, and, second, because there are always more questions, questions directly linked to the events onscreen and the individuals living through them, than there are answers; *Hour of the Wolf*, by contrast, remains primarily a concatenation of acts and images which, though frequently striking in themselves, never cohere into a solid whole. Genre films have their exigencies

as do straight dramas, and mixing the two forms successfully requires a steadier hand than Bergman displays here.

11. The entire sequence is brilliantly constructed. As we hear the song of the blind beggar from outside, Gray follows Fettes to the door of the stable and watches him leave, framed the whole while by the stable door. A reverse shot, likewise through the door, links Fettes and the passing singer. In both cases the visual emphasis is on the constraints encircling everyone here. We hear, but do not see, the murder. As the camera stares motionlessly, the singer passes through an arch into the darkness. Gray's cab follows; after a few moments the singer's voice is suddenly cut off, and the scene slowly fades into silence. The poor quite literally are not allowed even a voice in this world.

12. Indeed, one of the film's few weaknesses is a minimally developed suggestion that Dr. MacFarlane's putative housekeeper (who is actually his secret wife) has "second sight," allowing her to foresee dark and terrible events. This component could have been dropped utterly without loss, as it has no genuine impact on what follows its revelation, save as a convenient, if improbable, means of getting Fettes out of the house while MacFarlane carts in Gray's body.

13. His first name is John, which we see chalked on the door of his stable, but no one uses it. The whole name — John Gray — suggests through its anonymity someone who is as much a shadow of his external function as a full human being. He even identifies himself as "Cabman Gray" when first meeting Fettes. Gray is, as his name portends, already halfway to the darkness in which the film will end.

14. Joseph, it should be noted, represents monetary greed at its starkest; he also demonstrates the perils of exceeding one's expertise; stepping from the role of servant to that of blackmailer merely assures his prompt death.

15. Leemann, p. 107.

16. John Clute, *Science Fiction: The Illustrated Encyclopedia* (London: Dorling Kindersley, 1995), p. 262.

17. Bernard M. Baruch, *Baruch: The Public Years* (New York: Holt, Rinehart, and Winston, 1960), pp. 369, 370, 371. This was by no means the only such plan offered at this; many others, from various sources and of

varying degrees of credibility, achieved at least some public discussion during the late 1940s.

18. Gregg Herken, *The Winning Weapon: The Atomic Bomb in the Cold War, 1945–1950* (New York: Alfred A. Knopf, 1980), p. 171.

19. Robin Wood, *Howard Hawks* (Detroit, MI: Wayne State University Press, 2006), p. 103. Wood sees the film as showing a greater respect for the scientists than I do and have here described; Carrington, he claims, "is never made absurd" (p. 105). This is true only at the level of behavior; Carrington's intellectual arguments are so illogically constructed that their absurdity is almost self-evident. Regardless of nuances of portrayal, though, both Wood and I agree on the overall depiction of the scientists as not fully developed as human beings. Wood refers to "the tendency of the scientific outlook to inhibit emotional development" (*Ibid.*). He does not question the similarly inhibiting effects on emotional maturity of military training. The more extended point is that too great an emphasis on *any* aspect of human consciousness carries with it the likelihood of damage to other, equally important, aspects of being human.

20. Rennie was then virtually unknown to film audiences, and thus represented mystery. Spencer Tracy was reportedly interested in the part of Klaatu, and Claude Rains was actively considered for it. Although either would no doubt have provided an excellent performance, each would have brought far too much face recognition to be believable.

21. There is a marvelous little scene just prior to Harley's return in which two doctors discuss Klaatu's apparent physiological normality. One, commenting specifically on Klaatu's lungs, asks the other how old he takes Klaatu to be. Thirty-five to thirty-eight, the second answers. No, says the first, he is almost eighty; "Life expectancy is a hundred and thirty." The second doctor is astonished, and queries how this could be. "Says their medicine is that much more advanced," explains his counterpart, as he offers him a cigarette. Needless to say, we never see Klaatu smoking. His people, as he says, have learned to live without stupidity.

22. Klaatu's wound is cured by nothing the earthly doctors do, but through the use of a salve he carries himself.

23. The name Carpenter, and Klaatu's message of peace, along with his eventual death and resurrection, suggest parallels with central aspects of Christian beliefs, parallels amply commented upon elsewhere. While there are links (no doubt intentional), the significance of these should not be overestimated, as the differences are even greater. Klaatu works no miracles for the edification of the credulous, and it is difficult to imagine Jesus Christ appealing to scientists for assistance, even if such had existed in his day. *The Day the Earth Stood Still* is at heart a profoundly humanistic film, and its religious resonances should be understood in this context. Note here the commentary which we hear in the background as Klaatu discovers the name he will use for the rest of the film: it consists of scientific speculation regarding his planet of origin, but we hear distinctly the assertion that "all reputable scientists warn us against jumping to hasty conclusions."

24. Albert Einstein, *Out of My Later Years* (New York: Philosophical Library, 1950), p. 138.

25. *Ibid.*, p. 142.

26. Although there were always exceptions, such as *Earth vs. the Flying Saucers* (Fred F. Sears, 1956) — in which Hugh Marlowe as the scientist who saved the planet was the romantic lead — many later films would emphasize the eccentric or quirky aspect of the scientists portrayed, making them into doddering old charmers who had to be tended carefully, or monomaniacs of one sort or another, harmless or troublesome as the plot demanded. Edmund Gwenn in *Them!* (Gordon Douglas, 1954) is a prime example of the latter. Cecil Kellaway in *The Beast from 20,000 Fathoms* (Eugène Lourié, 1953), who dies while commenting on the dentition of the dinosaur which is eating him, represents the harmless monomaniac, while Bela Lugosi in *Bride of the Monster* (Edward D. Wood, Jr., 1955) is a characteristic version of the more troublesome type. Rarely did the more pleasant scientists do more than add some humor, or perhaps a cover for necessary jargon. The military men solved the problem with military means.

As the 1950s unfolded, the menacing beings were increasingly likely to be ordinary earthly creatures, often insects, enlarged by radiation from atomic tests. This eventually led to an emerging awareness of a central contradiction: the atomic experiments, though of necessity led by scientists, were being conducted at the behest of the military, which fact weakened the plausibility of the portrayal of the military as the principal, or even sole, force staving off the attackers. Thus there are exceptions to the portrayal of scientists as largely irrelevant, especially after the launch of *Sputnik* by the Soviet Union startled the American public into something of an awareness of the link between scientific and technological achievement. In *The Deadly Mantis* (Nathan Juran, 1957), for example, the scientists cooperate with the military on something of an equal footing, although it is, of course, the heroic Air Force officer rather than the stolid paleontologist who gets the girl at the end.

More interesting is *The Monolith Monsters* (John Sherwood, 1957), in which the military does not appear at all, save in the distantly related form of a small-town police chief and a couple of patrol officers. Nor would military intervention be of any value; the problem is not, despite the title, a monster at all, but rather a natural process: extraterrestrial siliceous rocks which grow exponentially when exposed to water, and which would eventually, if unstopped, cover at least much of North, Central, and South America. The difficulty here is solved entirely by scientists using conventional research methods, albeit very small scale ones. The result is a film which concentrates on the process of solution instead of the conflict with the invaders.

The Monolith Monsters is in some ways a distant ancestor of *The Andromeda Strain*, though not as complex in its portrayal of the relations between scientists and the political structure within which they work. Interestingly, though, there is a small nod in this direction via a suspicion — barely voiced but still visible — of the presumptive social preeminence of money. When the paper boy is asked to round up all the kids with bicycles to help distribute the evacuation notices (the power having been cut off by the process of the monoliths), he tells the police chief and newspaper editor that the kids will want to know how much they're being paid. Brusquely ordered to tell them that this is "police business," he quickly acquiesces, but the chief ponders the situation disapprovingly for a moment before the action resumes: "Kids nowadays have to get paid for everything." Soon afterwards, it is *his* turn to raise monetary concerns; the geologist who is the leading figure in combating the advance of the rocks has realized that dynamiting the nearby dam is the only possible way of stopping them, and the chief reacts forcefully: "You can't do that! It's privately owned!" The scientist dismisses the concern in light of the impending disaster, and the chief, after a dramatic pause, tells him where to find the necessary explosives. These are minor elements, yet like much of the film are atypical of their genre.

27. Just as Alfred Hitchcock used variable staircase lengths in *Notorious*, depending on the emotional needs of the scenes, Wise plays with location here. Klaatu's saucer is within walking distance of the rooming house, yet the taxi ride toward it covers a considerable portion of Washington, D.C. Physical reality gives way to the demands of the drama — a fact missed by most viewers of the film, as they are responding by now to the situation rather than its setting.

28. Carlos Clarens, *An Illustrated History of the Horror Film* (New York: Capricorn Books, 1968), p. 127. Among Clarens's other errors, he claims that Klaatu's message involves stopping atomic testing (it does not, as he is unconcerned with what the people of Earth do to themselves), that electrical power is stopped for a day rather than half an hour, that Klaatu is watched by the F.B.I. (he is not), and that ordinary people are peaceful at heart, as opposed to their leaders (whereas part of the problem is precisely the mix of political attitudes Klaatu encounters). Clarens also misquotes the phrase Helen uses to stop Gort. To be fair, Clarens was writing well before home video made repeated viewing of films easy, but such a fact does not mitigate the dubious grasp he has on the film's content.

29. Albert Einstein, *Ideas and Opinions* (New York: Crown Publishers, 1963), p. 163.

30. Thomson, *op. cit.*, p. 66. Interestingly, this assessment appears in the entry on Harry Belafonte but finds no echo in the dismissive entry on Wise himself.

31. See, for example, Robert G. Porfirio, "No Way Out: Existential Motifs in the Film Noir," *Sight and Sound*, 45.4 (Autumn 1976): 212–217; 213. Regarding the credits for the screenplay of *Odds Against Tomorrow*, it should be noted that Polonsky's credit could

not originally be given onscreen due to his having been blacklisted during the McCarthy era (it has been silently added in the DVD release), and that John O. Killens, who did receive credit originally, had nothing to do with the final script.

32. Keenan, p. 108.

33. Note the subtle linkage of the children, as yet untrammeled by rigid social roles, with positive morality; the group of kids is racially mixed, something to which no attention is drawn (which, outside of the purposes of critical analysis, is as it should be). *Odds Against Tomorrow* is a grim film, but it does contain clues as to ways forward.

34. This is among the many small links drawn between Slater and Ingram; fifteen dollars is also the amount Ingram has in his wallet when he arrives in Melton.

35. Another clue to this emptiness is provided by the fact that during her interlude with Slater she leaves her baby unattended upstairs.

36. Georges Bataille, *Death and Sensuality: A Study of Eroticism and the Taboo* (New York: Ballantine, 1969; first published in 1962), pp. 166–167.

37. George Meredith, *Rhoda Fleming* (Boston: Roberts Brothers, 1891), p. 176.

38. Burke would have done well to listen to Ingram and to pay attention to the scenery; in the first shot of the street on which they are traveling we see, next door to each other, a residential hotel offering "Transient Housekeeping Facilities" and a funeral parlor. Burke's future is indeed both transient and funereal.

39. There is another, less dramatic but still pointed, semantic irony here. Ingram refers to staying out of the "watermelon patch," alluding to a strange stereotype regarding African American gustatory enjoyment. We have already heard another reference to watermelon, this time from Earl; in his first resistance to Burke's proposal he comments, "I never stole nothin' in my life —'cept maybe a watermelon when I was a boy on the farm."

40. Keenan, p. 109.

41. There is another difference. *Odds Against Tomorrow* contains what is one of Wise's very few clearly Christian images. As the medic contemplates the corpses, we see behind him a telephone pole leaning at an angle against a harshly gray sky; the reference to the crucifixion of Jesus Christ, and pre-

sumably thereby to the merciful teachings associated with Christ, seems clear. No further attention is drawn to the reference; the film ends with a close-up on a sign bearing a warning: "STOP. DEAD END." This is followed by a tilt down to a small pool of water, closing the visual circle with which the film began.

42. Keenan, p. 108.

43. The credits, interestingly enough, give only the last names of the male characters and only the first names of the females; the only exception, apart from minor roles listed descriptively (e.g., Police Chief, Girl in Bar, and Soldier in Bar), is the hoodlum whose portrayal codes him as homosexual. Even a film devoted to condemning bigotry cannot fully escape the ingrained stereotypes of its era.

It is also worth noting that Burke, the instigator of the robbery, is utterly unconnected with any woman at all. He himself comments that he has a large dog in a small apartment because "I never had a wife." His reasoning is obscure, but he recognizes that he is missing something important.

44. Martha Nussbaum, *Sex and Social Justice* (New York: Oxford University Press, 1999), p.161.

45. Wise did something similar in both *The Captive City*, and, though to more lighthearted purposes, in *Destination Gobi* (1953); in the latter film the camera itself peers into ostensibly secret files belonging to the Navy as a means of inaugurating the story.

46. This, by the way, indicates more of Stone's naïveté. The nuclear strike for which he has almost cavalierly called would violate major agreements between the United States and the Soviet Union, and would thus require that the Soviets be alerted and given an explanation. "Then," a cabinet official comments, "they'll ask a flock of questions." A colleague adds a disturbing corollary: "Some we don't want answered." Science does not take place in a political vacuum, and scientists who ignore this fact, of whom there are many, are often given rude, or even violent, awakenings.

47. The principal exception to this is his antagonistic relationship with Ruth Leavitt. The motivation for this is not clear as to its purpose in the screenplay, save perhaps as a means of showing, a) that Hall is not perfect, and, b) that he can overcome his own dislikes in the service of medicine (he attends to her

during her grand mal seizure). The mutual dislike could have been omitted without loss, I think.

Chapter Three

1. Timothy 6:10.
2. Robert Sklar, *A World History of Film* (New York: Harry N. Abrams, 2002), p. 279.
3. Raymond Chandler, *Trouble Is My Business* (New York: Ballantine), 1980, p. viii.
4. Porfirio, *op. cit.*, p. 213.
5. His name also foreshadows his doom; a mart is an ox or cow which has been fattened in preparation for slaughter.
6. Ayn Rand, *Capitalism, the Unknown Ideal* (New York: New American Library, 1966), p. 288. (All emphases are Rand's.)
7. Rand's books still sell hundreds of thousands of copies a year, many of them, oddly enough, to individuals she would have utterly despised, yet her actual influence, especially intellectually, is minimal. Probably many of those who read her books enjoy them for the same reasons that audiences are prone to identification with the criminals in noir films: to the degree that the consequences for others of one's actions are of little or no concern, one is free of any constraints, and there is an excitement in the idea of being free of all constraints and all consequences (I explore this more fully later in the chapter). Rand's books, being free of the constraints of the Production Code, are thus free to depict quite drastic behaviors which proceed with neither negative consequence to the character nor concern for those whose lives are destroyed by those actions. Rand's contempt for the powerless is vast and frequently expressed.
8. As Hazel Barnes noted, Rand's philosophy "claims to be a humanism and to reaffirm the essential worth and dignity of the human being. In reality it is one more form of evasion, seeking to escape the vision of what it really means to be human." (Hazel Barnes, *An Existentialist Ethics* [New York: Alfred A. Knopf, 1969], pp. 140–141.) Although not intended as a comprehensive refutation of Rand's philosophy, the chapter devoted to her ideas is a very effective examination of some of the many the hidden assumptions and contradictions found therein.
9. John Kenneth Galbraith, *The Affluent Society* (Boston: Houghton Mifflin, 1958), p. 160.

10. Hobbes, *op. cit.*, p. 186.
11. Erich Fromm, *To Have or to Be?* (New York: Continuum, 1997), p. 6.
12. *Ibid.*, p. 81.
13. *Ibid.*, p. 78.
14. Films such as these, if my analysis is correct, invert Sigmund Freud's formulation regarding the appeal of invincible heroes in popular fiction and drama: "This significant mark of invulnerability very clearly betrays— His Majesty the Ego, the hero of all daydreams and all novels." What we see here instead might be called His or Her Majesty the Id, the dark forces urging us toward destruction, of others and of self. We act out the destruction vicariously yet retain our personal security; even where the work concerned ends without a ray of hope for the characters (as, for example, *Odds Against Tomorrow*), the range of destruction is still controlled by the form of the work itself. (The Freud quotation is from *On Creativity and the Unconscious: Papers on the Psychology of Art, Literature, Love, Religion*. Edited by Benjamin Nelson [New York: Harper & Row, 1958], p. 51).
15. Gary Collins, "The Meanest Man in the Movies." In Ted Sennett, ed., *The Movie Buff's Book* (New York: Pyramid Books, 1975), pp. 18–23; p. 18.
16. Something like this, I suspect, underlies Aristotle's famous but mysterious conception of catharsis, in which emotions, being potentially dangerous to the smooth functioning of the *polis*, are things to be purged.
17. Simone de Beauvoir, *The Second Sex*. Translated by H. M. Parshley (New York: Alfred A. Knopf, 1957), p. 643.
18. Mrs. Kraft and Helen both sarcastically dismiss most men as "turnips." Where one seeks self-realization through another, one needs the other to be as forceful as possible. It is not uncommon to find the weak who have internalized the values of the strong, dismissing others among the weak. Helen's comment to Sam that he is not a turnip is, if only she knew it, another signal of the dangers ahead.
19. Robin Morgan, *The Demon Lover: On the Sexuality of Terrorism* (New York: Norton, 1989), p. 197. (All emphases hers.)
20. Mrs. Perth is immediately curious, and thrilled to hear that the case involves murder. Where a person's life lacks internal worth (or where circumstances are such as to

starve them of opportunities for self-development) vicarious excitement becomes increasingly important. This is echoed shortly afterward, when Mrs. Kraft tells Arnett that Laury Palmer "had the best time of anybody I ever knew," and that "just hearing her tell about her doings was all the fun I had left in life."

21. Herbert Marcuse, *Eros and Civilization: A Philosophical Inquiry into Freud* (New York: Vintage, n.d.), pp. 98–99.

22. Paul Sawtell's score plays a role here as well, from the anguished brass and high strings as Helen agonizes over her confusion to the solo violin parodying conventional love music as she makes her decision in favor of Sam. Sawtell's score is generally subdued, in keeping with Wise's low-key approach overall, but here it is allowed a central part in the emotional drama.

23. Morgan *op. cit.* p. 195. (Emphasis hers.)

24. There is a great deal of following in this film; the decisions of most of the characters are shaped, if not outright controlled, by the actions of others.

25. The camera will move once more in association with Mrs. Kraft: when she gets up to see Helen out and spits on her. Mrs. Kraft may have succumbed to greater force, or the threat thereof, but she still retains at least some moral independence—for what that may be worth in such a corrupt world.

26. Is there a specifically homosexual subtext here? I confess I can't see one. While Sam is straddling Mart and thrusting a knife into his belly (the upward shots into Sam's grim visage derive from similar shots of Lawrence Tierney in his break-through film *Dillinger* [Max Nosseck, 1945]), the killing itself is straightforward, unaccompanied by any bodily movements, beyond the arm movement as the knife is driven home, indicative of physical involvement. The knife is, of course, arguably a phallic symbol, and one might proceed from its relatively unimpressive size to assert that some point about Sam's sexual insecurities or even actual inabilities is being implied, but there is no visual emphasis on it to support such a viewing. Given the reasons for the killing, Sam's hyper-masculine possessiveness of "his" women, and the utter lack of anything else to suggest a physical relationship between him and Mart, I would argue that there is nothing further hidden in their relationship.

27. Ecclesiastes 7:26. The proper text from the King James version reads, "And I find more bitter than death the woman, whose heart is snares and nets, and her hands as bands; whoso pleaseth God shall escape from her; but the sinner shall be taken by her."

28. De Beauvoir, p. 668.

29. Marcuse, *Eros and Civilization*, p. viii.

30. There is more than a touch of F. Scott Fitzgerald here: "Let me tell you about the very rich. They are different from you and me. They possess and enjoy early, and it does something to them, makes them soft where we are hard, and cynical where we are trustful, in a way that, unless you were born rich, it is very difficult to understand. They think, deep in their hearts, that they are better than we are because we had to discover the compensations and refuges of life for ourselves. Even when they enter deep into our world or sink below us, they still think that they are better than we are." F. Scott Fitzgerald, "The Rich Boy," in *The Short Stories of F. Scott Fitzgerald*, ed. Matthew J. Bruccoli (New York: Scribner, 1989), pp. 335–366; p. 336.

31. Proverbs 13:15 ("transgressor" is more commonly translated in the plural).

32. Wood, *op. cit.* p. 169.

Chapter Four

1. Eric Hoffer, *Working and Thinking on the Waterfront: A Journal: June 1958–May 1959* (New York: Harper and Row, 1969), p. 150.

2. Most sources attribute Bullard's death to a heart attack, but Loren Shaw, who has no reason to lie in this regard, tells Dudley that Bullard died of a stroke.

3. Although Julius Steigel does not object to Caswell's actions, he does appear to enjoy unsettling his certainties. As they leave the building shortly afterward, he congratulates Caswell, suggesting that the only way there could be trouble is if the dead man is not Bullard. Caswell, startled, grows nervous, but cannot speak while on the elevator, as his machinations might be overheard, a fact of which Steigel apprises him with silent gestures, all the while wearing a small smile. As they exit the elevator, Caswell reminds Steigel that he saw the body as well. "I'm an old man, Mr. Caswell," Steigel comments, clearly enjoying Caswell's discomfiture; "my eyes don't see easy money so good any more." Stheli's

performance is a delight, and the entire exchange is one of the many incidental pleasures afforded by the film.

4. Lehman's script is remarkable in its evocation of character through word choice. No other character would use the dated contraction "'twas," but for Alderson it is entirely appropriate, summing up in a word his old-fashioned nature. Likewise highlighted here is the importance of proper casting; Walter Pidgeon is superb as Alderson, nowhere more so than here, and one need merely imagine his switching roles with any of the other players to see the radical shift in the tone and quality of the film which would have resulted. The same is true of most of the other parts and their players.

5. Quoted in Reginald Pound, *Arnold Bennett: A Biography* (Port Washington, NY: Kennikat Press, 1972), p. 7. The nature of the family background of the potential candidates is, of course, speculative, but the evidence indicates that Lehman has been careful to balance them. Alderson clearly comes from wealth, and the implication is that Caswell does also. Shaw does not, Dudley almost certainly does not (there is a suggestion that he married into money and has been regretting it ever since), and Jesse Grimm presumably worked his way up through the plant (he knows "every brick, every machine, every inch of every production line," knowledge obtained without the aid of "the boy-wonders and slide rule experts," as he reminds his wife). Walling's case is less clear, although the implication is that he is middle class rather than as wealthy as some of the others. On the grounds of class origin, therefore, Shaw would appear to have the leading edge in the competition.

6. And it is a very hierarchical company, as we see in a brief scene when Bullard's telegram is brought to the Tower. The telegram messenger is told by the elevator operator to wait in the elevator, as "*I* deliver all messages to executive suite." But no sooner does he reach the upper floor than his manner becomes quite deferential in Miss Martin's presence. Another sign of Walling's qualifications for the presidency is that he, alone among the other executives, speaks with, and listens to, the workers in the Tredway factory.

7. There is a further clue in the scene immediately preceding this one, in which the various vice-presidents are awaiting Bullard's arrival. A series of cuts shows each of them sitting at the conference table, concluding with a shot of Bullard's empty chair, which looks remarkably like a tombstone awaiting engraving. Bullard's absence and death are tied together effortlessly.

8. Significantly, the table had been brought in just before the meeting for the express purpose of holding the ballot envelopes; it was not a normal part of the furniture of the board room.

9. William Morris, *The Political Writings of William Morris*, ed. A. L. Morton (New York: International Publishers, 1973), p. 50. The lecture in which Morris discusses these topics first occurred in 1877.

10. *Ibid.*, pp. 50–51.

11. It is in moments like this that *Executive Suite* displays considerable kinship with C. P. Snow's superb 1951 novel *The Masters*. The latter, about the power struggles over the succession at the head of a Cambridge University college, is a remarkably humane and understanding portrayal of the intense emotions the desire for such comparatively trivial positions and honors can generate.

12. Something of the possibilities faced by Mary is suggested, through a coincidence of timing and casting, in the situation of Max, also played by William Holden, in Sidney Lumet's *Network* (1976). Max has what appears to be a conventionally happy marriage which exists vaguely alongside his great success as the head of a network news department, a marriage which founders on the rock of his intense affair with a younger woman, an affair generated by the increasing emptiness in Max's professional life. Max's wife even refers, in an unconscious echo of Mary Walling's question to her husband, to "all the senseless pain that we have inflicted on each other." There can be no question of influence here, but the parallels are illuminating.

13. Erich Fromm, *The Art of Loving* (New York: HarperCollins, 2000), p. 19.

14. *Ibid.*, p. 43. Fromm adds, "If a person loves only one other person and is indifferent to the rest of his fellow men, his love is not love but a symbiotic attachment, or an enlarged egoism." As he adds, "This attitude can be compared to that of a man who wants to paint but who, instead of learning the art, claims that he has just to wait for the right object, and that he will paint beautifully when he finds it."

15. *Ibid.*, p. 101.

16. James Monaco, *How to Read a Film: Movies, Media, Multimedia*, 3d ed. (New York: Oxford University Press, 2000), p. 46.

Chapter Five

1. Smedley D. Butler, *War Is a Racket* (Gainesville, FL: Crises Press, 1995), p. 1. Smedley D. Butler (1881–1940) was the commanding officer of the China Expeditionary Force of the United States Marine Corps beginning in March of 1927, and thus would have been on duty during the latter part of *The Sand Pebbles*. Already suspicious of the political and economic motives behind foreign interventionism, he became increasingly so following his retirement from the Marines in 1931. He originally published *War Is a Racket* in 1935, by which time his outspoken opposition to foreign wars, combined with his equally outspoken advocacy of a strong military for defense purposes, earned him a prominent place in the public eye. As his biographer Hans Schmidt notes, "He was always the patriot and battling marine, never the sniveling pacifist or convoluted ideologue. The marriage of extreme left-wing and right-wing themes enhanced his warrior method of attack" (Hans Schmidt, *Maverick Marine: General Smedley D. Butler and the Contradictions of American Military History* [Lexington: University Press of Kentucky, 1987], p. 232). Probably Butler's most famous claim was, "I feel I might have given Al Capone a few hints. The best *he* could do was to operate his racket in three city districts. We Marines operated on three *continents*" (quoted in *Ibid.*, p. 231).

2. Preproduction was so complex that Wise was able to fit in another entire film while *The Sand Pebbles* gestated — the little something called *The Sound of Music*. In fact, studio funding for *The Sand Pebbles* was part of the deal he made to direct *The Sound of Music*.

3. The fact that Chien, an otherwise minor character, is the first to die is not irrelevant. He is killed by that which he does not understand, and what kills him is the symbol of the entire structure of control which suffuses the film. It is the Chinese who are the first victims of imperialism, though by no means the last.

4. More plausibly than in the book, in which the battle appears to occur with scarcely any deaths among the Americans.

5. This is not, strictly speaking, the beginning of the film. Like several others among Wise's films, *The Sand Pebbles* opens with an overture. Unlike that in *Star Trek: The Motion Picture*, which literally enunciates one of the central themes of the film, the preludial music for *The Sand Pebbles* appears merely to serve the more traditional purpose of quieting the audience and creating a general mood.

6. This is echoed in the distribution of names. We never learn Captain Collins's first name at all. Holman's is Jake, but he is at least as frequently called simply "Holman" (or occasionally, insultingly, "Ho-Mang"). But Burgoyne is never called by his last name, nor is his real first name of any significance; he has thus, at least to a degree, escaped the rigidity of nomenclature with which the military is so bound up.

7. This entire sequence is so smoothly and elegantly done that it almost passes notice, but watched closely it can be seen as a marvel of editing and camera technique, the sort of thing which almost makes one despair of *writing* about film.

8. The Shore Patrol officer's function as an agent of the patriarchal power hierarchy is emphasized by the thick phallic baton he wields with evident relish.

9. The other man, it will quickly be noted, is sporting a large phallic cigar; the traditionally masculine power of money is here virtually equated with rape, the power of acquiring and using women.

10. Not only was this true in 1926 as regards Western sailors in China, it was also true, in 1966, that in several of the United States interracial marriages were illegal. Not until 1967, in the *Loving v. Virginia* decision, did the United States Supreme Court rule that such laws were unconstitutional. Gay marriages, of course, remain illegal, as of this writing, in most jurisdictions. Legal hurdles to legitimate love remain common across the world.

11. It is odd that political conservatism is commonly associated with something called "family values"; the very natures of capitalism and military expansionism, both beloved by conservatives, are such as to break apart families on a large scale. Nor indeed is love allowed to determine family in conservative

eyes, but rather a commitment to breeding, along proper lines. It is yet another irony in *The Sand Pebbles* that Maily is pregnant with a child wanted by both partners but which would have been considered, in the eyes of society and society's laws, "illegitimate" had it lived. Life is valued proportionally to its usefulness to the system.

12. Po-Han is daring to drink coffee out of a cup used by the crew members; one of the hallmarks of capitalism is the emphasis placed on possession, even of seemingly trivial objects. Again, this is not entirely irrational but a sign of the warping of rationality by a corrupt system; where one has virtually nothing, even little possessions take on a tremendous symbolic importance.

13. It may be objected that Wise and Anderson have stacked the deck by concentrating on individual, rather than collective, action. This is not entirely accurate in any case, but what if it were? Consider the possibilities available. The crew has been deliberately infantilized, or worse, by the nature of military discipline, which is intended to reduce individual initiative in favor of an unthinking collectivity (on the *San Pablo*, military drills are held "every day except Sunday"). As a result, as Collins acknowledges after witnessing a fight on deck stemming from the enforced inactivity while the *San Pablo* is effectively under siege, "The men are not responsible. They have to be protected." They are not responsible precisely because their professional training is completely inadequate for such a situation; they do not have the reserves of personality necessary to overcome it peaceably, and therefore revert to the violence for which they have been trained. We see this several times: in the fight sequence, in the Maily auction, and in the near mutiny with its repeated chant of "Holman, come down." Collective action by the crew could effectuate only in perverted forms of something which is itself already perverted.

On the other hand, the Chinese *are* acting collectively, at least to a degree. The problem, though, is that they (like virtually everyone else, then and now) are still acting within the mode of competitive political entities. There is no clear way to distinguish among the collectives, since each is largely dominated by a single leader or group, and thus collective only in the loosest sense. It is difficult to see how, whether in 1926, 1966, or 2006, a full-

scale collectivism could be attained which also retained genuine individualism. There are many stages yet to be crossed before reaching that point (one of which is, as I will demonstrate, adumbrated, however tentatively, in *The Sand Pebbles*).

14. In what has been reported as Wise's original version the segment is far more poignant in its implications. Po-Han had been shown earlier working on the engine to shouts of "Hammer! Hammer!" as he battered at a recalcitrant part. Thus it is not simply that he is a tool of Holman's, but rather that he is becoming almost literally a part of the machinery of imperialism. The so-called road-show version of the film has been released on DVD, but no such scene appears. As there are elements found in the shorter standard theatrical release missing from the (very faded) road-show print, it may be that this scene was excised from the material used for the DVD release, or filmed but cut before the theatrical release.

15. This would be late March of 1927, at which time Smedley Butler was taking command of the U.S. forces in China. For a good short account of the events of the period, see Schmidt, *op. cit.*, Chapter 13, pp. 173–201.

16. Jean-Paul Sartre, *What Is Literature?* translated by Bernard Frechtman (New York: Harper Colophon, 1965), p. 283.

17. At the end of 1966, as *The Sand Pebbles* was entering wide release, the CIA estimated North Vietnamese casualties from bombing raids at 24,000, with 18,000 of those being civilians; the death toll among soldiers on all sides was probably in the vicinity of 50,000. The fighters are doing what they have been trained to do; the question is when such training will no longer be central to society.

18. The escape with Maily is also all downhill, signifying Frenchy's approach to a similar understanding (as explicated above). Frenchy, too, acts on his new understanding, with similarly fatal results.

19. Again, note the care with which moral balance is maintained. Collins's order to Holman to train a new coolie is what leads Holman to Po-Han and thence to his own less racist attitude. In a self-contradictory social system it is unlikely that anyone will be entirely a villain or entirely a hero.

20. We will encounter this physically wrenching expression of grief again, in *A*

Storm in Summer, when Abe Shaddick confronts his own self-willed isolation.

21. Machinery intended to be used at the mission, but which has never even been opened; the metaphor is evident.

22. I say "ambiguous" because, first, there is no certainty that the ship will not be stopped by Chinese forces along the river; and, second, the ship is now under the command of Ensign Bordelles, who has shown no recognition whatsoever that he understands the complexities of the situations he has faced, or even that he recognizes the existence of such complexities. He stands, all too clearly, for the vast majority of individuals, military or civilian, within the imperialist world. He and his ilk may yet win out, but so long as there are Shirley Eckerts to challenge them, there is hope.

23. Holman eventually realized this as specifically related to Po-Han, but never expanded upon that understanding.

Chapter Six

1. André Bazin, *What Is Cinema?* Vol. II, trans. Hugh Gray (Berkeley: University of California Press, 1972), p. 130.

2. Which is not to condemn the useful: a guide to assembling a stove which was written in strict Petrarchan sonnet form might be fascinating to contemplate but would likely be confusing and annoying as a set of instructions. It is also sometimes the case, even with works of art, that their practical effect for a time justifiably overwhelms their aesthetic impact: *Uncle Tom's Cabin,* for example, is not an especially well-written novel, but had it been more literary it might not have had the success it did in stimulating vital changes in public opinion regarding slavery. These sorts of works retain a historical significance which eventually outweighs their aesthetic importance; it is possible to study the ante-bellum American novel with scarcely a reference to *Uncle Tom's Cabin,* but much less easy to study ante-bellum politics without acknowledging its impact. Similarly, the moral status of a work may come to outweigh its aesthetic value (*cf.* Griffith's *The Birth of a Nation* for a powerful example of this; even most of those who defend it as a film cannot avoid expressing revulsion regarding its political stance, and many writers prefer to ignore it and concentrate on *Intolerance* instead).

3. These introductory remarks are meant to point toward later aspects of my discussion of this film; they are most assuredly not meant as a comprehensive theory of aesthetic evaluation. It should be evident that a multilayered work of art can be approached along the lines I have indicated in several ways simultaneously; one can be reacting emotionally to one aspect even while appreciating another one intellectually. One's eventual evaluative stance may well be modified over time as different understandings, based on different balances of emotional and intellectual comprehension, evolve, so that for any work of art, but especially the greatest works, there is no finality, only a provisional resting point, in evaluation(s). Such resting points are necessary, however, for without them we could never say anything about the works of art at all. For minor works the resting points are rarely changed; for major ones they can and do shift on a frequent basis.

4. The network told one studio executive, "They would not buy the series because they didn't think they could sell the program to enough sponsors. The 'too cerebral' excuse was put out to save network face." Or so says one version of the story; see David Alexander, *Star Trek Creator: The Authorized Biography of Gene Roddenberry* (New York: Roc, 1994), p. 224.

5. The central plotline of *Star Trek: The Motion Picture* is taken, without acknowledgment, from the television episode "The Changeling," by John Meredyth Lucas, which was first aired on September 29, 1967; elements suggestive of other episodes also appear. The important point, though, is not what similarities exist but how the differences, of which there are many, are developed. The original episode is a good 50-minute television science fiction drama with no resonances beyond itself; the film is far more complex both visually and dramatically.

For fan reactions, see the discussions at any *Star Trek* web site or at the film's entry on the Internet Movie Database (IMDb.com); almost invariably the few defenders of the film are treated dismissively, and usually, in typical internet fashion, vigorously abused as well, for their opinions. For a critical dismissal of the film as simply a bloated television episode, see *Harlan Ellison's Watching* (Los Angeles: Underwood-Miller, 1989), p. 143. For a contrary example of a reaction by a critic who was not a fan of the television series, see Vincent Canby: "I doubt anyone who saw it could possibly confuse this film with those shards of an earlier, simpler, cheaper television era" (*New York Times*, December 19, 1979, p. 14).

6. The situation of *Star Trek: The Motion Picture* on home video is messy. Prior to Wise's completion of the film in 2001, the video and laser disk releases were of the unfinished version; the initial DVD release, appropriately called the "Director's Edition," was of the finished version. But Paramount, apparently having no intention of ever releasing the finished film theatrically, paid only for digital image resolution which would look acceptable on small screen televisions. When widescreen televisions and high-definition digital video became common soon afterwards, it was instantly obvious that the level of resolution in the updated effects was simply too low to be watchable. The studio's solution, which had the twin advantages of saving money and requiring no commitment to artistic integrity, was simply to re-release the previous version, as if Wise had never finished the film at all (!). At this writing, therefore, only the original DVD release accurately reflects the director's intentions. This is all the more ironic in that *Star Trek: The Motion Picture* is the only one of the many films in that franchise which is clearly conceived throughout as a true large screen film by a director deeply familiar with such things.

7. Details regarding the production of the film may be found in Susan Sackett and Gene Roddenberry, *The Making of Star Trek: The Motion Picture* (New York: Wallaby, 1980).

8. From an interview published originally in *Playboy*, reprinted in Stephanie Schwam, ed., *The Making of 2001: A Space Odyssey* (New York: The Modern Library, 2000), pp. 272–300; p. 274.

9. As one illustration, consider the appearance of the Jupiter astronauts as they emerge from the pod: the helmets, seen from above, make them resemble some sort of alien life form rather than anything recognizably human.

10. It should go without saying that this is not an evaluative point, but a comparative one. What is at issue here is whether or not *Star Trek: The Motion Picture* is, as some of its critics have charged, a derivative film. It is not, despite a few superficial similarities,

precisely because those similarities are in the service of a vision that is virtually the opposite of its predecessor.

11. Technically, Ilia is a Deltan, a member of an alien species, but the points being made in the film have very much to do with the essence of humanity, regardless of the external attributions of a given individual.

12. *Solaris* is a very complex film; these few remarks are meant only to make points in regard to its relation to *Star Trek: The Motion Picture*, not as a summation of its many aspects. An entire, and no doubt lengthy, essay could be written on the thematic and philosophical connections between the two masterpieces alone.

13. I had intended to provide musical illustrations allowing readers to more easily follow the ensuing discussion, in which Goldsmith's score is of fundamental importance. Unfortunately, the six examples, totaling 23 measures of music drawn from a score lasting well over an hour, evidently would be considered too extensive a citation and might threaten the profit structure of Hal Leonard Music, the copyright holder, thereby entailing legal action on the part of the corporation. I supplied 15 pages of material in order to apply for permission to cite these 23 measures, only to learn both that this wasn't enough and that I would be expected to pay fees to cite the music in any case (imagine an author being required to pay a movie studio for quoting 23 words— not even complete sentences—from a film under discussion!). I apologize to the reader for the consequent obscurity of certain points; two measures of music can take many words to describe, and even then be captured only imperfectly.

14. One of the very few quibbles which may be provoked by the Director's Edition is that the original black screen has been replaced by a moving field of stars. While the shift is minor, it does subtly undercut the tension being created here. Unfortunately, the decision was probably a practical one; in the theater the audience must accept whatever the film offers, whereas at home two minutes of black screen would simply be a prompt for the fast forward button. At least they did not adopt the practice, found in many other DVD releases of films with overtures, of showing the word "Overture" printed over a still shot while the music plays.

15. Bazin, *op. cit.*, p. 132. Consider also

Roger Ebert's comment on Tarkovsky's *Solaris*: "[Tarkovsky] uses length and depth to slow us down, to edge us out of the velocity of our lives, to enter a zone of reverie and meditation. When he allows a sequence to continue for what seems like an unreasonable length, we have a choice. We can be bored, or we can use the interlude as an opportunity to consolidate what has gone before, and process it in terms of our own reflections" (Roger Ebert, "Tarkovsky's 'Solaris,'" Chicago *Sun-Times*, January 19, 2003).

16. Leemann, p. 123.

17. It may be noted that *Star Trek: The Motion Picture* operates, in its gradual unfolding, in much the same manner as do most aesthetic responses. We begin with an emotional response (to the music unaccompanied by image, and the image unaccompanied by meaning) and gradually fill in the gaps in our intellectual comprehension as we acquire new information regarding the relevant structural and thematic elements. These, in turn, shift our understandings of the emotional elements, and vice versa. Eventually we are able to assess what we have seen on its own terms as well as ours, and can evaluate both the work and our understanding of it. Evaluation, where it is not a matter of pure practicality, always involves aesthetic judgment; where we cannot imaginatively appreciate what we are experiencing, we cannot claim genuine understanding.

18. Both here and in the Klingon sequences, the respective alien languages are spoken, with translations provided via subtitles; the verbal action in *Star Trek: The Motion Picture* thus takes place in three languages.

19. One of the central tensions of the character as developed in the television series came as a result of Spock's biological heritage; the child of a Vulcan father and a human mother, he fought hard to restrain his human emotions in the service of Vulcan logic. The film makes his struggle clear but wastes no time explaining its origins.

20. The amulet, despite having several parts, is in fact a solid unit; the pattern, therefore, is no accident.

21. It is a mark of how widely known the character was by this time that at no point in the ensuing scene is Kirk's name mentioned, but only his new rank (in the television series he was a captain).

22. The long highway sequence in Tarkovsky's *Solaris* serves the same purpose, but is generally agreed to lack the cinematic weight necessary for its function. Nonetheless, it is worth noting how each of the three films uses similar materials for similar purposes yet reaches a quite dissimilar position from the others, intellectually and emotionally.

23. A recurrent motif, small but of great relevance to the film's overall utopianism, comes in the form of information being provided by, or in answer to questions from, minor characters; in this world, everyone has something of professional significance to contribute, has a part to play in attaining the eventual success of the mission (and, by implication, of others to come). Unfortunately, these minor parts are too frequently played by amateur actors (in some cases, apparently people with connections to the production [business] side of the film), with a concomitant lessening of the impact of the performance. More happily, the assembled crew of the *Enterprise* in the recapitulation of the Epsilon 9 encounter with V'Ger is played almost entirely by fans of the original television series, a generous method of saluting the people without whose support of the series—new and in syndication—*Star Trek: The Motion Picture* would likely never have been made. The social setting of a film has seldom if ever been so directly acknowledged within the film itself.

24. Another subtle clue to Decker's ultimate place in the narrative is provided by the fact that it was Kirk who recommended him for the command position. It was thus Kirk who operated as a controlling factor even in this apparently climactic moment in Decker's career. This power imbalance will be reversed at the film's climax.

25. In most cases, *Star Trek: The Motion Picture* can be appreciated entirely on its own. Occasionally, as here, some of the humor rests on an awareness of the characters as developed in the television series. There, McCoy was shown as continually suspicious, not always without reason, of the transporter technology.

26. Among these is a shot of sunrise over the Earth, as seen from space. This, in particular, is not a debt to *2001*; rather, it has been a part of the vocabulary of space travel films since Fritz Lang's *Frau im Mond* (1929). The melodramatic plot of Lang's film, com-

bined with things now unfairly seen as ludicrous (the presence of breathable air on the moon, for example), has obscured the fact that his film was the first great celebration of the potential of technology as an aid to human aspirations beyond the Earth. The parallel with *Star Trek: The Motion Picture* should not be exaggerated, but neither should it be ignored.

27. McCoy has even warned him of the relevant professional concerns, concerns Kirk has, in his hubristic haste, forgotten: "Jim, you're pushing. Your people know their jobs." Kirk would have done well to listen.

28. Another subtle visual detail differentiates between Kirk, who is learning, and the Klingons, who refused to learn at all: during the Klingon attack the bridge of the leading ship was lit with dull red lights; at the onset of the encounter between the *Enterprise* and the alien the *Enterprise*'s bridge is similarly lit, but Kirk explicitly calls for "standard lighting," which proves to be far less murky.

29. Indeed, even feigned communication is better than none, for the act of feigning at least requires that we acknowledge another's being.

30. That the shadows are accidental, created by the fact that the onstage light source for the special effect was not as strong as the effect itself implied, is by now of little import; the film's creative energies are such that it can absorb such happy accidents thematically.

31. Ernest Ferlita, *The Theatre of Pilgrimage* (New York: Sheed and Ward, 1971), p. 35. *Star Trek: The Motion Picture* is very much a pilgrimage, albeit in a humanist sense.

32. St. Bonaventure, *The Mind's Road to God*, trans. George Boas (New York: Liberal Arts Press, 1953), p. 8. He will further identify these as "the corporeal, the spiritual, and the divine" (*Ibid.*).

33. Kirk, in the television series, if faced with a similar situation, would now solve it with a few well-placed kisses. Love and understanding, freed of the exigencies of network television scheduling, require rather more complex, and lengthier, means to achieve their goals.

34. Iris Murdoch, *The Fire and the Sun: Why Plato Banished the Artists* (Oxford: Oxford University Press, 1978), p. 34.

35. Harlan Ellison, a particularly harsh critic of this film, mistook this particular shot for a continuity error, failing to note the presence, or significance, of the mirror. See Ellison, *op. cit.*, pp. 144–45.

36. Persis Khambatta's acting earlier in the film is uneven, but here it is superb; despite the many jokes about mechanical actors, it is difficult to play a machine, and even harder to make the transitions between machine and human state plausible. She does both very well, and her performance adds a great deal to the scene.

37. Judith Butler, *Subjects of Desire: Hegelian Reflections in Twentieth-Century France* (New York: Columbia University Press, 1987), p. 8.

38. In fact, we actually see that he learns more than this, but in such a jumble that neither he nor the audience realizes that the climax of the film has already been revealed.

39. Here again the deeper truths of the film override the demands of external reality. It is unlikely that the ship's commanding officer would leave it for any but the direst of reasons at such a point, but it is very much the case that a friend so closely tied to Spock would do so.

40. The single greatest visual flaw in the completed film occurs here; a brief shot of the entirety of V'Ger passing by. The image, in contrast to those of the *Enterprise* and the surface of V'Ger which were so carefully developed earlier, has absolutely no presence or sense of massiveness; it looks exactly like what it is: a computer-generated picture. The original shot replaced by this one was far more impressive: the Earth seen between two extrusions from the surface of V'Ger, momentarily creating the sense that V'Ger was larger than the Earth itself, thus visually anticipating the vast destructive power which V'Ger soon prepares to unleash. Presumably this new shot was a gift to the effects team which aided the film's completion, but all it does is illustrate the difference between those who are willing to allow a sense of mystery and those who demand that every detail be shown, between imagination and fact. This brief image is a flaw precisely in its insistence on presenting every detail, by which insistence it not only undercuts but contradicts the overall development of the film. Fortunately, it is a *brief* image, and can soon be dismissed from memory.

41. An important philosophical flaw in *Star Trek: The Motion Picture* is its overly male-centered structure, nowhere more ob-

vious than here. A genuine utopian future will include an equally genuine balance between genders, and this we do not see here; although Ilia is certainly a vital character, she is rarely presented as taking an active role in the proceedings, unlike the men. Given the circumstances of the film's creation, I do not see how this problem could have been fully overcome. The main roles, stemming from a pre-existing television series, could not be changed in any significant manner (such as recasting them for gender balance). While Decker could certainly be played by a woman, the resultant shift in emphasis would (even assuming it could have been accepted as a key aspect of a big-budget film by anyone in Hollywood in 1979) probably have ended up seeming either purely titillating or aggressively separatist, neither option conveying the underlying utopian vision (and the second possibly being misunderstood altogether as simply a peculiar, and unsuccessful, plot gimmick). We are, in ways which I will consider below, free to imagine another film altogether, of course, one free of this flaw, but whether such a film could have been made within the given circumstances by *anyone* in 1979 remains, I think, a serious question. I do not say this to dismiss the concerns about the film's masculine bias, but rather to argue that one must acknowledge possibilities, or their absence, as well as actualities in assessing any work of art. This said, it is unfortunate that no reference to a potential female answerer was included in Spock's summation.

42. Herbert Marcuse, *Eros and Civilization*, pp. 102–103.

43. There is yet another balance of motion here. As Kirk informed Decker of his assumption of command, he took a single abrupt step toward Decker. As Decker challenged Kirk in the latter's quarters following the near-destruction of the *Enterprise*, he took a single abrupt step toward Kirk. As the Ilia-probe appealed to Decker, "The creator must join with V'Ger," it took a step toward Decker.

These disjunctive motions, indicative of underlying power imbalances (and thus a lack of cooperation), are echoed but smoothed out in the complementary camera motions bringing Ilia and Decker together.

44. Herbert Marcuse, *One-Dimensional Man: Studies in the Ideology of Advanced Industrial Society* (Boston: Beacon Press, 1969), p. 127.

45. McCoy even refers to having "delivered a baby," thus linking the events here with Wise's frequent use of children as an indicator of future hopes and possibilities.

46. It is a sheer coincidence that the ship's identification number, 1701 (already famous from the television series), prominently visible at the beginning of this shot, add up to nine, but it is one of those happy coincidences which, as I have already pointed out above, the film's creative energy simply absorbs.

47. Marcuse, *The Aesthetic Dimension*, p. 8.

48. Butler, *op. cit.*, p. 31.

49. Whitehead, *Adventures of Ideas*, p. 329.

50. *Ibid.*, p. 330.

51. This is, I think, the reason for the otherwise mysterious appeal of truly wretched films, for which there appears to be a sizeable audience. In watching these films, we not only imagine ways in which they could be better, we imagine ways in which *we* could have made them more competently, even with the same materials; we are thereby allowed a space in which to exercise, if not genuine creativity (which requires actual encounters with the potentially recalcitrant materials essential to the given art form), at least the beginnings of creative imagination. In a world in which the forms of entertainment and human interaction are ever more rigorously controlled and shaped by external forces, forces increasingly hostile to the growth of serious art and genuine individual freedom, such an opportunity to exercise one's creativity will have an undeniable attraction.

52. Marcuse, *Aesthetic Dimension*, p. 72.

Bibliography

Adorno, Theodor W. *Prisms*. Translated by Samuel and Shierry Weber. Cambridge, MA: MIT Press, 1983.

Alexander, David. *Star Trek Creator: The Authorized Biography of Gene Roddenberry.* New York: Roc, 1994.

Barnes, Hazel. *An Existentialist Ethics.* New York: Alfred A. Knopf, 1969.

Baruch, Bernard M. *Baruch: The Public Years.* New York: Holt, Rinehart, and Winston, 1960.

Bataille, Georges. *Death and Sensuality: A Study of Eroticism and the Taboo.* New York: Ballantine, 1969.

Bazin, André. *What Is Cinema?* Vol. II. Translated by Hugh Gray. Berkeley: University of California Press, 1972.

Beauvoir, Simone de. *The Second Sex.* Translated by H. M. Parshley. New York: Alfred A. Knopf, 1957.

Bergman, Ingmar. *The Magic Lantern: An Autobiography.* Translated by Joan Tate. New York: Viking, 1988.

Bonaventure, St. *The Mind's Road to God.* Translated by George Boas. New York: Liberal Arts Press, 1953.

Bruccoli, Matthew J., ed. "The Rich Boy." In *The Short Stories of F. Scott Fitzgerald*, pp. 335–366. New York: Charles Scribner's Sons, 1989.

Butler, Judith. *Subjects of Desire: Hegelian Reflections in Twentieth-Century France.* New York: Columbia University Press, 1987.

Butler, Smedley D. *War Is a Racket.* Gainesville, FL: Crises Press, 1995.

Chandler, Raymond. *Trouble Is My Business.* New York: Ballantine, 1980.

Clarens, Carlos. *An Illustrated History of the Horror Film.* New York: Capricorn Books, 1968.

Clute, John. *Science Fiction: The Illustrated Encyclopedia.* London: Dorling Kindersley, 1995.

Collins, Gary. "The Meanest Man in the Movies." In *The Movie Buff's Book*, edited by Ted Sennett, pp. 18–23. New York: Bonanza, 1975.

Durgnat, Raymond. *Films and Feelings.* Cambridge, MA: MIT Press, 1967.

Einstein, Albert. *Ideas and Opinions.* New York: Crown, 1963.

_____. *Out of My Later Years.* New York: Philosophical Library, 1950.

Ellison, Harlan. *Harlan Ellison's Watching.* Los Angeles: Underwood-Miller, 1989.

Ferlita, Ernest. *The Theatre of Pilgrimage.* New York: Sheed and Ward, 1971.

Freud, Sigmund. *On Creativity and the Unconscious: Papers on the Psychology of Art, Literature, Love, Religion.* Edited by Benjamin Nelson. New York: Harper & Row, 1958.

Fromm, Erich. *The Art of Loving.* New York: HarperCollins, 2000.

_____. *To Have or to Be?* New York: Continuum, 1997.

Gado, Frank. *The Passion of Ingmar Bergman.* Durham, NC: Duke University Press, 1986.

Galbraith, John Kenneth. *The Affluent Society.* Boston: Houghton Mifflin, 1958.

Herken, Gregg. *The Winning Weapon: The*

Atomic Bomb in the Cold War, 1945–1950. New York: Alfred A. Knopf, 1980.

Hobbes, Thomas. *Leviathan.* London: Penguin, 1980.

Hoffer, Eric. *In Our Time.* New York: Harper and Row, 1976.

_____. *Working and Thinking on the Waterfront: A Journal: June 1958–May 1959.* New York: Harper and Row, 1969.

Horney, Karen. *The Neurotic Personality of Our Time.* New York: Norton, 1937.

Kael, Pauline. *Going Steady.* New York: Bantam, 1971.

Keenan, Richard C. *The Films of Robert Wise.* Lanham, MD: Scarecrow Press, 2007.

Leemann, Sergio. *Robert Wise on His Films: From Editing Room to Director's Chair.* Los Angeles: Silman-James Press, 1995.

Lukács, Georg. *Realism in Our Time: Literature and the Class Struggle.* New York: Harper Torchbooks, 1971.

Lumet, Sidney. *Making Movies.* New York: Alfred A. Knopf, 1995.

Marcuse, Herbert. *The Aesthetic Dimension: Toward a Critique of Marxist Aesthetics.* Boston: Beacon Press, 1978.

_____. *Eros and Civilization: A Philosophical Inquiry into Freud.* New York: Vintage, n.d.

_____. *One-Dimensional Man: Studies in the Ideology of Advanced Industrial Society.* Boston: Beacon Press, 1969.

Meredith, George. *Rhoda Fleming.* Boston: Roberts Brothers, 1891.

Monaco, James. *How to Read a Film: Movies, Media, Multimedia.* Third Edition. New York: Oxford University Press, 2000.

Morgan, Robin. *The Demon Lover: On the Sexuality of Terrorism.* New York: Norton, 1989.

Morris, William. *The Political Writings of William Morris.* Edited by A. L. Morton. New York: International Publishers, 1973.

Murdoch, Iris. *The Fire and the Sun: Why Plato Banished the Artists.* Oxford: Oxford University Press, 1978.

Nathan, George Jean. Section XV in *Living Philosophies,* pp. 221–233. New York: Simon and Schuster, 1931.

Nussbaum, Martha. *Sex and Social Justice.* New York: Oxford University Press, 1999.

Porfirio, Robert G. "No Way Out: Existential Motifs in the Film Noir." *Sight and Sound,* Vol. 45, #4 (Autumn 1976), pp. 212–217.

Pound, Reginald. *Arnold Bennett: A Biography.* Port Washington, NY: Kennikat Press, 1972.

Rand, Ayn. *Capitalism, the Unknown Ideal.* New York: New American Library, 1966.

Sackett, Susan. *The Hollywood Reporter Book of Box Office Hits.* New York: Billboard Books, 1990.

_____, and Gene Roddenberry. *The Making of Star Trek: The Motion Picture.* New York: Wanderer Books, 1980.

Sartre, Jean-Paul. *What Is Literature?* Translated by Bernard Frechtman. New York: Harper Colophon, 1965.

Schmidt, Hans. *Maverick Marine: General Smedley D. Butler and the Contradictions of American Military History.* Lexington: University Press of Kentucky, 1987.

Schwam, Stephanie, ed., *The Making of 2001: A Space Odyssey.* New York: The Modern Library, 2000.

Singer, Irving. *Ingmar Bergman, Cinematic Philosopher: Reflections on His Creativity.* Cambridge, MA: MIT Press, 2007.

Sklar, Robert. *A World History of Film.* New York: Harry N. Abrams, 2002.

Thompson, Frank. *Robert Wise: A Bio-Bibliography.* Westport, CT: Greenwood Press, 1995.

Thomson, David. *The New Biographical Dictionary of Film.* New York: Alfred A. Knopf, 2002.

Truffaut, François. *The Films in My Life.* Translated by Leonard Mayhew. New York: Simon and Schuster, 1978.

Watts, Anthony J. *Japanese Warships of World War Two.* Garden City, NY: Doubleday, 1970.

White, Patricia. "Female Spectator, Lesbian Specter: *The Haunting.*" In *Sexuality and Space,* pp. 130–161. Edited by Beatriz Colomina. Princeton Papers on Architecture #1. New York: Princeton Architectural Press, 1992.

Whitehead, Alfred North. *Adventures of Ideas.* New York: Macmillan, 1954.

Wood, Robin. *Howard Hawks.* Detroit, MI: Wayne State University Press, 2006.

Index